BECOMING NEW

A DOCTRINAL COMMENTARY ON THE WRITINGS OF PAUL

ROBERT L. MILLET

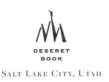

DESERET BOOK

Salt Lake City, Utah

Also by Robert L. Millet

Whole in Christ
I Saw a Pillar of Light
The Holy Spirit
The Atoning One
Whatever Happened to Faith?
Precept upon Precept
Men of Covenant
Living in the Millennium
Living in the Eleventh Hour
Lehi's Dream
Coming to Know Christ
Making Sense of the Book of Revelation
Talking with God
Men of Influence
Holding Fast
Men of Valor
What Happened to the Cross?
Are We There Yet?
Getting at the Truth
Grace Works
When a Child Wanders

© 2022 Robert L. Millet

All rights reserved. No part of this book may be reproduced in any form or by any means without permission in writing from the publisher, Deseret Book Company, at permissions@deseretbook.com. This work is not an official publication of The Church of Jesus Christ of Latter-day Saints. The views expressed herein are the responsibility of the author and do not necessarily represent the position of the Church or of Deseret Book Company.

Deseret Book is a registered trademark of Deseret Book Company.

Visit us at deseretbook.com

Library of Congress Cataloging-in-Publication Data
CIP on file
ISBN 978-1-63993-066-1

Printed in the United States of America
Lake Book Manufacturing, Inc., Melrose Park, IL

10 9 8 7 6 5 4 3 2 1

CONTENTS

Abbreviations iv
Preface v
Introduction: "A Chosen Vessel". 1
The Epistle to the Romans. 18
The First Epistle to the Corinthians 69
The Second Epistle to the Corinthians 144
The Epistle to the Galatians 179
The Epistle to the Ephesians 221
The Epistle to the Philippians 250
The Epistle to the Colossians 269
The First Epistle to the Thessalonians 286
The Second Epistle to the Thessalonians 300
The First Epistle to Timothy 309
The Second Epistle to Timothy 333
The Epistle to Titus 348
The Epistle to Philemon 356
The Epistle to the Hebrews 360
Conclusion: The Lengthening Shadow of Paul 430
Sources 435
Index 445

ABBREVIATIONS

ESV	English Standard Version of the Bible
JST	Joseph Smith Translation of the Bible
KJV	King James Version of the Bible
KNT	N. T. Wright's Kingdom New Testament Translation
NASB	New American Standard Bible
NRSV	New Revised Standard Version
REB	Revised English Bible

PREFACE

For many Latter-day Saints, the Apostle Paul is a stranger, an enigma, and his epistles are too often viewed with confusion, reticence, and even suspicion. In my many years of teaching the writings of Paul, I have noticed an interesting phenomenon among students. Because Paul places such a strong emphasis on justification by faith and salvation by grace, a surprising number of Latter-day Saints perceive him to be a kind of ancient Protestant. But the resurrected Savior said of the converted Saul of Tarsus, "He is a chosen vessel unto me" (Acts 9:15). Many in the religious world consider Paul to be the greatest Christian missionary of all time, but it is *what he taught*, particularly in his epistles, that we will concern ourselves with in this book.

Paul's testimony of Jesus, the message of salvation in Christ, and the assurance that men and women can become new creatures in Christ (see 2 Corinthians 5:17)—these matters are as current, relevant, and needed in the twenty-first century as they were in the first century. In other words, Paul has something to say to Latter-day Saint Christians and, for that matter, to all Christians in our day. Interestingly, the Prophet Joseph Smith drew upon Paul's writings in some of his sermons and offered a surprising amount of insight into them. In addition, latter-day revelation, coupled with clarifying messages from modern prophets and apostles, provides additional commentary on much of Paul's writings.

Readers can get a feel for how often Brother Joseph spoke of Paul's ministry or offered insight into his epistles by simply browsing the Sources section at the end of this book. Bringing all this information together into one grand package has been a labor of love for me.

This book will focus principally on doctrinal truths that come through Paul's teachings, including eternal principles that transcend culture and time and place; singular insights into the Savior and His atoning work; and distinctive doctrine found nowhere else in holy scripture. The fire that Paul sought to ignite in the souls of the former-day Saints is the same fire that Paul's apostolic successors today seek to ignite in the souls of Latter-day Saints.

This is a book I have desired to write since the time I fell in love with Paul and his letters in the summer of 1976. It was in a graduate course at Brigham Young University taught by Professor Robert J. Matthews. The class was made up of about forty seminary and institute personnel from throughout central Utah. Each class was a spiritual treat. Brother Matthews was not what I would call an exuberant teacher, bubbling over with enthusiasm and entertaining all in attendance. Rather, his was a quiet and gentle way of teaching, but one that was filled with the Spirit of God. He opened our eyes to sacred truths that we had never seen before in our own private readings of Paul's letters.

In our class that summer, we read much of the biblical text and engaged Paul with new eyes. Few, if any, of the students walked out of class at the end of the hour proclaiming: "Wow! Robert Matthews is amazing. His gospel knowledge is stunning. His insights are unbelievable!" No, but I suspect that many of my graduate-student colleagues felt just what I did: what I wanted most was to walk over to the Harold B. Lee Library, find a quiet place, sit down, and pore over the scriptural texts more carefully. Often what I felt was a strong desire to pray, to plead with the Lord to open my eyes and enlighten my understanding to sacred truths that could be understood and appreciated only through the power of the Holy Spirit. I can still remember that when I returned home each day, I would sit in the living room holding my scriptures, with several books on my lap or at my side: the Joseph Smith Translation of the Bible; Elder Bruce R. McConkie's *Doctrinal New Testament Commentary*, volumes 2 and 3; and Sidney B. Sperry's *Paul's Life and Letters*, a book Brother Matthews recommended that we consult regularly.

That fall, my Latter-day Saint seminary students and I read and studied the New Testament, and by midyear we turned to, among other scriptural texts, the Pauline epistles, and I attempted to unfold Paul's letters to my high school students. A year later I was asked to be the institute director at Florida State University and the Church Educational System coordinator for six stakes in Florida and Georgia. And, of course, I chose to teach the second half of the New Testament as one of the first courses in my large evening class. Six years later (in 1983) I was invited to join the Religious Education faculty at Brigham Young University and was assigned—can you believe it?—to teach the second half of the New Testament during the summer term. Following my time as Brother Matthews's student and then later as his colleague, I continued to glean precious insights from him, one who had for decades reserved a special place in his heart for the Apostle Paul.

I believe most sincerely that an intense study of the writings of Paul is needed and that a careful search of the doctrine taught by Paul can both deepen faith in the Lord Jesus Christ and enhance the spirituality of members of The Church of Jesus Christ of Latter-day Saints. It will also equip the Saints to speak more intelligently and comfortably with other Christians. Further, my own experience is that once I better understood Paul's teachings, I was able to engage the scriptures of the Restoration with an even greater zeal and confidence, given that the recurring themes and doctrinal refrains are much the same across the standard works. My hope is that you will come to better appreciate and love the Apostle Paul, a "chosen vessel" of the Lord, and, most important, that a careful study of his teachings will literally change your lives.

Introduction

"A CHOSEN VESSEL"

T>HE MAIN CHARACTER OF this book, the author of the epistles, was likely born at about the same time as Jesus of Nazareth. His Hebrew name was Saul, being called, no doubt, after the king of Israel who preceded David. His Roman or Latin name was Paulus or Paul, first mentioned by Luke, the author of the Acts of the Apostles (Acts 13:9). Paul's hometown was Tarsus of Cilicia (Acts 9:11; 22:3). New Testament scholar N. T. Wright explained:

> Tarsus, a noble city in Cilicia, ten miles inland on the river Cydnus in the southeast corner of modern Turkey, was on the major east-west trade routes. (The major landmass we think of today as Turkey was divided into several administrative districts, with "Asia" as the western part, "Asia Minor" as the central and eastern part, "Bithynia" in the north, and so on). . . .
>
> Tarsus could trace its history back two thousand years. World-class generals like Alexander the Great and Julius Caesar had recognized its strategic importance; the emperor Augustus had given it extra privileges. It was a city of culture and politics, of philosophy and industry. Among these industries was a thriving textile business, producing material made from goats' hair, used not least to make shelters. This may well have been

the basis of the family business, tentmaking, in which Saul had been apprenticed and which he continued to practice.[1]

Citing the work of the ancient geographer Strabo, F. F. Bruce added that "the people of Tarsus were avid in the pursuit of culture. They applied themselves to the study of philosophy, the liberal arts and the 'whole round of learning in general'—the whole encyclopedia—so much so that Tarsus in this respect at least surpassed even Athens and Alexandria, whose schools were frequented more by visitors than by their own citizens. Tarsus, in short, was what we might call a university city."[2]

SAUL THE PHARISEE

Like King Saul, Saul of Tarsus was of the tribe of Benjamin (Philippians 3:5), one of the smallest of Jacob's twelve tribes. When it came to his religious beliefs and practices, Saul was, like his father, a Pharisee (see Acts 23:6). Historians have estimated that there were approximately six thousand Pharisees in the land during the time of Jesus and Paul.[3] Keep in mind that the Pharisees believed in spirits, angels, life after death, and the resurrection of the dead. They not only believed in the Torah itself but also accepted the oral traditions of the elders who had, through the generations, sought to interpret and intuit the meaning and application of scripture. Of his background, Paul described himself as "circumcised the eighth day, of the stock of Israel, of the tribe of Benjamin, an Hebrew of the Hebrews; as touching the law, a Pharisee." Indeed, he was a very conservative Pharisee (Philippians 3:5–6; Acts 26:5).

To Jewish leaders, Paul explained that he was "brought up in this city [i.e., Jerusalem] at the feet of Gamaliel, and taught according to the perfect manner of the law of the fathers, and was zealous toward

---

1. Wright, *Paul: A Biography*, 33–36.
2. Bruce, *Paul: Apostle of the Heart Set Free*, 34–35.
3. Anthony J. Saldarini, "Pharisees," in Freedman, *Anchor Bible Dictionary*, 5:293.

God" (Acts 22:3). "Gamaliel was one of the greatest rabbis of the period," explained Wright. "Under his guidance, Saul would have studied the scriptures themselves, of course, and also the unwritten Torah, the steadily accumulating discussions of finer points that would grow as oral tradition and be codified nearly two hundred years later in the Mishnah."[4]

The fascinating thing about Gamaliel, however, is that he was a disciple of Hillel, the head of one of the most significant schools of Jewish thought, and a very liberal one at that. Hillel's conservative counterpart was Shammai. While Saul of Tarsus was no doubt shaped and schooled intellectually in many ways by Gamaliel, he was also a staunch follower of the school of Shammai and thus much more conservative than his beloved teacher.[5] One thing is sure: by his own assessment, Saul excelled in his studies, standing head and shoulders above those of his own age (see Galatians 1:14).

CONVERSION

There are three accounts of the conversion of Saul, one in Acts 9, one in Acts 22, and one from the testimony of Paul himself, found in his defense before King Agrippa II (Acts 26). We are actually introduced indirectly to Saul of Tarsus by Luke, the author of both the Gospel of Luke and the Acts of the Apostles. Luke wrote that Saul was holding the coats or cloaks of those involved in the stoning of the powerful preacher Stephen (Acts 7:58). In Acts 9, Luke picks up Saul's narrative by explaining that he, "yet breathing out threatenings [i.e., hostility] and slaughter against the disciples of the Lord, went unto the high priest [in Jerusalem], and desired of him letters to Damascus to the synagogues, that if he found any of this way [i.e., followers of Jesus; see Acts 22:4], whether they were men or women, he might bring them

---

4. Wright, *Paul: A Biography*, 35.
5. See Bruce, *Paul: Apostle of the Heart Set Free*, 49–51; Wright, *Paul: A Biography*, 35–36.

bound unto Jerusalem" (Acts 9:1–2). Saul was determined to root out those he perceived to be apostates, Jews who were abandoning the law of Moses and converting to Christianity.

Regarding this event, Professor Douglas Campbell wrote that Saul "had been conducting the ancient equivalent of police sweeps in Jerusalem and the surrounding region of Judea, and we shouldn't sugarcoat this: Paul was the leader of a death squad. Such was his zeal." Campbell continued, "He wanted to pursue these deviants [i.e., Jewish apostates] wherever they had fled, even to foreign cities. At some point in AD 34 he started out for Damascus to hunt down any fugitives there that he could find. But God had other ideas."[6]

As Saul and his party made their way to Damascus, a light from heaven knocked him to the ground (he may have been riding a donkey or a horse). He then heard a voice that inquired: "Saul, Saul, why persecutest thou me? And [Saul] said, Who art thou, Lord [i.e., distinguished sir, respected one]? And the Lord said, I am Jesus whom thou persecutest: *it is hard for thee to kick against the pricks*" (Acts 9:3–5). These last words must have had a haunting ring to them. When cattle, for instance, resist being guided by kicking against the pricks, they essentially fight against a barb or goad (a pointed protrusion), and as they do so, they are pricked again and again. Their rebellion brings even greater pain. It was as if Jesus were saying to the persecutor, "You continue to rebel, to fight me and those who represent me, and in the process, you make life ever more painful and unpleasant for yourself."

Through the centuries, serious students of Paul and his letters have debated whether Saul felt sadness or sorrow or even guilt as he made his way to Damascus. Many years ago, President David O. McKay wrote beautifully and compellingly of this most significant moment in the future Apostle's life:

---

6. Campbell, *Paul: An Apostle's Journey*, 15.

Damascus is about one hundred and fifty miles north of Jerusalem, so it would take Saul and his attendants about a week to travel the distance. Perhaps during those few days of comparative leisure, he began to wonder whether what he was doing was right or not. Perhaps the shining face of the dying Stephen [Acts 7:54–60] and the martyr's last prayer [verse 60: "Lord, lay not this sin to their charge"] began to sink more deeply into his soul than it had done before. Little children's cries for their parents whom Saul had bound began to pierce his soul more keenly, and make him feel miserably unhappy as he looked forward to more experiences of that kind in Damascus. Perhaps he wondered whether the work of the Lord, if he were really engaged in it, would make him feel so restless and bitter. He was soon to learn that only the work of the evil one produces those feelings, and that true service for the Lord always brings peace and contentment.[7]

Professor Craig L. Blomberg wrote:

[Paul] talks repeatedly about a major turnaround in his life, from being an arch-persecutor of the followers of Jesus to becoming one of Jesus's staunchest supporters and most zealous missionaries (Galatians 1:13–14; Philippians 3:4b–11). Scholars debate whether this is properly called a conversion or merely a special call and commissioning within Paul's revolutionized understanding of Judaism, but there is no doubt about the extent of his change (see especially Galatians 1:11–17). All that he once trusted in as pleasing God he began to count as "dung" (Philippians 3:8, KJV). Instead of leading the charge to purify Judaism from the apostasy of Jewish followers of Jesus, he himself endured enormous amounts of persecution

---

7. McKay, *Ancient Apostles*, 120.

and physical torture for the sake of promoting the gospel of Jesus Christ (see especially 2 Corinthians 11:23b–33).[8]

There is no question whatsoever that Saul of Tarsus loved his God and was doing what he felt was his duty in defending the Jewish faith against this rising cult of Jesus followers. He believed in his cause, and he was most effective at what he was doing. Despite his missteps, the divine light of truth had been striving within Saul. The God of Abraham, Isaac, and Jacob knew of Saul's goodness, his devotion, his tenacity, and his deepest desires to please the Almighty, but his zeal needed to be redirected by Him who is "the way, the truth, and the life" (John 14:6). To echo Paul's own words, he had been zealous in his efforts, but he lacked knowledge (Romans 10:2). Saul was right in wanting to serve Jehovah, the only true God, but he was painfully wrong in his grasp of who that one true God was.

THE PEOPLE PAUL ENCOUNTERED

During his ministry, Paul met various groups and types of people. First, there were those who had been Jews all of their lives, most of whom viewed the Jewish-Christians as apostates. Second, there were Jews who had received the gospel of Jesus Christ and accepted Jesus as the promised Messiah. Third, there was a group of people called "proselytes," Gentiles who had converted to the Jewish faith and culture (through baptism, circumcision for males, and a willingness to offer sacrifice). Fourth, there were those who were known as "God-fearers." These individuals were attracted to Jewish teachings and customs and were clearly moved by what they encountered among the Jews, but had not formally converted to the faith. They could often be found lingering around the Jewish synagogues. One writer indicates that "God-fearers" is probably more correctly translated as "God-worshippers," meaning "worshippers of the one true God. . . . The God-worshippers

---

8. Blomberg, *New Testament Theology*, 179.

attended synagogue and socialized with Jews, so they were the more accessible group of pagans for Paul . . . to approach."[9]

Fifth, there was a group who came to be known as the "weak brethren." These were converts to Christianity who were still growing into the faith and were often easily shaken in their faith. Paul mentioned these people frequently in his letters, encouraging the branch leaders to be kind and caring, patient and understanding, with the ones who needed to be "remembered and nourished by the good word of God" (Moroni 6:4)—that is, those who required careful and kindly fellowshipping.

CITIZENSHIP

Significantly, Paul was a freeborn citizen of the Roman empire, which awarded him privileges and opportunities that he would not otherwise have enjoyed. Roman citizenship meant that a person had the right to vote, hold office, make contracts, own property, have a lawful marriage, have one's children born as citizens, and have the right to a speedy trial if ever accused of a crime. Having been arrested by the Jews, "Paul said unto the centurion that stood by, Is it lawful for you to scourge a man that is a Roman, and uncondemned? When the centurion heard that, he went and told the chief captain, saying, Take heed what thou doest: for this man is a Roman. Then the chief captain came, and said unto him, Tell me, art thou a Roman? He said, Yea. And the chief captain answered, With a great sum obtained I this freedom. And Paul said, But I was free born" (Acts 22:25–28).

How would someone know that Paul was a Roman citizen, other than by asking him? "In Rome, citizens would wear a toga, but it is highly unlikely that Paul was doing so on this occasion [i.e., speaking with the centurion] (even supposing that his clothes were recognizable after his near lynching). The other mark, which we may be sure Paul

---

9. Campbell, *Paul: An Apostle's Journey*, 25.

kept safe about his person all along, perhaps on a chain or string, was the small wooden badge (known as a *diploma*) that, much like a passport, gave official details of who he was and where his citizenship was registered."[10]

OUTWARD APPEARANCE

What did Paul look like? What did he sound like? Writing of what others had said about him, he observed: "For his letters, say they, are weighty and powerful; but his bodily presence is weak" (2 Corinthians 10:10). A nineteenth-century Roman Catholic scholar offered the following: "Sources of information are both scanty and late. Yet as the passing descriptions of the great Apostle which have come down to us agree in several particulars, it cannot be denied that to some extent they give us correct data respecting St. Paul's countenance. They all agree in speaking of his small stature, his long face with high forehead, aquiline nose [i.e., hooked, shaped like an eagle's beak], close and prominent eyebrows. Other features mentioned are partial baldness, grey beard, a clear complexion, and a winning manner."[11]

The beloved nineteenth-century Anglican scholar, Frederick W. Farrar, author of the *Life of Christ*, wrote: "The reader must judge whether any truth may have trickled into the various accounts through centuries of tradition. As they do not contradict, but are rather confirmed by the earliest portraits which have been preserved, we may perhaps assume from them this much, that St. Paul was short, that he had a slight stoop in the shoulders, that his nose was aquiline, that his thin hair was early 'sable silvered.' We may also conjecture that his face was pale, and liable to a quick change of expression."[12]

Joseph Smith provided the following description of Paul in 1841. Note the specificity: "He is about five feet high; very dark hair, dark

---

10. Wright, *Paul: A Biography*, 357.
11. Gigot, *Outlines of New Testament History*, 326–27.
12. Farrar, *Life and Work of St. Paul*, 2:758.

complexion; dark skin; large Roman nose, sharp face; small black eyes, penetrating as eternity; round shoulders; a whining voice, except when elevated, and then it almost resembled the roaring of a lion. He was a good orator, active and diligent, always employing himself in doing good to his fellow man."[13]

MISSIONARY EFFORTS

Paul was raised as a Jew, and so he knew who the Jews were, what they believed, and how and where they worshipped. Whenever Paul entered a city or community, he first determined if there was a Jewish synagogue there. If so, he looked for opportunities to meet with and preach to the Jews in their house of study and worship (see Acts 13:1–5; 17:1–4; 18:4). Paul "preached Christ in the synagogues, that he is the Son of God" (Acts 9:20). If the Jews there did not receive him, the Apostle offered the gospel of Jesus Christ to the Gentiles. Many of Paul's sermons to the Jews were patterned after Stephen's great discourse—marching through Israelite history, citing or quoting from the ancient prophets, and showing how Jesus of Nazareth was the true and ultimate fulfillment of the prophecies, particularly of the promises Jehovah had made to Abraham and his descendants. Although the Acts of the Apostles contains details of Paul's three principal missionary journeys (see Acts 13–14; 16–18; 18:23–21:14), some of his epistles provide details of these journeys not found in Acts. We will address some of Paul's greatest challenges as a missionary in our study of his epistles.

LETTERS (EPISTLES)

Professor Frank F. Judd wrote that "when Paul was unable personally to revisit a particular group of saints, he sometimes sent others to inquire concerning their well being. . . . Sometimes, in lieu of

---

13. Joseph Smith, in "Discourse, 5 January 1841, as Reported by William Clayton"; punctuation and spelling standardized.

personally returning or having one of his companions return to a congregation, Paul would simply send a letter. After the composition was complete, Paul would then send the letter to its recipients. Since there was no real postal service for anyone but government officials in Paul's day, he would have the letter delivered by one or more of his trusted associates."[14]

We must keep in mind that the Epistles of Paul are regulatory correspondence—apostolic counsel to the branches of the Christian church, not systematic theologies: "Paul's 14 epistles found in our present New Testament were written to members of the Church who already had some knowledge of the gospel. They are not evangelistic [i.e., do not primarily serve a missionary purpose]; rather, they are regulatory in nature. The arrangement is neither chronological, geographical, or alphabetical, but by length, in descending order from the longest (Romans) to the shortest (Philemon)."[15] Hebrews is placed at the end of the list because many New Testament scholars through the centuries have questioned its Pauline authorship. Below is a list, in approximate chronological order, of Paul's epistles, grouped under major events in Paul's ministry.

Approximate Chronological Order

First Missionary Journey (AD 45–48)
    No known epistles

Second Missionary Journey (AD 50–51)
    1 Thessalonians (probably from Corinth)
    2 Thessalonians (probably from Corinth)

Third Missionary Journey (AD 55, 57)
    1 Corinthians (probably from Ephesus)
    2 Corinthians (from Ephesus or Philippi)

---

14. Judd, "Epistles of the Apostle Paul," 419–20.
15. Bible Dictionary, "Pauline Epistles," 743.

Galatians (from Corinth)

Romans (from Corinth)

(The epistles to this point heavily emphasize Jewish-Christian relationships and problems. This is particularly true of Paul's defense of his apostolic calling in reaction to the Judaizers, agitators who still clung to the law of Moses, and of his teachings that emphasized faith and grace as opposed to the works of the law.)

First Roman Imprisonment (AD 60, 62)
    Colossians
    Ephesians
    Philemon
    Philippians
    Hebrews

Between Roman Imprisonments (AD 64, 65)
    1 Timothy (from Macedonia or Laodicea)
    Titus (from Ephesus or Nicopolis)

Second Roman Imprisonment (AD 65, 67)
    2 Timothy

(The epistles written during the Roman imprisonments are concerned less with Jewish-Christian problems and more with Gentile-Christian problems, principally with the influences of Greek philosophy and Hellenism in general.)

THE AUTHORSHIP OF HEBREWS

I have chosen to include Hebrews as one of Paul's letters. Many scholars in the early eastern Church simply assumed that Paul was the author. Clement of Alexandria (AD 50–ca. 213), for example, believed that Hebrews was Pauline. In the West, both St. Jerome (AD 347–420) and St. Augustine (AD 354–430) were persuaded that, because Hebrews was in the canon of scripture, the letter must have been written by an Apostle, namely, Paul. In the medieval church, Thomas Aquinas (ca. AD 1225–1274) agreed with Clement of Alexandria and assumed Pauline authorship, although he felt the letter was penned by Luke. Since the sixteenth century (following the Protestant Reformation), however, scholars have in general rejected Pauline authorship based mainly on the argument that the style and content of the work differs somewhat from the other Pauline epistles.

Origen (AD 184–253) expressed his opinion on the matter as follows: "For my own part, if I may state my opinion, I should say that the thoughts are the apostle's but that the style and composition are the work of someone who called to mind the apostle's teaching and wrote short notes, as it were, on what his master [Paul] said. If any church, then, regards this epistle as Paul's, let it be commended on this score; for it was not for nothing that the men of old have handed it down to us as Paul's."[16] Indeed, over the years various authors of Hebrews have been proposed: Clement of Rome, Barnabas, Apollos, Luke, Silas, Epaphras, and Priscilla.[17]

A modern Roman Catholic scholar, Raymond Brown, wrote that "it is enough here to say that the arguments against Pauline authorship are that he nowhere makes any personal reference to himself (although Timothy is mentioned in 13:23), and that its literary style is quite unlike other undoubtedly Pauline writings."[18]

Two Latter-day Saint authors, Professors Sidney B. Sperry[19] and Richard Lloyd Anderson, both believed Paul to be the author of Hebrews. The latter observed: "Hebrews has the same manuscript credentials as other letters of Paul, but its distinctive nature produced

---

16. Quoted in Eusebius, *History of the Church*, book 6, p. 202, par. 25.
17. See Wright and Bird, *New Testament in Its World*, 712–13; Hagner, *Encountering the Book of Hebrews*, 20–23.
18. Brown, *Message of Hebrews*, 15; for an extensive discussion, see Bruce, *Epistle to the Hebrews*, xxxv–xlii.
19. Sperry, *Paul's Life and Letters*, 268–72.

unnecessary skepticism among ancient and modern scholars. Yet trends are not necessarily truths. Of all the arguments against authorship, style is the most easily misused. The Gettysburg address is remarkably unlike most of Lincoln's speeches but of course was authored and delivered by him. . . . Since Hebrews was widely considered one of Paul's letters a century after his death, why is there any doubt? . . . Must the most creative writer of the New Testament fit one literary mold?"[20]

In writing of Paul's letters in general, N. T. Wright insisted:

> Three things have to be said about Pauline style. First, those who have done computer analysis of these things have tended to say that most of the letters came from him. Second, Paul's surviving letters are in fact so short, by comparison with most literary products from the ancient world, that it is hard to be sure we have enough to make a valid comparison. Third, it is easy for critics to be too wooden in their view of *how this or that person ought to write*. It is perfectly possible for the same person to write, in the same week, a learned article for a journal, a speech for a political meeting, a children's talk, and perhaps some scraps of poetry. *Small variations in style—and that is all that they are in the case of the Pauline letters—are to be expected when the same person faces different situations.* . . .
>
> Some earlier generations thought that Paul wrote the Letter to the Hebrews. *The standard objection to this*—that the theology of the letter is so unlike Paul's—*is considerably overstated.*[21]

One Bible scholar offered an unusual possibility regarding Hebrews. He noted that "we know so little about its historical context. I think Hebrews was originally a sermon, noteworthy for its elegant Greek and rhetoric, that eventually was edited in order to fit the format

---

20. Anderson, *Understanding Paul*, 198, 200.
21. Wright, *Paul: A Biography*, 285, 394, emphasis added.

of an epistle, but that is far from the only suggestion. We can't be sure by whom, to whom, when, where, or why it was written."[22]

The Prophet Joseph Smith spoke of Paul as the author of Hebrews[23] and identified him as such in his inspired translation of the Bible. I am prone to believe that Hebrews was, in fact, written by Paul. Although there are several doctrinal matters that are quite distinctive to Hebrews (such as the temple, animal sacrifice, Jesus and Melchizedek, and the Aaronic and Melchizedek Priesthoods), there are other topics or themes in Hebrews that are easily identified in some of Paul's other epistles. For example:

- Hebrews 1:2 (Christ made the worlds—see Ephesians 3:9; Colossians 1:16.)
- Hebrews 2:8 (All will eventually be put under Christ—see 1 Corinthians 15:27–28.)
- Hebrews 2:9 (Christ suffered death for all—see 2 Corinthians 5:21; Galatians 3:13.)
- Hebrews 4:2 (The gospel was preached to the ancients—see Galatians 3:8.)
- Hebrews 4:16; 10:19 (We are invited to come boldly to the throne of grace—see Ephesians 3:12.)
- Hebrews 5:12–14 (The proper occasion for milk and meat—see 1 Corinthians 3:1–2.)
- Hebrews 10:38 (The just shall live by faith—see Romans 1:17; Galatians 3:11.)
- Hebrews 12:1 (Competing in an athletic contest—see Philippians 2:16; Galatians 2:2; 5:7; 2 Timothy 4:7.)
- Hebrews 13:3 (Comparing the Church to a human body—see 1 Corinthians 12:12–27.)
- Hebrews 13:9 (Caution against being carried away by strange

---

22. Svartvik, "Dangerous Book," 35.
23. Joseph Smith, in "Letter to the Church, circa March 1834."

doctrine—see 2 Corinthians 11:3; Ephesians 4:11–15; Colossians 2:8.)
- Hebrews 13:17 (We should obey those who rule over us—see Romans 13:1–2.)
- Hebrews 13:21 (God is working in you—see Ephesians 2:8–10; Philippians 2:12–13.)

I suppose it is possible that a close associate or disciple of Paul could have written Hebrews, drawing upon many of the Apostle's teachings that had been recorded. But until I encounter more convincing evidence otherwise, I will assume Pauline authorship of all fourteen epistles.

ALTERNATE BIBLE TRANSLATIONS

In my doctoral work in a religious studies program, it was very clear from the start that any effort to bring to class or draw upon the King James Version of the Bible (KJV) was highly discouraged and even scoffed at by professors as being naïve and shortsighted. The King James Version was treated much like a rather eccentric older cousin at a family reunion—a member of the family to be sure, but one whose contribution to the occasion is questionable and whose company is to be avoided. In religious studies programs, seminaries, and divinity schools throughout the world, this is the fare on which inquiring and impressionable young minds are invited to dine. This means that large numbers of college and university professors, and perhaps more seriously, an even larger number of ministers and priests, assume their academic posts or their pastoral duties with an established prejudice against the King James Version. And, sadly, students and congregations will be the poorer because of it.

Alister McGrath wrote: "In popular Christian culture, the King James translation is seen to possess a dignity and authority that modern translations somehow fail to convey. Even four hundred years after the six companies of translators began their long and laborious task, their efforts continue to be a landmark for popular Christianity. Other translations will doubtless jostle for place in the nation's bookstores in the twenty-first century. Yet the King James Bible retains its place as a literary and religious classic, by which all others continue to be judged."[24]

I love the King James Version because it lifts my spirit, feeds my soul, and enlightens my mind; I have not always had the same experience with other translations. For those who are eager to point out the antiquated words of the King James Version, I recommend that you study the footnotes found in the Latter-day Saint edition more carefully, in which Hebrew and Greek alternate renderings are provided and idiomatic expressions are explained, thereby allowing readers to derive meaning similar to what might be found in more recent translations.

Now, having sung the praises of the King James Version, I have in this book chosen to include alternate translations occasionally, principally when the language or expressions in the King James are vague and when marginal notes in the Latter-day Saint edition still leave the meaning unclear. These translations include the New Revised Standard Version (NRSV), the Revised English Bible (REB), the New International Version (NIV), the New American Standard Bible (NASB), the English Standard Version (ESV), and a translation by respected New Testament scholar N. T. Wright, known as the Kingdom New Testament (KNT). Finally, I will occasionally draw upon a wonderful paraphrase of the text done by Eugene Peterson, known as *The Message*.

HOW TO USE THIS COMMENTARY

There is no substitute for reading, searching, pondering, and praying over the scriptures themselves. We all need to appreciate that the greatest commentary on scripture is scripture. Beyond the scriptures,

---

24. McGrath, *In the Beginning*, 300.

I will draw upon Joseph Smith's Translation of the Bible (JST); the scriptures of the Restoration; sermons by the Prophet Joseph Smith in which he quotes or paraphrases or offers explanations of Paul's writings; the words of modern apostles and prophets and other Church leaders; the work of trusted Latter-day Saint writers; and occasionally insights from devoted Christian scholars of other faiths. This commentary has been written, therefore, with the hope and understanding that the reader will first read and reflect on the scriptural passages and then turn to the commentary for possible additional insight.

The reader will notice that I occasionally use square brackets throughout the book. Text enclosed in the brackets are alternate translations or clarifications, such as those contained in the marginal notes found in the Latter-day Saint edition of the King James Bible. Often, words and passages are placed in italics to emphasize their significance; unless otherwise noted, these instances of emphasis have been added and are not in the original sources.

THE EPISTLE TO THE ROMANS

Paul's letter to the Saints in Rome is probably quoted or paraphrased more among Christians than any of Paul's other epistles. Romans was written from Corinth in about AD 55–57 and has been referred to as the "granddaddy" of all Paul's writings and teachings. Romans contains some of the most beautiful expressions and explications of the doctrine of Christ, also known as the gospel. Romans is not easy reading, to be sure, but when read prayerfully and humbly, the messages and lessons are stimulating to the mind and spiritually transformative.

"THE GOSPEL OF GOD" (1:1–2)

The salvation of souls is a work in which each member of the Godhead is intimately involved and eternally committed. Elohim, who is God, the Eternal Father; Jesus Christ, who is the Only Begotten Son of God in the flesh; and the Holy Ghost, who is the representative and witness of the Father and the Son—these three are perfectly united and forevermore linked in bringing to pass the immortality and eternal life of the children of God (Moses 1:39). While the Father, Son, and Holy Ghost are one in numerous ways (see John 10:30; 17:21; 2 Nephi 31:21; Alma 11:44; 3 Nephi 11:23–25; Doctrine and Covenants 20:28), there is a hierarchy among these three holy beings. God the

Father is preeminent, the senior member and presiding officer in this divine presidency.

The plan of salvation, the great plan of happiness, is the plan of the Father, taught and declared by Him in our first estate. Therefore the gospel is first and foremost the gospel of God (see Romans 15:16; 1 Thessalonians 2:2, 8; 1 Peter 4:17). We also call this plan the gospel of Jesus Christ because Jehovah—who is Jesus Christ—was the one who, in our premortal existence, was the chief advocate and proponent of the plan and because He was the one sent to earth by the Father to put into effect the terms and conditions of this divine plan.

GRACE AND PEACE TO YOU (1:7)

Paul uses this expression in practically every letter he writes to the various branches of the Church. It is an endearing greeting that is in many ways a plea, a prayer of sorts, in which the Apostle yearns for his beloved Saints to enjoy (1) the grace of God—the Almighty's gifts and blessings and strengthening power; as well as (2) the Almighty's peace—His comfort, His settled and restful influence, and His liberating power.

"I AM NOT ASHAMED" (1:13–16)

Those who have gained a witness or conviction of the gospel of Jesus Christ and have been truly converted—have had their hearts changed and renewed by the power of God's Holy Spirit—proceed through life unhindered and unaffected by the alluring distractions of the devil or the chants and ridicule of those who refuse to listen to the word of truth. Those who have truly been converted possess a quiet confidence, a deep assurance, an anchor. This righteous state impels them to be far more concerned with being proper than politically correct, with being acceptable to God than admired by the world. Each of us hears regularly from the citizens of this raucous crowd, and to the extent that we have chosen first and foremost the kingdom of God, we will, like Lehi, "[heed] them not" (1 Nephi 8:33). Paul knew only too well, just as we should, that once he had accepted Jesus as the Messiah and received His gospel, he had left neutral ground; there was no turning back, no turning around, no retreating. It was the kingdom of God or nothing! Not being ashamed of the gospel—the very power of God unto salvation—and the Lord's Church that administers it results in a humble boldness, a wise fearlessness, and a quiet confidence to face whatever may come.

"THE JUST SHALL LIVE BY FAITH" (1:17; HEBREWS 10:38)

The Apostle then teaches us that, through the gospel of Jesus Christ, the righteousness of God is revealed "through faith on his name" (verse 17, JST). That is, through their faith in Christ, His disciples are lifted and renewed by the righteousness of God. The Book of Mormon can be particularly helpful in better understanding what Paul means when he speaks of the righteousness of God or Christ. Lehi seemed to have had this in mind when he explained to his son Jacob: "I know that thou art redeemed." Why was Jacob redeemed? Was it because he was such a fine young man? Was it because he was basically a "chip off the old block"? Was it because he was helpful and dependable like his older brother Nephi?

All of these things were certainly true of Jacob, but notice what comes next from Lehi: "I know that thou art redeemed, *because of the righteousness of thy Redeemer*" (2 Nephi 2:3). In short, Jacob was bound for glory because of the goodness, the righteousness, of Jesus Christ. It was Aaron, the son of King Mosiah, who taught that because men and women are fallen, they cannot merit anything of themselves (Alma 22:14). The prophets and preachers in the Book of Mormon speak often of merit, but seldom is there a reference to the merits of men and women. Why? Because no matter how good and noble we seek to be, we cannot be saved or redeemed through our own works. We are saved, as Father Lehi taught, by the merits, mercy, and grace of the Holy Messiah (2 Nephi 2:8; see also 2 Nephi 31:19; Alma 24:10; Helaman 14:13; Moroni 6:4).

Although good works matter a great deal, for they are our way of expressing our love and gratitude to a gracious God and a Savior, we cannot perform enough of them to save ourselves. Nor do our good works in any way "repay" the Savior for what He has done for us. We will always and forever be in His debt. We show our love for and demonstrate our gratitude to the Father and the Son by striving to keep the commandments (John 14:15).

Romans 1:17 is a significant passage of scripture for another reason: while Martin Luther was pondering this passage ("the just shall live by faith"), the concept of justification by faith dawned on him. The result was a significant part of the Protestant Reformation—a revolt against the Roman Catholic Church, its priestly hierarchy, its almost nonuse of the Bible, its sale of indulgences, and in general, much of what Luther and his Reformation associates felt were abusive practices and corrupt doctrine.[1] In many ways, the Reformation opened the way for an eventual Restoration in which the fullness of the gospel would once again be on earth, together with revealed doctrine and divine priesthood authority.[2]

GOD'S WRATH AGAINST UNGODLINESS (1:18–32)

These fifteen verses contain, in my view, one of the strongest pure denunciations of sin anywhere in scripture. An alternate translation of the first two verses reads, "For the wrath of God is revealed from

---

1. For a classic treatment of Luther's discovery of Romans 1:17 and the ensuing revolution, see Bainton, *Here I Stand*, 49–50.
2. For more on how the Reformation paved the way for the Restoration, see Joseph Fielding Smith, *Progress of Man*, 237; Joseph Fielding Smith, *Doctrines of Salvation*, 1:174–75; *Teachings of Spencer W. Kimball*, 426–27; *Teachings of Thomas S. Monson*, 132–33; Packer, *Mine Errand from the Lord*, 388–89; McConkie, *Millennial Messiah*, 90–93, 400–401; McConkie, *New Witness for the Articles of Faith*, 672–74.

heaven against all ungodliness of men, *who by their unrighteousness suppress the truth. For what can be known about God is plain to them, because God has shown it to them*" (verses 18–19, ESV). Or, in another translation, "For the anger of God is unveiled from heaven against all the ungodliness and injustice performed by people *who use injustice to suppress the truth.* What can be known of God, you see, is plain to them, since God has made it plain unto them. Ever since the world was made, his eternal power and deity have been seen and known in the things he made. As a result, they have no excuse: they knew God, but didn't honor him as God or thank him" (verses 18–21, KNT). In short, those who are honest-hearted, unafraid of truth, and willing to set aside their own wisdom and excessive dependence on the rational mind and merely attend to the beauty and order of the cosmos, have "seen God moving in his majesty and power" (Doctrine and Covenants 88:47).

When we read in verse 24 that "God gave them up to uncleanness through the lusts of their own hearts," we are reminded that God will force no person to heaven; His children possess moral agency, and He thus allows them to choose, even to choose unwisely, often painfully and tragically, and thus reap the whirlwind of consequences. The result is idolatry: those who make unwise choices end up worshipping the creations of God rather than the Creator Himself. Then follows a condemnation of sins such as fornication, covetousness, maliciousness, envy, deceit, backbiting, disobedience to parents, and murder.

I am persuaded that if first-century Paul were living today, he would offer counsel that would be in harmony with what twenty-first century apostles and prophets teach regarding the law of chastity. A modern prophet, President Russell M. Nelson, explained to Brigham Young University students: "God has not changed His law of chastity. Requirements to enter the temple have not changed." He added that "because we feel the depths of God's love for His children, we care deeply about every child of God, regardless of age, circumstance, gender, sexual orientation, or other unique challenges."³

N. T. Wright has written:

> When God gives human beings responsibility he means it. The choices we make, not only individually but as a species, are choices whose consequences God, alarmingly, allows us to explore. He will warn us; he will give us opportunities to repent and change course; but if we choose idolatry we must expect our humanness, bit by bit, to dissolve. When you worship the God in whose image you are made, you reflect that image more brightly and become more fully and truly human. When you (and by "you" I mean the human race as a whole, not simply individuals) worship something other than the living God, something that is itself merely another created object, and hence subject to decay and death, you diminish that image-bearingness, that essential humanness.⁴

NO RESPECTER OF PERSONS (2:3–11)

God loves all of His children perfectly. A person who is outside the Christian faith, for example, who is decent and upright, who strives to the best of his or her ability to be a positive influence in society, to be true to what we know as the Judeo-Christian ethic, enjoys the approbation of the Creator of heaven and earth. On the other hand, a man or woman who knowingly violates the Ten Commandments, be they Latter-day Saint or otherwise, and who has not yet seared their conscience, will usually feel inner conflict, guilt, alienation, and general unhappiness.

Now, while God is no respecter of persons, those who strive to keep His commandments do receive his approbation in the form of blessings. Nephi observed that "the Lord esteemeth all flesh in one; [but] he

---

3. Nelson, "Love and Laws of God."
4. Wright, *Paul for Everyone*, 1:23.

that is righteous is favored of God" (1 Nephi 17:35). "Favored" here does not mean preferred over another but rather in a position to be blessed by God. Our Father in Heaven does not cease to love us when we stray. Thus even though He loves the wicked man as much as he loves the devoted woman, there are things He simply cannot do for the sinner that are given freely to the faithful. A modern revelation states, "If you keep not my commandments, the love of the Father shall not continue with you, therefore you shall walk in darkness" (Doctrine and Covenants 95:12). To be clear, this does not mean that God ceases to love the wayward, but rather that a sinful person cannot enjoy the sweet benefits of feeling and enjoying the love of God in his or her heart.

JUDGED ACCORDING TO THE LIGHT WE HAVE (2:12–15)

No one will be condemned for not keeping a law or abiding by a standard of which they are ignorant. Paul explains that "where no law is, there is no transgression" (Romans 4:15). Or as Jacob, son of Lehi, declared, "Where there is no law given there is no punishment; and where there is no punishment there is no condemnation; and where there is no condemnation the mercies of the Holy One of Israel have claim upon them, because of the atonement; for they are delivered by the power of him. For the atonement satisfieth the demands of his justice upon all those who have not the law given to them" (2 Nephi 9:25–26).

At the same time, we are taught that every person who is born into this world comes with a native endowment we know as the Light of Christ or the Spirit of Jesus Christ (see John 1:9; Moroni 7:16; Doctrine and Covenants 84:46). This light is the source of reason, judgment, moral values, and conscience. All are expected to follow this light and to obey its promptings. If they do so, they will in time (either in this life or the next) be led to the fullness of the covenant gospel, where through baptism and the reception of the gift of the Holy Ghost, they will obtain a higher light (Doctrine and Covenants 84:46–48).

Paul thus writes that when the Gentiles obey the laws of God, even when they are unaware of those laws, they are "a law to themselves." That is, "when Gentiles who do not have the Law do instinctively the things of the Law, these . . . show the work of the Law written in their hearts" (verses 14–15, NASB). In this sense, then, even the Gentiles were expected to be true to the light they have, even when they did not know the tenets of the law of Moses.

> What then of the Gentiles who do not have the Law? Paul proceeds to show that they know enough about what is right and what is wrong for them to be judged by the same general principle. . . . Doing by nature things required by the law refers to those occasions when a Gentile does something that is also prescribed in the law. Thus he may honor his parents or refrain from stealing. He does these things by nature. . . . The Gentile does not have the law revealed in the Old Testament, but his conduct shows that he knows right. God is at work in him. He knows enough of "law" to be guilty when he sins, even though he may not know the God who prescribes right conduct, or even that there is a God that prescribes it.[5]

THE CIRCUMCISION OF THE HEART (2:28–29)

The commandment to circumcise male infants at the age of eight days came to Abraham. Circumcision was a token of the covenant God made with the Father of the Faithful, one of many identity markers for the descendants of Abraham, and a deeply significant reminder concerning the accountability of children. "I will establish a covenant of circumcision with thee, and it shall be my covenant between me and thee, and thy seed after thee, in their generations; that thou mayest know forever that *children are not accountable before me until they are eight years old*" (Genesis 17:11, JST; compare Doctrine and Covenants 68:27).

Paul's point is that circumcision alone does not make one a Jew,

---

5. Morris, *Epistle to the Romans*, 121, 124, 125.

any more than living the Word of Wisdom makes one a Latter-day Saint. He then teaches a marvelous lesson: it is the circumcision of the heart, the cleansing and purification of the soul, that makes one a true Israelite. It is the lifelong effort to sanctify one's very being that makes that person a part of "an holy nation, a peculiar people," a society that is engaged in "the praises of him who hath called you out of darkness into his marvellous light" (1 Peter 2:9).

ADVANTAGES OF BEING A JEW (3:1–2)

Having made the point that circumcision is not an end in itself but rather the means to a grand end, Paul asks, essentially, "So what's the value of being a Jew? Why is it such an important matter?" His answer is straightforward: unto the Jews were committed "the oracles of God," meaning the revelations of God through prophets. It was unto the Jews that Jehovah revealed Himself as the one true and living God. It was unto the Jews that the words of the prophets were delivered. It was unto the children of Israel that the Ten Commandments were given. It was to the descendants of Abraham that the priesthood, the gospel of Jesus Christ, blessings of the temple, and sealing power were delivered (Abraham 2:9–11; Doctrine and Covenants 124:37–39; 132:39). And most important, it was first to the Jews that the Messiah, the Anointed One, the Savior of humankind, was sent.

ALL ARE UNDER SIN (3:9–18, 23)

"Just as a man does not really desire food until he is hungry," President Ezra Taft Benson taught, "so he does not desire the salvation of Christ until he knows why he needs Christ. No one adequately and properly knows why he needs Christ until he understands and accepts the doctrine of the Fall and its effect upon all mankind."[6] To use another analogy, a person does not see the need to take her medicine if she does not understand that she is ill. One does not delight in a

---

6. Benson, *Witness and a Warning*, 33.

solution unless he appreciates the difficulty of the problem. Good news is always much more appreciated when we know what the bad news is.

Thus, before Paul teaches and testifies to the Roman Saints of the work of salvation undertaken by Jesus Christ, the Apostle senses the need to write of the plight of fallen humanity. He begins by observing that when it comes to the people on earth, "they are all under sin" (verse 9). We live in a fallen world. Life is difficult. Men and women are frequently bruised and beaten by the vicissitudes of life, worn down by life on a telestial planet. Earthquakes and tsunamis and tornados wreak havoc on our world. Adults and children contract diseases. The body decays with the passing of time. Death dogs the steps of every person who is born.

The scriptures of the Restoration make it clear that even though the Fall was a vital part of the great plan of the Eternal God (see 2 Nephi 2:24–26)—as much a foreordained act as Christ's intercession—our state, including our relationship to and contact with God, changed dramatically when Adam and Eve partook of the forbidden fruit. Although we understand that we are not accountable for Adam and Eve's act in Eden and will not be punished for it (see Articles of Faith 1:2), it would be foolish to suppose that we are *unaffected* by it.

JUSTIFICATION BY FAITH (3:9–22)

The children of our Father in Heaven have been sent to earth on a mission—to learn, to grow, to gain experience, to face and overcome opposition, to practice self-control. We come to earth to be proved (see Abraham 3:24–26), to see if we, now having a veil of forgetfulness across our minds, can exercise faith in the Lord Jesus Christ and in the Father's plan of salvation. We come into this second estate to repent and improve and to learn how to have our souls sanctified from sin and our hearts purified from worldliness. We come here to learn to be a *just*, meaning a *righteous*, person.

When the restored Church was organized, the Savior stated: "And we know that justification through the grace of our Lord and Savior

Jesus Christ is just and true; and we know also, that sanctification through the grace of our Lord and Savior Jesus Christ is just and true, to all those who love and serve God with all their mights, minds, and strength" (Doctrine and Covenants 20:30–31). It is as though the Lord was saying there is a true doctrine of justification, as well as a true doctrine of sanctification, both of which come through the goodness and grace of the Savior and the faithfulness of the sons and daughters of God. To be *justified* means to be forgiven of sin, pardoned, pronounced innocent, and placed once again in a proper relationship with Deity. *Sanctification* comes to members of the Savior's Church who strive to be true to their covenants and do so faithfully until the end of their lives. It is the ongoing process by which, through the cleansing power of the Holy Spirit, the very nature of men and women is changed—made pure and holy. Sanctification is to be freed from the *effects* of sin.

Elder D. Todd Christofferson pointed out that "justification and sanctification are at the center of God's gracious plan of salvation." Speaking of justification, he continued that "pardon comes by the grace of Him who has satisfied the demands of justice by His own suffering, 'the just for the unjust, that he might bring us to God' (1 Peter 3:18). He removes our condemnation without removing the law. We are pardoned and placed in a condition of righteousness with Him. We become like Him, without sin. We are sustained and protected by the law, by justice. We are, in a word, *justified*. Thus, we may appropriately speak of one who is justified as pardoned, without sin, or guiltless."

Elder Christofferson explained further that "to be sanctified through the blood of Christ is to become clean, pure, and holy. If justification removes the punishment for past sin, then sanctification removes the stain or effects of sin. . . . This marvelous pardon that relieves us of the punishment that justice would otherwise exact for disobedience and the purifying sanctification that flows are best described as gifts. . . . Given the magnitude of the gift of grace, we would never suppose, even with all the good we could possibly do in this life, that we had earned it. It is just too great."⁷ In speaking of those who will inherit the highest heaven, the celestial glory, the Lord declared: "These are they who are *just* men [and women] *made perfect through Jesus the mediator of the new covenant*, who wrought out this perfect atonement through the shedding of his own blood" (Doctrine and Covenants 76:69).

Section 20 of the Doctrine and Covenants teaches, as did the Apostle Paul, that justification comes, not just through keeping the commandments of the Lord, but as a gift from a gracious and loving Lord. In other words, while we strive to keep the Lord's laws and statutes—that is, to perform the works of righteousness—there should be no misunderstanding as to how one is justified; it is by the goodness and grace of the Lord. Now, because no one—save Jesus only—will walk earth's paths without committing sin, we cannot be justified or saved by our works or by law. Our only hope is to hold tenaciously to and lean forevermore on the One who *did* keep God's law perfectly, the only person who could rightly be saved by law or by works. In other words, our only hope is to be justified and saved *by faith*.⁸

PROPITIATION FOR THE PENITENT (3:23–28)

My colleague Stephen Robinson pointed out many years ago that the children of God find themselves on the horns of a spiritual dilemma. Paul teaches: "For all have sinned, and come short of the glory of God" (verse 23). And in the preface to the Doctrine and Covenants, the Lord declared: "I the Lord cannot look upon sin with the least degree of allowance" (Doctrine and Covenants 1:31). "In other words," Brother Robinson noted,

> all human beings, even the best among us, have committed sins or have displayed imperfections that are incompatible with

---

7. Christofferson, "Justification and Sanctification," 22.
8. An excellent discussion of this matter is found in Lund, "Salvation: By Grace or by Works?" 20–22.

the celestial standard and that God cannot tolerate. Here as elsewhere, Paul implies that there are only two categories: For him either you are perfect or you are a sinner in some degree. There is no middle ground. . . .

Now from these two facts—God's absolute demand for perfection and our absolute inability to come up with it—one conclusion is inescapable: *we* cannot be allowed to dwell in the presence of God, sinful and imperfect beings as we are. This contradiction between God's demands and our inability to carry them out represents the most serious problem with the direst consequences in all the universe.[9]

There's the problem. But Jesus Christ is the solution.

Paul emphasizes that through Christ we are "justified freely by his grace through the redemption that is in Christ Jesus" (verse 24). Or, stated more perfectly, we are "justified *only* by his grace through the redemption that is in Christ Jesus" (JST).

Paul continues by stating that God the Father "hath set forth [Christ] to be a propitiation through faith in his blood" (verse 25). *Propitiation* is a word that is rarely used in our day. Other translations (NIV, NRSV) render this term as "sacrifice of atonement," or as we would say, "atoning sacrifice." "Therefore we conclude," Paul adds, "that a man is justified by faith alone without [i.e., apart from] the deeds of the law" (verse 28, JST). By faith alone. Faith is never completely alone, however, since true saving faith implies and cannot be separated from faithfulness, from obedience and dedicated discipleship.

ABRAHAM WAS JUSTIFIED BY FAITH (4:1–8, 21–25)

Paul draws upon Father Abraham to make his point, illustrating how the principle of justification by faith works. Paul reasons thus: If Abraham had been justified by works, then the Father of the Faithful

---

9. Robinson, *Believing Christ*, 2–3; emphasis in original.

could boast in his own spiritual success. In verses 2 and 3, Paul then reminds us of what Moses wrote: "And [Abraham] believed in the Lord; and [God] counted it to him for righteousness" (Genesis 15:6). Paul then makes a statement that could easily be misunderstood and even wrested by persons whose motives are less than pure: "Now to him that worketh is the reward not reckoned of grace, but of debt. But to him that worketh not, but believeth on him that justifieth the ungodly, his faith is counted for righteousness" (verses 4–5). The Joseph Smith Translation of this passage brings clarity: "Now to him who is justified by the law of works, is the reward reckoned, not of grace, but of debt. But to him *that seeketh not to be justified by the law of works, but believeth on him who justifieth not the ungodly,* his faith is counted for righteousness." That is to say, if people declare that they have been justified by their works, then what they are really saying is that God is in their debt, that God owes them for what they have done. On the other hand, if they declare that they have been justified, not by works but by faith, their faith is a righteous faith and that righteousness is placed on their celestial account.

Paul then introduces us to the word *impute*. To impute means to put on one's ledger, to place on one's account, or to credit that person. He then quotes the Psalms: "Blessed is he whose transgression is forgiven, whose sin is covered. Blessed is the man unto whom the Lord imputeth not iniquity, and in whose spirit there is no guile" (Psalm 32:1–2). When we break the laws of God, God imputes to us sin with its consequences; figuratively speaking, He places it on our spiritual ledger. On the other hand, those who demonstrate true faith in God, through both belief and behavior, have righteousness and its consequences imputed to them. And this brings us closer to the grand principle Paul is seeking to teach us: those who have faith in Jesus Christ—who totally trust Him, have complete confidence in Him, and are ever ready to rely upon Him—have the righteousness of Christ placed upon their ledger (see the discussion of Romans 1:17 herein).

The Lord pleads our cause on the basis of *His merits*. We are saved through *His works* and *His mercy and grace* (see 2 Nephi 2:8; Alma 24:10). And what does He require? "Wherefore, Father, spare these my brethren *that believe on my name*, that they may come unto me and have everlasting life" (Doctrine and Covenants 45:5). What a person trusts in, what he or she relies on—these are excellent indicators of one's spiritual maturity. Like the infant who grasps and clings to objects with selfish immaturity, we are prone to be stingy with our lives, to insist on doing things our way, to chart a course that we want to pursue, to insist on having complete control. While we labor in the flesh, we are subject to a kind of mortal myopia, a tragic shortsightedness in regard to eternal things. Yet, in our heart of hearts we know that God's ways are higher than ours and His thoughts and judgments so much grander than our own (see Isaiah 55:8–9).

President Ezra Taft Benson declared: "Men and women who turn their lives over to God will discover that He can make a lot more out of their lives than they can. He will deepen their joys, expand their vision, quicken their minds, strengthen their muscles, lift their spirits, multiply their blessings, increase their opportunities, comfort their souls, raise up friends, and pour out peace."[10]

JUSTIFICATION BRINGS PEACE (5:1)

Simon Peter, Paul's apostolic colleague, teaches: "Humble yourselves therefore under the mighty hand of God, that he may exalt you in due time: *casting all your care upon him; for he careth for you*" (1 Peter 5:6–7). We all know that we can cast our burdens upon the Lord because He cares for us—because He loves us. Peter is basically counseling us: "Quit worrying. Don't be so anxious. Stop wringing your hands. Let Jesus take the burden while you take the peace. Trust him." I once heard someone express the following (I wish I knew the source): "Grace represents God's acceptance of me. Faith represents my acceptance of God's acceptance of

---

10. *Teachings of Ezra Taft Benson*, 361.

me. Peace is my acceptance of me." C. S. Lewis wrote, "Thus if you have really handed yourself over to Him, it must follow that you are trying to obey Him. But *trying in a new way, a less worried way*."[11]

RECONCILED BY HIS DEATH, SAVED BY HIS LIFE (5:8–10)

Many times while serving as a priesthood leader, I have met with members of the Church who harbor their sin for an extended period; they bear a crushing weight. When I ask why they wait so long to begin the process of repentance, the answers are all somewhat different, but the essence of their replies has been the same: "I wanted to get right with God, to be more worthy before I met with you." But the Savior doesn't ask us to wait until we are cleansed from sin, until we are "worthy," to heal us, to remit our sins and purify our hearts. We are, one and all, invited to come unto Him as we are.

The *Random House College Dictionary* defines the word *reconcile* as follows: "to cause to cease hostility or opposition; to cause (a person) to accept or be resigned to something not desired; to harmonize or settle (a quarrel)." From Latin, the term means literally "to sit again with."[12] As a parent and grandparent I can appreciate especially the literal meaning of the word. On a few occasions through the years, when my wife and I have had sober conversations or confrontations with one of our children, at a particularly difficult moment, the child has stood up and begun to walk out of the room. One of us has inevitably responded: "Come back here, please. Sit down with us. Let's work this out." Then after conversing about tough issues, apologies, and resolves, we all left the room together. We were *reconciled*.

Jesus the Christ came to earth to reconcile fallen, mortal, and sinful men and women to an exalted, immortal, and sinless God. Through applying the principles of the Savior's gospel—faith, repentance, baptism, receiving the gift of the Holy Ghost, and enduring faithfully to the end

---

11. Lewis, *Mere Christianity*, 131 (book 3, chap. 12).
12. Quoted in Nelson, *Perfection Pending*, 165–66.

of one's life—we are able to have our sins forgiven, our hearts changed, our desires educated, and our souls transformed. We are then in a position to be with and abide comfortably in the presence of our Father in Heaven. We are reconciled to Him (see 2 Nephi 10:24; 25:23).

According to Paul's words in verse 10, we are "reconciled to God by the death of his Son" and then "saved by his life." That is, we are brought back, united with the Father through the atoning work of Jesus, through His sufferings and death. Jesus did not, however, come to earth just to die for us; He came to *live in us*. Having died to the old man of sin (see Romans 6:6), we are brought back to life, spiritually resuscitated, as God's Holy Spirit once again takes up residence within our souls.

WE HAVE RECEIVED THE ATONEMENT (5:11)

The King James Version renders verse 11, "And not only so, but we also joy in God through our Lord Jesus Christ, by whom we have now received the atonement." The English word *atonement* occurs only once in that form in the King James Version of the New Testament. It might be misleading, however, to suggest that this is the only time the word is used. Rather, the Greek word is rendered repeatedly as *reconcile* or *reconciliation* (such as in Romans 5:10; 11:15; 2 Corinthians 5:18; Colossians 1:20; Hebrews 2:17). The Hebrew word translated as *atone* was *Kafar*, meaning "to cover." The Arabic or Aramaic word translated as *atone* is *Kafat*, meaning "to embrace."

The Savior's reconciliation "covers" our sins, much as a tablecloth might cover a table or as a friend might offer to "cover" the cost of a lunch meeting. Or the word might also be used to connote the embrace that accompanies the reconciliation of previously divided parties. The latter usage is illustrated in Lehi's farewell to his family. He testifies that "the Lord hath redeemed my soul from hell; I have beheld his glory, and *I am encircled about eternally in the arms of his love*" (2 Nephi 1:15; see also Mormon 5:11). In this dispensation, the Redeemer implored His Latter-day Saints: "Be faithful and diligent in keeping the commandments of God, and I will *encircle thee in the arms of my love*" (Doctrine and Covenants 6:20).

"Through the atonement accomplished by Jesus Christ," Elder James E. Talmage wrote, "a redeeming service, vicariously rendered in behalf of mankind, all of whom have become estranged from God by the effects of sin both inherited and individually incurred—the way is opened for a reconciliation whereby man may come again into communion, and be made fit to dwell anew and forever in the presence of his Eternal Father. This basal thought is admirably implied in our English word, 'atonement,' which, as its syllables attest, is *at-one-ment*."[13] Indeed, the At-one-ment is a process of bringing together that which has been separated—namely, the children of God from God.

THE OFFENSE OF ONE, THE JUSTIFICATION OF MANY (5:18–19)

Because of Adam and Eve's violation of the commandment not to partake of the forbidden fruit, spiritual death passed upon *all men and women*; we were separated from God and from things of righteousness. Even so, by the perfect obedience and righteousness of *one man*—Jesus Christ, our Lord—*all men and women* have the opportunity to overcome the effects of the Fall and be made righteous.

"SHALL WE CONTINUE IN SIN?" (6:1–2, 15)

After we begin to understand better the beautiful message of the grace of God, we can see it everywhere. The scriptures place a repetitive emphasis on the goodness and mercy and divine grace made available through our Lord's suffering, death, and Resurrection. Though this doctrine is marvelous and uplifting, teaching it can indeed be a risk, one that is as real in the twenty-first century as it was in the first century when it was presented by the Apostle Paul. Gospel liberty is very appealing, but what is a godsend and a breath of fresh air to one who

---

13. Talmage, *Jesus the Christ*, 23; emphasis in original.

is doing her best but falling short becomes a temptation to continue in sin to another looking for shortcuts or flirting with evil.

Paul's question here to the Saints in Rome is quite simple. He essentially asks, "Now, since we understand that justification comes by faith in Christ and that salvation comes by the grace of Christ, should we then regularly take occasion to sin, knowing that the Savior is ever willing to forgive, knowing that faith and salvation are the gifts of God?" Paul answers his own question: "God forbid," meaning "May it not be!" Why? Because by so doing, we "despite [i.e., insult] . . . the Spirit of grace" (Hebrews 10:29). We treat the Lord's sufferings and death in our behalf as though they were paltry and insignificant offerings. We mock the very God who extends His hand to us always and everlastingly. A true Saint, one who is growing and delighting in the goodness and grace of our Lord, is eager to keep the commandments and to be steadfast and immovable, because he or she is looking for every way possible to express gratitude and demonstrate love to the Father and the Son for the unspeakable gift they proffer us.

"BAPTIZED INTO HIS DEATH" (6:3–10; COLOSSIANS 2:12–17)

Paul now begins to explain how the ordinance of baptism, a rite necessary for entrance into the Church and kingdom of God (see John 3:3–5; 2 Nephi 31:5–7), points to a greater and grander reality. A true believer participates in a public ceremony, attesting that he or she is fully committed to a life in Christ. In being baptized, the new Christian publicly professes a belief in Christ's Atonement and Resurrection. At the heart of the baptismal covenant is a sacred agreement to be united with Christ in both death and life. First, sincere newcomers to the Christian life enter the waters of baptism fully intending to undergo a mighty change: to turn away from (repent of) a life of selfishness and sin, to put to death the old man of sin (verse 6).

Baptism by immersion is in the similitude of the Crucified One being placed in the tomb of Joseph of Arimathea. Baptized persons come forth out of the water to what Paul calls a "newness of life" (verse 4), born from above, quickened as pertaining to things of righteousness. This is, of course, in similitude of the Son of God rising from the tomb on that first Easter morning, resurrected and glorified (see Doctrine and Covenants 128:12–13). In the words of Alma the Elder, those who are "baptized in the name of the Lord" become "a witness before him that [they] have entered into a covenant with him, that [they] will serve him and keep his commandments, that he may pour out his Spirit more abundantly upon [them]" (Mosiah 18:10).

The King James Version renders Paul's words, "For if we have been planted together in the likeness of his death, we shall be also in the likeness of his resurrection" (verse 5). In another translation this passage reads: "For if we have been united with him in a death like his, we shall certainly be united with him in a resurrection like his" (ESV). Paul continues, "Our old man is crucified with him, that the body of sin might be destroyed," or, perhaps, "rendered powerless" (verse 6, KJV, NIV).

The Atonement of Jesus Christ took place once (see verse 10), and that was in Jerusalem of Judea in about AD 33 or 34. While its effects are indeed infinite in scope (timeless, reaching to all that Christ created), Jesus suffered in Gethsemane and on Golgotha for the sins of humanity once, and He rose from the dead one time. He will suffer for sin no more, die no more, nor will He be resurrected again. The Resurrection is the inseparable union of body and spirit (Doctrine and Covenants 93:33–34).

SERVANTS (SLAVES) OF THE ONE WE OBEY (6:16–18)

Jesus offered the chilling warning that "whosoever committeth sin is the servant of sin" (John 8:34). Any person who persists or continues in sin, who rebels against God's law and remains in an unrepentant state, becomes a slave to sin (compare 1 John 3:6, 9). The Apostle Peter wrote, "While [the wicked] promise them liberty, they themselves are the servants of corruption: for of whom a man is overcome, of the same is he brought in bondage" (2 Peter 2:19). Unhealthy or inappropriate actions, if not confronted and corrected, become habitual. They result in addictive patterns, and as time passes, these chains of hell become more confining and the individual becomes more bound and controlled by his or her own behaviors or attitudes.

PAUL BEFORE AND AFTER CHRIST (7:1–25)

Chapter 7 of Romans has resulted in more misunderstanding about Paul and about the human race in general than almost any other chapter of scripture. A cursory reading will cause most persons unfamiliar with the Pauline epistles to shake their heads and wonder how in the world the Apostle Paul managed to garner so much attention through the years, as well as how he could possibly have been so admired and respected by Christians through the centuries. As it reads in the King James Version or, for that matter, most any other translation, we see poor, old, pitiful Paul—a weak, simpering, and pathetic excuse of a man whose life is completely out of control; a man who never does what he should do and always seems to be doing what he shouldn't.

My late colleague Robert J. Matthews wrote: "As rendered in the KJV, Paul is sinful, carnal, and wicked even after years in the apostleship, and knows not how to do good, or even what is good. The JST rewords the passage in such a way as to show the difference between Paul's life while under the law of Moses and his life after he found and obeyed the gospel of Christ."[14] In the Joseph Smith Translation, Paul explains that when he was living under the law of Moses, he was carnal, but through the gospel, including receiving its covenants and ordinances, he has become spiritual. Most important, the Joseph Smith Translation states that it is "only in Christ" that he learned how to be a good man and that "through the assistance of Christ," Paul subdues the sin within him (verses 19, 22, JST).

---

14. Matthews, *Behold the Messiah*, 341.

NO CONDEMNATION FOR THOSE
WHO ARE "IN CHRIST" (8:1, 5–11)

Paul uses some form of the phrase "in Christ" well over one hundred times in his letters. This matter is clearly dear to his heart, a subject that he feels should be emphasized again and again. But what does "in Christ" mean? To his beloved Corinthian Saints, the Apostle writes simply that "we have the mind of Christ" (1 Corinthians 2:16). This expression is closely related to a person being "in Christ."

Fallen and unredeemed mortals tend to focus on whatever brings them attention, acclaim, prominence, pleasure, or power. From their perspective, they are the center of the universe, while all other people or circumstances exist merely to meet their carnal needs and pamper their ever-expanding egos. They are gripped and ensnared by pride. Carnal or natural men or women take their cues from the world about them, and they are largely externally driven. They are enemies to God and to themselves, since they work at cross-purposes to the Father's plan for the happiness and salvation of His children (Mosiah 3:19; Alma 41:10–11).

On the other hand, once people have determined to come unto Christ, have experienced godly sorrow for their sins, and have confessed and forsaken those sins, the Savior of Souls is more than eager to forgive and forget (see Mosiah 26:30; Doctrine and Covenants 58:42–43). Following repentance and baptism (and continual repentance for those are who already members), they are entitled to enjoy what President Wilford Woodruff called the greatest gift of God as pertaining to mortality—the gift of the Holy Ghost.[15] The Holy Ghost is a sanctifier. By virtue of the atoning blood of Jesus Christ shed in Gethsemane and on Golgotha, the Spirit of God, who is the agent of the new birth, the midwife of conversion, is able to purge the penitent

---

15. *Discourses of Wilford Woodruff*, 5.

individual from worldliness and wayward actions, thoughts, and feelings and from self-centeredness, pride, and unholy ambition.

The repentant man or woman will then begin to see the world—and certainly the people in it—with new eyes. He or she strives to think as the Lord would think, to feel what the Lord would feel, and to act as the Lord would act. In short, these individuals seek to have an eye single to the glory of God (Matthew 6:22; Doctrine and Covenants 88:67). Such people are said to be "in Christ." John the Beloved put it simply: "*Hereby know we that we dwell in him, and he in us, because he hath given us of his Spirit*" (1 John 4:13; see also John 17:21; 2 Corinthians 5:17). In a revelation received by the Prophet Joseph Smith in May 1831, the Lord said, "And the Father and I are one. I am in the Father and the Father in me; and *inasmuch as ye have received me, ye are in me and I in you*" (Doctrine and Covenants 50:43). This divine indwelling relationship allows the Saints to have the mind of Christ.

Chapter 8 begins with Paul's declaration that "there is therefore now no condemnation to them which are in Christ Jesus, who walk not after the flesh, but after the Spirit. For the law of the Spirit of life in Christ Jesus hath made me free from the law of sin and death" (verses 1–2). In other words, the way you and I can know that we are not under condemnation, but rather under the grace or approbation of God, is that we have and enjoy the Holy Spirit in our lives. Thus when Paul explains that to be carnally minded is death (compare 2 Nephi 9:39), he is emphasizing that to be in sin, to have gone contrary to the mind and will of the Lord, is to live under condemnation, while to be spiritually minded is "life and peace" (verse 6). Whenever Paul refers to "the flesh," he is not merely referring to the physical body; rather, he is referring to mortality, fallenness, and life in this telestial world.

"WAITING FOR THE ADOPTION" (8:14–23)

Those who have come alive to the things of the Spirit, who have had their spiritual eyes opened and their hearts attuned to matters pertaining to the Lord and His gospel—these are the sons and daughters of God. John the Beloved wrote that Christ "came unto his own, and his own received him not. But as many as received him, *to them gave he power to become the sons of God*, even to them that believe on his name" (John 1:11–12). This same language is used by the Savior in our own dispensation. He declared that "as many as receive me, to them will I give power to become the sons of God, even to them that believe on my name" (Doctrine and Covenants 11:30). And Orson Pratt was informed that "Jesus Christ your Redeemer . . . so loved the world that he gave his own life, that as many as would believe might become the sons of God" (Doctrine and Covenants 34:1, 3).

Some readers might ask at this point, "If we accept the Savior, how will we be given *power to become* the sons and daughters of God? Aren't we already His spirit children? Isn't He the Father of our spirits?' And of course the answer is yes; God is the Father of our spirits (see Numbers 16:22; 27:16; Hebrews 12:9). The verses cited above, however, speak of those persons who accept Jesus Christ and His gospel as *being given the power to become* the children of God. This power is the power of redemption, the power of the Lord's Atonement, the power that derives from the gospel of Jesus Christ, the "power of God unto salvation" (Romans 1:16).

To say this another way, those who come unto Christ by covenant and through the saving ordinances become the sons and daughters of God *by adoption*. They are adopted into the royal family of God. This is essentially the testimony that Joseph Smith and Sidney Rigdon bore in the vision of the degrees of glory, when they attested that by and through Christ "the worlds are and were created, and *the inhabitants thereof are begotten sons and daughters unto God*" (Doctrine and Covenants 76:24). They are begotten by redemption and spiritual regeneration. This is what King Benjamin had in mind when he spoke to those who had heard his magnificent sermon, been deeply moved by the Spirit, and then covenanted to be obedient to God and His commandments. They became, in the words of Benjamin, "the children of Christ, his sons, and his daughters; for behold, this day he hath spiritually begotten you" (Mosiah 5:7). Thus to be born again is to enter into a new family relationship, to take upon us the family name (the name of Christ), and to receive the divine charge to be true and faithful to that holy name and all that it represents. It is to become Christians in the fullest sense.

Paul continues: "For I reckon that the sufferings of this present time are not worthy to be compared with the glory which shall be revealed in us. For the earnest expectation of the creature waiteth for the manifestation of the sons of God" (verses 18–19). Put another way, "This is how I work it out. The sufferings we go through in the present time are not worth putting in the scale alongside the glory that is going to be unveiled for us. Yes: creation itself is on tiptoe with expectation, eagerly awaiting the moment when God's children will be revealed" (KNT).

PRAYER IN THE SPIRIT (8:26–27)

Most of us are well aware that God the Father is the ultimate object of our worship and that our prayers should be directed to Him. And we know that we are to pray to the Father in the name of the Son. But perhaps we are not quite as familiar with the idea that our prayers, in order to meet the divine standard, should be prompted, guided, and empowered by the Holy Spirit. In other words, as with all forms of divine communication—including sermons, gospel lessons, and so forth—prayers can be carried out under the direction of the third member of the Godhead. Prayer is not, and should not be, merely a product of our own thoughts and feelings. Prayer is intended to engender communion with Deity, to create a dialogue, not a monologue.

"He that asketh in the Spirit asketh according to the will of God; wherefore it is done even as he asketh" (Doctrine and Covenants 46:30). "And if ye are purified and cleansed from all sin, ye shall ask whatsoever you will in the name of Jesus and it shall be done. But know this, it shall be given you what you shall ask" (Doctrine and Covenants 50:29–30). "Let my servants, Joseph Smith, Jun., and Sidney Rigdon, seek them a home, as they are taught through prayer by the Spirit" (Doctrine and Covenants 63:65). Each of these passages suggests that divine instruction that can come through prayer. The Lord may choose, through His Spirit, to teach us what we should pray for and to actually provide the words for our supplication.

Why would we need God to give us the very words we should use in addressing Him? As Paul explains, "The Spirit also helpeth our infirmities: for we know not what we should pray for as we ought: but the Spirit itself maketh intercession for us with groanings which cannot be uttered" (verse 26), or more correctly, "with striving which cannot be expressed."[16] Generally, we pray for our wants, when in truth it would be wiser and more beneficial to pray for our needs. Often, however, we are unable to discern what is most critical in our lives—what thoughts and feelings and yearnings lie deep within our soul that are not readily accessible to the conscious mind. Clearly we need help.

The Holy Ghost can, if we are open and teachable and patient, make known to us the things of greatest import, the matters upon which God would have us ponder and reflect and pray. If we will be still, quiet, attentive, and sensitive during our prayers, we may find our words reaching beyond our thoughts. This is what occurred with the Nephites as they prayed to the risen Lord in the New World (see 3 Nephi 19:24).

In speaking of this marvelous topic, Elder Neal A. Maxwell pointed out:

> Only with the help of the Holy Ghost can we be lifted outside the narrow little theater of our own experience, outside

---

16. Joseph Smith, Journal, February 2, 1843.

our selfish concerns, and outside the confines of our tiny conceptual cells. . . . .

God sees things as they really are and as they will become. We don't! In order to tap that precious perspective during our prayers, we must rely upon the promptings of the Holy Ghost. With access to that kind of knowledge, our circles of concern will expand. The mighty prayer of Enos began with understandable self-concern, moved outward to family, then to his enemies, and then outward to future generations.[17]

Elsewhere Elder Maxwell taught: "In our deepest prayers, when the agency of man encounters the omniscience of God, we sometimes sense how provincial our petitions really are. We perceive that there are more good answers than we have good questions, and that we have been taught more than we can tell, for the language used is not that which tongue can transmit."[18]

"ALL THINGS WORK TOGETHER" (8:28)

In modern revelation, the same Lord who inspired His servant Paul inspired His servant Joseph Smith: "Search diligently, pray always, and be believing, and all things shall work together for your good, if ye walk uprightly and remember the covenant wherewith ye have covenanted one with another" (Doctrine and Covenants 90:24). The Lord also stated: "Therefore, be ye as wise as serpents and yet without sin; and *I will order all things for your good*, as fast as ye are able to receive them" (Doctrine and Covenants 111:11).

God does not send all of the trials that come into our lives. Some trials come simply because we live in a fallen, telestial world. Some we bring upon ourselves through foolish decisions, and others come to us as a result of other persons' unwise or even evil misuse of their

---

17. Maxwell, "What Should We Pray For?" 45–46.
18. Maxwell, *All These Things Shall Give Thee Experience*, 9.

moral agency. Paul's message here, a message echoed beautifully in Restoration scripture, is that God can cause things to work together for our good. Being omniscient, omnipotent, and—by the power of his Holy Spirit—omnipresent, our Father in Heaven can, if we will let Him, turn the most miserable of life's losses toward our eventual gain.

This is what Lehi meant when he consoled his son Jacob: "Jacob, my firstborn in the wilderness, thou knowest the greatness of God; and he shall consecrate thine afflictions for thy gain" (2 Nephi 2:2). That same Jacob observed, "Look unto God with firmness of mind, and pray unto him with exceeding faith, and he will console you in your afflictions" (Jacob 3:1). And it was in Liberty Jail that the Prophet Joseph Smith penned a letter to the Saints in which he pleaded to God for divine intervention. The Lord's response was "My son, peace be unto thy soul; thine adversity and thine afflictions shall be but a small moment" (Doctrine and Covenants 121:7). Truman G. Madsen reminded us "that 'small moment' turned out to be five more years of incredible struggle. But comparatively, it was a small moment. And that, I submit to you, is a real force in facing suffering. To believe, better, to know that this lonely or crushed or deprived or pain-wracked condition won't last forever; that it will somehow, somewhere be over, is a balm of comfort. Without it, certain kinds of suffering would be unbearable."[19]

Later, after reviewing every conceivable horrendous situation into which Joseph might be thrust, the Savior said to the Prophet, "Above all, if the very jaws of hell shall gape open the mouth wide after thee, know thou, my son, that all these things shall give thee experience, and shall be for thy good" (Doctrine and Covenants 122:7). "Life is an obstacle course," Brother Madsen observed. "And sometimes it is a spook alley. But the before was a time for visioning the after. And some of our prayers are like the gambler's, 'Give me the money I made you promise not to give me if I asked for it.' What does a true friend do in such a

---

19. Madsen, *Four Essays on Love*, 82–83.

case? God will honor our first request, to let us go through it; and He will provide you with . . . the way to make it bearable. More, to make it productive."[20]

WHOM GOD KNEW, HE PREDESTINED (8:29–30)

The Greek word rendered *predestined* in verse 29 could just as well have been rendered *fore-appointed* or *foreordained*. I have been impressed with other translations of verse 29:

> For *those who God knew before ever they were, he also ordained to share the likeness of his Son*, so that he might be the eldest among a large family of brothers. (REB)

> Those he foreknew, you see, he also *marked out in advance* to be shaped according to the model of the image of his son, so that he might be the firstborn of a large family. (KNT)

> God knew what he was doing from the very beginning. *He decided from the outset to shape the lives of those who love him* among the same lines as the life of his Son. The Son stands first in the line of humanity he restored. (*The Message*)

We are also blessed to have the Prophet Joseph's inspired translation of this passage. What follows is verses 29–30:

> For him whom he did foreknow, he also did predestinate to be conformed to his own image, that he might be the firstborn among many brethren. Moreover, him whom he did predestinate, him he also called; and him whom he called, him he also sanctified; and him whom he sanctified, him he also glorified. (JST)

Note that here, the Prophet, under inspiration, altered the passage

---

20. Madsen, *Four Essays on Love*, 83.

to help us understand that *it was Christ whom God foreknew*, that He (Christ) might be conformed to the image of God the Father. Further, this inspired rendering clarifies that Paul was speaking of Christ's calling, sanctification, and glorification.

Looking at this passage from another angle, we can appreciate that in at least one sense there was a predestination in God's plan. Joseph Smith taught: "The whole of the chapter [Romans 9] had reference to the priesthood and the house of Israel; and *unconditional election of individuals to eternal life*"—that is, predestination as it was taught by St. Augustine, Luther, Calvin, and so on—"*was not taught by the apostles.*" Now attend to these important words: "God did elect or predestinate, that *all those who would be saved, should be saved in Christ Jesus, and through obedience to the gospel*; but he passes over no man's sins, but visits them with correction, and if his children will not repent of their sins, he will discard them."[21] In other words, what is fixed and unalterable from all eternity to all eternity is that the only way by which men and women can be saved is through the Atonement and Resurrection of the Lord Jesus Christ. That grand truth is set in stone.

"WHO SHALL SEPARATE US?" (8:35–39)

Three great foundational stones, doctrine upon which the plan of salvation rests, are (1) the love of God (see John 3:16; 1 Nephi 11:16–17; Doctrine and Covenants 34:1–3); (2) the righteousness of God (see 2 Nephi 2:3; Matthew 6:33; Romans 10:1–4); and (3) the mercy and grace of God (see 2 Nephi 2:6–8; Alma 24:10; Helaman 14:12–13). It is the first of these—the love of God—that Paul speaks of here in beautiful and uplifting prose and praise. What must a child of God do to cause the Savior's love to cease? What sin or misdeed must one commit? How low must a person descend into depravity to reach that lowly plain where the love of God is not found? Recall the Prophet Joseph's

---

21. Joseph Smith, in "Discourse, 16 May 1841, as Published in *Times and Seasons.*"

tender invitation that "there is never a time when the spirit is too old [or has descended to the deepest of spiritual depths] to approach God. All are within the reach of pardoning mercy, who have not committed the unpardonable sin."[22]

Elder Jeffrey R. Holland quoted the Savior's words at His Last Supper: "Peace I leave with you, my peace I give unto you. . . . Let not your heart be troubled, neither let it be afraid" (John 14:27). "I submit to you," Elder Holland observed, "that may be one of the Savior's commandments, that is, even in the hearts of otherwise faithful Latter-day Saints, almost universally disobeyed; and yet I wonder whether our resistance to this invitation could be any more grievous to the Lord's merciful heart. . . . Just because God is God, just because Christ is Christ, they cannot do other than care for us and bless us and help us if we will but come unto them, approaching their throne of grace in meekness and lowliness of heart. They can't help but bless us. They have to. It is their nature."[23]

THE ELECTION OF ISRAEL (9:1–5)

Chapter 9 and portions of chapters 10 and 11 address the doctrine of election. Election and foreordination are very closely linked. According to the Guide to the Scriptures, "Based on premortal worthiness, God chose those who would be the seed of Abraham and the house of Israel and become the covenant people (Deuteronomy 32:7–9; Abraham 2:9–11). These people are given special blessings and duties so that they can bless all the nations of the world (Romans 11:5–7; 1 Peter 1:2; Alma 13:1–5; Doctrine and Covenants 84:99). However, even these chosen ones must be called and elected in this life in order to gain salvation."[24] This is election.

---

22. Joseph Smith, in "Discourse, 3 October 1841, as Published in *Times and Seasons*."
23. Holland, *Trusting Jesus*, 68.
24. Guide to the Scriptures, "Election," 72.

Brother Joseph pointed out that "the election here spoken of is pertaining to the flesh and has reference to the seed of Abraham, according to the promise God made to Abraham [see Genesis 12:3; Abraham 2:8–11]. To them belong the adoption and the covenants. . . . The election of the promised seed still continues, and in the last days they shall have the priesthood restored unto them, and they shall be the 'saviors on mount Zion' [see Obadiah 1:21], the 'ministers of our God' [see Isaiah 61:6]. . . . The whole of this chapter had reference to the priesthood and the house of Israel."[25]

NOT ALL ISRAEL IS ISRAEL (9:6–8; COMPARE GALATIANS 3:7–14, 26–29)

Not all Latter-day Saints are true Latter-day Saints. Neither are all Roman Catholics or all Jehovah's Witnesses or all Muslims or all Baptists what their name, label, or religious affiliation imply they are. Why? Because sometimes our speech or behavior slip below the line of acceptance and what we say or do is not what people have come to expect from members of that particular tradition. What Paul states here would certainly have ruffled the feathers of the leaders among the Pharisees or Sadducees: just because a person can demonstrate by genealogical descent or cultural affiliation that they are Jewish does not necessarily mean that they have been loyal to the royal within them—that is, have been true members of the house of Israel.

At the close of his second book, Nephi addressed himself to the Jews: "And now behold, my beloved brethren, I would speak unto you; for I, Nephi, would not suffer that ye should suppose that ye are more righteous than the Gentiles shall be. For behold, *except ye shall keep the commandments of God ye shall all likewise perish*; and because of the words which have been spoken ye need not suppose that the Gentiles are utterly destroyed." Nephi then gets at the heart of the matter: "For behold, I say

---

25. Joseph Smith, in "Discourse, 16 May 1841, as Published in *Times and Seasons*."

unto you that as many of the Gentiles as will repent are the covenant people of the Lord; and *as many of the Jews as will not repent shall be cast off; for the Lord covenanteth with none save it be with them that repent and believe in his Son, who is the Holy One of Israel*" (2 Nephi 30:1–2).

Professor Hugh Nibley explained that "the gospel of repentance is a constant reminder that the most righteous are still being tested and may yet fall, and that the most wicked are not yet beyond redemption and may still be saved."[26] On another occasion, Brother Nibley explained: "Who is righteous? Anyone who is repenting. No matter how bad he has been, if he is repenting, he is a righteous man. There is hope for him."[27]

NO UNRIGHTEOUSNESS WITH GOD (9:10–15)

Jehovah spoke a profound truth to Isaiah: "For my thoughts are not your thoughts, neither are your ways my ways. . . . For as the heavens are higher than the earth, so are my ways higher than your ways, and my thoughts than your thoughts" (Isaiah 55:8–9). For this reason it is foolish and profoundly arrogant for men and women on earth to question God's omniscience; to judge His goodness; or to demand to know why He allows this or why He permits that, why there is so much suffering in the world, why holocausts and hurricanes and tsunamis and terrors are a part of mortal existence, when, in fact, our Heavenly Father is supposed to be a loving God. We grasp so little. Much of the time we mortals do not see things as they really are, but rather *as we are*. Is there unrighteousness with God? Of course not.

What did the Lord mean when He stated that "Jacob have I loved, but Esau have I hated" (verse 13)? Or what did Samuel the Lamanite have in mind when he declared that the Nephites "have been a chosen people of the Lord; yea, the people of Nephi hath he loved. . . . But behold . . . , the Lamanites hath he hated because their deeds have been evil continually, and this because of the iniquity of the tradition

---

26. Nibley, *Prophetic Book of Mormon*, 461–62.
27. Nibley, *Approaching Zion*, 301.

of their fathers" (Helaman 15:3–4)? This language is certainly strong. One would assume that the Lord did not mean to convey that He actually hated Esau and his descendants, at least not in the same sense that mortal men hate one another. Rather, these scriptures indicate that because of the rebellion of the families of Esau (and the family of Laman), because they rejected the light and spurned the association with God they might have enjoyed through the Spirit, they alienated themselves from the love of the Father. It is not that God did not love them, but that He is simply unable to bless or favor them in the same way He can those who choose the right.

John the Beloved wrote: "Whoso keepeth [God's] word, in him verily is the love of God perfected: hereby know we that we are in him. . . . Love not the world, neither the things that are in the world. If any man love the world, the love of the Father is not in him" (1 John 2:5, 15). Once again, a person who loves the world—who has given himself or herself up to the pleasures and passions of the world—is incapable of feeling and enjoying the glorious and soul-satisfying love of God. God does not, however, ever cease to love His children.

GENTILES MADE RIGHTEOUS BY FAITH (9:30–32; 10:1–4)

This section is a sobering message to Paul's own people, the Jews. Those who subscribed to the law of Moses, continuing to observe all of the 613 laws and assuming these "works" made them approved of the heavens, were painfully mistaken. They sought to become perfectly righteous on their own through their own grit and willpower—through their meticulous observance of outward ordinances and performances. In short, they attempted to save themselves by their own works.

In speaking of Paul's challenge in teaching the gospel, Elder Bruce R. McConkie asked,

> What words shall we choose to offer to the world the blessings of a freely given atoning sacrifice?
> On the one hand, we are preaching to Jews who, in their

lost and fallen state, have rejected their Messiah and who believe they are saved by the works and performances of the Mosaic law.

On the other hand, we are preaching to pagans—Romans, Greeks, those in every nation—who know nothing whatever about the Messianic word, or the need for a Redeemer, or of the working out of the infinite and eternal atonement. They worship idols, the forces of nature, the heavenly bodies, or whatever suits their fancy. As with the Jews, they assume that this or that sacrifice or appeasing act will please the Deity of their choice and some vague and unspecified blessings will result.

Can either the Jews or the pagans be left to assume that the works they do will save them? Or must they forget their little groveling acts of petty worship, gain faith in Christ, and rely on the cleansing power of his blood for salvation?

They must be taught faith in the Lord Jesus Christ and to forsake their traditions and performances. Surely we must tell them they cannot be saved by the works they are doing, for man cannot save himself. Instead they must turn to Christ and rely on his merits and mercy and grace.[28]

Paul commends the Jews for their zeal but questions the depth of their understanding of God and the salvation that is found only in Christ. For centuries they sought to establish their own righteousness, when in fact men and women become righteous only through relying upon and trusting in the righteousness of the Redeemer of all humankind (2 Nephi 2:3, 6–8).

FAITH COMES BY HEARING (10:9–17)

Before any person can receive the message of salvation—the message that Jesus Christ is the only name by which salvation can come

---

28. McConkie, "What Think Ye of Salvation by Grace?" 47–48.

(Acts 4:12; Mosiah 3:17)—he or she must first encounter the message. That encounter may take place by reading and studying holy writ, or it may come through hearing the spoken word of God (John 1:1–2, 14; Doctrine and Covenants 93:1–9). Paul declares that "if thou shalt confess with thy mouth the Lord Jesus, and shalt believe in thine heart that God hath raised him from the dead, thou shalt be saved" (verse 9). Similarly, "whosoever shall call upon the name of the Lord shall be saved" (verse 13).

"So then faith cometh by hearing, and hearing by the word of God" (verse 17). Or, as Joseph Smith put it, "Faith comes by hearing the word of God through the testimony of the servants of God. That testimony is always attended by the Spirit of prophecy and revelation."[29] The early elders of the restored Church were taught that "the existence of God became an object of faith in the early age of the world. And the evidences which these men had of the existence of a God, was *the testimony of their fathers* in the first instance." Thus "it was *human testimony*, and human testimony only, that excited this inquiry, in the first instance, in their minds. It was the credence they gave to the testimony of their fathers, this testimony having aroused the minds to inquire after the knowledge of God; the inquiry frequently terminated, indeed always terminated when rightly pursued, in the most glorious discoveries and eternal certainty."[30]

Confessing that Jesus is the Christ or calling upon His name entail far more than uttering a few well-spoken words. Confessing and calling upon Christ are expressions of one's faith in Him. As we will see again and again, true faith is always manifest in *faithfulness*—in one's obedience, how one lives and keeps the commandments of the Lord, and the extent to which one's actions toward other people are consistent with what Jesus taught and how He lived (see Matthew 7:21–23; John

---

29. Joseph Smith, in "Discourse, between circa 26 June and circa 2 July 1839, as Reported by Wilford Woodruff"; punctuation and spelling standardized.
30. *Lectures on Faith*, 2:33, 56; pp. 17, 24.

14:15; James 2:19–20). A Christian is not just a person who can spout off correct theology or who can defend the faith by rational argument alone. Christianity must be lived, must be experienced. Orthodoxy (correct teaching) is surely desired, but orthopraxy (a proper walk and talk) is the most powerful indication that one has accepted the gospel of Jesus Christ.

A person's witness must demonstrate to Christian and non-Christian alike that the gospel of Jesus changes lives, transforms women and men into new creatures, and motivates them to be kinder and more gracious, more charitable and service oriented. In short, the depth of a person's profession of faith, one's confession of Christ as Lord and Savior and Redeemer, manifests itself in the performance of what we call "good works." These good works include receiving the principles and ordinances of the gospel, gathering regularly and consistently with the Saints to worship God through partaking of the sacrament of the Lord's Supper, singing hymns and anthems of praise, and receiving spiritual nourishment through hearing and rejoicing in the good word of God. "And why call ye me, Lord, Lord," Jesus asked, "and do not the things which I say?" (Luke 6:46).

We are saved through the sacrifice of Jesus the Christ. Salvation is thus the greatest of all the gifts of God (2 Nephi 2:4; Doctrine and Covenants 6:13; 14:7). "Salvation cannot be bought with the currency of obedience," Elder Dieter F. Uchtdorf explained. "It is purchased by the blood of the Son of God." He continued,

> If grace is a gift of God, why then is obedience to God's commandments so important? Why bother with God's commandments—or repentance, for that matter? Why not just admit we're sinful and let God save us? Brothers and sisters, we obey the commandments of God—out of love for Him! . . .
>
> Therefore, our obedience to God's commandments comes as a natural outgrowth of our endless love and gratitude for the

goodness of God. *This form of genuine love and gratitude will miraculously merge our works with God's grace.* . . . Grace is a gift of God, and our desire to be obedient to each of God's commandments is the reaching out of our mortal hand to receive this sacred gift from our Heavenly Father.[31]

ISRAEL IS NOT CAST AWAY (11:1, 5, 11, 17–21)

Having scolded his own people for their centuries-long effort to save themselves, Paul circles back to a vital principle: Israel is God's chosen people, and He simply will not let them go. That's the mystery couched within the allegory of Zenos in the Book of Mormon (see Jacob 4:15; 5:77), and what Jacob, son of Lehi, meant when he proclaimed, "How merciful is our God unto us, for he remembereth the house of Israel, both roots and branches [i.e., both ancestry and posterity]; and he stretches forth his hands unto them all the day long; and they are a stiffnecked and a gainsaying people; but *as many as will not harden their hearts shall be saved in the kingdom of God*" (Jacob 6:4).

Ancient Israel wearied and tested the patience of Jehovah; they grumbled, murmured, and complained constantly to Moses, the Lawgiver and leader of Israel; they moved in and out of apostasy through the generations, forsook worshipping the only true God, and went whoring after false gods; and, finally, they rejected the true Messiah, the Stone of Israel, the one who is "the great, and the last, and the only sure foundation, upon which [they] can build" (Jacob 4:15–16). Yet the God of Abraham, Isaac, and Jacob will, in His infinite goodness and perfected patience, find a way to gather and restore His people (1) to Jesus Christ, the true Messiah, His gospel, His doctrine, and His Church; and (2) to the lands of their inheritance, or the congregations of the Saints (see 1 Nephi 15:13–16; 2 Nephi 6:8–11; 9:2; 10:7).

---

31. Uchtdorf, "Gift of Grace," 109–10.

And why is the God of Israel willing to do this? In speaking to ancient Israel just before he was translated and taken into heaven, Moses explained that

> thou art an holy people unto the Lord thy God: the Lord thy God hath chosen thee to be a special people unto himself, above all people that are upon the face of the earth. The Lord did not set his love upon you, nor choose you, because ye were more in number than any people; for ye were the fewest of all people: But because the Lord loved you, and because he would keep the oath which he had sworn unto your fathers [i.e., the Abrahamic covenant], hath the Lord brought you out [of Egyptian captivity] with a mighty hand, and redeemed you out of the house of bondmen, from the hand of Pharaoh king of Egypt. Know therefore that the Lord thy God, he is God, the faithful God, which keepeth covenant and mercy with them that love him and keep his commandments to a thousand generations. (Deuteronomy 7:6–9)

There is, however, a deeper and more profound reason why God will keep His promises to Israel, a reason that few on earth understand. It is what Paul calls "the election of grace" (verse 5) and has reference to our first estate, our premortal existence. Following our birth as spirit sons and daughters of God, and with our endowment of agency, we grew and developed and progressed in that premortal state according to our desires for truth and righteousness. The scriptures teach that some exercised exceedingly great faith and performed many good works (see Alma 13:3). The Lord states many were among the noble and great ones (Abraham 3:22–23), certainly implying a gradation of faithfulness and that some were less noble and some even ignoble.

Though the Saints are often prone to speak at length of individual foreordination to positions, callings, or assignments in the Church, perhaps one of the greatest foreordinations or elections, based on premortal faithfulness, is foreordination to lineage and family. Certain individuals come to earth through a designated channel, through a lineage that entitles them to specified blessings but also carries burdens and responsibilities. This entails what my colleague Brent L. Top called "a type of collective foreordination—a selection of spirits to form an entire favored group or lineage." He added, "Although it is a collective foreordination it is nonetheless based on individual premortal faithfulness and spiritual capacity."[32] In the words of Elder Melvin J. Ballard, Israel is "a group of souls tested, tried, and proven before they were born into the world. . . . Through this lineage were to come the true and tried souls that had demonstrated their righteousness in the spirit world before they came here."[33]

"THE WISDOM AND KNOWLEDGE OF GOD" (11:33–36)

Our God is God. He possesses every gift, every quality, every divine attribute in perfection. There is no power, no might, no truth that He does not possess. Not only does God love all of His children, He knows them, one by one. He has known us for a near infinite period of time, and so He knows our talents, our gifts, our capacities, as well as our weaknesses and our less than noble inclinations.

God's work and glory is to bring to pass the immortality and eternal life of every soul (Moses 1:39), but He cannot save us in our sins (Alma 11:34, 37; Helaman 5:10), nor will He force any man or woman to heaven. Our Father in Heaven will, as we sing in a hymn, "call, persuade, direct aright, and bless with wisdom, love, and light, in nameless ways be good and kind, but never force the human mind."[34] The Almighty will always and forevermore honor our moral agency. Yet He who knows the end from the beginning will also orchestrate the times, places, events, and comings and goings of individuals and

---

32. Top, *Life Before*, 144.
33. *Melvin J. Ballard: Crusader for Righteousness*, 218–19.
34. "Know This, That Every Soul Is Free," *Hymns*, no. 240.

whole nations so as to provide optimal circumstances for His children to do and become their very best (see Deuteronomy 32:7–9; Acts 17:24–27).

PRESENTING A LIVING SACRIFICE (12:1–2)

King David, at a time of grief and terrible guilt, having complicated his adultery with Bathsheba by arranging for her husband, Uriah, to be killed, cried out to the Almighty from the depths of his soul: "Have mercy upon me, O God, according to thy loving-kindness: according unto the multitude of thy tender mercies blot out my transgressions. . . . Create in me a clean heart, O God; and renew a right spirit within me." Then come these marvelous and instructive words: "For thou desirest not [animal] sacrifice; else would I give it: thou delightest not in burnt offering. *The sacrifices of God are a broken spirit: a broken and a contrite heart, O God, thou wilt not despise*" (Psalm 51:1, 10, 16–17; compare 3 Nephi 9:19–20; Doctrine and Covenants 59:9).

Hardened hearts—hearts that because of sin or spiritual neglect can no longer perceive the workings or impressions of God's Holy Spirit—must be broken. That is, they must be sorrowful, submissive to a higher will, humble and penitent, and willing to place on the sacrificial altar the pride and ego and self-promotion that so often stand in the way of genuine spirituality and personal peace of mind. Women and men must be willing to repent and seek forgiveness from Him who knows the hearts and minds of all. Indeed, every one of us as true Christians, is called upon to come unto Christ and "offer [our] whole souls as an offering unto him, and continue in fasting and praying, and endure to the end; and as the Lord liveth [we] will be saved" (Omni 1:26).

In the words of the Apostle Paul, this kind of sacrifice is our "reasonable service" (verse 1), or as rendered elsewhere, our "spiritual worship" (ESV, NRSV, NIV). In other words, sacrificing our will is one of the ways we worship God. As we learn in modern revelation, our effort to receive grace and grow spiritually from grace to grace, just as Jesus Himself did—that is, to emulate the only truly perfect being to walk the earth—is indeed the essence of true worship (Doctrine and Covenants 93:12–19).

Then come these magnificent words from Paul. "And be not conformed to this world: but be ye transformed by the renewing of your mind, that ye may prove what is that good, and acceptable, and perfect will of God" (verse 2). Or, in other words, "Don't let yourselves be squeezed into the shape dictated by the present age. Instead, be transformed by the renewing of your minds, so that you can work out what God's will is—what is good, acceptable, and complete" (verses 1–2, KNT). We do not take our cues from, nor do we form our values based upon, the fickle and ever-changing ways of a secular society. We look to holy scripture and the living prophets and apostles for guidance and direction.

A CALL TO CHRISTIAN CHARITY
(12:9–18, 20–21; 13:6–10; 14:10–13)

These verses basically reiterate what our Savior taught to His followers in the Sermon on the Mount in Galilee (Matthew 5–7) and in His sermon at the temple in Bountiful (3 Nephi 12–14). We know that Paul spent a good bit of time, both after his conversion and throughout his ministry, with those who had known Jesus best, particularly with the men who had been called as His Apostles. They had walked and talked with the Master for three years; they had listened with keen interest to His sermons; and they had heard His quiet counsel to individuals He healed and lifted and reoriented.

Instructing his listeners to "be not wise in your own conceits" (verse 16) reaffirms Paul's advice not to think of ourselves more highly than we should (Romans 12:3).

Two bits of counsel that would be true and extremely valuable in any dispensation are found in verses 18 and 21: "If it be possible, as much as lieth in you, live peaceably with all men," and "be not overcome of evil, but overcome evil with good."

BE SUBJECT TO THE POWERS THAT BE
(13:1–6; COMPARE HEBREWS 13:17)

The Joseph Smith Translation of Romans 13:1–2 reminds us that a given passage of scripture may be rendered in more than one way. One example is how Moroni's version of Malachi 4:5–6 (in Doctrine and Covenants 2 and Joseph Smith—History 1:36–39) differs from what we read in the King James Version. To be sure, there is nothing doctrinally incorrect about Malachi 4:5–6, but Moroni's rendition delivers sacred doctrine concerning the "promises made to the fathers" that is not obvious in the King James Version. This understanding helps us appreciate that far more important than the ancient texts themselves is the spirit of revelation that lies behind the texts and the translation.

Hence, Romans 13:1–2 provides counsel to the followers of Christ to be subject to civic officers and established government (KJV) *and* to be submissive to those called and charged to lead the Lord's Church (JST). As to the former, a confirming message came through the Prophet Joseph Smith in August 1831: "Let no man break the laws of the land, for he that keepeth the laws of God hath no need to break the laws of the land. Wherefore, be subject to the powers that be, until he reigns whose right it is to reign [i.e., Christ, the King of kings], and subdues all enemies under his feet" (Doctrine and Covenants 58:21–22). Why should we follow this counsel? Because we have been instructed that "governments were instituted of God for the benefit of man; and that [God] holds men accountable for their acts in relation to them, both in making laws and administering them, for the good and safety of society" (Doctrine and Covenants 134:1). Not *all* governments are necessarily good, for clearly any government that is totalitarian or that robs its citizens of their moral agency is *not* of God. But rule by government in general has divine approval. Therefore it is appropriate to pay tribute or taxes to the government (see Romans 13:6).

As to being subject to the leaders of the Church, Paul declares: "Let every soul be subject unto the higher powers. For there is no power in the church but of God: the powers that be are ordained of God. Whosoever therefore resisteth the power, resisteth the ordinance [i.e., law or statute] of God: and they that resist shall receive to themselves damnation. . . . For, for this cause pay ye your consecrations unto them; for they are God's ministers, attending continually upon this very thing" (Romans 13:1–2, 6, JST).

NOW IS OUR SALVATION NEARER (13:11–12)

These two verses make clear that when it comes to mortals, salvation is not an event as much as it is a process. As we strive to do our duty through keeping the commandments of God and trusting in the redemptive labors of our Savior, we grow in spiritual graces. Do Latter-day Saints believe that men and women enjoy the benefits of salvation only in the world to come? Is there no sense in which we may be saved in the present, in the here and now? Though we quickly acknowledge that most scriptural references to salvation seem to point toward that which comes in the next life, we do have within our theology principles and doctrine that suggest a form of salvation *in this life*. Perhaps the most obvious illustration is when a member of the Church lives a faithful life, endures to the end, and passes the tests of mortality and then eventually gains the assurance of eternal life (see Doctrine and Covenants 6:13; 14:7; 50:5). As Joseph Smith taught, when we exercise saving faith and demonstrate our willingness to serve God at all hazards, we eventually, in this life or the next, receive the promise of eternal life (see Doctrine and Covenants 58:2).[35]

---

35. *Words of Joseph Smith*, 5.

Those who have been sealed to eternal life are no doubt fully aware of the fact that they must stay faithful to the end, but even so, they know assuredly that if they were to die suddenly, their salvation is secure. They are saved, or to put it another way, they are *living in a saved condition*. Thus there is a condition or state you and I may attain in this mortal life in which salvation hereafter is promised; the Day of Judgment is essentially advanced.

As we will discuss in our consideration of 2 Corinthians and Ephesians, the same Holy Spirit of Promise who searches the hearts of men and women, who ratifies and approves and seals ordinances and lives, serves, as Paul indicates, as the "earnest of our inheritance" (Ephesians 1:14). When the Spirit is with us, we know that we are on course and that our lives are approved of God. We know that we are in Christ, in covenant, when the Spirit is with us. If we live in such a way that we can take the sacrament worthily, hold and use a current temple recommend, and maintain the gift and gifts of the Spirit, then we are in line with our duty; we are approved of the heavens, and if we were to die suddenly, we would go into paradise and eventually into the celestial kingdom.

The Joseph Smith Translation of 1 John 3:9 confirms, "Whosoever is born of God *doth not continue in sin*; for the Spirit of God remaineth in him; and he cannot continue in sin, because he is born of God, *having received that holy Spirit of promise*."

President Dallin H. Oaks also spoke on the meaning of salvation:

> As Latter-day Saints use the words *saved* and *salvation*, there are [several] different meanings. According to some of these, our salvation is assured—we are already saved. In others, salvation must be spoken of as a future event. . . . But in all of these meanings, or kinds of salvation, salvation is in and through Jesus Christ. . . .
>
> The short answer to the question of whether a faithful

member of The Church of Jesus Christ of Latter-day Saints has been saved or born again must be a fervent "yes." Our covenant relationship with our Savior puts us in that "saved" or "born again" condition meant by those who ask this question.[36]

"We do not work out our salvation in a moment," Elder Bruce R. McConkie observed. "It doesn't come to us in an instant, suddenly. Gaining salvation is a process." He then paraphrased Romans 13:11 ("now is our salvation nearer than when we believed") as follows: "We have made some progress along the straight and narrow path. We are going forward, and if we continue in that direction, eternal life will be our everlasting reward."[37]

The God-fearing live always in a spirit of repentance. A modern prophet, President Russell M. Nelson, instructed the Saints:

> Nothing is more liberating, more ennobling, or more crucial to our individual progression than is a regular, daily focus on repentance. Repentance is not an event; it is a process. It is the key to happiness and peace of mind. When coupled with faith, repentance opens our access to the power of the Atonement of Jesus Christ.
>
> Whether you are diligently moving along the covenant path, have slipped or stepped from the covenant path, or can't even see the path from where you are now, I plead with you to repent. Experience the strengthening power of daily repentance—of doing and being a little better each day.
>
> When we choose to repent, we choose to change! We allow the Savior to transform us into the best version of ourselves. We choose to grow spiritually and receive joy—the joy

---
36. Oaks, "Have You Been Saved?"
37. McConkie, "Jesus Christ and Him Crucified," 398.

of redemption in Him. When we choose to repent, we choose to become more like Jesus Christ![38]

NEVER ALLOW FOOD TO DESTROY OUR NEIGHBOR
(14:14–17, 21; 15:1; COMPARE 1 CORINTHIANS 8:8–13; 10:27–32)

One of the perplexing questions faced by the Saints of the first century was whether they should eat meat that had once been offered in sacrifice to false gods. Throughout his epistles, Paul seems to provide varied answers, probably because of individual circumstances. On some occasions he points out that since there is only one true God and since the gods to which the meat had been offered do not in fact exist, eating such meat should be of no consequence whatsoever. On other occasions, Paul offers a kindly caution to seasoned and settled members of the Church. He counsels them that while in the long run it doesn't matter one whit what may have been sacrificed to false gods, there are times when eating such meat might prove spiritually harmful to others—namely, the less-seasoned members, such as very recent converts or those he designates as "weak brethren."

This is a sweet and tender request on the part of this remarkable Apostle of the Lord Jesus Christ. It manifests clearly Paul's decency, goodness, and deep love for his beloved Saints and his sensitivity to members of all types. In other words, "If one who is not yet strong in the faith should see you consuming foods that had been offered to alien gods, it may confuse them, upset them, and deflect them from the gospel path. Surely this is not something you would wish to have happen. So be wise, be careful what you consume; you never know who may be watching." An excellent summary reads, "It is good neither to eat flesh, nor to drink wine, nor any thing whereby thy brother stumbleth, or is offended, or is made weak" (verse 21). Why? Because "the

---

38. Nelson, "We Can Do Better and Be Better."

kingdom of God is not meat and drink; but righteousness, and peace, and joy in the Holy Ghost" (verse 17).

BEARING THE INFIRMITIES OF THE WEAK (15:1–7; COMPARE GALATIANS 6:2; JAMES 2:8; MOSIAH 18:8)

With all that the followers of Christ are charged to do in our day—pray, search the scriptures, teach and learn the gospel, attend church, take the sacrament, pay tithes and offerings, and so on—there is no assignment more central to the Christian life than that of loving our neighbors and ministering in holy ways to them, even as our Exemplar Jesus Christ did in both the Old and New Worlds. In Paul's words, we are to "bear the infirmities of the weak" (verse 1), not to be seen of others, but out of a charitable heart (see Matthew 6:1–8, 16–18).

Indeed, how the Savior's followers treat others, both within and beyond the household of faith, is a sure sign of whether the gospel of Jesus Christ—what James calls "pure religion" (James 1:27)—has truly taken root in their souls. Speaking and listening well to one another; handling ourselves in a Christlike manner during tense or troublesome situations; avoiding undue criticism; refusing to take offense or judge unrighteously; reacting graciously to one whose beliefs are different from our own; being attentive and sensitive to those who do not feel included, are lonely, or are despairing—these are the marks of a true Christian. The King James Version of verse 7 reads, "Wherefore receive ye one another, as Christ also received us to the glory of God." Indeed, love for one another is the Lord's barometer of righteousness (see John 15:12–13).

HOW BOTH JEWS AND GENTILES ARE BLESSED (15:8–11; GALATIANS 3:14)

Under God's plan His sons and daughters come to earth at a specified time and under circumstances that will allow them the greatest opportunities to grow and mature spiritually. Our Father in Heaven operates within a divine timetable, setting forth when the fullness of the gospel of Jesus Christ, with all of its blessings, will be given to different groups of people while on earth. When Jesus entered mortality in what we call the meridian of time, He made the gospel available to the people of the house of Israel. In His charge to His chosen Twelve, He said, "Go not into the way of the Gentiles [i.e., those not of the lineage of Jacob], and into any city of the Samaritans enter ye not: but go rather to the lost sheep of the house of Israel" (Matthew 10:5; compare Matthew 15:24). That is, the message, covenants, and ordinances of salvation went first to Israel; Jesus was sent principally to the Jews. An alternate translation of Romans 15:7–8 reads, "In a word, accept one another as Christ accepted us, to the glory of God. Remember that Christ became a servant of the Jewish people to maintain the faithfulness of God by making good his promises to the patriarchs" (REB).

In what we know as the Abrahamic covenant, God promised the Father of the Faithful that his posterity would be as the sand upon the seashore, as innumerable as the stars in the heavens (Genesis 13:14–16; 15:5–6; 17:1–8). As we learn in modern revelation, Abraham was promised that his family would receive the gospel, the priesthood, an endless and eternal posterity, and a land of inheritance and that through his posterity the people throughout the earth would be blessed (Abraham 2:8–11, 19). Jesus's presentation of the gospel to the house of Israel was a part of the fulfillment of the Abrahamic covenant.

As the risen Lord prepared to ascend into heaven in the Old World, He delivered a new and expanded charge to the Apostles. According to Matthew's account, the Savior said, "*Go ye therefore, and teach all nations*, baptizing them in the name of the Father, and of the Son, and of the Holy Ghost" (Matthew 28:19). Mark renders the Lord's words as follows: "*Go ye into all the world, and preach the gospel to every creature*" (Mark 16:15). When the time came to fulfill that enlarged assignment, God sent an angel to Cornelius, the Roman centurion, and a vision to Peter, the senior Apostle, indicating to both that the time had arrived for the blessings of the fullness of the gospel of Jesus Christ to be taken to the Gentiles (Acts 10). In time, Saul of Tarsus was stopped in his tracks on his way to Damascus and received a call to be "the minister of Jesus Christ to the Gentiles" (Romans 15:16; see also 11:13).

AVOID THOSE WHO ARE DIVISIVE (16:17–20)

Chapter 16 begins with Paul's request that Phebe, clearly a faithful member of the Church, send greetings to the members of the Church in Rome. Roman Catholic scholar Joseph A. Fitzmyer wrote:

> Paul now includes in his letter of recommendation to Phoebe greetings to various persons in the Roman church, mentioning at least twenty-four people by name. Indirectly, Paul is commending himself on his coming visit to Rome. . . .
>
> In the letters that Paul has written to churches that he himself founded he rarely greets individuals as he does here. That may have been because he did not want to single out individuals and neglect others. In any case, the difference that one notes now undoubtedly comes from the fact that this letter is being sent to Rome, to a congregation that he did not found personally, but in which he knows that a number of Christian friends reside.[39]

Paul then offers a warning to the leaders of the Church in Rome: "Now I beseech you, brethren, mark [i.e., watch, beware of] them which cause divisions and offenses [i.e., stumbling blocks, scandals] contrary to the doctrine which ye have learned; and avoid them. For they that are such serve not our Lord Jesus Christ, but their own belly [i.e., appetites]; and by good words and fair speeches deceive the hearts of the simple [i.e., innocent, guileless]" (verses 17–18). The damage that is done to the Church through factions and schisms is reviewed in more detail in the discussion of 1 Corinthians 1 herein. For now, let's

---

39. Fitzmyer, *Romans*, 734.

keep in mind that the Spirit of the Lord unifies people, while the spirit of Satan divides, distracts, deludes, and, if not addressed and eradicated, destroys spirituality and the peace that ought to exist among the followers of the Prince of Peace.

Priesthood leaders in the wards and branches of the Church must keep a close watch for such mischief. It may come in the form of persons riding their particular gospel hobbyhorse over and over in the meetings of the Church—for example, the imminent destruction of America, the specific time of the Savior's Second Coming, faddish interpretations of the Word of Wisdom, an excessive zeal for overwhelming spiritual experiences, and so on. It may manifest itself in the woman who insists on dominating the discussions in Sunday School or Relief Society, or in the man who constantly contradicts and spreads controversy among the Saints. As Paul explains in another epistle, "The fruit of the Spirit is love, joy, peace, longsuffering, gentleness, goodness, faith, meekness, temperance" (Galatians 5:22–23). Whatever or whoever prevents the outpouring of the Holy Spirit upon those who come to church to learn and to be edified must be corrected. As Joseph Smith taught from Liberty Jail: "*None but fools will trifle with the souls of men.*"[40]

---

40. Joseph Smith, in "Letter to the Church and Edward Partridge, 20 March 1839"; spelling standardized.

THE FIRST EPISTLE TO THE CORINTHIANS

1 Corinthians seems to have been written in about AD 55–57 to the Saints at Corinth, the provincial capital of southern Greece. 1 Corinthians is filled with significant doctrine and wise counsel. While the behavior of many in the Corinthian congregation obviously reflected positively on what it means to be a Christian or follower of Jesus, it is also clear that other members of the Church struggled to maintain Christian beliefs and behavior. Three letters were apparently written by Paul to his beloved fellow Saints in Corinth, one of which is now lost (see 1 Corinthians 5:9).

A PLEA FOR UNITY (1:10–17)

Word reached Paul that extensive division, disunity, and even contentions had arisen among the Saints in Corinth. This troublesome message was either delivered in person or mentioned in a letter to Paul from the household of Chloe, presumably a prominent member of the Church in Corinth, possibly in whose home the Saints met to worship. At this time, Paul was in Ephesus. N. T. Wright's translation renders verses 11–15 as follows: "You see, my dear family, Cloe's people have put me in the picture about you—about the fact that you are having quarrels. What I'm talking about is this. Each one of you is saying, 'I'm with Paul!' 'I'm with Apollos!' 'I'm with Cephas!' 'I'm with the

Messiah!' Well! Has the Messiah been cut up into pieces? Was Paul crucified for you? Or were you baptized into Paul's name? I'm grateful to God that I didn't baptize any of you, except Crispus and Gaius, so that none of you could say that you were baptized into my name" (KNT).

Many of the members of the Corinthian congregation seem to have been caught up in a kind of hero worship of different leaders of the Church. Perhaps these Saints showed partisanship because these noteworthy and impressive leaders and teachers had taught or baptized them. Certain Saints may also have been attracted to different leaders' style and approach to teaching the gospel—their eloquence and powerful oratory.

Language like "I am of Paul," "I am of Apollos," "I am of Cephas (Peter)," and, appropriately, "I am of Christ" suggests that different factions or schisms had developed. The situation might be analogous to a group of Latter-day Saints sitting around a table and expressing who their favorite General Authorities are, although the case with the Corinthian Saints was much more serious than that. Let us suppose that certain members of the restored Church choose to study and teach and focus solely on the words of their particular champion. There are the David O. McKay Saints and the Joseph Fielding Smith members; the Marion D. Hanks followers and the Bruce R. McConkie fans; the Boyd K. Packer crowd and the Thomas S. Monson collection. Each of these chosen servants is different in his own way—all gifted, powerful, and effective witnesses of the Lord Jesus Christ, each appealing to different kinds of Latter-day Saints.

I have always been sobered by a section of Proverbs 6, particularly verses 16–19: "*These six things doth the Lord hate: yea, seven are an abomination unto him:* a proud look, a lying tongue, and hands that shed innocent blood, an heart that deviseth wicked imaginations, feet that be swift in running to mischief, a false witness that speaketh lies." And now note the last one: "and *he that soweth discord among brethren.*" When the risen Lord ministered among His American Hebrews, He explained sternly that "he that hath the spirit of contention is not of me, but is of the devil, who is the father of contention, and he stirreth up the hearts of men to contend with anger, one with another" (3 Nephi 11:29). In modern revelation we are counseled by the Lord: "I say unto you, be one; and if ye are not one ye are not mine" (Doctrine and Covenants 38:27).

In the vision of the three degrees of glory, given to Joseph Smith and Sidney Rigdon in February 1832 (Doctrine and Covenants 76), the Lord spoke of the kinds of people who would inherit the celestial, terrestrial, and telestial kingdoms. Among those who receive the glory likened unto the stars (the telestial, or lowest), Christ listed such persons as those who receive neither the fullness of the gospel nor the testimony of Jesus; whose wickedness is not of such magnitude as to constitute the sin against the Holy Ghost; who are thrust down to hell in the postmortal spirit world; who inherit the last resurrection, the resurrection of the unjust; and who are liars, sorcerers, adulterers, and whoremongers (Doctrine and Covenants 76:82–85, 101, 103).

There is one other classification of telestial persons: "For these are they who are of Paul, and of Apollos, and of Cephas. These are they who say they are some of one and some of another—some of Christ and some of John, and some of Moses, and some of Elias, and some of Esaias, and some of Isaiah, and some of Enoch" (Doctrine and Covenants 76:99–100).

The Spirit of God will not dwell among a people who are divided, contentious, argumentative, or schismatic, nor with those who sow discord among their brothers and sisters of the faith. A person who creates such a division partakes of the spirit of him who rebelled in the beginning against God the Father and His plan (see Revelation 12:7–9; Doctrine and Covenants 29:36–38; Moses 4:1–4; Abraham 3:22–28). Such a woman or man is a divided soul, a double-minded member of the Lord's Church, and thus one who is unstable in all his or her ways (see James 1:8).

Verse 17 of chapter 1 might easily be misunderstood by readers: "For Christ sent me not to baptize, but to preach the gospel: not with wisdom of words, lest the cross of Christ should be made of none effect." Didn't the Messiah send Peter, James, John, and Paul into the world to bring people into His Church through conversion and baptism? Of course He did. Paul isn't here stating that he doesn't care whether his investigators commit to be baptized. He cares very much, but he was not sent into the world to make a record for himself, to focus unduly on the numbers of converts, or to be acknowledged as the greatest Christian missionary of all time. Rather, he was sent out to teach of the nature and plight of fallen humanity and the absolute inability of women and men to rid themselves of sins or sinfulness. This is accomplished in one way and one way only—through accepting the message of the gospel of Jesus Christ; applying the precious blood of Christ through faith, repentance, and baptism by water and the Spirit; and faithfully keeping covenants until the end.

THE SCANDAL OF THE CROSS (1:18–27)

Paul tends to use certain key words to connote a greater or broader concept. For example, the word *circumcision* conveys much more than the rite performed on eight-day-old male children, a token of the covenant given to Father Abraham (see Genesis 17). The term comes to connote Jewishness, Judaism, and life under the law of Moses with the onerous expectations of obedience to the 613 commandments of Torah. Similarly, the word *cross* in reference to the Crucifixion of Jesus comes to mean more than simply the mode of torture and execution. *Cross* is also a sign, a token of the Savior's Atonement. To say that one believed in and taught the cross was to say that one accepted the reality of Christ's suffering and death as having divine redemptive power. But this was no easy sell to those whom Paul and his Christian associates bore witness. Indeed, it was scandalous.

For example, Paul reminds the Corinthian Saints that the risen Lord sent him "to preach the gospel: not with wisdom of words, lest the cross of Christ should be made of none effect. For the preaching of the cross is to them that perish foolishness; but unto us which are saved it is the power of God. . . . For the Jews require a sign, and the Greeks seek after wisdom: but we preach Christ crucified, unto the Jews a stumblingblock, and unto the Greeks foolishness" (verses 17–18, 22–23). Why would the Jews and the Greeks have been so put off by the idea of a crucified savior? Well, for one thing, Moses had written that any person who is hanged on a tree is cursed by God (Deuteronomy 21:23). What, then, do we make of the outlandish Christian claim that God cursed the one who claimed to be God? This implies, in one sense, that God cursed Himself! Ridiculous. Irony of ironies: the one who had come into the world as the Tree of Life, the Tree of Blessing, hung and bled and suffered and died on the tree of cursing, the tree of death. "From both the Greek and Roman points of view, the stigma of crucifixion made the whole notion of the gospel claiming Jesus as the Messiah an absolute absurdity," pastor and teacher John MacArthur has written.

A glance at the history of crucifixion in first-century Rome reveals what Paul's contemporaries thought about it. It was a horrific form of capital punishment, originating, most likely, in the Persian Empire, but other barbarians used it as well. The condemned died an agonizingly slow death by suffocation, gradually becoming too exhausted and traumatized to pull himself up on the nails in his hands, or push himself up on the nail through his feet, enough to take a deep breath of air. King Darius crucified three thousand Babylonians. Alexander the Great crucified two thousand from the city of Tyre. Alexander Janius crucified eight hundred Pharisees, while they watched soldiers slaughter their wives and children at their feet.

> This sealed the horror of the crucifixion in the Jewish mind. Romans came to power in Israel in 63 B.C. and used crucifixion extensively. Some writers say authorities crucified as many as thirty thousand people around that time. Titus Vespasian crucified so many Jews in A.D. 70 that the soldiers

had no room for the crosses and not enough crosses for the bodies. It wasn't until 337, when Constantine abolished crucifixion, that it disappeared after a millennium of cruelty in the world.[1]

New Testament scholar Martin Hengel pointed out:

> To believe that . . . the mediator at creation and the redeemer of the world, had appeared in very recent times in out-of-the-way Galilee as a member of the obscure people of the Jews, and even worse, had died the death of a common criminal on the cross, could only be regarded as a sign of madness. The real gods of Greece and Rome could be distinguished from mortal men by the very fact that they were *immortal*—they had absolutely nothing in common with the cross as a sign of shame . . . and thus of the one who was "bound in the most ignominious fashion" and executed in a shameful way.[2]

Nevertheless, when Paul came to the Corinthians, he "came not with excellency of speech or of wisdom, declaring unto you the testimony of God. For I determined not to know any thing among you," he wrote, "save Jesus Christ, and him crucified" (1 Corinthians 2:1–2). References to the cross are made many times throughout the writings of Paul (for example, Romans 6:3–6; Galatians 2:20; 6:14; Ephesians 2:14–16; Philippians 3:17–18; Colossians 1:18–20; 2:10, 13–14).

Clearly, the doctrine of the cross, meaning the doctrine of the Atonement of Jesus Christ, was right where it needed to be—at the heart and core of Paul's teachings. Neither the scandal of the *cross*—a word that was not even acceptable in polite Roman company—nor the absurdity of a dying Messiah could hinder the Apostle to the Gentiles

---

1. MacArthur, *Hard to Believe*, 26–27.
2. Hengel, *Crucifixion*, 6–7.

from delivering his witness of Christ to the ends of the known world. He was not ashamed of the gospel, which included our Lord's sufferings and death on the cross (see Romans 1:16).

Notably, in the first few Christian centuries, the cross was not considered a virtuous or admirable symbol but rather a terrifying reminder of what Jesus and many thousands of others had ignominiously suffered. In fact, some scholars report that the cross did not appear in churches as a symbol of veneration until AD 431. Crosses on steeples did not appear until 586, and it was not until the sixth century that crucifixes were sanctioned by the Roman church.

The Bible does not stand alone in testifying of the significance of the cross. The scriptures of the Restoration bear a like witness with the Bible (see, for example, 1 Nephi 11:33; Jacob 1:8; 3 Nephi 27:13–14; Moroni 9:25; Doctrine and Covenants 21:9; 35:2; 46:13–14; 53:2; 138:35). We do not have the space here to list all of the passages in the Book of Mormon and modern scripture that speak of the vital need for Christ's suffering *and death*. That is to say, it was not just His suffering but also His death—on the cruel cross of Calvary—that was an indispensable element of the atoning sacrifice (see Alma 21:9; 22:14; Moses 7:47, 55).

We have no quarrel with those who speak reverently of the cross, for so did those whose writings compose a significant portion of the New Testament and those who spoke or wrote what is contained in our own scriptural records. The cross is a symbol. The key is not to become obsessed with the symbol, but to allow the symbol to point beyond itself toward that which is of deepest significance. Thus we do not worship Moroni; we look upon those statues on the tops of temples and are reminded that, through the instrumentality of Moroni and a whole host of divine messengers, the everlasting gospel of Jesus Christ has been restored to the earth (see Revelation 14:6–7). When we see a CTR ring, we are reminded that followers of the Good Shepherd must do more than talk the talk; we must walk the walk, conforming our lives to the pattern He has shown and in a way befitting true disciples. In that spirit, President Joseph F. Smith reminded us that "having been born anew, which is the putting away of the old man sin, and putting on of the man Christ Jesus, *we have become soldiers of the Cross*, having enlisted under the banner of Jehovah for time and for eternity."[3]

HOW THE THINGS OF GOD ARE KNOWN (2:9–14)

In verse 9 Paul writes: "Eye hath not seen, nor ear heard, neither have entered into the heart of man, the things which God hath prepared for *them that love him.*" What a marvelous promise! That expression is a comforting assurance to each of us, a reminder that while there are moments of intense joy and peace in this world, the glories and feelings and transcendent associations of a future world are even grander. These powerful and encouraging words were spoken first by Isaiah and, incidentally, in a slightly different manner. "For since the beginning of the world," Isaiah declared, "men have not heard, nor perceived by the ear, neither hath the eye seen, O God, beside thee, what he hath prepared *for him that waiteth for him*" (Isaiah 64:4; compare Doctrine and Covenants 133:45).

To *wait* on the Lord is closely related to having *hope* in the Lord. *Waiting on* and *hoping in* the Lord are scriptural phrases that focus not on frail and faltering mortals but rather on a sovereign, omniscient, and omni-loving God who fulfills His promises to the people of promise in His own time. Hope is more than worldly wishing. It is expectation, anticipation, assurance. We wait on the Lord because we have hope in Him. "For we through the Spirit wait for the hope of righteousness by faith" (Galatians 5:5). Thus, we wait on the Lord—not in the sense that we sit and wring our hands and glance at our clocks repeatedly, but

---

3. Joseph F. Smith, *Gospel Doctrine*, 91; an outstanding book on the subject of the cross of Christ is John Hilton III's *Considering the Cross: How Calvary Connects Us with Christ.*

rather we exercise patience in His providential hand, knowing full well, by the power of the Holy Ghost, that our Heavenly Father will soon transform a darkened world in preparation for the personal, thousand-year ministry of His holy Son (see 1 Corinthians 1:4–8).

While saving faith is always built upon that which is true (see Alma 32:21)—something that really took place (whether that be Jesus's rise from the tomb or Joseph Smith's First Vision)—true believers will never allow their faith to be held hostage by what science or philosophy or human reason has or has not discovered at a given time. We can know, for example, that Jesus fed the five thousand, healed the sick, raised the dead, calmed the storm, and rose from the dead—not because we have physical evidence for each of those miraculous events (we do not) or even because we can read of these things in the New Testament, which we accept as true. Rather, we know these things actually happened because the Spirit of the Living God bears witness to our spirits that Jesus of Nazareth did all that the scriptures say He did and much more (John 20:30–31; 21:25).

In a very real sense, *believing is seeing*. Members of the Church need not feel ill-equipped, inadequate, or embarrassed when they cannot produce and display the gold plates or know exactly how the Prophet of the Restoration translated the ancient Egyptian papyri. No Latter-day Saint should ever feel hesitant to bear testimony of those truths that are seen only with the "eye of faith" (Alma 5:15; 32:40; Ether 12:19). In the end, the only way the things of God *can and should be known* is by the power of the Spirit of God. These things are what the scriptures call the "mysteries of God" (Alma 12:9–11; Doctrine and Covenants 42:61; 63:23).

"When we seek the truth about religion," President Dallin H. Oaks stated, "we should use spiritual methods appropriate for that search: prayer, the witness of the Holy Ghost, and study of the scriptures and the words of modern prophets. I am always sad when I hear of one who reports a loss of religious faith because of secular teachings. Those who once had spiritual vision can suffer from self-inflicted spiritual blindness."[4]

"WE HAVE THE MIND OF CHRIST" (2:16)

The Prophet Joseph Smith and some of his associates taught the early elders of the Church profound truths in what we know as the *Lectures on Faith* in the winter of 1834–35. In perhaps the most doctrinally dense of the lectures (lecture 5), the members of the School of the Elders were taught that Jesus Christ "is called the Son because of the flesh, and descended in suffering below that which man can suffer; or, in other words, suffered greater sufferings, and was exposed to more powerful contradictions than any man can be [see Hebrews 12:3]. But, notwithstanding all this, he kept the law of God, and remained without sin . . . and having overcome, received *a fulness of the glory of the Father, possessing the same mind with the Father, which mind is the Holy Spirit*, that bears record of the Father and the Son."

The elders were then given a remarkable and soul-stirring promise—all those who keep God's commandments would be be "*filled with the fulness of the mind of the Father; or, in other words, the Spirit of the Father*, which Spirit is shed forth upon all who believe on his name and keep his commandments." All those who keep His commandments "shall grow up from grace to grace, and become heirs of the heavenly kingdom, and joint heirs with Jesus Christ; *possessing the same mind, being transformed into the same image or likeness*."[5]

What do we learn from these words? Mortal men and women, the sons and daughters of Almighty God, may, through cultivating and retaining the Holy Spirit in their lives, gain the mind of the Father, which is also the mind of Christ. In other words, as we earnestly strive to enjoy the constant companionship of the Holy Ghost—as we live so that the Spirit can dwell with us, comfort us, teach us, chasten us, and sanctify

---

4. Oaks, "Truth and the Plan."
5. *Lectures on Faith*, 5:2; pp. 59–60.

us—we gain the mind of Christ. We begin, bit by bit, line upon line, and precept upon precept, to see and feel as our Savior sees and feels. We begin to reason and reflect as He does. We come to love and nurture others as He does. We gradually come to recognize and reject falsehood and shun secondary causes as we cleave unto truth and righteousness and delight in and dedicate our time and resources to primary causes. We gain the mind of Christ as our eye becomes single to the glory of God, as God's light is manifest more and more in our countenances (see Matthew 6:22; Alma 5:14; Doctrine and Covenants 88:67).

MILK BEFORE MEAT, BUT MEAT (3:1–4; HEBREWS 5:12–14)

Some foods are not only inappropriate but dangerous for an infant to eat. So it is with our spiritual digestive system and our growth to spiritual maturity. Just as it would be unwise for a college student with very little background in high school science to jump into an organic chemistry class, so too must we be careful about what, how, and when we study. There is, in a manner of speaking, a system of gospel prerequisites. President Boyd K. Packer explained: "Teaching prematurely or at the wrong time some things that are true can invite sorrow and heartbreak instead of the joy intended to accompany learning. . . . The scriptures teach emphatically that we must give milk before meat. The Lord made it very clear that some things are to be given only to those who are worthy. It matters very much not only *what* we are told but *when* we are told it."[6]

The Savior taught that gospel prerequisites should be observed when teaching or learning sacred things (Matthew 7:6–7). After having spoken of the profound truths associated with His own suffering in Gethsemane and thus of our need to repent, the Lord warned in a modern revelation: "And I command you that you *preach naught but repentance*, and show not these things unto the world until it is wisdom in me. For they cannot bear meat now, but milk they must receive;

---

6. Packer, *Let Not Your Heart Be Troubled*, 107–8; emphasis in original.

wherefore, they must not know these things, lest they perish" (Doctrine and Covenant 19:21–22). A person who knows very little about our doctrine, for example, will probably not understand or appreciate our teachings concerning temples, sealing powers, eternal life, or the capacity of women and men to become like our Father in Heaven.

The instruction to teach nothing but repentance does not mean that the only topic we should pursue or address in a Church meeting is repentance; rather, to teach nothing but repentance is to teach the gospel of Jesus Christ, which is all about repentance, progression, and refinement. The Prophet Joseph Smith observed, "If we start right, it is easy to go right all the time; but if we start wrong, we may go wrong, and it [will] be a hard matter to get right."[7] When a proper foundation has been laid, the truth can then flow more freely.

Milk must come before meat. As we grow in understanding and holiness, it is vital that we grow steadily and surely, feeding regularly and consistently upon the fundamental and foundational doctrine of salvation. Too often members of the Church, supposing that they are deeper and stronger than they really are, make an effort to feast upon heavy meat—doctrinal matters that are clearly beyond the purview of what is taught by apostles and prophets today—well before they are ready to do so. Generally speaking, people who want to spend the bulk of their study time well beyond the standard works, who feel that the scriptures and the words of living prophets are too elementary for them, may be traversing an unsure and often perilous path. Such persons may sow discord in a ward rather than build unity and strengthen the Saints.

The leaders of the Lord's Church have a much clearer perspective on what should and should not be taught than most of us will ever have. By traveling throughout the earth and meeting regularly with the Saints, they sense the "bearing capacity" of the people, what we are and

---

7. Joseph Smith, in "Discourse, 7 April 1844, as Reported by *Times and Seasons*."

are not prepared to receive. For that reason, we should teach what the apostles and prophets teach (see Mosiah 18:18–19; 25:21; Doctrine and Covenants 52:9).

On the other hand, while our growth in understanding should be gradual and sustained, we must also stretch, expand our views, and open our minds to new truths and new applications. That is, we need to partake of milk before meat, but eventually we need meat. "For when for the time ye ought to be teachers," Paul wrote, "ye have need that one teach you again which be the first principles of the oracles of God; and are become such as have need of milk, and not of strong meat. For every one that useth milk is unskilful in the word of righteousness: for he is a babe. But strong meat belongeth to them that are of full age"—or, in other words, are spiritually and intellectually mature—"even those who by reason of use have their senses exercised to discern both good and evil" (Hebrews 5:12–14).

We must be willing to think, to open ourselves to new insights, to broaden our scope, to pray for deeper understanding, if we truly desire to make a difference in the kingdom of God in the years ahead. It is one thing to respond to a difficult question by saying, "I don't know the answer to your question, but I know the gospel is true." That's a noble approach, to be sure. If we don't know, then we don't know, and we should not try to bluff our way through things. How much more powerful, however, is an answer like this one: "That's a good question. Let me answer your question first, and then let me bear my testimony of the things I do know." The Lord and His Church desperately need members who are committed to the faith and have a testimony of the gospel. Of even greater worth, however, are those who know the gospel is true and also *know the gospel.*

No matter the depth of our personal searching for the meat of the plan of salvation, true spiritual maturity will be manifest in our continued return to the milk that provided substance and sustenance for our souls in our formative years. Many have a deep love and appreciation for the scriptures now that they simply could not have anticipated thirty years ago. They treasure the words of living apostles and prophets today as of much greater worth than silver and gold. Those most to be admired, the men and women who are some of the finest teachers in the Church, are people who, despite the breadth and depth of their knowledge, are devoted to the standard works of the Church and have a great desire to teach the portion of the word the Lord has allotted for us today (see Alma 12:9–11; Doctrine and Covenants 71:1). For them, as for those they teach so ably and well, the simple has become profound.

GOD GIVES THE INCREASE (3:5–9)

Verses 5–6 in the King James Version read as follows: "Who then is Paul, and who is Apollos, but ministers by whom ye believed, even as the Lord gave to every man? I have planted, Apollos watered; but God gave the increase." This is Paul's way of deferring to the Lord, appropriately, the miracle of spiritual growth for all people. As mortals, you and I do the best we can to teach the gospel in such a way that light and truth and understanding may come to the listener. Subsequently, a teacher or Church leader reinforces what was said earlier and even supplements it with insights that expand the listener's mind and inspire the soul. The listener is growing, bit by bit, spiritually maturing because of the power of the word delivered by a servant of God (see Alma 31:5).

Let there be no misunderstanding, however, regarding the real source or cause of such growth—it is the Lord. It is the power of the Lord. The New American Standard Bible renders verse 6 as, "I planted, Apollos watered, but God was causing the growth." The Revised English Bible reads, "I planted the seed, and Apollos watered it; but God made it grow." And one study Bible offers this insight: "Paul's work was of a pioneer nature, preaching where no one had ever preached before. Apollos watered. Apollos worked in the established church, teaching and encouraging the converts Paul had won."[8] Our Heavenly Father, who is indeed the Father of Lights (James 1:17), opens the eyes, deepens the understanding, and inspires, lifts, and transforms the individual—all by means of His Holy Spirit.

THE ONLY SURE FOUNDATION (3:10–11)

Some people build upon the foundation of financial security. They become obsessed with making more and more money—with investments, with portfolios, with expanding their already bulging granaries. "Take heed, and beware of covetousness," the Savior counseled. "For a man's life consisteth not in the abundance of the things which he possesseth" (Luke 12:15). Our Lord also posed these haunting questions: "For what is a man profited, if he shall gain the whole world, and lose his own soul? or what shall a man give in exchange for his soul?" (Matthew 16:26).

Some people build upon esteem, popularity, or public acknowledgement and acclaim by doing whatever they can to cause others to admire them, to lift them up. We learn in modern revelation that one of the reasons many are called but few are chosen is that some people's "hearts are set so much upon the things of this world, and aspire to the honors of men" (Doctrine and Covenants 121:34–35). Indeed, we could list humanism, intellectualism, scientism, ethical relativism, atheism, and a whole host of other distractions that turn people's heads away from the Lord Jesus Christ and His kingdom on earth. These subtle distractions lure individuals away from the covenant path and onto the broad road that leads to destruction (see Matthew 7:13–14).

Just prior to his death, Helaman, grandson of Alma, delivered parting counsel to his own sons Nephi and Lehi. Like all of his prophetic predecessors, he counseled them to keep the commandments of God; to be true to their names, honoring those who had once borne those

---

8. *New International Version Study Bible*, 1927.

names; and to lay up for themselves treasures in heaven, seeking to qualify for that everlasting inheritance that the scriptures call eternal life. After offering further counsel, that mighty prophet-leader voiced this divine directive: "And now, my sons, remember, remember that it is upon the rock of our Redeemer, who is Christ, the Son of God, that ye must build your foundation; that when the devil shall send forth his mighty winds, yea, his shafts in the whirlwind, yea, when all his hail and his mighty storm shall beat upon you, it shall have no power over you to drag you down to the gulf of misery and endless wo, because of the rock upon which ye are built, which is a sure foundation, a foundation whereon if men build they cannot fall" (Helaman 5:12).

How, then, do we build on Christ? In a day when the winds blow and the waves beat upon our ship, how do we navigate our course safely into the peaceful harbor? How do true disciples of Christ know the way, live the truth, and gain that abundant life (see John 14:6)? The prophets have counseled us to (1) seek for, accept, and experience the Lord's healing grace; (2) search the scriptures; (3) teach His doctrine; (4) sustain His latter-day servants and hearken to their words; (5) maintain a believing heart; and (6) have hope in Christ—the sweet anticipation of life eternal.

THE CHURCH IS THE TEMPLE OF GOD (3:16–17)

Paul speaks of "the temple of God" in both chapters 3 and 6. A close look at the context of chapter 3 suggests that here he is speaking of the Church of Jesus Christ and not the human body. Indeed, later in this epistle, Paul refers to the Church as "the body of Christ" (1 Corinthians 12:27). New Testament scholar Gordon D. Fee has written:

> The imagery of the church as God's temple . . . is a pregnant one both for the Jewish Paul and the Gentile Corinthians. The word used (*naos*) refers to the actual sanctuary, the place of the deity's dwelling. . . . For Paul the imagery reflects the OT

[Old Testament] people of God. They are his people among whom he chose to "dwell" by tabernacling in their midst. . . .

The imagery of the church as temple would have been easily understood by the Corinthians as well, although perhaps not with its rich OT overtones. . . . Paul is calling their attention to the fact that since there is only one God, he can have only one temple in Corinth, and they are it. They became that new temple by the fact that "God's Spirit lives in you." Most likely, Paul meant by this not that the Spirit dwelt in each one of them, true as that would be for him (compare 6:19), but that the Spirit of God "lives in your midst." That is, Paul is here reflecting on the church as the corporate place of God's dwelling, who, when gathered in Jesus's name, experiences the presence and power of the Lord Jesus in their midst (5:4–5).[9]

When I was called to serve as the bishop of our ward in the late 1970s, the stake president laid his hands upon my head, ordained me to the office of bishop, set me apart as the bishop of my family's ward, and then offered very direct counsel. In fact, he said something that quickly got my attention. As I can recall, he stated, "There is a great deal of sin in your ward, and you must attend to it. As you meet with the Saints, seek to understand which members of your ward need special direction and which ones stand in need of serious repentance." The president then added, "As you do so, you will begin to see and feel the spirituality of the ward increasing." While it took a while to get to know the members better, to uncover unconfessed serious sins, and to assist those in transgression in getting back on the covenant path, the stake president's promise was realized. Not only did the members of the bishopric see the difference, but many ward members commented on the fact that they felt the Spirit of God much stronger and more frequently as they came to church and participated in the worship services.

---

9. Fee, *First Epistle to the Corinthians*, 146–47.

Some eighty years before the Savior came to earth, members of the Church of Jesus Christ in the New World fell into sinful practices such that "the wickedness of the church was a great stumbling-block to those who did not belong to the church; and thus *the church began to fail in its progress*" (Alma 4:9–10). The Lord's Church and kingdom are no stronger than the obedience and faithfulness of its members. When persons of other faiths encounter members of our Church who have chosen to violate the laws of God, their inappropriate actions and attitudes reflect directly on the Church. When they see worldly behavior by those who claim to have come out of the world of darkness into the light (see 1 Peter 2:9), it is extremely difficult for them to believe our doctrine or accept our religion and way of life as restored Christianity (see Alma 39:11). In order for the Lord's Church to accomplish the good that it is destined to accomplish, members of that Church must always and forever be purifying their lives through repentance and forgiveness.

"JUDGE NOTHING BEFORE THE TIME" (4:1–5)

Toward the end of His powerful Sermon on the Mount, Jesus delivered to His Apostles crucial counsel for them to teach to the people: "Judge not unrighteously, that ye be not judged," the Lord declared, "but judge righteous judgment. For with what judgment ye judge, ye shall be judged: and with what measure ye mete, it shall be measured to you again" (Matthew 7:1–2, JST). Later in his ministry, Jesus charged His disciples to "judge not according to your traditions, but judge righteous judgment" (John 7:24, JST). To His New World disciples, Christ declared, "And know ye that ye shall be judges of this people, according to the judgment which I shall give unto you, which shall be just." And now note what follows: "Therefore, what manner of men [and women] ought ye to be? Verily I say unto you, even as I am" (3 Nephi 27:27).

Almost always when members of the Church quote this verse, they use it to illustrate the divine directive for us to become like Jesus, our Exemplar—that is, we ought to live the way He lived. And that statement is just as true and powerful as it can be. True Christians strive to be like our Lord in how they think, speak, treat others, and so on. But the context of that dynamic command indicates that we are to be like Jesus and to *judge righteously—that is, to judge as He does.* We can only do this as we follow the dictates and direction of the Holy Ghost (see Doctrine and Covenants 11:12).

The great prophet and record keeper Mormon explained to his people that they should not "judge that which is evil to be of God, or that which is good and of God to be of the devil." And just how does one go about making such discriminations? Mormon continues: "For behold, the Spirit of Christ [or Light of Christ] is given to every man [and woman], that [they] may know good from evil; wherefore, I show unto you the way to judge; for every thing which inviteth to do good, and to persuade to believe in Christ, is sent forth by the power and gift of Christ; wherefore ye may know with a perfect knowledge it is of God" (Moroni 7:14, 16).

Regarding judging others, President Dallin H. Oaks pointed out that there are two kinds of judgments—intermediate judgments and final judgments: "I believe that the scriptural command to 'judge not' refers most clearly to [the] final judgment, as in the Book of Mormon declaration that 'man shall not . . . judge; for judgment is mine, saith the Lord' (Mormon 8:20)."[10] On the other hand, each of us must make intermediate judgments almost every day of our lives—how we will spend our time, with whom we will spend our time, whether to watch a questionable video, where we will go and where we will not go, who we will date and who we will not.

"FOOLS FOR CHRIST'S SAKE" (4:9–10)

In some ways, the more we learn about our Heavenly Father's plan of salvation, about Jesus Christ and His gospel, and about how the

---

10. Oaks, "'Judge Not' and Judging," *Ensign*, August 1999.

Savior's Atonement took place and how we may incorporate it into our individual lives, the deeper our conviction of the restored gospel becomes. We begin to sense more deeply within our souls our inadequacies, that we are ignorant, incapable, and utterly dependent upon God for our lives, our daily bread, and the very air we breathe. King Benjamin put it poignantly when he taught that "if [we] should serve him with all [our] whole souls yet [we] would be unprofitable servants" (Mosiah 2:21).

In writing about this rather unsettling expression, "ye would be unprofitable servants," Elder Gerald N. Lund explained that "God is perfect—in knowledge, power, influence, and attributes. He is the Creator of *all* things! What could any person—or all people together for that matter—do to bring profit (that is, an increase in assets, status, or benefits) to God? . . . That we are his children and that he loves us is undeniable, and that situation puts us in a status far above any of his other creations. But *we must somehow disabuse ourselves of any notion that we can bring personal profit to God by our actions*. That would make God indebted to men, which is unthinkable."[11]

Jacob, the brother of Nephi, taught a profound truth when he declared, "And whoso knocketh, to him will [God] open; and the wise, and the learned, and they that are rich, who are puffed up because of their learning, and their wisdom, and their riches—yea, they are they whom he despiseth; and save they shall cast these things away, and *consider themselves fools before God*, and come down in the depths of humility, he will not open unto them" (2 Nephi 9:42). To consider ourselves as fools before God is to acknowledge our limitations, our inabilities, our inadequacies, and our sins and shortcomings. It is to be spiritually open and transparent before an omniscient and omni-loving God. It is a humbling but healthy exercise. Alma instructed his faithful son Shiblon simply to "acknowledge your unworthiness before God at

---

11. Lund, *Jesus Christ: Key to the Plan of Salvation*, 120–21.

all times" (Alma 38:14). Those who are personally persuaded that they "have it all together," and that they perfectly perceive things as they really are, are the ones most in need of a course correction, reorientation, and pardoning mercy (see John 9:39–41).

Surely part of coming to know our Lord and Savior is coming to know who He is and what He has done. The more we learn of Him and the more we search the prophets and ponder on the revelations, the clearer it becomes that we must develop two attitudes or perspectives toward Jesus Christ. These points of view seem to be almost in tension, perhaps even in opposition to one another. The first is this: a major indicator of our spiritual development is the growing realization that Christ is God; under the direction of the Father, He is the Creator and Governor of all things; His redemptive labors are infinite and eternal in scope; He has power over life and death and over the very elements that make up our world and an infinite number of other worlds; He is the King of kings and the Lord of lords; in order to come unto Him and to *stand* before Him, we must first *fall* to our knees in an attitude of adoration, praise, awe, and worship. Some of the greatest men and women who have ever inhabited this planet were persons who came to know and acknowledge their "own nothingness, and his goodness and longsuffering towards [them], unworthy creatures" (Mosiah 4:11; see also 2 Nephi 4:17–19; Ether 3:2). It seems that the closer a man or woman comes to the Lord, the more sensitive and attentive he or she is to those flaws of the flesh, those imperfections of the soul, those sins against charity that are a part of every one of us. Such persons gladly and unhesitatingly confess the Lord's majesty and glory and, at the same time, their own unworthiness before Him.

The second attitude is a growing desire to be close to Christ, to spend time with Him, to enjoy communion with Him. The Apostle John bore witness that he and his apostolic colleagues had heard and seen, looked upon, and touched the Lord Jesus Christ. John reported this so "that ye also may have fellowship with us: and truly our fellowship is with the Father, and with his Son Jesus Christ." John then offered the comforting and reassuring invitation that "if we walk in the light, as he is in the light, we have fellowship one with another, and the blood of Jesus Christ his Son cleanseth us from all sin" (1 John 1:3, 7). As modern disciples of the Savior, we desire to enjoy fellowship with Him and with His Father, the Almighty Elohim. Thus when we speak of the Atonement of Jesus Christ, the greatest act of mercy and love in all eternity, we must of necessity speak of that intercession, that reconciliation, as being both *infinite* and *intimate*.

WICKEDNESS MUST BE CONFRONTED (5:1, 4–5)

In this chapter, it appears that Paul has learned, either by letter or direct report, of an especially grievous situation in Corinth. A young man has presumably been involved in an inappropriate sexual relationship and perhaps has even married his stepmother. Paul comments that this is the kind of sin that one would never even see among the Gentiles, those who are without the light and truth of the gospel of Jesus Christ. Elder Bruce R. McConkie wrote: "Such marriages were forbidden by the Mosaic Code under penalty of excommunication (Leviticus 18:6, 8–9). Paul endorses the Mosaic prohibition, describes the intimacies resulting from such unions as fornication, condemns his Corinthian brethren for winking at the offense, and directs the excommunication of the offender. If the sinner were left in the Church, Paul reasons, his influence, as leaven, would spread throughout the whole Church. The Church must, therefore, purge out this old leaven of wickedness and replace it with a new influence or leaven of righteousness."[12]

The leaders of the Corinthian branch are told to "deliver such an one unto Satan for the destruction of the flesh, that the spirit may be saved in the day of the Lord Jesus" (verse 5). That is, they are to excommunicate this person and thereby deliver him up to what the scriptures

---

12. McConkie, *Doctrinal New Testament Commentary*, 2:335.

call "the buffetings of Satan until the day of redemption" (Doctrine and Covenants 78:12; 82:21; 104:9; 132:26). In short, the sinner's severance from the Church will cost him the companionship of the Holy Ghost, that sanctifying and comforting companionship enjoyed by those who walk in the light and maintain their place on the covenant path. The one in need of sore repentance must then battle against evil influences without the buffering and strengthening influence of the Spirit. When genuine and sincere repentance has taken place, that individual may then receive forgiveness, once again enjoy the precious gift of the Holy Ghost, and walk in the light, as God and Christ are in the light (see 1 John 1:7; Mosiah 4:3).

"To be 'destroyed in the flesh' [Doctrine and Covenants 132:26] means exactly that," said President Joseph Fielding Smith, speaking of very serious sins that could cost a person his or her membership in the Lord's Church. "We cannot destroy men in the flesh, because we do not control the lives of men and do not have power to pass sentences upon them which involve capital punishment [see Doctrine and Covenants 134:10]. In the days when there was a theocracy on the earth, then this decree was enforced. What the Lord will do in lieu of this, because we cannot destroy in the flesh, I am unable to say, but it will have to be made up in some other way."[13]

AVOIDING EXCESSIVE AND UNNECESSARY LITIGATION (6:1–8)

Paul expresses his frustration and disappointment that members of the Corinthian branch are choosing to take their disputes or disagreements with one another to civil courts when they could be settled more amicably by dealing with one another as brothers and sisters in the faith. He asks: "Do ye not know that the saints shall judge the world? and if the world shall be judged by you, are ye unworthy to judge the

---

13. Joseph Fielding Smith, *Doctrines of Salvation*, 2:96–97.

smallest matters? Know ye not that we shall judge angels? how much more things that pertain to this life? . . . Is it so, that there is not a wise man among you? no, not one that shall be able to judge between his brethren? But brother goeth to law with brother, and that before the unbelievers" (verses 2–3, 5–6).

President Dallin H. Oaks—himself not only an ordained Apostle but also a former attorney, professor of law, and state supreme court judge—offered wise counsel on this matter in his writings to the Latter-day Saints. To begin, President Oaks rejected two extremes on this matter of Christians and litigation: (1) that "a conscientious Christian can never use the courts to resolve disputes"; and (2) "that there are no religious restraints on participating in litigation, thus succumbing to the popular notion that every wrong must have a legal remedy." He pointed out what ought to be obvious: "It is common knowledge that our courts are overloaded and that the number of lawsuits has increased in recent years at a rate far greater than the growth of population."

President Oaks added that "there is no dispute over the proposition that the increasing use of civil courts to resolve private disputes is exceedingly costly to the private disputants and to the public purse. Other costs . . . include the effects on society of millions of private acts by persons seeking to protect themselves from a lawsuit rather than pursuing what is best for their patient, their partner, and so forth. This category includes medical practitioners who abandon the healing arts because of the cost of malpractice insurance or who prescribe marginally necessary but highly expensive diagnostic techniques in the practice of what is called defensive medicine."

Finally, President Oaks outlined several principles that should guide Latter-day Saints in determining whether a civil action should be taken in a particular case: (1) forgive (see Mark 11:25–26; Doctrine and Covenants 64:9–11; 98:5–11, 20–22, 33–37); (2) pursue private settlement (see 3 Nephi 12:23–24, 39; Matthew 18:15; Doctrine and Covenants 42:88; (3) eliminate revenge (see Mormon 8:20; Moroni

9:20); (4) consider the effect of civil action upon those being sued (see Matthew 7:12); and (5) think of responsibilities instead of rights.[14]

In addressing how civil disputes may have been handled in Paul's day, President Oaks noted, "If these courts followed Roman procedures, as seems probable, then a criminal proceeding could be initiated by the accuser's taking an oath. In order for his testimony to be heard in civil or criminal cases, a witness would also have to take an oath. *In these pagan courts, such oaths might have required sacrifices to pagan gods.*"[15] This last statement can help us appreciate Paul's frustration with arguments or disputes being handled before what he calls the unjust and unbelievers (verses 1, 6).

OUR BODIES ARE THE TEMPLE OF GOD (6:18–20; 7:23)

If any people in the world should understand and take seriously prophetic counsel about the importance of our physical bodies, it is the Latter-day Saints. It is clear that faithful Saints in the meridian of time understood the nature of the human body and its vital place in the plan of salvation, the great plan of happiness. To be sure, they understood that the effects of the Fall are very real—men and women are fallen creatures and the body is fallen. At the same time, the Apostle Paul, who labored so diligently to dispel error among those who misunderstood the purpose of the physical body, writes: "What? know ye not that your body is the temple of the Holy Ghost which is in you, which ye have of God, and ye are not your own? For ye are bought with a price" (verses 19–20).

We know from scripture and from the Prophet Joseph Smith that the resurrection, or inseparable union of body and spirit (see Doctrine and Covenants 138:17), is a part of our glorified condition following death; that the spirit and the body constitute the soul of man; that "the resurrection from the dead is the redemption of the soul" (Doctrine and Covenants 88:15–16); that when we are raised from the dead, we

---

14. Oaks, *Lord's Way*, 155–58, 169–86.
15. Oaks, *Lord's Way*, 162.

will receive our own bodies—complete, whole, and perfected (see Alma 11:43; 40:23); that we are resurrected with a glorified body adapted and capacitated to dwell in a kingdom of that same glory (celestial, terrestrial, or telestial; see Doctrine and Covenants 88:28–31); and that the inseparable union of body and spirit is the only way to receive a fullness of joy (see Doctrine and Covenants 93:33; 138:17). And perhaps no teaching of the restored gospel could do more to establish a proper understanding of and appreciation for the physical body than the one that explains that "the Father has a body of flesh and bones as tangible as man's" (Doctrine and Covenants 130:22). God, our Eternal Heavenly Father, is a corporeal being, and it was "in the image of his own body" that Adam and Eve were formed (Moses 6:9).

In two sermons Joseph Smith declared: "That which is without body, parts and passions is nothing. There is no other God in heaven but that God who has flesh and bones. . . . *We came to this earth that we might have a body and present it pure before God in the Celestial Kingdom. The great principle of happiness consists in having a body.* The Devil has no body, and herein is his punishment. . . . All beings who have bodies have power over those who have not."[16] Only months later, Joseph taught: "They who have tabernacles have power over those who have not."[17]

Pastor Timothy Keller explained that in 1 Corinthians 6, Paul laid down a clear behavioral rule for sex: "Flee *porneia* [i.e., sexual immorality] (verse 18). The word *pornos* is usually translated as 'sexual immorality' in modern translations, but that is too general and doesn't convey the sharp and clear meaning it had for Paul and readers of the New Testament. The word meant any sexual intimacy outside an exclusive marriage relationship, not only adultery but premarital sex."[18]

---

16. Joseph Smith, in "Discourse, 5 January 1841, as Reported by William Clayton."
17. Joseph Smith, in "Discourse, 16 May 1841, as Reported by Unidentified Scribe"; spelling standardized.
18. Keller, *Hope in Times of Fear*, 145.

What did Paul mean when he wrote that our body is the temple of God? Each of us is born with the Light of Christ, or Spirit of Jesus Christ. This light is innate, inborn, a part of our soul that is a permanent link with the Almighty. One of the manifestations of the Light of Christ is conscience, a kind of moral monitor that impresses upon us what is right and what is wrong, what is good and what is evil, what is important and what is unimportant. Those who heed and hearken to the impressions and guidance of this light are led to a higher light, the gift of the Holy Ghost, which comes following our baptism at the hands of ordained administrators. Just as a house of the Lord, a temple, has within it God's Holy Spirit because of what goes on within those sacred precincts, so our physical body has within it the Spirit of the Lord, to the extent that we remain worthy of the Spirit's power and influence.

Just as no sane person would dare to defile the holy temple by committing acts that are unclean or impure within it, no man or woman who is interested in spiritual things, who desires to remain close to our Heavenly Father and His Beloved Son, would ever think and act in ways that would offend the Spirit. Truly, as Paul explains, we "are not our own." Why? Because we have been "bought with a price," even a priceless and sacred sacrifice of the sinless Son of Man (6:19–20; 7:23).

Many of us have heard, perhaps hundreds of times, the marvelous words of Jesus Christ given through Joseph Smith to Oliver Cowdery and David Whitmer: "Remember the worth of souls is great in the sight of God" (Doctrine and Covenants 18:10). On scores of occasions I have asked university students or Sunday School class members, "Why is the worth of souls great?" Answers come quickly: We are children of God. We matter greatly to Him. Man and woman are the highest and grandest of God's Creation. All of these replies are true.

The language of the Lord in the revelation, however, suggests a related but slightly different response as to why the worth of souls is great: "For, behold, *the Lord your Redeemer suffered death in the flesh; wherefore he suffered the pain of all men, that all men might repent and come unto him*. And he hath risen again from the dead, that he might bring all men unto him, on conditions of repentance. And how great is his joy in the soul that repenteth!" (Doctrine and Covenants 18:11–13). Did you catch that? Do we understand why, according to the Savior Himself, the worth of souls is great? It is because an infinite and eternal price was paid for our release from sin and our deliverance from physical death. Truly, we are not our own, for we have been bought with a price.

"With your body being such a vital part of God's eternal plan," President Russell M. Nelson stated, "it is little wonder that the Apostle Paul described it as a 'temple of God' (1 Corinthians 6:19). Each time you look in the mirror, see your body as your temple. That truth—refreshed gratefully each day—can positively influence your decisions about how you will care for your body and how you will use it."[19] And Elder David A. Bednar explained, "Because a physical body is so central to the Father's plan of happiness and our spiritual development, Lucifer seeks to frustrate our progression by tempting us to use our bodies improperly. One of the ultimate ironies of eternity is that the adversary, who is miserable precisely because he has no physical body, entices us to share in his misery through the improper use of our bodies. The very tool he does not have is thus the primary target of his attempts to lure us to spiritual destruction."[20]

MARRIAGE AND MISSIONS (7:1–2, 5, 7–9, JST)

Through the centuries two sentiments have spread far and wide regarding Saul of Tarsus, who became Paul the Apostle: (1) he was a woman-hater; and (2) he was opposed to marriage. Both are incorrect, and the Joseph Smith Translation offers significant assistance in better understanding Paul. The King James Version of the Bible opens chapter 7 this way: "Now concerning the things whereof ye wrote unto me [in an earlier epistle]: It is good for a man not to touch a woman.

---

19. Nelson, "Decisions for Eternity."
20. Bednar, "We Believe in Being Chaste."

Nevertheless, to avoid fornication, let every man have his own wife, and let every woman have her own husband" (verses 1–2). A cursory reading seems to suggest that Paul is discouraging close associations between men and women. The Joseph Smith Translation of verse 1 inserts a few words that change everything. It reads: "Now concerning the things whereof ye wrote unto me *saying*, It is good for a man not to touch a woman. Nevertheless *I say* . . ." In reality, the Corinthians wrote to Paul that they concluded that a man should not touch a woman, to which Paul responds. This is a very different story.

Some New Testament scholars have suggested that many of the Corinthians had begun to incorporate what might be called "proto-Gnostic" ideas into their worldview. The Gnostics were an apostate, heretical group from the second and third centuries AD who claimed to be Christians but had very strange ideas about the gospel. The word *Gnostic* is taken from the word *gnosis*, which means "knowledge." But these people claimed a special, sacred, saving knowledge that only a select few possessed. This knowledge might be termed the esoteric teachings of Jesus, the more mysterious insights that the Savior presumably taught His Apostles when they were alone, matters that were not to be shared with the uninitiated. Among other beliefs, the Gnostics had a dualistic perspective, drawing a very solid line between the physical and the spiritual. The physical—for example, the physical body—was something to be shunned, rejected, and transcended. Spiritual teachings, on the other hand, were those matters that enlightened, elevated, informed, and sanctified. According to the Gnostics, grasping these private matters led one to greater light and truth and even salvation. (Let me emphasize that Gnosticism as a movement did not reach its full-blown influence within Christianity until the second and third centuries AD. But some early elements of this heresy seem to have existed in the days of the Apostle Paul.)

Now, because the physical was considered to be of little or no importance, something to be looked down upon and discarded, two contrasting points of view of the physical body evolved. First of all, because the body was disdained, some were drawn toward *hedonism*, wherein the body was something to be exploited. Every passion and appetite could be satisfied, including desires for gluttony, drunkenness, and hedonistic orgies and erotic activities of every kind. Over the centuries, a word developed that came to represent this form of uncontrolled behavior. A person who yielded to a life of pleasure seeking, demonstrating very little temperance or restraint, was said to have been "Corinthianized."

Secondly, some of those who were enticed by a Gnostic way of thinking, viewing the body as something to be shunned or transcended, were drawn toward *asceticism*, the belief that the body was to be tamed, controlled, reigned in, subject to strict discipline. This seems to be what is reflected in the first verse of chapter 7. Perhaps some of the Corinthian branch who had been exposed to this proto-Gnostic thinking (Gnosticism in its very earliest, undeveloped stages) devised a rule that a man was not to touch a woman. In response, Paul explained the God-ordained relationship of husband and wife and the proper place of sexual expression, within the bonds of marriage.

The King James Version of verse 5 reads as follows: "Defraud ye not one the other, except it be with consent for a time, that ye may give yourselves to fasting and prayer; and come together again, that Satan tempt you not for your incontinency." The Joseph Smith Translation replaces "*defraud* ye not one the other" with "*depart* ye not from the other." The message in this verse is straightforward and sound: husbands and wives should not be separated for long periods; it is simply unwise and is flirting with temptation. Paul's counsel is that when a husband and wife continue to spend long periods apart, they open themselves to the enticements of the world, the worldly, and the allurements of Satan. Those especially who wrestle with incontinence—those who have difficulty controlling their thoughts and behavior—should not tempt fate by remaining separated from their spouse.

In verse 7, Paul offers this thought: "I would that all men were even as I myself." Through the years, both laymen and scholars have assumed that Paul is here stating that he is unmarried—that he never married or that he is a widower. To me this interpretation is not only unnecessary but completely unjustifiable. Elder Bruce R. McConkie paraphrased Paul's comment in verse 7: "I would that all men understood the law of marriage, that all had self-mastery over their appetites, and that all obeyed the laws of God in these respects."[21]

Through the centuries, Christian scholars and church leaders consistently taught that Paul was not married and that marriage is too often a distraction from things of greater spiritual import. Note verse 26 in the King James Version: "I suppose therefore that *this is good for the present distress*, I say, that it is good for a man so to be [chaste]." The Joseph Smith Translation of this passage adds crucial perspective on what Paul is teaching in this epistle: "*I speak unto you who are called unto the ministry*. For this I say, brethren, the time that remaineth is but short, that ye shall be sent forth unto the ministry. Even they who have wives, shall be as though they had none; for *ye are called and chosen to do the Lord's work*" (1 Corinthians 7:29, JST).

Clearly Paul is not opposed to marriage. Robert J. Matthews summarized the value of the Joseph Smith Translation in understanding this otherwise difficult chapter:

> The JST makes many clarifications and corrections to the records about Paul. . . . The popular myth that Paul was opposed to marriage is corrected by the JST so that *his dictum that there is an advantage to remaining unmarried is limited to those on temporary mission assignments*. This practice was advocated by Paul for efficiency in the temporary ministry, and is similar to the practice of The Church of Jesus Christ of Latter-day Saints today in calling young men and women, unmarried,

---

21. McConkie, *Doctrinal New Testament Commentary*, 2:344.

to serve missions, and refrain from marriage while in the mission field. Paul's teachings about marriage were not for all Church members, any more than the policy for young missionaries to remain unmarried today is a permanent rejection of marriage. The JST restores the proper context.[22]

THERE IS ONE GOD (8:5–6)

The Prophet Joseph Smith explained that it is "the province of the Father to preside as the Chief or President, Jesus as the Mediator, and the Holy Ghost as the Testator or Witness."[23] As Elder Bruce R. McConkie stated, "In the ultimate and final sense of the word, there is only one true and living God. He is the Father, the Almighty Elohim, the Supreme Being, the Creator and Ruler of the universe. . . . Christ is God; he alone is the Savior. The Holy Ghost is God; he is one with the Father and the Son. But these two are the second and third members of the Godhead. The Father is God above all, and is, in fact, the God of the Son."[24]

The early brethren of this dispensation were taught in the School of the Elders that "God is the only supreme governor and independent being in whom all fullness and perfection dwell; who is omnipotent, omnipresent [by means of His Holy Spirit], and omniscient; without beginning of days or end of life; and that in him every good gift and every good principle dwell; that he is the Father of lights; in him the principle of faith dwells independently, and he is the object in whom the faith of all other rational and accountable beings center for life and salvation."[25]

However, Joseph Smith spoke of a way in which there is a plurality of gods. He discussed the doctrine of *theosis*, also known as deification or divinization. This powerful but little understood concept among

---

22. Matthews, *Behold the Messiah*, 340.
23. *Teachings of Presidents of the Church: Joseph Smith*, 42.
24. McConkie, *New Witness for the Articles of Faith*, 51.
25. *Lectures on Faith*, 2:2; p. 10.

many Christians is that mortal men and women may become more and more Christlike, becoming like God, our Eternal Father, as they apply the atoning blood of Christ, receive and comply with the covenants and ordinances of salvation and exaltation, and cultivate the gifts and fruit of the Spirit, thereby partaking of the divine nature (2 Peter 1:4).

John the Beloved addressed this grand and soul-expanding truth when he wrote: "Behold, what manner of love the Father hath bestowed upon us, that we should be called the [children] of God. . . . Beloved, now are we the sons of God, and it doth not yet appear what we shall be [in the Resurrection]: but we know that, *when he shall appear, we shall be like him*; for we shall see him as he is. And every man that hath this hope in him purifieth himself, even as he [i.e., Jesus Christ] is pure" (1 John 3:1–3; compare Moroni 7:48).

"Here, then, is eternal life," Brother Joseph explained, "to know the only wise and true God; and you have got to learn how to be Gods yourselves, and to be kings and priests to God, the same as all Gods have done before you, namely, by going from one small degree to another, and from a small capacity to a great one; from grace to grace, from exaltation to exaltation, until you attain to the resurrection of the dead, and are able to dwell in everlasting burnings, and to sit in glory, as do those who sit enthroned in everlasting power."[26] Note carefully, to be like God is to receive a fullness of priesthood blessings. It is to be a king or a queen, a priest or a priestess, and to receive the ordinances of the house of the Lord and to keep their associated covenants.

Our God is not possessive. He does not hoard His power, glory, and gifts. God has *the power and the desire* to extend His grace—including the gifts, fruit, and blessings of the Spirit—to His children, and He does not hesitate to do so. The scriptures do not speak of a barrier beyond which men and women cannot progress spiritually. Followers of Christ are not told by the writers and speakers in either ancient or modern

---

26. *Teachings of Presidents of the Church: Joseph Smith*, 221.

scripture that they can progress and grow and mature and develop "thus far and no more." To inherit exaltation is to gain godhood.

Although Latter-day Saints certainly accept the teachings of Joseph Smith regarding man becoming like God, we do not fully comprehend all that is entailed by such a bold declaration. Subsequent and even current Church leaders have spoken very little concerning which of God's attributes are communicable and which may be incommunicable—that is, (1) which qualities of Deity can be conveyed to glorified human beings, and (2) which may reside solely and forever with Almighty God.

While we believe that becoming like God is entailed in eternal life (see Doctrine and Covenants 132:19–20), we do not believe we will ever unseat or oust God, the Eternal Father, or His Only Begotten Son, Jesus Christ; those holy beings are and forever will be the Gods we worship. I am unaware of any authoritative statement in Latter-day Saint literature that suggests that men and women will ever worship any being other than the ones within the Godhead. We believe in "one God" in the sense that we love and serve one Godhead, one divine presidency, each member of which possesses all of the attributes of godhood in perfection (see Alma 11:44; Doctrine and Covenants 20:28).

THE LABORER IS WORTHY OF HIS HIRE (9:1–6, 9–11)

Sadly, Paul was required to expend too much of his time and energy defending himself, his apostolic calling, and his manner of life to the Corinthian Saints. They were much too critical of his appearance, his manner of speech, and the complexity and depth of his letters (see 2 Corinthians 10:10; 2 Peter 3:16). In addition, some of the Saints in Corinth were troubled by Paul receiving material assistance from the members in terms of meals, lodging, and so on.

In some ways, Joseph Smith, the Prophet of the Restoration, was much like Paul. He was often unable to devote time to study and ministry because of his need to earn money and feed his family. To Brother Joseph, the Lord declared: "For thou shalt devote all thy service in

Zion; and in this thou shalt have strength. Be patient in afflictions, for thou shalt have many; but endure them, for lo, I am with thee, even unto the end of thy days. *And in temporal labors thou shalt not have strength, for this is not thy calling. Attend to thy calling and thou shalt have wherewith to magnify thine office,* and to expound all scriptures, and continue in laying on of the hands and confirming the churches" (Doctrine and Covenants 24:7–9).

A revelation given to the Saints in February 1831 charged the members: "And if ye desire the glories of the kingdom, appoint ye my servant Joseph Smith, Jun., and uphold him before me by the prayer of faith. And again, I say unto you, that *if ye desire the mysteries of the kingdom, provide for him food and raiment, and whatsoever thing he needeth to accomplish the work wherewith I have commanded him*" (Doctrine and Covenants 43:12–13).

The principle here is simple: "He who is appointed to administer spiritual things, the same is worthy of his hire, even as those who are appointed to a stewardship to administer in temporal things" (Doctrine and Covenants 70:12; see also 72:14). In Paul's case, he asks a question with a bit of a barb. In essence, he states: "Look, we do not even muzzle the ox, in order that it may glean the wheat in the fields (Deuteronomy 25:4). Am I any less than an ox?"

"ALL THINGS TO ALL MEN" (9:20–23)

The Apostle Paul is one of the most versatile men in all of holy scripture. Through experience, education, and training, he became a minister of the gospel of Jesus Christ who was prepared to interest, fascinate, infuriate, and, most important, teach and edify all types of people. He knew Hebrew, the holy language of the Jews and the language of the scriptures; he knew Aramaic, the *lingua franca*, the common language spoken by the Jews since the time of their Babylonian captivity; and he knew Greek, the language in which the New Testament was written. Since he was brought up in a Gentile world, he was no doubt quite familiar with the doings of the *goyim* (i.e., the Gentiles or the nations), including the gods of the Greeks and the Romans.

Paul inevitably chronicles the lives of the great ones of the Old Testament, highlighting those Jewish heroes and heroines, and bears witness that Jesus of Nazareth is the fulfillment of ancient prophecies and, indeed, the Promised Messiah, the hope of Israel, the prophet like unto Moses (see Deuteronomy 18:18–19). "To the weak became I as weak, that I might gain the weak: I am made all things to all men, that I might by all means save some. And this I do for the gospel's sake, that I might be partaker thereof with you" (verses 22–23).

CHRIST IS THE ROCK (10:1–4)

In the opening verses of chapter 10, Paul teaches an extremely valuable lesson, one that was taught by Jehovah to Father Adam some four millennia before the meridian of time: "And behold, all things have their likeness, and all things are created and made to bear record of me, both things which are temporal, and things which are spiritual; things which are in the heavens above, and things which are on the earth, and things which are in the earth, and things which are under the earth, both above and beneath: all things bear record of me" (Moses 6:63). Nephi, son of Lehi, bore a similar testimony: "Behold, my soul delighteth in proving unto my people the truth of the coming of Christ; for, for this end hath the law of Moses been given; and all things which have been given of God from the beginning of the world, unto man, are the typifying of him" (2 Nephi 11:4).

Hence, Paul reminds us that many of the sacred moments in Israel's history are types and shadows of an even greater reality—namely, the sacred ministry and deeds of the Holy One of Israel. Such events include the *Shekinah*, or holy cloud that rested upon the tabernacle in the wilderness to alert the people that Jehovah was in His temple; the Israelites' miraculous crossing of the Red Sea on dry ground; the sending of the manna; and Moses striking the rock and bringing forth water. To say that the ancient Israelites of the Exodus "drank of that spiritual Rock," which, Paul explains, represents the Savior, Jesus Christ (verse 4), is to teach that many of them prized the words of Jehovah, including the counsel of His commissioned prophet Moses, and received the living water that comes from God through His Only Begotten Son, Jesus Christ. The Israelites drank of the spiritual rock, who is Christ, to the extent they partook of the blessings of that portion of the gospel available to them.

NEVER TEMPTED BEYOND WHAT WE CAN BEAR (10:12–14)

No one is spiritually invulnerable. No one is strong enough or wise enough to avoid and withstand the fiery darts of the adversary, at least not on our own. Satan is, as young Joseph Smith discovered, "an actual being from the unseen world, who had such marvelous power as I had never before felt in any being" (Joseph Smith—History 1:16). Thus the last thing in the world any follower of Christ should do is assume that "I can handle it" without a serious infusion of divine assistance. "Wherefore let him that thinketh he standeth take heed lest he fall" (verse 12).

In writing of verse 13, one New Testament scholar pointed out that this particular verse "is one of the better known in 1 Corinthians, having served generations of Christians as a word of hope in times of difficulty. But it is almost always cited in isolation from its present context. . . . There is no risk of their falling, he seems to be telling them in response to verse 12, as long as one is dealing with ordinary trials. God will help them through such. But they must therefore 'flee from idolatry' (verse 14) because by implication there is no divine aid when one is 'testing' Christ in the way they [i.e., the Corinthians] are doing."[27]

To put this another way, God is less likely to deliver persons from

---

27. Fee, *First Epistle to the Corinthians*, 460.

a trial or temptation they have unwisely and knowingly thrown themselves into. Prevention is far, far better than redemption. Thus an individual who has wrestled with drug addiction is not likely to receive miraculous deliverance when he or she has purposely reentered the drug den, surrounded by other addicts. Alma delivered a timeless truth when he charged the wicked people of Ammonihah to "*humble yourselves before the Lord, and call on his holy name, and watch and pray continually, that ye may not be tempted above that which ye can bear*, and thus be led by the Holy Spirit, becoming humble, meek, submissive, patient, full of love and all long-suffering; having faith on the Lord" (Alma 13:28–29).

In order for us to enjoy the strength against and deliverance from Satan's attacks, we must be humble and vigilant, ever watchful. Paul's apostolic colleague, Simon Peter, taught a similar truth: "The Lord knoweth how to deliver the godly out of temptations" (2 Peter 2:9). Jude, the half-brother of the Savior, offered a type of benedictory prayer when he stated, "Now unto him that is able to keep you from falling, and to present you faultless before the presence of his glory with exceeding joy, to the only wise God our Saviour, be glory and majesty, dominion and power, both now and ever. Amen" (Jude 1:24–25).

HEAD COVERINGS (11:3–15)

One of the major challenges in understanding the teachings of Paul in his epistles is being able to separate what might be called eternal principles—matters that are always true and always relevant, no matter the situation or circumstances—and specific cultural laws and traditions. This is particularly true when we are striving to understand Paul's comments about women, men's and women's attire, and women's contributions in the meridian Church of Jesus Christ. In the twenty-first century, much progress has been made in promoting women's rights, their voices, their perspectives, and their vital importance in The Church of Jesus Christ of Latter-day Saints. We still have miles to travel, however, on this road of gender equality before we can rest. Hence it is awkward and, for some, off-putting to read Paul's words on these matters.

Our first illustration of this challenge is found in verses 3–15 of chapter 11 regarding head coverings during worship services. Verse 3 reads as follows: "But I would have you know, that the head of every man is Christ; and the head of the woman is the man; and the head of Christ is God." Most scholars agree that this is a statement about honor or authority—namely, that every one of us, even the Lord Jesus Christ, is answerable to someone. Later, in the fifth chapter of Ephesians, we find Paul teaching that the wife is subject to the husband, but the husband is also subject to the wife. This is implied in Ephesians 5:21, where Paul counsels the married couple to "[submit] yourselves one to another in the fear of God."

Paul writes in verse 4 of 1 Corinthians 11 that "every man praying or prophesying, having his head covered, dishonoureth his head." One commentary observes that this phrase in Greek

> means "down from the head" and may refer to either long hair that hangs loose (verses 14–15), or to a veil that covers the face, or to a piece of cloth pulled over the head (like a modern shawl or scarf) that leaves the face revealed. As background for understanding Paul's point in this verse, Roman men sometimes practiced the custom of pulling the loose folds of their toga over their head as an act of piety in the worship of pagan gods. Paul thus draws on the example of this pagan custom (which everyone in the Corinthian church would have thought absurd) to make the point that men should not dishonor Christ by praying according to pagan custom (8:4). He then uses the idea to prepare the way for his argument that it is equally absurd for wives to pray or prophesy in public with their heads uncovered.[28]

---

28. *English Standard Version Study Bible*, 2206–7.

Verse 5 states, "But every woman that prayeth or prophesieth with her head uncovered dishonoureth her head: for that is even all one as [i.e., one and the same as] if she were shaven." The same commentary explains that "a married woman who uncovered her head in public would have brought shame to her husband. The action may have connoted sexual availability or may simply have been a sign of being unmarried."[29] Continuing on, verse 10 states, "For this cause ought the woman to have power on her head because of the angels." It was generally felt that angels were present at the worship services and thus that a woman would want to present herself in a modest and respectful manner.

The revered commentator J. R. Dummelow explained that "some of the female Corinthian converts [had] discontinued this practice [covering their heads] in Christian worship, thus practically claiming equality with men. Now St. Paul himself taught that there can be no male and female: for ye are all one in Christ Jesus (Galatians 3:28). . . . But *just as in the case of slavery* (7:21), *Christianity did not come to abolish existing social conditions*. It has done much to improve the condition of women, but has done so gradually."[30]

As N. T. Wright put it, some of the women in Corinth "had decided to remove their normal head covering, perhaps also unbraiding their hair, to show that in the Messiah they were free from the normal social conventions by which men and women were distinguished. . . . Perhaps to the Corinthians' surprise, Paul doesn't congratulate the women on this new expression of freedom. He insists on maintaining gender differentiation during worship." Wright added that another dimension to the problem may well be that, at that time in Corinth, women who appeared in public without some kind of head covering were prostitutes. According to one, rather humorous, explanation, "If the watching world discovered that the Christians were having

---

29. *English Standard Version Study Bible*, 2207.
30. Dummelow, *Commentary on the Holy Bible*, 909.

meetings where women 'let their hair down' in this fashion, it could have the same effect on their reputation as it would in the modern West if someone looked into a church and found the women all wearing bikinis."[31]

MEN AND WOMEN ARE INTERDEPENDENT (11:11)

Each of the members of the Godhead is committed to the growth, expansion, perfection, and exaltation of all of the children of God. There are no favorites in the sense that They do not love one person more than another, nor do They love one gender more than another. Men are not more important to the work of the Lord than women, nor are women more important to the work of the Lord than men.

It is vital that we understand that the ultimate blessings associated with the holy priesthood cannot be had by a man alone. The highest blessings of the temple come to a man and a woman, husband and wife, together. President Charles W. Penrose, a counselor to President Joseph F. Smith, stated that "when a woman is sealed to a man holding the Priesthood, she becomes one with him. . . . The glory and power and dominion that he will exercise when he has the fullness of the Priesthood and becomes a 'king and a priest unto God,' she will share with him."[32] For that matter, every woman and man in the Church can and should attend carefully to the word of the Lord concerning the oath and covenant of the Melchizedek Priesthood (see Doctrine and Covenants 84:33–44). They should magnify their callings and enjoy the sanctifying and renewing powers of the Spirit as they do so; they should receive the Lord's servants and sustain them loyally and beware concerning themselves. They should give diligent heed to the words of eternal life, live by every word of God, and, in general, be true and faithful to their covenants, particularly those covenants made in the house of the Lord. They should also seek to understand how to

---

31. Wright, *Surprised by Scripture*, 74.
32. Charles W. Penrose, in Conference Report, April 1921, 24.

receive power in the priesthood. One who strives in this life to abide by these conditions, whether male or female, whether currently married or single, will in the life to come reap the everlasting rewards.

We are now on the path leading to life eternal, the covenant path, and we need to stay on that path. We are in training here for what will come and what will be expected of us hereafter. Indeed, it is a rigorous training program through which God expects His daughters and sons to pass, and the Master does not apologize for requiring much of those to whom much has been given (see Doctrine and Covenants 82:3). If we live in a manner that would allow the Holy Ghost to be a regular and eventually a constant companion (see Doctrine and Covenants 121:46), then we will begin to learn the spirit of revelation and acquire those gifts and attributes that will bring unspeakable peace in this life and equip us to dwell comfortably and joyously with God and Christ and our eternal family in exaltation and glory.

If we learn to lead and govern gently and lovingly in this life, we will have the opportunity to rule hereafter. John the Revelator beheld a sublime vision: "And I saw thrones, and they sat upon them, and judgment was given unto them. . . . Blessed and holy is he that hath part in the first resurrection: on such the second death hath no power, but *they shall be priests [and priestesses] of God and of Christ, and shall reign with him a thousand years*" (Revelation 20:4, 6).

HOW HERESIES ARE USEFUL (11:18–19)

When we speak of a person's doctrinal teachings as being *orthodox*, we mean that he or she is teaching doctrine that is not at variance with accepted truths. The word itself means literally "having the right opinion." The opposite term is *heresy*—literally, a choice one makes to a particular school of thought or course of action—or as we use the word today, a choice to depart from the proper or accepted belief. It is to accept a belief or choose a path that is *unorthodox*.

Paul indicates that the word *heresy* has reached him and that there are divisions or schisms or factions among the Corinthian Saints (verse 18), which of course we encountered in our discussion of chapter 1. "For there must be also heresies among you," Paul continues, "that they which are approved may be made manifest among you" (verse 19). Another way of saying this is to remark that heresies cause the faithful, the obedient, the Church member who is teaching sound doctrine, to stand out—to shine, as it were.

John the Beloved, writing during the early stages of the Great Apostasy, addressed his brothers and sisters in the faith as follows: "Little children, it is the last time," meaning the end of the age or the end of the Christian dispensation. "As ye have heard that antichrist shall come, even now are there many antichrists; whereby we know that it is the last time." Now note what follows: "They [i.e., the antichrists] went out from us, but they were not of us." In other words, the anti-Christs went out into the world claiming to be true followers of the Lord Jesus Christ, but they were not; they were not sent by the leaders of the Church. "For *if they had been of us, they would no doubt have continued with us*: but *they went out, that they might be made manifest that they were not all of us*" (1 John 2:18–19). Faithful representatives of the Lord, those who deliver orthodox messages of truth and light, do not leave the fold; they do not wander from the center of the faith; and they certainly do not preach a different gospel.

DISORDER WITHIN THE SACRAMENT SERVICE (11:20–22)

Paul now expresses his concern about another type of division that is taking place among the members of the branch. A tradition had developed in Corinth in which an *agape* (love) feast was held in conjunction with their sacramental service—what might be similar to a "dinner on the grounds" after church. That is, they gathered together to partake of bread and wine in remembrance of the Lord Jesus—His life, His teachings, His miracles, and especially His atoning death and glorious Resurrection—and then enjoyed a meal together. Unfortunately, some of the more well-to-do members brought their seven-course meals and were enjoying some serious eating. Also present were many of the poorer Saints, whose meal—if they brought one at all—was meager in comparison to the feasts being enjoyed by the wealthier members of the branch. The King James Version renders Paul's words in verse 20 as "When ye come together therefore into one place, this is not to eat the Lord's supper." The Joseph Smith Translation changes this to "When ye come together therefore, *is it not to eat the Lord's supper?*" In other words, "Isn't the main reason we come together as a branch to partake of the sacrament of the Lord's Supper?"

Of the division between the rich and the poor in Corinth, one scholar wrote:

> To understand Paul's critique, we need to understand the way meals worked within Corinthian society. Corinth had a clear hierarchy, an obvious social and economic ladder. Where you stood on that ladder depended on whether you had enough social capital to be considered "wise," "influential," and "of noble birth" (1:26). This social hierarchy could be a matter of life or death. Earning one of these labels meant that you were more likely to get the economic opportunities and social network on which your survival might depend.
>
> In Corinth, communal meals provided a primary way for individuals to claim their spot on the ladder or even move up the rung. Like middle-school cafeterias today, where you sat at the meal said a lot about where you stood in the social pecking order. Bringing more food or claiming a more honorable seat, for example, were strategies for trying to climb the ladder.
>
> This was all just business as usual in Corinth, but Paul declares that such behavior has no place in church. Because of the way this multiethnic, multiclass congregation humiliated the have-nots, they couldn't call what they were doing the

Lord's Supper at all. They were acting more Corinthian than Christian.[33]

REFLECTIONS ON THE LAST SUPPER (11:23–26)

In the closing hours of the ministry of the Son of God, Jesus celebrated the Passover with His beloved associates. The Passover meal essentially transformed into a sacred Christian ordinance that we know as the sacrament of the Lord's Supper (known in other Christian faiths as Communion or the Eucharist). Verses 23–26 of 1 Corinthians are believed to contain one of the oldest descriptions of what took place when Jesus met in the upper room with His Twelve Apostles. In fact, some New Testament scholars believe these words would have been available to the first-century Saints before the accounts in the synoptic Gospels were (see Matthew 26:17–30; Mark 14:12–26; Luke 22:7–20).

This brief account of the first sacramental service during the Savior's ministry confirms what many in the Christian world believe about partaking of the bread and wine (or water). Those who partake of it are to do so *in remembrance of the Lord Jesus*. Participants in the service are not literally partaking of the torn flesh and spilled blood of Jesus (a belief known as transubstantiation). Rather, followers of the Christ are charged to ponder upon, recall, and relive in our minds and hearts the price that had to be paid to win our souls.

Elder Jeffrey R. Holland reminded us:

> Every ordinance of the gospel focuses in one way or another on the atonement of the Lord Jesus Christ, and surely that is why this particular ordinance [i.e., the sacrament] with all its symbolism and imagery comes to us more readily and more repeatedly than any other in our life. . . .
>
> If remembering is the principal task before us, what might

---

33. Rhodes, "Paul and Prejudice," 43.

come to our memory when those plain and precious emblems are offered to us? . . . We could remember Christ's miracles and his teachings, his healings and his help. We could remember that he gave sight to the blind and hearing to the deaf and motion to the lame and the maimed and the withered. . . .

On some days we will have cause to remember the unkind treatment he received, the rejection he experienced, and the injustice—oh, the injustice—he endured. . . .

When those difficult times come to us, we can remember that Jesus had to descend below all things before he could ascend above them, and that he suffered pains and afflictions and temptations of every kind that he might be filled with mercy and know how to succor his people in their infirmities.[34]

TAKING THE SACRAMENT WORTHILY (11:26–30)

The risen Lord gave stern counsel to the leaders of the Nephite people: "And now behold, this is the commandment which I give unto you, that ye shall not suffer any one knowingly to partake of my flesh and blood unworthily, when ye shall minister it; for whoso eateth and drinketh my flesh and blood unworthily eateth and drinketh damnation to his soul; therefore if ye [i.e., the leaders of the Church] know that a man is unworthy to eat and drink of my flesh and blood ye shall forbid him" (3 Nephi 18:28–29).

Because not one of us walks our mortal paths without sin, without flaw, we should and must live in a state of constant repentance. That is, when we do commit sin, we "speedily repent and return unto [God], and find favor in [His] sight, and be restored to the blessings which [the Lord] hast ordained to be poured out upon those who shall reverence [the Lord] in [His] house" (Doctrine and Covenants 109:21).

---

34. Holland, "This Do in Remembrance of Me"; see also Doctrine and Covenants 88:6; 122:8; Alma 7:11–12.

And how do we do that? When we do stray from what we know to be right and true, we need to go to our Heavenly Father in prayer, doing so in the name of Jesus Christ, and then pray and earnestly plead for God to forgive us.

Paul instructs the Corinthians (and us, by extension) that "as often as ye eat this bread, and drink this cup, ye do shew [i.e., proclaim, announce] the Lord's death till he come" (verse 26). Surely no more powerful and comforting assurance could be given to us than "As often as my people repent will I forgive them their trespasses against me" (Mosiah 26:30). Many years ago, Elder Melvin J. Ballard of the Quorum of the Twelve Apostles asked:

> How can we have spiritual hunger? Who is there among us that does not wound his spirit by word, thought, or deed, from Sabbath to Sabbath? . . . If there is a feeling in our hearts that we are sorry for what we have done; if there is a feeling in our souls that we would like to be forgiven, then the method to obtain forgiveness is not through rebaptism. . . . It is to repent of our sins, to go to those against whom we have sinned or transgressed and obtain their forgiveness, and then repair to the Sacrament table where, if we have sincerely repented and put ourselves in proper condition, we shall be forgiven, and spiritual healing will come to our souls. It will really enter into our being.[35]

But what if we are unsure that we are worthy to partake? Elder John H. Groberg of the Seventy taught:

> If we desire to improve (which is to repent) and are not under priesthood restriction, then, in my opinion, we are worthy. If, however, we have no desire to improve, if we have no intention of following the guidance of the Spirit, we must ask: Are we worthy to partake, or are we making a mockery of the

---

35. Ballard, sermon, June 1, 1919.

very purpose of the sacrament, which is to act as a catalyst for personal repentance and improvement? . . . If we remember the Savior and all he has done and will do for us, we will improve our actions and thus come closer to him, which keeps us on the road to eternal life. . . .

Those who would deny themselves the blessing of the sacrament by not attending sacrament meeting or by not thinking of the Savior during the services surely must not understand the great opportunity to be forgiven, to have his Spirit to guide and comfort them! What more could anyone ask? As we worthily partake of the sacrament, we will sense those things we need to improve in and receive the help and determination to do so. No matter what our problems, the sacrament always gives hope.[36]

One of the more sobering verses in this section of the epistle is verse 30: "For this cause [i.e., partaking of the sacrament unworthily] many are weak and sickly among you, and many sleep." Paul isn't speaking symbolically here. He means what he says: sinning against the sufferings and death of the Redeemer is serious business, which can eventually result in illnesses (see Alma 14:6; 15:3) and even physical death.[37] Moroni's counsel to those who read the Nephite-Jaredite record is that we "do all things in worthiness, and do it in the name of Jesus Christ, the Son of the living God; and if ye do this, and endure to the end, ye will in nowise be cast out" (Mormon 9:29).

WE COME TO KNOW BY REVELATION (12:3)

As chapter 12 of 1 Corinthians begins, Paul indicates that he does not want his associates in the faith to be ignorant of the workings of the Holy Ghost. Verse 3 states, "Wherefore I give you to understand,

---

36. Groberg, "Beauty and Importance of the Sacrament."
37. See McConkie, *Doctrinal New Testament Commentary*, 2:365–66; Fee, *First Epistle to the Corinthians*, 565.

that no man speaking by the Spirit of God calleth Jesus accursed: and that *no man can say* that Jesus is the Lord, but by the Holy Ghost." The meaning of the first part of verse 3 is fairly obvious: no one who has and enjoys the influence of the Spirit of God can call Jesus accursed. The third member of the Godhead will never speak harshly against the second member of the Godhead. But the second half is a bit more muddled. Anyone can literally "say" that Jesus is Lord. Even the devils of hell can do that (see Mark 1:34; James 2:19). Hence, in both the Joseph Smith Translation[38] and in sermons he delivered, Joseph corrected 1 Corinthians 12:3 to read that "*no man can know* that Jesus is the Lord, but by the Holy Ghost."[39]

As discussed in our consideration of chapter 2, the things of God may be *known*. Knowledge, especially knowledge of spiritual realities, can be recognized in ways that far transcend what we may learn through the five natural senses. One can *know* that Jesus walked on water, cast out demons, restored sight to the blind, and raised the dead—not just because these miracles are recorded in scripture, but by the confirming power of God's Holy Spirit. One can *know* that God, the Eternal Father, and Jesus Christ, the Son of God, appeared to the boy Joseph Smith in the Sacred Grove in 1820—not only because Joseph said They did, but by means of the convincing power of the Spirit. One can *know* that The Church of Jesus Christ of Latter-day Saints is in very deed the restoration of first-century Christianity—not only by the amount of good its people do throughout the world or because of its continuing growth and expanding influence, but by means of the revealed witness that comes to one's soul through the work of the third member of the

---

38. This change in the Joseph Smith Translation is not contained in the Latter-day Saint edition of the King James Bible but is on the Joseph Smith Translation manuscripts.
39. Joseph Smith, in "History, 1838–1856, volume C-1 Addenda," 26; see also Joseph Smith, in "Discourse, 28 April 1842," and "Minutes and Discourse, 28 April 1842."

Godhead (see 1 Nephi 22:2; Jacob 1:6; 4:8; Ether 4:11; Moroni 10:5; Doctrine and Covenants 11:13–14; 42:61; 46:13; 101:16).

SPIRITUAL GIFTS IN THE CHURCH (12:4–30)

One of the signs of the Lord's true Church is what we call the gifts of the Spirit. These spiritual endowments are granted to the Lord's people as an illustration of His love for us. No one of us is capable of carrying out our duties in the Church in a faithful manner without divine grace, without the loving assistance of our Heavenly Father. As Paul illustrates in chapter 12, the gifts of the Spirit are given to bless the Church of Jesus Christ and, more particularly, the body of Christ—those who are members of that Church. In modern revelation we learn that every member has been given at least one spiritual gift, and some enjoy many of those gifts. Section 46 of the Doctrine and Covenants also states that one of the main purposes of these gifts is to help the Saints avoid being deceived (Doctrine and Covenants 46:8, 11).

Paul lists various of these spiritual gifts: wisdom, knowledge, faith, healing, the working of miracles, prophecy, discernment, tongues, and the interpretation of tongues. In the Book of Mormon, Moroni adds to this list the gifts of teaching wisdom, teaching knowledge, and beholding angels and ministering spirits. Section 46 of the Doctrine and Covenants adds the gift of a testimony of Jesus Christ, a conviction that He is the Son of God and was crucified for the sins of the world; the gift of a believing heart, the spiritual capacity to believe on the words of those who do know; and the gift of the faith to be healed.

Though many spiritual gifts are described in scripture, there is an almost infinite variety of gifts that the Lord can and will bestow upon His children. Elder Marvin J. Ashton taught: "Let us review some of these less-conspicuous gifts: the gift of asking; the gift of listening; the gift of hearing and using a still, small voice; the gift of being able to weep; the gift of avoiding contention; the gift of being agreeable; the gift of avoiding vain repetition; the gift of seeking that which is righteous; the gift of not passing judgment; the gift of looking to God for guidance; the gift of being a disciple; the gift of caring for others; the gift of being able to ponder; the gift of offering prayer; the gift of bearing a mighty testimony; and the gift of receiving the Holy Ghost."[40]

These gifts are signs of the true Church, evidences that God is indeed working through and with a people (see Mark 16:15–18). Spiritual gifts are the signs and wonders and miracles that are always found among the Lord's covenant people. They are indeed a sign of the Lord's true Church. The Apostle Paul compares the various gifts to parts of the human body or the body of Christ, the Church. The Church provides a gathering place for individuals to share their gifts. Since every member of the Church has at least one spiritual gift, participation in the Church allows us to draw upon all these various gifts and graces. Brother Jones may have the gift of healing, Sister Backman the gift of wisdom, Brother Brown the gift of teaching, and Sister Young the gift of discernment. "Therefore, let every man stand in his own office, and labor in his own calling; and let not the head say unto the feet it hath no need of the feet; for without the feet how shall the body be able to stand? Also the body hath need of every member, that all may be edified together, that the system may be kept perfect" (Doctrine and Covenants 84:109–10).

In verses 22–23, Paul teaches a principle that is vital when it comes to desiring spiritual gifts: those gifts that are the most dramatic, and even sensational, are not necessarily the most important ones. While such gifts as discernment, wisdom, knowledge, faith, and a believing heart may not attract much attention, they are crucial for acquiring a testimony and living a life devoted to spiritual things. In an editorial in the Church newspaper *Times and Seasons*, Joseph Smith addressed this particular principle. Referring to 1 Corinthians 12, the Prophet wrote:

---

40. Ashton, "There Are Many Gifts."

There are several gifts mentioned here, yet which of them all could be known by an observer at the imposition of hands? The word of wisdom, and the word of knowledge, are as much gifts as any other, yet if a person possessed both of these gifts, or received them by the imposition of hands, who would know it? Another might receive the gift of faith, and they would be as ignorant of it. . . .

The greatest, the best, and the most useful gifts would be known nothing about by an observer. It is true that a man might prophesy, which is a great gift, and one that Paul told the people—the Church—to seek after and to covet [1 Corinthians 14:29], rather than to speak in tongues; but what does the world know about prophesying?[41]

THE PERFECT AND PERFECTING GIFT (12:31–13:13)

The Apostle Paul calls upon members of the Lord's Church to "covet earnestly the best gifts" (verse 31). In speaking of the vital importance of seeking for and enjoying the gifts of the Spirit, President George Q. Cannon declared:

> We find, even among those who have embraced the Gospel, hearts of unbelief. How many of you, my brethren and sisters, are seeking for those gifts that God has promised to bestow? How many of you, when you bow before your Heavenly Father in your family circle or in your secret places, contend for these gifts to be bestowed upon you? How many of you ask the Father, in the name of Jesus, to manifest Himself to you through these powers and these gifts? . . . There is not that diligence, there is not that faith, there is not that seeking for the

---

41. Joseph Smith, "Gift of the Holy Ghost," 824–25.

power of God that there should be among a people who have received the precious promises we have. . . .

If any of us are imperfect, it is our duty to pray for the gift that will make us perfect. Have I imperfections? I am full of them. What is my duty? To pray to God to give me the gifts that will correct these imperfections. . . . No man ought to say, 'Oh, I cannot help this; it is my nature.' He is not justified in it, for the reason that God has promised to give strength to correct these things, and to give gifts that will eradicate them.[42]

Paul then adds: "And yet shew I unto you a more excellent way" (verse 31). While the breakdown of the scriptures into chapters and verses is ever so helpful in referencing selected passages, here the division between chapters 12 and 13 is arbitrary. Why? Because the "more excellent way" is the gift or fruit of charity, which is discussed beautifully in chapter 13.

Chapter 13 begins with a rather bold and direct remark from Paul: "Though I speak with the tongues of men and of angels, and have not charity, I am become as sounding brass, or a tinkling cymbal" (verse 1). This is rendered elsewhere as follows:

> If I speak in the tongues of mortals and of angels, but do not have love, I am a noisy gong or a clanging cymbal. (NRSV)

> If I speak in human languages, or even in those of angels, but do not have love, then I've become a clanging gong or else a clashing cymbal. (KNT)

> If I speak with human eloquence and angelic ecstasy but don't love, I'm nothing but the creaking of a rusty gate. (*The Message*)

---

42. "Discourse by President George Q. Cannon," 259–61; see also Cannon, *Gospel Truth*, 154–55.

Charity, the purest form of love, the pure love of Christ (see Moroni 7:47), Godlike love, is much more than an emotion. It is a fruit of the Spirit (see Galatians 5:22), a divine endowment that is "bestowed" by the Lord (see Moroni 7:48). Charity has been defined as "the highest, noblest, strongest kind of love, not merely affection; the pure love of Christ. It is never used to denote alms or deeds or benevolence, although it may be a prompting motive."[43]

After quoting verse 1 of chapter 13, Joseph Smith offered a bit of commentary: "Don't be limited in your views with regard to your neighbor's virtue, but beware of self-righteousness, and be limited in the estimate of your own virtues, and not think yourselves more righteous than others; you must enlarge your souls towards each other if you would do like Jesus and carry your fellow creatures to Abraham's bosom."[44]

On another occasion, the Prophet taught that "there is a love from God that should be exercised toward those of our faith, who walk uprightly, which is peculiar to itself, but it is without prejudice; it also gives scope to the mind, which enables us to conduct ourselves with greater liberality towards all that are not of our faith, than what they exercise towards one another. These principles approximate nearer to the mind of God, because [they are] like God, or Godlike."[45]

In reading verse 2, some would suppose that if they had the gift of prophecy, understood the mysteries of God, and possessed the faith needed to move mountains, they would also enjoy the pure love of Christ in their lives. Paul adds that if he gave away all that he possessed to feed the poor and even sealed his witness through a martyr's death but did not have charity, such noble and certainly commendable endeavors would not be sufficient to ensure one's eternal life.

---

43. Bible Dictionary, "Charity," 632.
44. Joseph Smith, in "History, 1838–1865, volume C-1 Addenda," 41; punctuation standardized.
45. *Teachings of Presidents of the Church: Joseph Smith*, 146–47.

"The ultimate purpose of the gospel of Jesus Christ," Elder Bruce C. Hafen explained,

> is to cause the sons and daughters of God to become as Christ is. Those who see religious purpose only in terms of ethical service in the relationship between man and fellowmen may miss that divinely ordained possibility. It is quite possible to render charitable—even "Christian"—service without developing deeply ingrained and permanent Christlike character. Paul understood this when he warned against giving all one's goods to feed the poor without true charity. . . . We can give without loving, but we cannot love without giving. If our vertical relationship with God is complete, then, by the fruit of that relationship, the horizontal relationship with our fellow beings will also be complete. We then act charitably toward others, not merely because we think we should, but because that is the way we are.[46]

Verses 4–7 describe the Lord Jesus Christ beautifully because He is the embodiment of charity, the prototype of a being filled with charity. Charity, or rather the charitable person:

1. **Suffers long; bears all things.** Charitable persons are endowed with a portion of the love of God and thus, to some degree, with the patience and perspective of God toward people and circumstances. Their vision of here and now (the present) is greatly affected by their glimpse of there and then (the future).

2. **Is kind.** Charity motivates us to goodness, to benevolence, and to sensitivity toward others' needs. People are the focus.

3. **Envies not.** Those who love the Lord and are filled with His love are much less prone to concern themselves with acquisitions or the accolades of others. Their joy is full in Christ (see Doctrine and

---

46. Hafen, *Broken Heart*, 196–97.

Covenants 101:36). They find happiness in simple pleasures and delight in God's goodness to them.

4. **Is not puffed up; seeks not one's own.** Charitable people seek diligently to turn attention away from themselves and toward God. They eagerly acknowledge the hand of the Lord in all things and hesitate to take personal credit for accomplishments.

5. **Is not easily provoked.** Those filled with the love of Christ are meek; they have a quiet but pervasive poise under provocation.

6. **Thinks no evil.** The minds of charitable individuals are on things of righteousness, and they desire that which builds and strengthens and encourages.

7. **Rejoices not in iniquity but rejoices in the truth.** Charitable persons are repulsed by sin, though anxious to fellowship and lift the sinner. They are pained by the waywardness of the world and labor tirelessly to extend gospel assistance to those who stray from the path of peace.

8. **Believes all things.** Those possessed of charity are not naïve or gullible; they are simply open to truth. They enjoy the spiritual gift of a believing heart. Therefore, all things work together for their good (see Doctrine and Covenants 90:24).

9. **Hopes all things.** Their hope is in Christ, a quiet but dynamic assurance that even though they are imperfect, they are on course, that the Lord is pleased with their lives, and that eternal life is at the end of their path.

10. **Endures all things.** No matter what the true followers of Christ are required to pass through, they proceed as called. Neither the shame of the world nor the threat of physical death can deter those who are bent upon enjoying the love of God everlastingly.

One who has studied all of the books within the scriptural canon of The Church of Jesus Christ of Latter-day Saints will notice how similar Paul's words in 1 Corinthians 13 are to Mormon's words in Moroni 7. In an address delivered just months before his death, Elder Bruce R. McConkie stated, "Both Paul and Mormon expounded with great inspiration about faith, hope, and charity, in many cases using the same words and phrases. . . . It does not take much insight to know that both Mormon and Paul had before them the writings of some Old Testament prophet on the same subjects."[47]

Verses 8–11 of chapter 13 describe how charity matures the true followers of the Son of God. It is as if Paul is calling upon the Corinthians to grow up spiritually, to cease speaking or understanding as a child, and instead to seek for and rejoice in charity, the love of God, the highest and holiest of divine attributes and gifts. It is, however, Mormon who provides understanding that charity has a sanctifying influence upon the souls of those who are possessed of it: "Wherefore, my beloved brethren [and sisters], pray unto the Father with all the energy of heart, that ye may be filled with this love, which he hath bestowed upon all who are true followers of his Son, Jesus Christ; that ye may become the sons of God; that when he shall appear we shall be like him, for we shall see him as he is; that we may have this hope; that we may be purified even as he is pure" (Moroni 7:48).

In what I consider to be one of the most profound statements in all our literature regarding the love of God, Elder Jeffrey R. Holland wrote:

> It is instructive to note that the charity or "the pure love of Christ," we are to cherish can be interpreted two ways. One of its meanings is the kind of merciful, forgiving love Christ's disciples should have one for another. That is, all Christians should try to love as the Savior loved, showing pure redeeming compassion for all. Unfortunately, *few, if any, mortals have been entirely successful in this endeavor*, but it is an invitation that all should try to meet.
>
> The greater definition of "the pure love of Christ," however, is not what we as Christians try but largely fail to demonstrate toward others but rather what Christ totally succeeded

---

47. McConkie, "Doctrinal Restoration," 18.

in demonstrating toward us. True charity has been known only once. It is shown perfectly and purely in Christ's unfailing, ultimate, and atoning love for us. . . .

This does not in any way minimize the commandment that we are to try to acquire this kind of love for one another. We should "pray unto the Father with all the energy of heart that [we] may be filled with this love." We should try to be more constant and unfailing, more long-suffering and kind, less envious and puffed up in our relationships with others. As Christ so lived, so should we live, and as Christ loved so should we love. But the "pure love of Christ" Mormon spoke of is precisely that—*Christ's love*. With that divine gift, that redeeming bestowal, we have everything; without it we have nothing and ultimately are nothing, except in the end "devils [and] angels to a devil."[48]

SEEK THE GIFT OF PROPHECY (14:1–5)

Paul points out that not all of the gifts of the Spirit are of equal spiritual value and that some of the gifts, though "less comely" (1 Corinthians 12:23) or attractive or enviable, are in fact among the most valuable. He encouraged the meridian Saints, for example, to seek earnestly to obtain the gift of prophecy. When the man or woman on the street is asked what is meant by prophecy, most will refer to the ability to know and speak of things in the future. And that is certainly one dimension of the spirit of prophecy. When the people of King Benjamin had heard their king's powerful address, they indicated that they had "*great views of that which is to come; and were it expedient, we could prophesy of all things*" (Mosiah 5:3).

There is a broader and more common use of the word *prophecy*—namely, the gift to speak the word of God by the gift and power of the

---

48. Holland, *Christ and the New Covenant*, 336–37.

Holy Spirit. In writing of the sons of Mosiah, Mormon pointed out that "they were men of a sound understanding and they had searched the scriptures diligently, that they might know the word of God. But this is not all; they had given themselves to much prayer, and fasting; therefore they had the spirit of prophecy, and the spirit of revelation, and when they taught, they taught with power and authority of God" (Alma 17:2–3).

John the Revelator taught a powerful principle in very few words. "The testimony of Jesus," he wrote, "is the spirit of prophecy" (Revelation 19:10). In other words, one who has by revelation, through the workings of God's Holy Spirit, gained a witness and conviction that "Jesus Christ is the Son of God, and that he was crucified for the sins of the world" possesses the spirit of prophecy (Doctrine and Covenants 46:13).

THE GIFT OF TONGUES (14:6–28)

There are different manifestations of the gift of tongues. When a person speaks the Adamic language, or language of God, he or she is speaking in tongues. In the Prophet Joseph's inspired translation of the Bible, we learn of Adam's son Seth and Seth's son Enos, who had this gift of tongues: "And then began these men to call upon the name of the Lord, and the Lord blessed them; and a book of remembrance was kept, in the which was recorded, *in the language of Adam*, for it was given unto as many as called upon God to write by the spirit of inspiration; and by them their children were taught to read and write, having *a language which was pure and undefiled*" (Moses 6:2–6). Enoch later explained that "a book of remembrance we have written among us, according to the pattern given by the finger of God; and it is given in our own language" (Moses 6:46).

"The first man placed upon this earth," President Joseph Fielding Smith wrote, "was an intelligent being, created in the image of God, possessed of wisdom and knowledge, with power to communicate his thoughts in a language, both oral and written, which was superior to anything to be found on the earth today. . . . The first man was instructed by the best Teacher man ever had, for he was taught of God, and spoke the language of the Most High, in which angels conversed. This language he taught to his children."[49]

Elsewhere President Smith explained: "It is stated in the Book of Ether that Jared and his brother made the request of the Lord that their language be not changed at the time of the confusion of tongues at the Tower of babel. Their request was granted, and they carried with them the speech of their fathers, the Adamic language, which was powerful even in its written form, so that the things Moroni wrote 'were mighty even . . . unto the overpowering of man to read them' [Ether 12:24]. That was the kind of language Adam had and this was the language with which Enoch was able to accomplish his mighty work [Moses 7:13]."[50]

Very early in this dispensation, this type of tongues was manifest. In the fall of 1832, Heber C. Kimball and Brigham Young made their way to Kirtland, Ohio, to meet the Prophet Joseph. They found Joseph chopping wood with some of his brothers. "Here my joy was full at the privilege of shaking the hand of the Prophet of God," Brigham recalled, "and I received the sure testimony, by the spirit of prophecy, that he was all that any man could believe him to be, as a true prophet. He was happy to see us, and made us welcome."

That evening the men came into the Smith home and had a powerful discussion "upon the things of the kingdom." As Brigham retold, "Joseph called upon me to pray. In my prayer I spoke in tongues, which gift I had previously received and exercised." When the prayer was over, the brethren "flocked around [Joseph] and asked his opinion concerning the gift of tongues that was upon me. He told them that it was the pure Adamic language." The Prophet explained that the gift "is of God,

---

49. Joseph Fielding Smith, *Progress of Man*, 39.
50. Joseph Fielding Smith, *Way to Perfection*, 69.

and the time will come when Brother Brigham Young will preside over this Church."[51]

This same kind of gift of tongues was prevalent in the pentecostal season surrounding the dedication of the Kirtland Temple (January through May of 1836). Those who rose and spoke in tongues were not speaking German or French or Spanish, but instead the language of God.

A second manifestation of the gift of tongues is when an individual, inspired and empowered by the Holy Ghost, begins to speak a known but foreign language, one he or she did not know previously. This is what took place on the day of Pentecost some fifty days following the Resurrection of Jesus Christ, as recorded in the second chapter of the Acts of the Apostles. A variation of this gift is what Latter-day Saint missionaries experience every day throughout the world. Young missionaries, as well as seasoned couples, begin to learn a foreign language and acquire linguistic skills and cultural insight in a relatively short period, thus equipping them to present the message of the restored gospel in the language of the people, by the power of the Holy Spirit.

A third manifestation of the gift of tongues is described by Nephi, son of Lehi. "I know that if ye shall follow the Son [of God], with full purpose of heart, acting no hypocrisy and no deception before God, but with real intent, repenting of your sins, witnessing unto the Father that ye are willing to take upon you the name of Christ, by baptism. . . . Behold, then shall ye receive the Holy Ghost; yea, then cometh the baptism of fire and of the Holy Ghost; and *then can ye speak with the tongue of angels*, and shout praises unto the Holy One of Israel" (2 Nephi 31:13). In the next chapter Nephi returns to this subject. He asks: "And now, how could ye speak with the tongue of angels save it were by the Holy Ghost? *Angels speak by the power of the Holy Ghost; wherefore, they speak the words of Christ*" (2 Nephi 32:2–3). In other

---

51. In Andrus and Andrus, *They Knew the Prophet*, 34.

words, when an individual seeks for and obtains the power of the Spirit, what she or he speaks is what Nephi here calls "the tongue of angels."

Paul commends those who have enjoyed the gift of tongues but warns them that such a gift has a limited utility and may do more to mystify and even repel those not of the faith than entice them. Joseph the Prophet took a similar course. He noted that "there are only two gifts that could be made visible—the gift of tongues and the gift of prophecy. These are things that are the most talked about, and yet if a person spoke in an unknown tongue, according to Paul's testimony, he would be a barbarian to those present. They would say that it was gibberish."[52]

Indeed, rather than recommend that people acquire the gift of tongues, the Prophet offered far more caution: the Saints should be careful lest they be deceived;[53] it is not necessary for tongues to be taught to the Church;[54] because the devil will often take advantage of the innocent and unwary, anything taught in the Church by the gift of tongues is not to be received as doctrine;[55] and it is the smallest gift of all but the one most sought after.[56]

Brother Joseph also provided sound and solid counsel to avoid the drama and sensationalism that we so often witness in our own Spirit-starved world: "The Lord cannot always be known by the thunder of His voice; by the display of His glory, or by the manifestation of his power; and those that are the most anxious to see these things, are the least prepared to meet [i.e., receive] them."[57] Paul puts it succinctly: "What is it then? I will pray with the spirit, and I will pray with the understanding also: I will sing with the spirit, and I will sing with the understanding also" (verse 15).

---

52. *Teachings of Presidents of the Church: Joseph Smith*, 121.
53. *Teachings of Presidents of the Church: Joseph Smith*, 383.
54. *Teachings of Presidents of the Church: Joseph Smith*, 383.
55. *Teachings of Presidents of the Church: Joseph Smith*, 384.
56. Joseph Smith, "Gift of the Holy Ghost," 825.
57. Joseph Smith, "Gift of the Holy Ghost," 825.

WOMEN SPEAKING IN THE CHURCH (14:34–35)

Verses 34 and 35 of chapter 14 are difficult, even painful, to many who read the New Testament. Let's take a few moments and try to view Paul's words in their context. One highly regarded student of the New Testament wrote of the unusual and even paradigm-shifting nature of the Resurrection of Jesus. This monumental moment in salvation history is odd because of "the presence of the women as the principal witnesses. Whether we like it or not, women were not regarded as credible witnesses in the ancient world. When the tradition had time to sort itself out and acquire the fixed form we already find in Paul's quotation of it in 1 Corinthians 15, the women were quietly dropped; they were apologetically embarrassing. But there they are in all four gospel stories, front and center, the first witnesses, the first apostles. Nobody could have made them up."[58]

E. P. Sanders has written that "Paul's theology contained the potential for social revolution. He thought that 'There is neither Jew nor Greek, there is neither slave nor free, there is neither male nor female; for you are all one in Christ Jesus.' (Galatians 3:28.) Yet this was not a social program. . . . *To women he accorded equality in many ways* (1 Corinthians 7:4; 11:8–12), *yet he wanted the usual distinction of sexual roles to be maintained* (1 Corinthians 14:33–36). The appointed 'time [had] grown short' and the form 'of this world [was] passing away' (1 Corinthians 7:29–31). *There was not time to remake society.*"[59]

Professor Douglas Campbell provides a related explanation for verse 34: "As we have seen in 11:2–16, and as we read at length in 1 Corinthians 14, women are fully entitled to speak under the influence of the Spirit in tongues or in prophecy. It's just that they are not to question and to interrupt other people speaking in church. They are not to interrogate the preacher. Consequently, Paul never silences women in

---

58. Wright, *Surprised by Hope*, 55.
59. Sanders, *Paul: A Very Short Introduction*, 12.

church altogether. Far from it. He silences those sitting in the pews. So in fact most churches today have followed this advice to the letter—although most of the men must now remain silent as well."[60]

THAT WHICH IS OF FIRST IMPORTANCE (15:1–11)

The gospel of Jesus Christ is the good news, the glad tidings that deliverance from sin, death, and hell has been made available to us as a gracious gift of God. His Beloved Son "so loved the world that he gave his own life, that as many as would believe might become the sons [and daughters] of God" (Doctrine and Covenants 34:3; see also John 3:16). These opening verses of the fifteenth chapter of 1 Corinthians set forth what the gospel of Jesus Christ is and what it entails. Scholars agree that these verses are among the earliest teachings concerning the Savior's redeeming work.

The King James Version of verse 3 reads, "For I delivered unto you first of all that which I also received, how that Christ died for our sins according to the scriptures." Notice the clarification in the English Standard Version: "For I delivered to you *as of first importance* what I also received: that Christ died for our sins in accordance with the Scriptures" (see also NIV, NRSV). No doubt Joseph Smith had these precious verses in mind when he responded to a question: "What are the fundamental principles of your religion?" The Prophet replied, "The fundamental principles of our religion is the testimony of the apostles and prophets concerning Jesus Christ, that he died, was buried, and rose again the third day and ascended up into heaven; and *all other things [which pertain to our religion] are only appendages to these.*"[61]

Many years ago, President Boyd K. Packer delivered a significant address entitled "The Mediator." "Know this," President Packer testified, "Truth, glorious truth, proclaims there is . . . a Mediator. . . . Through Him mercy can be fully extended to each of us without offending the

---

60. Campbell, *Paul: An Apostle's Journey*, 110.
61. Joseph Smith, in "*Elders' Journal*, July 1838," 44; punctuation standardized.

eternal law of justice. This truth is the very root of Christian doctrine." Now notice what follows: "You may know much about the gospel as it branches out from there, but *if you only know the branches and those branches do not touch that root, if they have been cut free from that truth, there will be no life nor substance nor redemption in them.*"[62]

In other words, if the Son of God had not atoned for the sins of the world and made the immortality of the soul possible through His Resurrection, there would be

- no gospel of Jesus Christ, no good news, no glad tidings, no plan of salvation for the children of God.
- no need for a Church of Jesus Christ.
- no priesthood and thus no need for the saving principles and ordinances of the gospel.
- no redemption of the dead in the postmortal spirit world.
- no kingdoms of glory hereafter.
- no eternal marriage or perpetuation of the family beyond the grave.
- no need for spiritual gifts, wonders, and miracles.
- no need for revelation, either personal or institutional.

The list could go on and on. If there were no plan of salvation, if there were no Christ, if Jesus had not suffered for the sins of the world in Gethsemane and on Golgotha, and if He had not risen triumphantly from the tomb, the plans and purposes of the Almighty would have been thwarted and all of creation would be utterly wasted.

The Resurrection of the Son of God was the capstone to our Lord's infinite and eternal Atonement and, to be sure, one of the most attested events in human history. By combining the testimonies of Matthew, Mark, Luke, and John, we learn that after the resurrected Lord had ministered to Mary Magdalene and the other women who followed Him (John 20:11–18; Matthew 28:1–10; Mark 16:1–11), He appeared to

---

62. Packer, "Mediator."

Simon Peter (verse 5) and to the two disciples on the road to Emmaus (Mark 16:12; Luke 24:13–32). He also revealed Himself to the assembled Apostles in the upper room (Luke 24:33–53; John 20:19–29), to the Apostles at the Sea of Galilee (John 21), to more than five hundred disciples (verse 6), and to Saul of Tarsus on the road to Damascus (verse 8; Acts 9, 22, 26). Finally, Latter-day Saints understand that several months after His ascension into heaven He appeared to his "other sheep" in the New World (3 Nephi 10:18; 15:16–17, 21–24; John 10:14–16).

NO RESURRECTION MEANS NO FORGIVENESS (15:12–17)

Based on this portion of 1 Corinthians, it appears that Paul has learned that some of the Corinthian Saints do not believe in the Resurrection, and, more specifically, do not accept the Resurrection of Jesus. As discussed in our consideration of chapter 7, persons with a Gnostic or proto-Gnostic perspective looked upon physical matter as evil and something to be discarded and rejected. Their reasoning often led to a conclusion like this: If corporeality and the physical body are worthless, why in the world would someone ever want to have their body once again, this time forever?

The prophet Jacob offered an answer to this question and rejoiced in the goodness of God and the vital intercession of the Savior: "O the wisdom of God, his mercy and grace! For behold, if the flesh should rise no more our spirits must become subject to that angel who fell from before the presence of the Eternal God, and became the devil, to rise no more. And our spirits must have become like unto him, and we become devils, angels to a devil, to be shut out from the presence of our God, and to remain with the father of lies, in misery, like unto himself; yea, to that being who beguiled our first parents, who transformeth himself nigh unto an angel of light" (2 Nephi 9:8–9). We might ask at this point: Why would we be subject to the devil if there had been no resurrection? What if we lived good and noble lives and were moral and upright in our dealings with our fellow beings?

The step in logic that Jacob skipped is illuminated by the Apostle Paul: "Now if Christ be preached that he [i.e., Jesus] rose from the dead, how say some among you that there is no resurrection of the dead? But if there be no resurrection of the dead, then is Christ not risen: and if Christ be not risen, then is our preaching vain, and your faith is also vain. . . . And if Christ be not raised, your faith is vain; *ye are yet in your sins*" (15:12–14, 17). That is to say, if Jesus did not rise from the dead—as He declared He would and as it had been prophesied for millennia—then why would we suppose that He has the power to forgive our sins? If He cannot overcome physical death, how can He enable us to overcome spiritual death?

THE RESURRECTION COMES TO ALL (15:19–23)

Our Father in Heaven bestows numerous blessings upon His children unconditionally, with nothing required on the part of the recipient. These blessings evidence the pure grace of God. Had there been no Atonement of Christ, because of the Fall of our first parents, this earth and all forms of life on it would have been shut out forever from the presence of the Eternal God; humankind would have been severed completely from the regenerating powers of the Spirit. Because of the love and mercy of the Holy One, however, God has planted within each one of His children the Light of Christ, or Spirit of Jesus Christ, "otherwise [we] could not abound" (Doctrine and Covenants 88:49–50; see also Doctrine and Covenants 11:28; 39:1–2; Mosiah 2:21). Thus the capacity to reason, judge, and know good from evil (through our conscience) is found within every child of God.

Moral agency is also made available to all persons through the Lord's Atonement (see 2 Nephi 2:26–27; compare 10:23; Helaman 14:30). People in all ages are thus able to "stand fast therefore in the liberty wherewith Christ hath made us free" (Galatians 5:1).

Further, those who live and die without gospel law or without understanding or accountability are not subject to the demands of God's justice (2 Nephi 9:25–26; see also Mosiah 3:11; 15:24; Moroni 8:22). This principle and benefit applies to little children who die before the time of accountability: they remain innocent before the Lord and are not subject to the tempter's power; they are assured of eternal life (see Moses 6:53–54; Moroni 8; Doctrine and Covenants 29:46–48; 93:38).

Finally, because of the ransoming power and intercessory role of our Redeemer, all men and women will receive the free gift of immortality—they will be raised from the dead to inherit a glorified physical body (see 1 Corinthians 15:21–22; Alma 11:40–44; Doctrine and Covenants 29:26). "All your losses will be made up to you in the resurrection," Joseph Smith testified, "provided you continue faithful. By the vision of the Almighty, I have seen it."[63]

GOD THE FATHER IS FOREVER SUPREME (15:24–28)

Over the years I have discussed the nature of the Godhead with scholars or church leaders of other Christian faiths, and many of those who have accepted the tenets of the early Christian creeds believe that God the Father and Jesus Christ are, and forevermore will be, equal in each and every category that might be named. I have suggested that the Gospel of John would certainly challenge that position and have stated categorically that the Son is subordinate to the Father (for examples, see John 5:19, 26, 30, 43; 6:38–39, 44; 7:16, 28–29; 8:26, 29, 38, 40; 10:25). The response I have received from these associates of other faiths is that while on earth Christ underwent a "temporary subordination." The scriptures, however, teach otherwise. Paul writes that Christ, when He has brought to an end the kingdoms of this world and destroyed every enemy, even death, He will have put "all things" beneath his feet. Paul clearly adds, however, that the words "all things" *do not include God the Father*. Then "shall the Son also himself be subject unto

---

63. *Teachings of Presidents of the Church: Joseph Smith*, 51.

him that put all things under him, that God [the Father] may be all in all" (15:24–28).

Elder Parley P. Pratt wrote that "the difference between Jesus Christ and His Father is this: one is subordinate to the other and does nothing of himself independently of the Father, but does all things in the name and by the authority of the Father, being of the same mind in all things."[64]

THE ANCIENTS PERFORMED BAPTISMS FOR THE DEAD (15:29)

The Revised English Bible translates verse 29 as "Again, there are those who receive baptism on behalf of the dead. What do you suppose they are doing? If the dead are not raised to life at all, what do they mean by being baptized on their behalf?" One Evangelical Christian commentator noted that "it is difficult to imagine any circumstances under which Paul would think it permissible for living Christians to be baptized for the sake of unbelievers in general. Such a view, adopted in part by the Mormons, lies totally outside the NT [i.e., New Testament] understanding both of salvation and of baptism."[65]

Indeed, many scholars who are not Latter-day Saints believe that in verse 29 Paul is denouncing or condemning the practice of baptism for the dead as heretical. This is a strange conclusion, given that Paul seems to be referring to the practice *to support the doctrine of the Resurrection*. In essence, he was asking, "Why are people performing baptism on behalf of their dead, if, as some propose, there will be no resurrection of the dead? If there is to be no resurrection, would not proxy baptisms be a waste of time?"

One student of the New Testament, a scholar not of our faith, wrote: "Paul has no reason to mention baptism for the dead unless he thought it would be an effective argument with the Corinthians, so

---

64. Pratt, *Key to the Science of Theology*, 20–21.
65. Fee, *First Epistle to the Corinthians*, 767.

presumably he introduced what he thought was an inconsistency in the Corinthians' theology. In this case, some at Corinth might have rejected an afterlife but practiced baptism for the dead, not realizing what the rite implied." In addition, "Because his mention [of the practice] could imply his toleration or approval of it, many have tried to distance Paul from baptism for the dead or remove features regarded as offensive from it. Some maintain that Paul . . . neither approved nor disapproved of the practice by referring to it. Yet it would have been unlike Paul to refrain from criticizing a practice he did not at least tolerate."[66]

On the afternoon of Tuesday, May 8, 1838, the Prophet Joseph answered a series of questions about the faith and practices of the Latter-day Saints. One of the questions was "If the Mormon doctrine is true, what has become of all those who died since the days of the Apostles?" Note Joseph's response: "All those who have not had an opportunity of hearing the gospel, and being administered to by an inspired man in the flesh, must have it hereafter, before they can be finally judged."[67] We cannot help but wonder if Joseph spoke of this doctrinal matter since the time of his vision of his brother Alvin more than two years earlier (see Doctrine and Covenants 137), but there is no record of such a conversation.

It appears the Prophet delivered his first public discourse on baptism for the dead at the funeral of a man named Seymour Brunson.[68] Simon Baker described the occasion:

> I was present at a discourse that the prophet Joseph delivered on baptism for the dead 15 August 1840. He read the greater part of the 15th chapter of Corinthians and remarked that the Gospel of Jesus Christ brought glad tidings of great joy, and then remarked that he saw a widow in that congregation that had a son who died without being baptized, and

---

66. DeMarius, "Corinthian Religion and Baptism for the Dead," 678–79.
67. Joseph Smith, in *"Elders' Journal,* July 1838," 43.
68. *Teachings of Presidents of the Church: Joseph Smith,* 472.

this widow [had read] the sayings of Jesus "except a man be born of water and of the spirit he cannot enter the kingdom of heaven." He then said that this widow should have glad tidings in that thing. He also said the apostle [Paul] was talking to a people who understood baptism for the dead, for it was practiced among them [see 1 Corinthians 15:29]. He went on to say that people could now act for their friends who had departed this life, and that the plan of salvation was calculated to save all who were willing to obey the requirements of the law of God. He went on and made a very beautiful discourse.[69]

After the meeting, a widow, Jane Nyman, was baptized vicariously for her son in the Mississippi River.[70]

Just one month later, on September 14, 1840, on his deathbed, Joseph Smith Sr. made a final request of his son Joseph Jr.—that someone be baptized on behalf of his eldest son, Alvin.[71] His second son, Hyrum, complied with that wish and was baptized vicariously in 1840 in the Mississippi River and again in 1841 in a baptismal font in the Nauvoo Temple.[72]

THE NATURE OF RESURRECTED BODIES (15:39–44)

As Jesus met with His beloved Apostles in the upper room, only hours before the agonies of Gethsemane, He taught a profound truth: "Let not your heart be troubled: ye believe in God, believe also in me. In my Father's house are many mansions: *if it were not so, I would have told you.* I go to prepare a place for you" (John 14:1–2). This is a most intriguing statement. The Savior seems to be saying, in essence, that it should be so obvious and self-evident that life hereafter consists of more than merely a heaven and a hell; if it were not so, He would

---

69. *Words of Joseph Smith*, 49.
70. See Baugh, "Practice of Baptism for the Dead Outside of Temples," 3–6.
71. See Lucy Mack Smith, *History of Joseph Smith by His Mother*, 308.
72. "Nauvoo Baptisms for the Dead," 145, 149.

have told us otherwise. Reason suggests that not all people are equally good, and thus not all good people deserve the same reward hereafter. Likewise, not all bad people are equally bad, and surely some are so bad they deserve to sink to the lowest pit in hell.

In verses 39–42, Paul speaks specifically of different kinds of resurrected bodies, mentioning here celestial bodies and terrestrial bodies. The Joseph Smith Translation of verse 40 adds *telestial* bodies. That something is missing from the New Testament manuscripts of verse 40 is evident in the fact that Paul in verses 41–42 writes of *three levels* of glorified bodies: "There is one glory of the sun, and another glory of the moon, and another glory of the stars: for one star differeth from another star in glory. So also is the resurrection of the dead."

One of the most glorious of all revelations ever given by God in heaven to men and women on earth was delivered to Joseph Smith and Sidney Rigdon in an upstairs room of the John Johnson home in Hiram, Ohio. The revelation is what Latter-day Saints know as the vision of the degrees of glory, received on February 16, 1832, and recorded in Doctrine and Covenants 76. "Nothing could be more pleasing to the Saints upon the order of the Kingdom of the Lord," Joseph Smith stated, "than the light which burst upon the world through the foregoing vision. Every law, every commandment, every promise, every truth, and every point touching the destiny of man, from Genesis to Revelation, . . . witness the fact that the document is a transcript from the records of the eternal world. . . . The rewards for faithfulness and the punishments for sins, are so much beyond the narrow-mindedness of men, that every man is constrained to exclaim: 'It came from God.'"[73]

Truly there are many mansions of the Father (John 14:1–2), and the Holy One of Israel has made provision for His people to attain hereafter the level of glory that they are willing to receive. The Prophet Joseph quoted the Savior about many mansions and then clarified: "It

---

73. Joseph Smith, in "History, 1838–1856, volume A-1," 183.

should be—'In my Father's kingdom are many kingdoms, in order that ye may be heirs of God and joint-heirs with me.'"[74]

VICTORY THROUGH CHRIST THE LORD (15:50–57)

Referencing Paul's statement that "flesh and blood cannot inherit the kingdom of God" (verse 50), the Prophet Joseph commented, "God Almighty Himself dwells in eternal fire; flesh and blood cannot go there, for all corruption is devoured by the fire. Our God is a consuming fire. When our flesh is quickened by the Spirit, there will be no blood in this tabernacle. Some dwell in higher glory than others."[75]

The Prophet also explained: "Flesh and blood cannot inherit the kingdom of God, or the kingdom that God inhabits, but the flesh without the blood, and the Spirit of God flowing in the veins in the stead of the blood. For blood is the part of the body that causes corruption. Therefore, we must be changed in the twinkling of an eye, or have to lay down these tabernacles and leave the blood vanish away. Therefore, Jesus Christ left his blood to atone for the sins of the world, that he might ascend into the presence of the Father. . . . The resurrection of the dead is devised to take away corruption and make man perfect."[76]

The Apostle Paul then discusses one of the great mysteries of salvation that can be understood only by and through the power of the Holy Ghost (see verses 51–52). The scriptures teach that when Jesus Christ returns to the earth in glory, the great Millennium will begin— one thousand years of peace and glory, in which Satan will be bound. "For I will reveal myself from heaven with power and great glory, with all the hosts thereof, and dwell in righteousness with men [and women] on earth a thousand years, and the wicked shall not stand" (Doctrine and Covenants 29:11).

---

74. Joseph Smith, in "History, 1838–1856, volume F-1," 19.
75. Joseph Smith, in "History, 1838–1856, volume F-1," 20.
76. Joseph Smith, in "Discourse, 12 May 1844, as Reported by George Laub," 22; punctuation and spelling standardized.

With the King of kings and Lord of lords will come all of the righteous who have died; they will return with their resurrected bodies: "And they who have slept in their graves shall come forth, for their graves shall be opened; and they. . . shall be caught up . . . to meet him; and all this by the voice of the sounding of the trump of the angel of God" (Doctrine and Covenants 88:97–98). Those faithful mortal women and men then living on earth will not die but will continue to live as mortals, albeit on a transfigured, glorified, and terrestrial earth. They will live in such a state until they arrive at the "age of man" (one hundred years, according to Isaiah 65:20). They will then be resurrected instantaneously ("changed in the twinkling of an eye")—transformed from mortality to glorified immortality (see Doctrine and Covenants 63:50–51; see also Mosiah 16:10; Alma 5:15; 40:2; 41:4).

Paul, basically expanding upon Isaiah's teachings, then challenges death and the grave: "O death, where is thy sting? O grave, where is thy victory? The sting of death is sin" (verses 55–56; compare Isaiah 25:8). In other words, death is especially painful and dreaded by those who enter the spirit world in an unrepentant state (see Galatians 6:7–8; Alma 41:3–4, 10–13). Further, without the grand and glorious Resurrection of the Son of God—He who was the "first-fruits of them that slept" (1 Corinthians 15:20)—the grave would be the eternal abode of all human flesh. "But thanks be to God, [who gives us] the victory through our Lord Jesus Christ" (verse 57).

HOPE FOR THE FUTURE DICTATES
OUR PRESENT LABOR (15:58)

Having set forth the doctrine of the Resurrection—the sweet assurance of the immortality of the soul, the comforting knowledge that life continues beyond the grave—Paul emphasizes that we have a grand perspective on how we should carry out the work of the kingdom of God on earth: "Therefore, my beloved brethren [and sisters], be ye steadfast, unmoveable, always abounding in the work of the Lord, forasmuch as ye know that your labour is not in vain in the Lord" (verse 58; compare Mosiah 5:15). Moroni offered a similar charge to his readers: "Wherefore, whoso believeth in God might with surety hope for a better world, yea, even a place at the right hand of God, which hope cometh of faith, maketh an anchor to the souls of men, which would make them sure and steadfast, always abounding in good works, being led to glorify God" (Ether 12:4).

N. T. Wright observed:

> To hope for a better future in this world—for the poor, the sick, the lonely and depressed, for the slaves, the refugees, the hungry and homeless, for the abused, the paranoid, the downtrodden and despairing, and in fact for the whole wide, wonderful, and wounded world—is not something *else*, something extra, something tacked on to the gospel as an afterthought. . . . It is a central, essential, vital, and life-giving part of it. . . .
>
> The point of the resurrection, as Paul has been arguing throughout the letter is that *the present bodily life is not valueless just because it will die.* God will raise it to new life. What you do with your body in the present matters because God has a great future in store for it. . . . What you *do* in the present—by painting, preaching, singing, sewing, praying, teaching, building hospitals, digging wells, campaigning for justice, writing poems, caring for the needy, loving your neighbor as yourself—*will last into God's future.* . . . They are part of what we call building for God's kingdom.[77]

---

77. Wright, *Surprised by Hope*, 191–93; emphasis in original.

THE SECOND EPISTLE TO THE CORINTHIANS

THE SECOND EPISTLE TO the Saints in Corinth was written from Ephesus in about AD 55–57. In this epistle, Paul expresses gratitude for the willingness of the Corinthian Saints to respond to some of his concerns mentioned in an earlier letter. He also offers a subtle apology for how strong his rebukes have been but then indicates that he is grateful that many of the members of the branch have been humbled and have experienced godly sorrow for their sins. Chapter 5 of this epistle contains some of the most profound teachings in all of scripture on the Atonement of Jesus Christ and the formation of ourselves as new creatures in Christ (5:17). Late in the epistle, Paul speaks of his painful "thorn in the flesh" and how his tenacious efforts to have it removed resulted in a spiritual maturity that could have come in no other way (12:7).

TURNING TO THE GOD OF COMFORT (1:3–5)

Some problems we encounter in this life are simply not solvable, at least not by mortals. Some distresses we experience cannot be relieved by the best-trained physicians, the most-capable therapists, or the very latest of "miracle" medications. There are times when our souls seem almost to be under attack by the "cunning and the snares and the wiles of the devil" (Helaman 3:29) or the "fiery darts of the wicked" (Doctrine and Covenants 27:17), occasions when our grit and willpower are absolutely ineffective in protecting ourselves and halting the evil assaults. There are times when our behavior slips below the Lord's standard of faithfulness, when we sin knowingly, when we feel so very alone. Our own efforts to fix the situation or repair the breach between God and ourselves, however, falls well short of what is needed and required for forgiveness. In other words, there are many, many times in our lives when we cannot "handle it" on our own.

Of the matter of forgiveness, President Boyd K. Packer spoke tenderly of Christ's gracious gift to us:

> Sometimes you cannot give back what you have taken because you don't have it to give. If you have caused others to suffer unbearably—defiled someone's virtue, for example—it is not within your power to give it back.
>
> If you cannot undo what you have done, you are trapped. It is easy to understand how helpless and hopeless you then feel and why you might want to give up, just as Alma did [at the time of his conversion; see Mosiah 27 and Alma 36].
>
> The thought that rescued Alma, when he acted upon it, is this: Restoring what you cannot restore, healing the wound you cannot heal, fixing that which you broke and you cannot fix is the very purpose of the atonement of Christ.
>
> When your desire is firm and you are willing to pay the "uttermost farthing" [Matthew 5:25–26], the law of restitution is suspended. *Your obligation is transferred to the Lord. He will settle your accounts.*[1]

"Blessed be God, even the Father of our Lord Jesus Christ, the Father of mercies, and the God of all comfort; who comforteth us in all our tribulation, that we may be able to comfort them which are in

---

1. Packer, "Brilliant Morning of Forgiveness."

any trouble, by the comfort wherewith we ourselves are comforted of God" (verses 3–4). Those who have been divinely comforted, who have received and delighted in heavenly help, who have been empowered to do what otherwise would be considered impossible—such persons are able to minister in higher and holier ways—to lift and liberate, to comfort and console, and to testify with authenticity of the transforming and enabling power of God Almighty.

"THE EARNEST OF THE SPIRIT"
(1:21–22; 5:5; COMPARE EPHESIANS 1:13–14)

One of the tenets of Reformed (Calvinist) theology is that once people have been "saved," they cannot thereafter "fall from grace"—that is, they cannot lose their salvation. At times when I have expressed our Latter-day Saint belief that one can, in fact, fall from grace (see Doctrine and Covenants 20:32), my conversation partner has responded with some form of the following: "Well then, you folks simply have no eternal security." How should we respond? Is there no way that we can know we are on course to inherit eternal life? Let's return to our text.

The "anointing" spoken of in verse 21 is the "unction," or anointing, of the Holy Spirit (see 1 John 2:20, 27). Paul here declares to the Corinthian Saints that God gives to His faithful children "the earnest of the Spirit in [their] hearts" (verse 22). When we live in such a manner that the Holy Ghost is our companion, when we enjoy the comfort and peace of the Spirit, when we experience the sanctifying and cleansing power of the Holy Ghost in our lives, and when we are prompted and guided by the third member of the Godhead—then we truly enjoy the blessings of the Savior's Atonement, living on what could be called "saving ground." Experiencing the Spirit is the way our Father in Heaven can let us know that we are on course and that our course is pleasing to Him.[2]

---

2. See *Lectures on Faith*, 3:5; p. 38; and 6:1–12; pp. 67–71.

What about the word *earnest*? How is Paul using it? *Earnest* as a noun is a token, pledge, promise, or assurance of something to come. Many of us have had the experience of paying "earnest money" toward a home we intend to purchase. The earnest money is a type of down payment that indicates we are serious about buying the home. The "earnest of the Spirit" is the Lord's "earnest money" on us, if you will, His token or pledge that He is serious about saving us and fully intends to do so. To put this another way, when we are enjoying the gift of the Holy Spirit, God is indicating that He is pleased with us, that the Savior's Atonement is working within us, that we are on course, that we are in covenant. We are in line to receive eternal life and exaltation.

In other words, the Holy Spirit is a type of spiritual barometer. Latter-day Saints can, in fact, have a kind of eternal security, a way of knowing that we will one day qualify to live with God and Christ and our families forever. We must pray, as latter-day prophets have counseled us, for the constant companionship of the Holy Ghost and then live in a manner befitting a person who sincerely desires to be eternally secure. We must reach that point of commitment and conversion in which we strive never to do anything that would offend our Lord and Savior and thus cost us the influence and guidance of His Spirit.

WE TRIUMPH IN CHRIST (2:14–16)

Consider an alternate translation of these rather difficult verses: "But thanks be to God, who always leads us into triumphant procession in Christ and through us spreads the fragrance of the knowledge of him. For we are to God the aroma of Christ among those who are being saved and those who are perishing. To the one we are the smell of death; to the other, the fragrance of life. And who is equal to such a task?" (NIV). Through His perfect life, His sufferings in Gethsemane and on Golgotha, and His triumph over the grave through His rise from the tomb, Jesus the Christ is the Victor, having conquered Satan, death, hell, and endless torment. Those who enjoy a victory with their

Savior are those who humble themselves and who confess their weakness and thus their need for redemption and deliverance. They bow the knee and confess the name that is above every name and strive to live as Jesus did.

THE TRUE GOSPEL EPISTLES (3:1–5)

The greatest evidence of the truthfulness and power of the restored gospel of Jesus Christ is not the rationality of the doctrine or the elevated perspective on where we came from, why we are here, and where we are going when we die—although such teachings are soul satisfying and comforting. The strongest indication that The Church of Jesus Christ of Latter-day Saints is indeed restored Christianity is not found solely in the number of convert baptisms throughout the earth, the building of meetinghouses and holy temples in countries throughout the globe—though such a pattern of growth is indeed impressive.

The surest indication that Jesus Christ stands at the head of the Church and is directing this Church through living apostles and prophets is the effect this restored gospel and the work of this restored Church has on its members—the quality of the lives of the Latter-day Saints themselves. In His marvelous Sermon on the Mount, Jesus taught that true prophets may be known by their fruits (Matthew 7:15–16)—that is, by the product of their preaching and prophecy. "In the ultimate sense," Elder Bruce R. McConkie taught, "the gospel is not written on tablets of stone or books of scripture, but in the bodies of faithful and obedient persons; the saints are, thus, living epistles of the truth, the books of whose lives are open for all to read."[3]

THE SPIRIT GIVES LIFE (3:5–6)

The Christian life is not and must not be characterized by mindless and heartless acts of service. Though we may not always feel overly motivated to work at the cannery or to minister to our brothers and

---

3. McConkie, *Doctrinal New Testament Commentary*, 2:414.

sisters, we should, of course, do our duty. It is always better to be obedient than slothful or disobedient. Some people say: "Given the way I feel right now, it would be better not to go to church." No, it's better to be at church; we will likely come to feel better about church once we're there. A member of the Church might say to his priesthood leader: "I simply don't want to be a ministering brother!" The leader might appropriately respond, "Well, that's okay. Go ahead and visit the families anyway. You have been called to serve them. Do your best. And *pray for the spirit of your calling.*" Doing our duty is a noble thing. It's the right thing to do.

There is, however, a higher motivation, a motivation borne of the Spirit, a motivation felt quite often by those who have sacrificed self on the altar and given themselves fully to Christ. Our Savior does not ask us to operate solely by sheer grit and willpower. Although we must be disciplined and deny ourselves of ungodliness—that is, keep ourselves from influences that degrade (Matthew 16:26, JST; Moroni 10:32)—the struggle against sin and the challenge to be anxiously engaged in good causes need not be undertaken by virtue of our own moral and physical strength. Jesus Christ stands ready to empower, energize, and motivate us.

We cannot sustain ourselves on written scripture alone, nor can we survive in a wicked world with the added benefit of prophetic declarations, handbooks, or resource manuals. The strength of this Church is found in the hearts and lives of its individual members, in the manner in which they seek for and obtain the mind of God through the instrumentality of the Holy Ghost. As members of the Church of Jesus Christ, our opportunity and our duty are to partake of the fruit of a living tree of life, to be governed by a living constitution. "Notwithstanding those things which are written," the Lord declared in a modern revelation, "it always has been given to the elders of my church from the beginning, and ever shall be, to conduct all meetings as they are directed and guided by the Holy Spirit" (Doctrine and

Covenants 46:2; see also 20:45; Moroni 6:9). The Church generally seeks to teach us guiding *principles*, but quite often it is the Holy Spirit who teaches us specific *practices*.

THE EYES OF THE CHILDREN OF ISRAEL WERE VEILED (3:12–16)

Paul tells us in verse 14 that the minds of many of the Jews, from the days of Moses to the first century, were blinded. This reminds us of the words of Jacob, son of Lehi: The Jews "were a stiffnecked people," he explained, "and they despised the words of plainness, and killed the prophets, and sought for things that they could not understand. Wherefore, because of their blindness, which blindness came by looking beyond the mark, they must needs fall" (Jacob 4:14).

Jesus the Messiah was the fulfillment of the law of Moses, the grand end to the law's myriad means. Those with spiritual insight—those who searched the law and sought for understanding through the power of God's Spirit—recognized the religion behind the ritual, the covenants behind the tokens. These persons began to press toward the mark, and the mark was Christ. Elder Dean L. Larsen of the Seventy offered the following insight:

> Jacob speaks of a people who placed themselves in serious jeopardy in spiritual things because they were unwilling to accept simple, basic principles of truth. They entertained and intrigued themselves with "things that they could not understand." They were apparently afflicted with a pseudosophistication and a snobbishness that gave them a false sense of superiority over those who came among them with the Lord's words of plainness. *They went beyond the mark of wisdom and prudence and obviously failed to stay within the circle of fundamental gospel truths which provide a basis for faith.* They must have reveled in speculative and theoretical matters that obscured for them the fundamental spiritual truths. As they became infatuated with

these "things that they could not understand," their comprehension of and faith in the redeeming role of a true Messiah were lost, and the purpose of life became confused.[4]

WHERE THE SPIRIT IS, THERE IS LIBERTY (3:17)

The third member of the Godhead is a revelator, teacher, testifier, comforter, warning voice, chastener, discerner, sanctifier, and sealer. He is also, under the direction of Jesus Christ, a liberator who frees us from the pull of sin, breaks the chains of addiction, and releases the restraining influences of false tradition. "Then said Jesus to those Jews which believed on him, If ye continue in my word, then are ye my disciples indeed [i.e., my real or genuine disciples]; and ye shall know the truth, and the truth shall make you free." Truly, "if the Son therefore shall make you free, ye shall be free indeed" (John 8:31–32, 36; compare Doctrine and Covenants 88:86).

CHANGED FROM GLORY TO GLORY (3:18)

The promises to those who keep the commandments and are true and faithful to their covenants are grand and glorious. "And we all, with unveiled face, beholding the glory of the Lord, are being transformed into the same image from one degree of glory to another," Paul writes. "For this comes from the Lord who is the Spirit" (verses 17–18, ESV). It was no doubt with this Pauline passage in mind that Charles Wesley penned what many consider to be his most magnificent hymn of praise, "Love Divine, All Loves Excelling." Here are the first and last verses of the hymn:

> *Love divine, all loves excelling,*
> *Joy of Heav'n to earth come down;*
> *Fix in us thy humble dwelling;*

---

4. Larsen, "Looking beyond the Mark."

All thy faithful mercies crown!
Jesus, Thou art all compassion,
Pure unbounded love Thou art;
Visit us with Thy salvation,
Enter every trembling heart.

. . .

Finish, then, Thy new creation;
Pure and spotless let us be;
Let us see Thy great salvation
Perfectly restored in Thee;
Changed from glory into glory,
Till in Heav'n we take our place,
Till we cast our crowns before Thee,
Lost in wonder, love, and praise.[5]

SATAN SEEKS TO BLIND US (4:4)

Paul here refers to Satan—the devil, the father of all lies (see 2 Nephi 2:18; 9:9)—as "the god of this world," or, more properly, the god of "this age." Indeed, whenever and wherever people choose knowingly to revel in wickedness, violate the commandments, turn a deaf ear to the warnings of the prophets, and, in general, deny and defy the true and living God, they have chosen to bow beneath another god, one bent on their destruction and their unhappiness.

Those who refuse to believe close themselves off from an understanding of things as they really are. Notice that one of the first things Nephi tells us about himself is that he has great desires to know the mysteries of God—those things that can only be known by the power of the Holy Ghost. "I did cry unto the Lord; and behold *he did visit me, and did soften my heart that I did believe all the words which had*

---

5. *Cokesbury Worship Hymnal*, no. 22.

been spoken by my father; wherefore, I did not rebel against him like unto my brothers" (1 Nephi 2:16). The visitation of the Spirit softens the heart, making it malleable, tender, and open to the ways and words of the Master. One would suppose that Nephi's heart was soft even before this experience, but it would appear that the closer we get to our Heavenly Father, the more open we are to His mind and will. Nephi's believing heart was at the foundation of his spiritual success; it made him what he was.

A believing heart is something for which to be deeply grateful, for it is less and less common in today's cynical and secular world. Many in our day are like the rising generation who lived many years after the time of King Benjamin. This generation refused to believe the righteous traditions of their fathers. "They did not believe what had been said concerning the resurrection of the dead, neither did they believe concerning the coming of Christ." Now note these penetrating words: "And now *because of their unbelief they could not understand* the word of God; and their hearts were hardened" (Mosiah 26:1–3). There are some things a skeptic will never make sense of. There are many things that a public doubter, a naysayer, a cynic, will never understand.

CHRIST, NOT PAUL, IS THE MESSAGE (4:5–7)

Paul wants to be very clear—neither he nor his ministerial associates have any interest in being acknowledged or idolized, nor do they preach and labor to draw attention to themselves. Indeed, their whole desire is to forevermore point those who are disciples of Christ toward Him who is the author and finisher—the Alpha and Omega, the beginning and end—of their salvation (see Hebrews 5:9; Moroni 6:4).

Verse 7 provides a wonderful insight into the heart and soul of the Apostle Paul: "But we have this treasure in earthen vessels, that the excellency of the power may be of God, and not of us." The Greek word translated as "earthen vessels" is *ostrikinos*, which means "baked clay," or as we might say, "clay pots." As one study Bible explains, these pots "were cheap, breakable, and replaceable, but they served necessary household functions. Sometimes they were used as a vault to store valuables, such as money, jewelry, or important documents. But they were most often used for holding garbage and human waste. The latter is the use Paul had in mind, and it was how Paul viewed himself—as lowly, common, expendable, and replaceable."[6] Such a comment reveals the greatness of Paul's soul and the unbounded reverence and awe he felt toward the Father and the Son.

DESPITE AFFLICTIONS, THE SAINTS PRESS ON (4:8–11, 16–18)

Few ministers of the gospel in the history of the world have encountered the kinds of challenges, roadblocks, setbacks, criticism, and persecution that Paul faced. From the time he was converted on the road to Damascus until he was beheaded in Rome—a period of approximately thirty years—his life was filled with trial and turmoil, persecution and pain, dismissal and discouragement. But through it all, this remarkable man maintained a persistence and an elevated perspective that enabled him to take it all in stride. He endured the stresses and strains of the here and now by focusing on the distant goal of life with Christ.

Few leaders of The Church of Jesus Christ of Latter-day Saints have spoken more of facing afflictions and adversity with the authenticity of personal experience than Elder Neal A. Maxwell of the Quorum of the Twelve Apostles. Consider some of the precious but poignant counsel from this beloved witness of Christ:

> Our life . . . cannot be both faith-filled and stress free.[7]
>
> For the faithful, our finest hours are sometimes during or just following our darkest hours.[8]

---

6. *MacArthur Study Bible*, 1722.
7. Maxwell, "Lest Ye Be Wearied and Faint in Your Minds."
8. Maxwell, "Great Plan of the Eternal God."

Adversity can increase faith or instead can cause the troubling roots of bitterness to spring up.[9]

The thermostat on the furnace of affliction will not have been set too high for us—though clearly we may think so at the time. Our God is a refining God who has been tempering soul-steel for a very long time. He knows when the right edge has been put upon our excellence but also when there is more in us than we have yet given.[10]

The storm fronts that come into our lives will not last forever. We can surmount the drifts of difficulties and we can hold out if we can maintain our perspective and faith. . . . Just as we know there is a sun just behind today's cloud cover, so we must not doubt the continued, watchful, and tutoring presence of The Son in spite of the stormy seasons in our lives.[11]

Verses 10–11 in the King James Version are not easy to understand: "Always bearing about in the body the dying of the Lord Jesus, that the life also of Jesus might be made manifest in our body. For we which live are alway delivered unto death for Jesus' sake, that the life also of Jesus might be made manifest in our mortal flesh." These verses remind us of what Paul wrote to the Romans: "Know ye not, that so many of us as were baptized into Jesus Christ were baptized into his death? Therefore we are buried with him by baptism into death: that like as Christ was raised up from the dead by the glory of the Father, even so we also should walk in newness of life" (Romans 6:3–4).

If we were to paraphrase Paul, we might render his words like this: "The sufferings and afflictions I undergo each day point me toward what our Lord and Savior suffered. And as I, His disciple, suffer in His name and, in a small measure, after the manner of His sufferings, so

---

9. Maxwell, "Lest Ye Be Wearied and Faint in Your Minds."
10. Maxwell, *All These Things Shall Give Thee Experience*, 46.
11. Maxwell, *Even as I Am*, 102–3.

I yearn to enjoy the life that He enjoys, that dynamic and everlasting life promised to those who are faithful and valiant in their testimony of Jesus."

Paul goes on to explain that even though our physical bodies are moving inexorably toward death, the "inward man," our eternal spirit, is maturing; expanding in understanding; and being cleansed, purified, and renewed. "Our light affliction"—the meager trials and adversities so common to this second estate—are miniscule when compared with our Lord's infinite suffering. And they last "but for a moment" and "worketh for us a far more exceeding and eternal weight of glory" (verses 16–17).

Paul then writes that "we look not at the things which are seen, but at the things which are not seen: for the things which are seen are temporal; but the things which are not seen are eternal" (verse 18). Another way of saying this is that we need to see all things, particularly our mortal trials and sufferings, with "an eye of faith." Alma asked the people of Zarahemla: "Do you exercise faith in the redemption of him who created you? *Do you look forward with an eye of faith, and view this mortal body raised in immortality, and this corruption raised in incorruption,* to stand before God to be judged according to the deeds which have been done in the mortal body?" (Alma 5:15). In writing of the ancient faithful, and specifically of the brother of Jared, Moroni observed that "there were many whose faith was so exceedingly strong, even before Christ came, who could not be kept from within the veil, but *truly saw with their eyes the things which they had [formerly] beheld with an eye of faith*, and they were glad" (Ether 12:19; compare Alma 32:40).

LOOKING TO THE GLORIOUS RESURRECTION (5:1–4)

The older we get and the more our physical bodies continue their trek toward decay and finally dissolution, the more we long for that "perfect day" (Doctrine and Covenants 50:24) when our spirits will be purified and refined in paradise and our physical bodies restored fully and gloriously in the Resurrection of the dead. "The soul shall be restored to the body," Alma explained, "and the body to the soul; yea, and every limb and joint shall be restored to its body; yea, even a hair of the head shall not be lost; but all things shall be restored to their proper and perfect frame" (Alma 40:23; see also 11:40–41). In his vision of the redemption of the dead, President Joseph F. Smith gave us a remarkably specific description of the resurrected body. Speaking of the faithful in paradise in the postmortal spirit world, he said: "Their sleeping dust was to be restored unto its perfect frame, bone to his bone, and the sinews and the flesh upon them, the spirit and the body to be united never again to be divided, that they might receive a fulness of joy" (Doctrine and Covenants 138:17).

In a sermon delivered in March 1842, Joseph Smith declared, "As concerning the resurrection, I will merely say that all men will come from the grave as they lie down, whether old or young; there will not be 'added unto their stature one cubit,' neither taken from it; all will be raised by the power of God, having spirit in their bodies, and not blood. Children will be enthroned in the presence of God and the Lamb with bodies of the same stature that they had on earth, having been redeemed by the blood of the Lamb; they will there enjoy the fulness of that light, glory and intelligence, which is prepared in the celestial kingdom."[12]

The nephew of the Prophet Joseph, President Joseph F. Smith, taught: "The spirit and the body will be reunited. We shall see each other in the flesh, in the same tabernacles we have here while in mortality. Our tabernacles will be brought forth as they are laid down, although there will be a restoration effected; every organ, every limb that has been maimed, every deformity caused by accident or in any other way, will be restored and put right. Every limb and joint will be

---

12. Joseph Smith, in "History, 1838–1856, volume C-1," 1297; punctuation and spelling standardized.

restored to its proper frame. We will know each other and enjoy each other's society throughout the endless ages of eternity, if we keep the law of God."[13]

"WE WALK BY FAITH" (5:6–10)

It is not uncommon to hear a Latter-day Saint remark that while we lived as spirits with our Heavenly Father, we walked by sight. But now on earth, with a veil of forgetfulness blocking the memory of our first estate, we walk by faith. We learn in the Book of Mormon, however, that in the premortal world we also walked by faith—faith in the Father's great plan of happiness (Alma 13:3), faith in the power of Jehovah's redemption, and faith in the overarching and undergirding love of God for His children.

And yes, in mortality we do indeed walk by faith. We "hope for things which are not seen, which are true" (Alma 32:21). We have faith that there is purpose in life, that our time on earth is not a colossal, cosmic accident. We have faith that, just beyond that thin veil that separates us from the immediate presence of Deity, the God of heaven hears our prayers and knows and understands the deepest longings of our souls. We have faith in the sense that we now view our life and the plans and purposes of God through an "eye of faith." We trust in things that we cannot see with our natural eyes but that the Holy Spirit confirms to our mind and heart. And we long for that glorious day when we will see things as they really are.

BECOMING NEW CREATURES IN CHRIST (5:17–21)

The gospel of Jesus Christ is all about change. To come unto Christ is to choose to be changed, to be transformed into a grander version of ourselves. Parley P. Pratt wrote of what takes place when one is born again, when he or she becomes a "new creature":

---

13. Joseph F. Smith, *Gospel Doctrine*, 447.

His mind is quickened, his intellectual faculties are aroused to intense activity. He is, as it were, illuminated. He learns more of divine truth in a few days than he could have learned in a lifetime in the best merely human institutions of the world.

His affections are also purified, exalted, and increased in proportion. He loves his Heavenly Father and Jesus Christ with a perfect love. He also loves the members of the Church, or the body of Christ, as he loves his own soul; while *his bosom swells with the tenderest sympathies and emotions of good will and benevolence for all mankind.* He would make any sacrifice that might be expedient to do good. He would lay down his life most cheerfully, without one moment's hesitation or regret, if required of him by the cause of truth. He also feels the spirit of prayer and watchfulness continually, and pours out his soul in the same, and finds he is answered in all things that are expedient.[14]

In a similar manner, Alma the younger taught that "all mankind . . . must be born again; yea, born of God, *changed from their carnal and fallen state, to a state of righteousness,* being redeemed of God, becoming his sons and daughters; and thus *they become new creatures*; and unless they do this, they can in nowise inherit the kingdom of God" (Mosiah 27:25–26).

We are told in this passage (verse 17) that "if any man be in Christ, he is a new creature: old things are passed away; behold, all things are become new." Paul uses some form of the expression "in Christ" well over a hundred times in his epistles. To be "in Christ" is to be in covenant with, in harmony with, and united to the Lord Jesus Christ. This link, this sacred unity, is accomplished by the sanctifying power of the Holy Spirit. The Apostle John wrote that "whoso keepeth his word, in him verily is the love of God perfected: hereby know we that *we are in*

---

14. Pratt, *Key to the Science of Theology*, 59–60.

him" (1 John 2:5). In short, "Hereby know we that we dwell in him, and he in us, because he hath given us of his Spirit" (1 John 4:13; see also 1 John 4:15; John 6:56; 17:20–21). In latter-day revelation the Savior spoke of His oneness with the Father, as well as the means whereby His followers could be one with Them: "And the Father and I are one. I am in the Father and the Father in me; and inasmuch as ye have received me, ye are in me and I in you" (Doctrine and Covenants 50:43).

Latter-day Saint philosopher Adam Miller explained beautifully that being "in Christ" is like being "in love":

> Something changes when you are in love. It's not just that a new person is added to your life, one person among many. It's that this new person changes for you what it means to be alive. Life is no longer just lived. Now, life is lived *in love*. You may keep the same job, have the same friends, and eat the same food, but something basic about why you do these things, or even *how* you do them, will have changed. . . . In love, life as a whole feels different. You see what you didn't use to see. You hear what you didn't use to hear. You care for things you'd ignored. You become capable of doing things that, last week, you weren't able to do.

Brother Miller says further, "Life in Christ is like this. In Christ, the way I live—my manner of living—is changed from the inside out. Like being in love, living in Christ changes what it means to be alive."[15]

Paul writes that "all things are of God, who hath reconciled us to himself by Jesus Christ, and hath given to us the ministry of reconciliation" (verse 18). Reconciliation is the process by which two persons or entities who were previously estranged or separated are reunited or brought back together. As followers of the Christ, we are called to "the ministry of reconciliation," which is the proclamation of the gospel of

---

15. Miller, *Early Resurrection*, 11–12; emphasis in original.

Jesus Christ, the good news and glad tidings that one need not remain in sin or be estranged from a loving Father and a redeeming Savior. One need not face the terrors of the world alone. For the Apostle, the message is "that God was in Christ, reconciling the world unto himself [by Jesus Christ], not imputing their trespasses unto them; and hath committed unto us the word of reconciliation" (verse 19). When we choose to repent, Christ no longer imputes, or records on our spiritual account, our sins and misdeeds. Why? Because "he who has repented of his sins, the same is forgiven, and I, the Lord, remember them no more" (Doctrine and Covenants 58:42).

Both full-time and member missionaries are charged by the prophets to take the message of salvation, the means of reconciliation, to the people of the world: "And again, I say unto you, I give unto you a commandment, that every man, both elder, priest, teacher, and also member, go to with his might, with the labor of his hands, to prepare and accomplish the things which I have commanded. And let your preaching be the warning voice, every man to his neighbor, in mildness and in meekness" (Doctrine and Covenants 38:40–41; see also 88:81).

Verse 21 of chapter 5 is one of the most profound pronouncements in all of scripture: "For he [i.e., God the Father] hath made him [i.e., Christ the Son] to be sin for us, who knew no sin; that we might be made the righteousness of God in him." As rendered in the King James Version, this verse can be a bit confusing. Here are some alternate translations:

> He made Him who knew no sin to be sin on our behalf, so that we might become the righteousness of God in Him. (NASB)

> Christ was innocent of sin, and yet for our sake God made him one with human sinfulness, so that in him we might be made one with the righteousness of God. (REB)

God put the wrong on him who never did anything wrong, so that we could be put right with God. (*The Message*)

This passage speaks of what many students of the New Testament call "the great exchange" or "the great reversal." When we come unto Christ, confess our sins, plead for forgiveness by virtue of His precious atoning blood, and forsake both sins and sinfulness, God the Father essentially takes away our sins and puts them upon the shoulders of Jesus Christ, who was never guilty of sin. We are then pardoned, exonerated, and pronounced innocent and clean, pure and undefiled, as though the sins had never been committed. We are justified.

Timothy Keller has written: "On the cross Jesus became, as it were, the very thing that was destroying us [i.e., sin]. He was treated as if he were sinful, and so he was cursed and put to death in our place. And now it is only as we in faith look at him on the cross—as we look at him becoming the sin that was killing us and taking the death that should have been ours—that we can be forgiven and healed. On the cross God turned the cross of death on sin into a blessing for us."[16]

Now let's be clear here. Jesus never violated the laws of God (see 1 Peter 2:22; Hebrews 4:15; 7:26, JST). He was sinless and perfect. But in the hours of His passion—His sufferings in the Garden of Gethsemane and on the cross of Calvary—He bore the sins of all humankind; thus *He became as though He were guilty of all sin*. He suffered the agony, the pain, and the awful sense of alienation from the loss of the Father's Spirit. He confronted what Elder Neal A. Maxwell called "the awful arithmetic of the Atonement."[17] In modern revelation we read the Savior's words: "I have overcome and have trodden the wine-press alone, even the wine-press of the fierceness of the wrath of Almighty God" (Doctrine and Covenants 76:107; see also 88:106; 133:50; Isaiah 63:3). Jesus faced the "wrath of Almighty

---

16. Keller, *Hope in Times of Fear*, 77.
17. Maxwell, "Willing to Submit."

God," or "drank the bitter cup," through experiencing the traumatic withdrawal of His Father's strengthening and sustaining Spirit. It was this withdrawal that caused Him to bleed from every pore (Mosiah 3:7; Doctrine and Covenants 19:15–19).[18]

"NOW IS THE DAY OF SALVATION" (6:1–2)

Paul emphasizes to the Corinthians that, as Christians, we are co-workers with the Lord Jesus in delivering the message of salvation to the people of the world and then doing our best to assist them in being true to the covenants they have made. He pleads that the members of the branch "receive not the grace of God in vain" (verse 1). This is a theme discussed in more detail in our study of the Epistle to the Galatians (specifically Galatians 1:6–8). Paul is basically saying, "You accepted the gospel of Jesus Christ when you first heard the word of truth and were baptized. You partook of the goodness and grace of God extended to you by the sufferings and death of our Lord. Why on earth would you allow yourselves to return to your old ways of thinking and acting? Why would you begin to trust once again in your dead works rather than in 'the merits, and mercy, and grace of the Holy Messiah'?" (2 Nephi 2:8).

"Behold, now is the accepted time," Paul writes. "Behold, now is the day of salvation" (verse 2). Students of the Book of Mormon will recognize here a concept developed in greater detail by Alma in his remarks to the Zoramites. "Yea, I would that ye would come forth and harden not your hearts any longer," Alma beckoned. "For behold, *now is the time and the day of your salvation*; and therefore, if ye will repent and harden not your hearts, *immediately shall the great plan of redemption be brought about unto you*. For behold, *this life is the time for men to prepare to meet God*; yea, behold the day of this life is the day for men to perform their labors" (Alma 34:31–32).

To enjoy the benefits and blessings of celestial living, we need not

---

18. See Brigham Young, in *Journal of Discourses*, 3:205–6; Holland, "None Were with Him."

wait until that "perfect day" (Doctrine and Covenants 50:24) when we are resurrected, glorified, and exalted in the highest degree of the celestial kingdom. We can do our best to rid ourselves of worldly thinking and acting and to live as nearly as we can to the example of the Christ. As we do so, the Lord will quicken us with "a portion of the celestial glory" in this life, and if we hold out faithful to the end of our days, He will, in the Resurrection, extend to us a fullness of celestial glory (Doctrine and Covenants 88:29).

BE NOT UNEQUALLY YOKED WITH UNBELIEVERS (6:14–18)

Earnest followers of the Savior face a particular challenge when interacting with worldly people. On the one hand, we have been charged by Christ to reach out to them, to assist them, to encourage them to live in harmony with the Judeo-Christian ethic, and to be obedient to the Ten Commandments. We have been commissioned to be the salt of the earth and the light of the world (see Matthew 5:13–14; 3 Nephi 12:13–14) and to be a leavening influence to people within and beyond our immediate circle. In His counsel to the Nephites, the risen Lord taught of the importance of ministering to such persons, "for ye know not but what they will return and repent, and come unto me with full purpose of heart, and I shall heal them" (3 Nephi 18:29–34).

On the other hand, we cannot allow those who flaunt immorality or promote indecency to draw us away from the high standards of the gospel of Jesus Christ. In seeking to help them, we must ensure that their negative influence on us is not stronger than our positive influence on them (see Mark 9:40–42, 44, JST).

In the end, every man and woman must know for themselves, must have a witness that is independent of others' convictions. In the end, we each rise or fall on our own. I cannot be saved on the basis of my parents' or grandparents' deep-seated faith. Just as the Lord's Church as an institution must "stand independent above all other creatures beneath the celestial world" (Doctrine and Covenants 78:14), so too must the disciples of the Lord receive their own spiritual confirmation of this work. It is this confirmation that will enable them to stand tall in defense of the gospel, particularly when others stumble or falter.

Sometimes it is difficult to make decisions regarding associating with others. For example, should we spend time with persons whose values or lifestyle are at odds with what we as Latter-day Saints know to be right and wrong? It requires serious spiritual work on our part to acquire the gift of discernment, the power to know whether we will be a blessing to the unbeliever or whether the unbeliever will prove to be a curse to us. Every situation is different, and so it is nearly impossible to establish a singular rule or guideline that would hold for all encounters. Jacob said it well: "O be wise; what can I say more?" (Jacob 6:12).

GODLY SORROW LEADS TO REPENTANCE (7:8–11)

More than three hundred years after the coming of the Messiah to the people in the New World, the young captain of the Nephite army, Mormon, had a moment of joy when he saw that "the Nephites began to repent of their iniquity." Shortly thereafter, however, Mormon's hopes were dashed as he began to realize that "their sorrowing was not unto repentance, because of the goodness of God; but it was rather *the sorrowing of the damned*, because *the Lord would not always suffer them to take happiness in sin.*" For one thing, "they did not come unto Jesus with broken hearts and contrite spirits, but they did curse God, and wish to die." Mormon then recorded these chilling words: "I saw that the day of grace was passed with them, both temporally and spiritually" (Mormon 2:10, 13–15).

"In worldly sorrow," one prominent Christian leader wrote, "you are sorry for the consequences of the sin, for your sake. *In true repentance you are sorry for the sin itself, for how it has wronged and grieved your Creator and Redeemer. In self-centered sorrow, you never come to hate the sin itself, and so when the consequences recede, the sin will roar back, as powerful within you as ever.* True repentance is fueled by grief for hurting the one we love, and that intensified love of Christ makes the sin appear hateful, and so it begins to lose its power over you."[19]

BECOMING RICH THROUGH CHRIST'S POVERTY (8:9)

The Apostle writes, "For ye know the grace of our Lord Jesus Christ, that, though he was rich, yet for your sakes he became poor, that ye through his poverty might be rich" (verse 9). The condescension of God (Jesus Christ), what many in the Christian world call the Incarnation, is indeed a marvel and an unspeakable blessing. We sing in a beloved hymn: "I marvel that he would descend from his throne divine to rescue a soul so rebellious and proud as mine, that he should extend his great love unto such as I, sufficient to own, to redeem, and to justify."[20]

In the prologue to John's Gospel, we read, "And the Word was made flesh, and dwelt among us, (and we beheld his glory, the glory as of the only begotten of the Father,) full of grace and truth" (John 1:14). The Greek words rendered "dwelt among us" are more graphic—as though John had written that the Word will "pitch His tent among us" or "camp out with us." Because Jesus was willing to descend to our fallen telestial world, you and I are able to ascend to celestial heights. Had He not come to earth and experienced pains, afflictions, infirmities, and temptations throughout His mortal life, He would not have been in a position to succor us in the midst of our trials and challenges (Alma 7:11–12; compare Hebrews 2:16–18; Doctrine and Covenants 62:1).

GOD LOVES A CHEERFUL GIVER (9:6–7, 15)

For a number of years the Saints in Jerusalem struggled with poverty, and so one of Paul's righteous obsessions was to collect funds from the various branches of the Church to assist the sufferers in the holy

---

19. Keller, *Hope in Times of Fear*, 103–4.
20. "I Stand All Amazed," *Hymns*, no. 193.

city. Paul explains to the Corinthians that "he which soweth sparingly shall reap also sparingly; and he which soweth bountifully shall reap also bountifully . . . for God loveth a cheerful giver. . . . Thanks be unto God for his unspeakable gift" (verses 6–7, 15). During His mortal ministry, Jesus taught: "Be ye therefore merciful, as your Father also is merciful. . . . *Give, and it shall be given unto you; good measure, pressed down, and shaken together, and running over*, shall men give into your bosom. For with the same measure that ye mete withal it shall be measured to you again" (Luke 6:36, 38).

In Matthew 6 Jesus spoke at some length about why we do things—that is, the motives behind our actions. He warned the Apostles and other followers against giving alms, praying, and fasting in order to be seen and admired by onlookers. Such persons, He stated, "have their reward" (Matthew 6:2, 5, 16; 3 Nephi 13:2, 5, 16). An important part of the quest for a pure heart is developing pure motives and desires. Surely one of the most significant requests disciples can make of their Heavenly Father is for a cleansing and purification of their motives, a greater desire to do the right things for the right reason. When the left hand does not know what the right hand is doing, it means there is no ulterior motivation, no hidden agenda, no selfish purposes for our actions. In one sense, then, the challenge of disciples is to rise above self, above self-regard.

SPIRITUAL WARFARE (10:3–6)

The war about which Paul is speaking is not a conflict that is waged with rifles and bayonets or grenades and missile launchers. It is a war that began in our premortal existence (see Revelation 12:7–9; Moses 4:1–4; Abraham 3:22–28; Doctrine and Covenants 29:36–37), a war of words and opinions, a war against truth and righteousness, a war over the souls of women and men. It is spiritual warfare, begun and perpetuated by Lucifer, the father of lies. "For though we walk in the flesh, we do not war after the flesh; (for the weapons of our warfare

are not carnal [i.e., physical], but mighty through God to the pulling down of strong holds;) casting down imaginations, and every high thing that exalteth itself against the knowledge of God, and bringing into captivity every thought to the obedience of Christ; and having in a readiness to revenge all disobedience, when your obedience is fulfilled" (verses 3–6). The matter of spiritual warfare is discussed in more detail in our commentary on the whole armor of God, worn by the Christian soldier (Ephesians 6:10–18).

RIGHTEOUSNESS IS MEASURED BY GOD'S STANDARDS (10:12–13, 17–18)

Paul here warns against becoming so self-assured that we begin to measure all things—good or evil, true or false, valuable or worthless—by our own standard of measurement. He speaks of people "measuring themselves by themselves, and comparing themselves among themselves." Such individuals, he adds, "are not wise." Such assessments and evaluations must be made "according to the measure of the rule which God hath distributed to us, a measure to reach even unto you" (verses 12–13).

President Joseph F. Smith spoke of "the proud and self-vaunting ones, *who read by the lamp of their own conceit; who interpret by rules of their own contriving;* who have become a law unto themselves, and so pose as the sole judges of their own doings."[21] Right and wrong, truth and falsehood are not determined by popular consensus. And sadly, they are not determined by legislation.

Ours is indeed a day spoken of by the prophet Isaiah, a time when many in society call good evil and evil good, "that put darkness for light, and light for darkness; that put bitter for sweet, and sweet for bitter! Woe unto them that are wise in their own eyes, and prudent in their own sight!" (Isaiah 5:20–21).

---

21. Joseph F. Smith, *Gospel Doctrine*, 373.

In a revelation received by Joseph the Prophet in September 1831, Jesus Christ taught a timely and timeless principle: "Behold, I, the Lord, have made my church in these last days like unto a judge sitting on a hill, or in a high place, to judge the nations. For it shall come to pass that *the inhabitants of Zion shall judge all things pertaining to Zion*" (Doctrine and Covenants 64:37–38). Paul summarizes by writing, "But he that glorieth, let him glory in the Lord. For not he that commendeth himself is approved, but whom the Lord commendeth" (verses 17–18).

MAINTAINING CHRISTIAN SIMPLICITY (11:2–4)

Some of the most effective gospel teachers are those who have searched and wrestled and stretched to come to a clearer understanding of a deep doctrinal concept. Then, when they truly grasp what the prophets or teachers intended to convey, they are able to teach profound truth simply and understandably. Elder Neal A. Maxwell explained that "the simpleness, the easiness of the gospel is such that it causes people to perish because they can't receive it. We like variety. We like intellectual embroidery. We like complexity. . . . As you increase the complexity of a belief system, you . . . create a sophisticated intellectual structure *which causes people to talk about the gospel instead of doing it*. But the gospel of Jesus Christ really is not complex. It strips us of any basic excuse for noncompliance, and yet many of us are forever trying to make it more complex."[22]

Paul's plea with the Corinthian Saints is essentially this: "Don't complicate the gospel of Jesus Christ. Don't despise the words of plainness. Don't allow yourselves to be drawn toward the mystical or the esoteric. Find joy and peace in the simple gospel." To complicate "the fundamental principles of our religion"[23] is tantamount to teaching "another gospel" (verse 4). Those who follow Paul's counsel, who

---

22. Maxwell, *"For the Power Is in Them,"* 48–49.
23. Joseph Smith, in *"Elders' Journal,* July 1838," 42–44.

search the scriptures diligently and attend carefully to the words of the apostles and prophets, begin to sense and discover great profundity within the simple and singular good news that salvation is in Christ.

PAUL'S PERSECUTION AND SUFFERING (11:22–30)

Too often Paul found it necessary to defend himself against the criticism of the Corinthians. Some critics have pointed out that Paul did not measure up to the status enjoyed by the first Apostles chosen by Jesus; he had not been one of the early witnesses of the Resurrection of Christ. Others found fault with his appearance and his manner of presenting the gospel. In addition, he was criticized by "false apostles," no doubt eloquent spokesmen who came among the Corinthians and who seem to have been well received by some. In the previous chapter, Paul voiced some of their complaints: "For his letters, say they, are weighty and powerful; but his bodily presence is weak, and his speech contemptible" (2 Corinthians 10:10). Two other translations render verse 10 as follows:

> For some say, "His letters are weighty and forceful, but in person he is unimpressive and his speaking amounts to nothing." (NIV)

> For they say, "His letters are weighty and strong, but his bodily presence is weak, and his speech of no account." (ESV)

Returning to chapter 11, we find Paul speaking in a way that is quite defensive, although certainly appropriate and called for: "Are they Hebrews? so am I. Are they Israelites? so am I. . . . Are they ministers of Christ? (I speak as a fool) I am more [i.e., 'so am I,' per the JST]; in labours more abundant, in stripes above measure, in prisons more frequent, in deaths oft" (verses 22–23). Paul is essentially replying, "I'm just as much a descendant of Abraham, Isaac, and Jacob as they are. I too am a minister of Jesus Christ, and I've suffered more than any of those other claimants. No one has worked harder and more diligently than I."

Paul then gets specific about his trials: "in stripes [i.e., afflictions, punishments] above measure, in prisons more frequent [see Acts 16:23; 21:33; 22:25; 24:27; 28:16, 30]; in deaths oft [i.e., times when his life was threatened: Acts 9:23; 21:31; 27:20, 42]. Of the Jews five times received I forty stripes save one [see Deuteronomy 25:2–3]. Thrice was I beaten with rods [see Acts 16:22–23], once I was stoned [Acts 14:19], thrice I suffered shipwreck [see Acts 27:9–10, 41–44], a night and a day I have been in the deep [Acts 27:42–44]; in journeyings often [such as his missionary journeys and his ministering to the Saints in present-day Turkey and Greece]" (verses 23–26). Paul then refers to perils among his own countrymen, the Jews, and the Gentiles—times of hunger and thirst and periods of fasting and of being cold and naked (verses 26–27). He adds the stresses, the strain, and the worry associated with "the care of all the churches"—that is, the various branches of the Church (verse 28). Finally, Paul mentions escaping through a window and being lowered in a basket in order to escape leaders of Damascus (verses 32–33; see also Acts 9:23–25).

PAUL GLORIES IN HIS SPIRITUAL EXPERIENCES (12:1–5)

Paul just chronicled the dangerous and exhausting circumstances through which he had passed in the years since his conversion. He now presents the most important area that should qualify him for the appreciation, respect, and recognition of the members of the Corinthian branch—namely, his many and varied spiritual experiences. No doubt few mortals have enjoyed a closeness and intimacy with angels and the risen Lord or received more divine guidance than Paul, the Lord's Apostle to the Gentiles.

Verse 1 reads, "It is not expedient for me doubtless to glory." Or as another translation reads, "It may do no good, but I must go on with my boasting; I come now to visions and revelations granted by the Lord" (REB). "I knew a man in Christ above fourteen years ago, (whether in the body, I cannot tell; or whether out of the body, I cannot tell: God knoweth;) such an one caught up to the third heaven" (verse 2). There are times when individuals are caught up into a heavenly vision and cannot discern whether they are actually brought to a certain place in person, in their bodies, or whether they have been transported in their minds, their bodies remaining where they were. Moses and Elijah, both translated beings at the time, appeared to Jesus and his three chief Apostles on the Mount of Transfiguration and conferred sacred keys of the priesthood (Matthew 17:1–3).[24]

Stephen, the powerful preacher, was permitted to see in a vision Jesus standing on the right hand of the Father (Acts 7:55). And God the Father and His Son, Jesus Christ, actually appeared in the Sacred Grove to young Joseph Smith in 1820.

Of the Three Nephites, Mormon wrote: "And behold, the heavens were opened, and they were caught up into heaven, and saw and heard unspeakable things. And it was forbidden them that they should utter; neither was it given unto them power that they could utter the things which they saw and heard; and whether they were in the body or out of the body, they could not tell" (3 Nephi 28:13–15). Joseph Smith employed similar language to describe his vision of the celestial kingdom: "The heavens were opened upon us, and I beheld the celestial kingdom of God, and the glory thereof, whether in the body or out I cannot tell" (Doctrine and Covenants 137:1).

To say that Paul saw the "third heaven" is to say that he was able to see the celestial kingdom, as Joseph Smith would do centuries later. The Prophet spoke of Paul's phenomenal experience: "Paul ascended into the third heavens, and he could understand the three principal rounds of Jacob's ladder [see Genesis 28:12–15]—the telestial, the terrestrial, and the celestial glories or kingdoms, where Paul saw and heard things which were not lawful for him to utter." And then, referencing

---

24. See Joseph Smith, in "Discourse, between circa 26 June and circa 4 August 1839–A."

his own experience with Sidney Rigdon as they beheld the vision of the degrees of glory (see Doctrine and Covenants 76), he stated: "I could explain a hundredfold more than I ever have of the glories of the kingdoms manifested to me in the vision, were I permitted, and were the people prepared to receive them."[25]

Paul adds that he was also "caught up into paradise"—the postmortal abode of the faithful spirits—"and heard unspeakable words, which it is not lawful for a man to utter" (verse 4). That is, he saw and heard things that were completely ineffable, sacred sights and sounds that could not be expressed in human language, as well as knowledge and understanding he was not permitted to share.

WE ARE STRENGTHENED BY GOD'S GRACE (12:7–10)

"And lest I should be exalted above measure," Paul hastens to add, "through the abundance of the revelations, there was given to me a thorn in the flesh, the messenger of Satan to buffet me, lest I should be exalted above measure. For this thing I besought the Lord thrice, that it might depart from me. And [the Lord] said unto me, *My grace is sufficient for thee: for my strength is made perfect in weakness.*" Paul then remarks: "Most gladly therefore will I rather glory in my infirmities, that the power of Christ may rest upon me. Therefore I take pleasure in infirmities, in reproaches, in necessities, in persecutions, in distresses for Christ's sake: for *when I am weak, then am I strong*" (verses 7–10).

No one really knows what Paul's "thorn in the flesh" was. Was it a lingering sickness, perhaps malaria, so common in places like Galatia, where Paul had labored previously? Was it a memory of his past, a hellish reminder of who he had been and what he had done? Was it an evil spirit that dogged his steps and wearied him in his ministry? Was it a medical condition, possibly problems with his eyes (see Galatians 4:13–15; 6:11)? Perhaps one day we'll know. But we do know that

---

25. Joseph Smith, in "History, 1838–1856, volume D-1," 1556; punctuation and spelling standardized.

whatever it was, it kept Paul humble and forced him to his knees often. His inabilities and his impotence in the face of this particular challenge were ever before him. I rather think that when Paul states that he "besought the Lord thrice" for the removal of the thorn that he is not describing merely three prayers but instead three seasons of prayer—extended periods of wrestling and laboring in the Spirit for a specific blessing that never came.

However, as he suggests, other kinds of blessings came—a closeness, a sensitivity, and an acquaintance with Deity and a sanctified strength that came through pain and suffering. When up against the wall of faith, shorn of self-assurance and feeling his finitude, a mere mortal received that strengthening power we know as the grace of the Lord Jesus Christ. As the Savior explained to Moroni, when we acknowledge and confess our weakness—not just our specific weaknesses or our individual sins, but our general weakness, our mortal limitation—and submit unto Him, He transforms weakness into strength (see Ether 12:27).

"Although the Savior could heal all whom He would heal," President Dallin H. Oaks explained, "this is not true of those who hold His priesthood authority. Mortal exercises of that authority are limited by the will of Him whose priesthood it is. . . . When the Apostle Paul sought to be healed from the 'thorn in the flesh' that buffeted him (2 Corinthians 12:7), the Lord declined to heal him. . . . Healing blessings come in many ways, each suited to our individual needs, as known to Him who loves us best. Sometimes a 'healing' cures our illness or lifts our burden. But sometimes we are 'healed' by being given strength or understanding or patience to bear the burdens placed upon us."[26]

The people who followed Alma were in bondage to wicked oppressors. When they prayed for relief, the Lord told them He would deliver them eventually, but in the meantime, He would ease their burdens

---

26. Oaks, "He Heals the Heavy Laden."

"that even you cannot feel them upon your backs, even while you are in bondage; and this will I do that ye may stand as witnesses . . . that I, the Lord God, do visit my people in their afflictions" (Mosiah 24:14). In this case the people did not have their burdens removed, but the Lord strengthened them so that "they could bear up their burdens with ease, and they did submit cheerfully and with patience to all the will of the Lord" (Mosiah 24:15). "Your struggles do not define you," Sister Reyna Aburto of the Relief Society General Presidency taught, "but they can *refine* you. Because of a 'thorn in the flesh,' you may have the ability to feel more compassion toward others."[27]

As Jacob, son of Lehi, affirmed: "Wherefore, we search the prophets, and we have many revelations and the spirit of prophecy; and having all these witnesses we obtain a hope, and our faith becometh unshaken, insomuch that we truly can command in the name of Jesus and the very trees obey us, or the mountains, or the waves of the sea." Now note these words: "Nevertheless, *the Lord God showeth us our weakness that we may know that it is by his grace, and his great condescensions unto the children of men, that we have power to do these things*" (Jacob 4:6–7). Or, as someone else put it, "The default mode of the human heart is to believe that it is *strength* that connects you to God, but the gospel says that it is *weakness* that connects you to God. Only to the degree that you see you are weak are you strong." Further, "all hard things, embraced in faithfulness to the one who did the same for us, will issue in greater good and glory. Through experiences of weakness we grow into a strength we would never have had otherwise, shedding enslaving allegiances and finding a new freedom."[28]

CHRISTIANS LIVE BY THE POWER OF GOD (13:4)

As he is about to close his second letter to his beloved Corinthian brothers and sisters in the faith, the Apostle Paul writes: "For though

---

27. Aburto, "Thru Cloud and Sunshine, Lord, Abide with Me."
28. Keller, *Hope in Times of Fear*, 105, 178.

he [i.e., Jesus Christ] was crucified through weakness, yet he liveth by the power of God. For we also are weak in him, but we shall live with him by the power of God toward you" (verse 4). Nephi taught prophetically that "the very God of Israel do men trample under their feet; I say, trample under their feet but I would speak in other words—they set him at naught, and hearken not to the voice of his counsels. . . . And the world, because of their iniquity, shall judge him to be a thing of naught; wherefore they scourge him, and he suffereth [i.e., permits, tolerates] it; and they smite him, and he suffereth it. Yea, they spit upon him, and he suffereth it, because of his loving kindness and his long-suffering towards the children of men" (1 Nephi 19:7, 9).

Indeed, the will of the Son was swallowed up in the will of the Father (see John 6:38; Mosiah 15:7; 3 Nephi 27:13–14). And as it is with our Savior, so it is with us. Joseph Smith and his associates taught the men in the School of the Elders that Jesus Christ "is the prototype or standard of salvation."[29] He set the pattern and marked the way. And as He was made strong through the power of our Heavenly Father, so we are made strong by and through the Father's divine Son. "For if you keep my commandments you shall receive of [God's] fulness, and be glorified in me as I am in the Father" (Doctrine and Covenants 93:20).

"EXAMINE YOURSELVES" (13:5)

"Examine yourselves," Paul writes, "whether ye be in the faith; prove [i.e., try, test] your own selves. Know ye not your own selves, how that Jesus Christ is in you, except ye be reprobates" (verse 5). "Search your hearts," the Prophet of the Restoration counseled the Saints, "and see if you are like God. I have searched mine and feel to repent of all my sins." Joseph went on to explain that "as far as we degenerate from God, we descend to the devil and lose knowledge, and without knowledge we cannot be saved, and while our hearts are filled

---

29. *Lectures on Faith*, 7:9; pp. 75–76.

with evil, and we are studying evil, there is no room in our hearts for good, or studying good. Is not God good? Yea, then you be good; if He is faithful, then you be faithful."[30]

When Paul says that "Jesus Christ is in you," he is referring to the fact that we are the temple of God and that the Holy Ghost is dwelling with us, as discussed in 1 Corinthians 6:19–20. Another translation of "Jesus Christ is in you, except ye be reprobates" is "Do you not realize that Jesus Christ is in you—unless, of course, you fail the test?" (NIV).

"WE CAN DO NOTHING AGAINST THE TRUTH" (13:8)

In the Church of Jesus Christ, specific policies, programs, or procedures may change from time to time, but certain truths are set, fixed, and immutable. They may not be altered by time or opinion. They are eternal absolutes. "God, our Heavenly Father—Elohim—lives," President Spencer W. Kimball testified.

> This is an absolute truth. All . . . of the children of men on the earth might be ignorant of him and his attributes and his powers, but he still lives. All the people of the earth might deny him and disbelieve, but he lives in spite of them. . . . In short, *opinion alone has no power in the matter of an absolute truth.* . . . The watchmaker in Switzerland, with materials at hand, made the watch that was found in the sand in a California desert. The people who found the watch had never been to Switzerland, nor seen the watchmaker, nor seen the watch made. The watchmaker still existed, no matter the extent of their ignorance or experience. If the watch had a tongue, it might even lie and say, "There is no watchmaker." That would not alter the truth.[31]

---

30. Joseph Smith, in "Discourse, 10 April 1842, as Reported by Wilford Woodruff"; punctuation and spelling standardized.
31. Kimball, "Absolute Truth," 138.

Without absolute truths and absolute values, without set and established principles within our personal and social experience, life would have no meaning and would prove chaotic; there would be few things upon which we could depend with certainty. President Rex E. Lee explained to Brigham Young University students that "there is nothing more important for each of you to do than build a firm, personal testimony that there are in this life some absolutes, things that never change, regardless of time, place, or circumstances. They are eternal truths, eternal principles, and . . . they are and ever will be the same yesterday, today, and forever."[32]

After Alma delivered a powerful address on spiritual rebirth to the people in Zarahemla, he inquired: "And now, my brethren, what have ye to say against this? I say unto you, if ye speak against it, it matters not, for the word of God must be fulfilled" (Alma 5:58).

---

32. Lee, "Things that Change and Things that Don't," 54.

THE EPISTLE TO THE GALATIANS

PAUL'S LETTER TO THE Galatian Saints is clearly one of the earliest of the fourteen epistles. This can be discerned by the nature of his counsel and condemnation of the Galatians' allegiance to and observance of the law of Moses. The epistle was written from Corinth in about AD 55–57. As the Bible Dictionary explains, Galatia is a "district in the center of Asia Minor [most of what is present-day Turkey], inhabited by tribes from Gaul who settled there in the 3rd century B.C. (Galatia was also the Greek name for Gallia, or Gaul.) . . . Some scholars think that Paul and Luke regard the cities of Antioch [of Pisidia, not to be confused with Antioch of Syria], Iconium, Lystra, and Derbe, visited by Paul on his first [missionary] journey, as part of Galatia and that it was to these towns that the epistle to the Galatians was addressed."[1] Because of some of its teachings about justification by faith and the fulfillment of the law of Moses, Galatians has been called "little Romans."

AN APOSTLE OF GOD, NOT MAN (1:1–5)

We begin our reading and study of Paul's epistle to the Galatians with his testimony of the divine call that has come to him. He

---

1. Bible Dictionary, "Galatia," 676–77.

identifies himself as "an apostle, (not of men, neither by man, but by Jesus Christ, and God the Father, who raised him [i.e., Christ] from the dead)" (verse 1). It is extremely difficult to determine at what point in Paul's ministry he was called to be an Apostle of the Lord Jesus Christ. Luke first refers to Paul and Barnabas being Apostles in his account of Paul's first missionary journey and, more specifically, when the two servants of God preach the gospel in Iconium, Lystra, and Derbe (Acts 13:50–51; 14:4, 14). The scriptures are silent regarding when Paul received his apostolic call, whether he was a member of the Quorum of the Twelve Apostles, or whether he was a special witness of the name of Christ in an at-large capacity.

President Joseph Fielding Smith offered his perspective: "We have no record that states that in the days of the apostles of old that any one was ever ordained to be an apostle and not to be a member of the Council of the Twelve. The Savior chose Twelve Apostles, and *this quorum was to continue*, according to the revelations [see Acts 1:15–26; Ephesians 4:11–16], but at no place has the Lord said that others more than the Twelve and a Presidency of three should be called. Paul was an *ordained apostle*, and without question he took the place of one of the other brethren in that council."[2]

Paul adds that the Savior "gave himself for our sins, that he might deliver us from this present evil world, according to the will of God and our Father" (verse 4). The Lamb of God, Jehovah, slain from the foundation of the world (see Revelation 13:8; Moses 7:47), offered in the premortal council of heaven to put into effect all of the terms and conditions of the Father's plan of salvation. Indeed, He would become its chief advocate and proponent, the Savior and Redeemer of all humankind. He said simply: "Father, thy will be done, and the glory be thine forever" (Moses 4:2). Or, as Abraham recorded this grand scene:

---

2. Joseph Fielding Smith, *Doctrines of Salvation*, 3:153; emphasis in original; see also McConkie, *Doctrinal New Testament Commentary*, 2:131.

"And the Lord [i.e., God the Father] said: 'Whom shall I send?' And one answered like unto the Son of Man [i.e., Jehovah]: Here am I, send me" (Abraham 3:27).

Jesus also "gave himself for our sins" through assuming the infinite burden of His atoning sacrifice. In ways that we can never comprehend at this stage of our eternal development, all of the sins and the effects of sin of all of God's children were placed upon the shoulders of this sinless, stainless, perfectly pure man, and He bore the burden and suffered the exquisite pain as though the sins and offenses were His own. He became our substitute, our stand-in. He thereby satisfied the demands of divine justice and ransomed us from the penalty of our transgressions and our misdeeds. The Only Begotten Son of God in the flesh gave Himself *for us* that He might give Himself *to us*.

WARNINGS AGAINST ANOTHER GOSPEL (1:6–8; 3:1–7)

As mentioned in the introductory sections of this book, Paul's earliest epistles—which includes the one to the Galatians—tend to deal largely with Jewish-Christian problems, while his later letters start to focus on the problems created by an unholy mingling of Christian doctrine and Greek philosophy. Truly one of the Apostle's most persistent and plaguing challenges was to keep both his Jewish-Christian converts and his Gentile-Christian converts focused on Jesus Christ and His liberating gospel and persuade them to leave behind the ordinances and performances of the law of Moses. Too many men and women who had been reared as Jews and later converted to the gospel of Jesus Christ were attempting to live out their Christian faith while at the same time holding tenaciously to Judaism and the laws and conditions of the old covenant.

This is the context for Paul's scathing remarks in the first chapter of his letter to the Galatian Saints. "I marvel that ye are so soon removed from him that called you into the grace of Christ unto another gospel: which is not another; but there be some that trouble you, and would pervert the gospel of Christ" (verses 6–7). Note a different translation of these verses: "I am astonished that you are so quickly deserting him who called you in the grace of Christ and are turning to a different gospel—not that there is another one, but there are some who trouble you and want to distort the gospel of Christ" (ESV).

It's as if Paul is saying: "It is hard for me to fathom that you have begun to ignore all that I have taught you; to treat lightly the sufferings and death of our Savior and Lord; to lay aside the doctrine and practices of the everlasting gospel; to backtrack spiritually; to return to life under the law, including the backbreaking and burdensome effort to keep all of the 613 commandments. I cannot understand why you would forget so quickly the joy and spiritual liberation that came into your life when you accepted the gospel of grace. It's as though you have been drawn into another gospel."

Those who had begun to lead away the stumbling Saints were known as the Judaizers, "agitators" or "troublemakers." In fact, the Greek word translated here as "trouble" means literally to "shake back and forth," or as we might say, to agitate or stir up problems. The Judaizers were actually attempting to persuade these Jewish Christians to hold on to many, if not most, of the tenets and practices of the law of Moses. And all of this is terribly upsetting, even demoralizing, to the Apostle. Paul issues this warning: "But though we, or an angel from heaven, preach any other gospel unto you than that which we have preached unto you, let him be accursed" (verse 8).

Paul's warning not to even take counsel from an angel of God if the angel preaches anything different from what Paul has taught is, of course, hyperbolic, an overstatement. Clearly an angel sent from the presence of God would never preach anything different from what God has revealed to his apostles and prophets. The Almighty would not work against Himself. The important point Paul is making here is that if any mortal should put forward some doctrine or practice that is at odds with the gospel of Jesus Christ, it is to be absolutely ignored and shunned.

THE GOSPEL PAUL PREACHED IS
NOT FROM MAN (1:10–16)

In spite of the views of radical historians or overreaching theologians who insist that Paul was the creator of Christianity, Paul here states humbly but convincingly the source of his gospel understanding and authority. He testifies that what he preached did not originate with him or, for that matter, with any man or woman. "For I neither received it of man, neither was I taught it, but by the revelation of Jesus Christ" (verses 11–12). It seems reasonable that Paul was taught the gospel, or at least given a foundation of the faith, by Ananias of Damascus or by disciples or Church members in that region (see Acts 9:17–22). Paul's point is simply that there are some things that cannot be taught by mortal men and women but can be known only by the spirit of revelation.

There were many things that Jesus could be taught only by His Father in Heaven (see Matthew 3:24–26, JST), through the power of the Holy Spirit. And so it was with Saul of Tarsus, who came to be known as Paul. Paul's conversion took place under the direction of the Lord Jesus Christ. His testimony came from God. His call and commission to be a "chosen vessel" (Acts 9:15) can be traced to heaven.

In order to dramatize just how far he has come in regard to spiritual things—to illustrate the major transformation of his life, thought, and behavior since that eventful day on the road to Damascus—Paul writes of his past: "For ye have heard of my conversation [i.e., conduct] in time past in the Jews' religion, how that beyond measure I persecuted the church of God, and wasted it: And profited in the Jews' religion above many my equals in mine own nation, being more exceedingly zealous of the traditions of my fathers" (verses 13–14). Stated differently: "You have heard, no doubt, of my earlier life in Judaism. I was violently persecuting the church of God and was trying to destroy it. I advanced in Judaism beyond many among my people of the same age, for I was far more zealous for the traditions of my ancestors" (NRSV).

Indeed, Saul of Tarsus was brought up as a devout, observant Jew. Like his fathers, he was a Pharisee—in fact, a Shammaite Pharisee and a very strict one at that. N. T. Wright explained: "Who were the Shammaites? A division had taken place within Phariseeism in the generation before Saul of Tarsus. During the reign of Herod the Great (36–4 BC) there arose two schools of thought within the already powerful movement, following the two great teachers of the Herodian period, Hillel and Shammai. We know them through dozens of discussions in the Mishnah (the codification of Jewish law, drawn together around AD 200), where almost always Hillel is the 'lenient' one, and Shammai is the 'strict' one. Their followers, likewise, argue issue after issue in terms of lenient and strict practices."[3]

Another respected Christian scholar pointed out: "Notice that Paul . . . is quite willing to say that he had advanced further than most of his peers in Judaism. He uses the term *anastrophen* to describe his former life. This term certainly refers more to orthopraxy [i.e., the practice or living out of the faith] than it does to orthodoxy [i.e., correct doctrine], but then early Judaism was much more of a way of living religiously than a set of doctrines to be believed."[4]

PAUL TRAVELS TO ARABIA (1:17)

Following his conversion and his baptism at the hands of Ananias, Paul preached the divine Sonship of Christ in the synagogues in Damascus. One can only imagine the stir of suspicion, doubt, and even disgust expressed by some of the Christians in Damascus. Seeing someone who had been a bitter enemy of the followers of Jesus now preaching the gospel of Jesus must have been more than many Christians could handle. Some of them cried out, "Is not this he that destroyed them which called on this name [i.e., the name of Jesus] in Jerusalem, and came hither for that intent, that he might bring them bound unto

---

3. Wright, *What Saint Paul Really Said*, 26.
4. Witherington, *Paul Quest*, 58.

the chief priests? But Saul increased the more in strength, and confounded the Jews which dwelt at Damascus, proving that this is very Christ" (Acts 9:19–22). In other words, Saul preached that Jesus of Nazareth was indeed the Messiah or Anointed One, the one foretold by the prophets.

Paul then writes that, in spite of his training and reputation, when the call came from God to be the apostle to the Gentiles (Romans 11:13; 15:16), he did not go to local members or leaders, nor did he even travel to Jerusalem to visit with Peter and the other leaders of the Church of Jesus Christ. "But I went into Arabia, and returned again unto Damascus" (verse 17; 2 Corinthians 11:32).

Why would Paul, at this early stage of his ministry, go to Arabia? First of all, we need to understand that Arabia is what we know today as Saudi Arabia, a gigantic land mass between the Red Sea and the Persian Gulf. "A first-century Jew from Jerusalem, however," Jerome Murphy-O'Connor explained, "in practice would have applied 'Arabia' to a much more restricted part of that vast area: namely, the modern kingdom of Jordan, plus both sides of the Gulf of Aqaba. This was the territory of the Nabataeans, whose king, Aretas IV [see 2 Corinthians 11:32–33], ruled from Petra."[5]

Scholars over the years have been divided on Paul's motivation for travelling to Arabia. One option, of course, is that Paul wanted to get started early in his new assignment to take the gospel to the Gentiles. Murphy-O'Connor wrote elsewhere that "Paul was trying to make converts. This first act subsequent to his conversion confirms his understanding of his conversion as a commission to preach the gospel among pagans."[6]

There is, however, another possibility for this journey. During Saul's conversion, his world was turned upside down. Every time I have

---

5. Murphy-O'Connor, *Paul: His Story*, 25.
6. Murphy-O'Connor, *Paul: A Critical Life*, 82.

read this portion of Galatians, I tend to ask myself: What was going on in the soul of Saul of Tarsus? What was he feeling? What kind of a conversion must this have been, in which he had to adjust his religious walk and talk 180 degrees—turn in the opposite direction than where he had been traveling? How must he have read the scriptures (the Old Testament) with new eyes? How does he fit Jesus of Nazareth into the role of the Messiah and the fulfillment of ancient prophecy?

Early in the twentieth century, Benjamin Willard Robinson of the Chicago Theological Seminary wrote that Paul "needed to adjust himself to his new situation, to think over the meaning of his call to Christian discipleship and missionary leadership. It would naturally require considerable time to formulate even in a general way the terms in which he might interpret the gospel of the Jewish Messiah to the nations of the empire."[7]

One of the most beloved Latter-day Saint biblical scholars was Professor Sidney B. Sperry at Brigham Young University. In offering his perspective on Paul's journey to Arabia, Dr. Sperry explained: "Saul's conversion was such an upsetting experience that he must have thought it necessary to seek retirement in a quiet place, think through his changed situation, and seek the spiritual instruction and uplift required for his coming mission to the Gentiles." While we cannot know many of the details of this one- to three-year period, "we can be sure that through prayer and meditation Saul came to peace with himself and his God in the desert place."[8]

PAUL VISITS JERUSALEM FOR A SHORT TIME (1:18–19)

After three years, Paul makes his way to Jerusalem, and there he meets with Peter and also James, the brother of the Lord. In suggesting what might have happened during those fifteen eventful days, Robert J. Matthews wrote:

---

7. Robinson, *Life of Paul*, 59.
8. Sperry, *Paul's Life and Letters*, 23–24.

The scriptures do not give us an account of what Saul talked about when he visited Peter and James. . . . We can only conjecture on what would have transpired between these brethren, but we conclude that in addition to discussing the scriptures and points of doctrine, Saul must have asked Peter many personal things about Jesus, and about events in the ministry that they shared for nearly three years. How thrilling to ask the chief Apostle about the time Jesus raised Lazarus from the dead, walked on the water, opened the eyes of one born blind . . . , suffered in the Garden of Gethsemane and visited with the eleven for forty days following his resurrection!

What an opportunity for Saul to ask James (the Lord's own half-brother) about Jesus as a boy, about Mary and Joseph and about other half brothers and sisters, as well as many other things that James would know firsthand![9]

PAUL REFERS TO THE JERUSALEM CONFERENCE (2:1–9)

The most detailed account of the extremely significant Jerusalem conference held in about AD 48–49 is written by Luke in Acts 15. But here, in the epistle to the Galatian Saints, Paul touches upon that gathering of Church leaders. He mentions specifically that fifteen years has passed since his conversion on the road to Damascus. Paul and Barnabas were either summoned to attend what came to be known as the Jerusalem conference, or, as intimated in verse 2, Paul may have been directed by revelation to be in attendance. Problems with the Judaizers or agitators—those Jewish Christians who felt the need, as baptized Christians, to hold to many of the tenets and practices of the law of Moses—continued to stir up the Saints and cause confusion among them.

Paul writes that he "communicated unto them that gospel which I

---

9. Matthews, *Unto All Nations*, 11–12.

preach among the Gentiles, but privately to them which were of reputation, lest by any means I should run, or had run, in vain" (verse 2). It appears that what Paul was doing was what we might term today as "setting his ducks all in a row"—communicating with Church leaders and prominent members of the Church before the conference began, informing them exactly what and how he had been preaching to the Gentiles. He would no doubt have explained to them that because many Gentile converts to the faith had not been a part of the Jewish tradition or culture, it was not necessary for male Gentile converts to be circumcised.

In his writings, the Apostle often uses key words to connote grander and broader concepts. For example, the word *cross* in reference to the Crucifixion of Jesus means more than simply the mode of torture and execution. It was a sign, a token, of the Savior's Atonement. To say that one believed in and taught the cross was to say that one accepted the reality of Jesus's suffering and death as having divine redemptive power. Similarly, in Paul's epistles the word *circumcision* conveys much more than the rite performed on eight-day-old male children or a token of the covenant given to Father Abraham. It connotes Jewishness, Judaism, and life under the law of Moses.

In verse 3, Paul makes a statement that might easily be misunderstood by students of the New Testament. He indicates that he and Barnabas took Titus with them to the conference, adding, interestingly, that he purposely did not have Titus circumcised. Using Titus as an illustration, Paul is emphasizing to the Church leaders that circumcision, like matters pertaining to the law of Moses, had been fulfilled and done away by Jesus Christ's atoning sacrifice. Thus it was no longer necessary for a male to be circumcised.

What complicates this picture, however, is what took place as Paul was about to begin his second missionary journey. First of all, Paul and Barnabas had a major disagreement—Barnabas wanted to have John Mark (who we know as Mark, the future author of the second Gospel) accompany them, but Paul was reluctant to do so since Mark had left the mission field early and returned home during the first mission (see Acts 13:13). Thus Barnabas and Mark decided to travel to Cyprus to preach the gospel, while Paul and Timothy, a convert from Lystra (see Acts 16:1–3), returned to strengthen the men and women whom he and Barnabas had brought into the Church on the first mission. Paul then took Timothy and had him circumcised before they left "because of the Jews which were in those quarters" (Acts 16:3), including Pamphylia, Antioch of Pisidia, Iconium, Lystra, and Derbe, all described in Acts 14. Paul sensed that if Timothy was not circumcised, the Jews they would encounter would be offended or would ignore them.

Is Paul being dishonest here? Duplicitous? Inconsistent? He insists that Titus *not* be circumcised but that Timothy *should* be circumcised. This seeming inconsistency was explained by one scholar who argued that Paul "saw a difference between *necessity and expediency*. With Titus it was an issue as to whether or not circumcision was essential to salvation. In this case Paul opposed it. With Timothy, it was a matter of rendering him acceptable to the non-Christian Jews in the vicinity of their mission. Paul was willing to allow circumcision as a concession, so that the Jews would be willing to listen to Timothy teach the gospel. This is an interesting and important distinction and reveals something of Paul's mind and method."[10]

In Galatians 2:4 we read: "But because of some pseudo-family members who had been secretly smuggled in, who came in on the side to spy on the freedom which we have in the Messiah, Jesus, so that they might bring us into slavery . . . I didn't yield authority to them, no, not for a moment, so that the truth of the gospel might be maintained in you" (KNT). Paul felt no pressure, in the presence of the Church's senior leadership, to dilute his message. He was straightforward and bold.

---

10. Matthews, *Unto All Nations*, 23.

Peter, James (the brother of the Lord), and John heard Paul's explanation of why he was conducting his missionary work as he did. It was agreed that while Peter (the senior Apostle within the Church) would oversee the preaching of the gospel of Jesus Christ to the Jews, Paul would oversee the preaching of the gospel to the Gentiles. "And when James, Cephas [i.e., Peter], and John, who seemed to be pillars, perceived the grace that was given unto me, they gave to me and Barnabas the right hands of fellowship; that we should go unto the heathen [i.e., Gentiles], and they [i.e., those under Peter's direction] unto the circumcision [i.e., Jews]" (verse 9).

PAUL CONFRONTS PETER (2:11–16)

Paul's letter continues by describing a later occasion when the Saints were gathered together in Antioch of Syria, a major missionary base for years, in what seems to be a kind of "dinner on the grounds." In the early stages of the meal, Peter sat and ate with the Gentile converts. When many of the Jewish Christians arrived, however, Peter left the table and went over and sat with the Jewish Christians. The scriptural account reads: "For before that certain came from James [who seems to be a significant leader among the Jewish Christians], he did eat with the Gentiles: but when they were come, he withdrew and separated himself, fearing them which were of the circumcision" (verse 12). Peter was in a very difficult position: he was trying to hold tenaciously onto the Jewish Christians, and it seems clear he was attempting to avoid a division within the Church of Jesus Christ. Paul, however, seems to have felt that Peter should have remained with the Gentile Christians.

Paul writes of his reaction to Peter's actions: "But when Peter was come to Antioch, I withstood him to the face, because he was to be blamed" (verse 11). Paul adds painfully that Barnabas also arose from the Gentile table and seated himself at the table of the Jews. In Paul's words, Barnabas "also was carried away with their dissimulation [hypocrisy]" (verse 13). The account continues, "But when I saw that they walked not uprightly according to the truth of the gospel, I said unto Peter before them all, If thou, being a Jew, livest after the manner of Gentiles, and not as do the Jews, why compellest thou the Gentiles to live as do the Jews?" (verse 14).

One study Bible describes this tender situation: "Interpreters differ in their explanations of this situation in this passage. One view is that the men who came from James (probably sent from the Jerusalem church by the Apostle James) encouraged Jewish Christians to eat separately and follow the kosher dietary laws. Peter decided to go along with this, perhaps not realizing that his example would make the Gentile Christians feel like second-class citizens in the church unless they followed Jewish dietary laws. . . . It implied that all Christians had to 'live like Jews' (verse 14) in order to be justified before God."[11]

What are we to make of this situation? The Prophet Joseph said simply: "Paul [was] contending with Peter face to face, with sound and irresistible arguments."[12] Elder Bruce R. McConkie wrote of this episode:

> Peter and Paul—both of whom were apostles, both of whom received revelations, saw angels, and were approved of the Lord, and both of whom shall inherit the fulness of the Father's kingdom—these same righteous and mighty preachers disagreed on a basic matter of church policy. Peter was the President of the Church; Paul, an apostle and Peter's junior in the church hierarchy, was subject to the direction of the chief apostle. But Paul was right and Peter was wrong. Paul stood firm, determined that they should walk "uprightly according to the truth of the gospel" [verse 14]; Peter temporized for fear of offending Jewish semi-converts who still kept the law of Moses.

---

11. *English Standard Version Study Bible*, 2247.
12. *Papers of Joseph Smith*, 2:117.

The issue was not whether the Gentiles should receive the gospel. Peter himself had received the revelation that God was no respecter of persons, and that those of all lineages were now to be heirs of salvation along with the Jews [Acts 10:34–35]. . . . Without question, if we had the full account, we would find Peter reversing himself and doing all in his power to get the Jewish saints to believe that the law of Moses was fulfilled in Christ and no longer applied to anyone either Jew or Gentile.[13]

DEAD TO THE LAW, ALIVE IN CHRIST (2:18–21)

Paul writes, "For if I build again the things which I destroyed, I make myself a transgressor" (verse 18). The Apostle understood very clearly that with the atoning sacrifice and Resurrection of the Son of God, the law of Moses had been fulfilled; the children of Israel—and certainly those who had come into the Church of Jesus Christ—were no longer required to observe the performances and ordinances of the law, for old things had passed away. The Saints of God were no longer to offer animal sacrifice, but now were to offer up to God a broken heart and a contrite spirit (see 3 Nephi 9:20). Paul could speak of the law in the past tense, for it was no longer a part of his social and religious life. In that sense the law had become dead to Paul. Nor should the law have continued to occupy the minds of those who had accepted the gospel of Jesus Christ. To return to that which had been done away and not make the necessary transition—of devoting oneself to the fullness of the gospel of Jesus Christ—was to be guilty of sin. As James explained: "Therefore to him that knoweth to do good, and doeth it not, to him it is sin" (James 4:17).

Paul continues, "I am crucified with Christ: nevertheless I live; yet not I, but Christ liveth in me: and the life which I now live in the flesh

---

13. McConkie, *Doctrinal New Testament Commentary,* 2:463–64.

I live by the faith of the Son of God, who loved me, and gave himself for me" (verse 20). This is a powerful and poignant verse of scripture. Every follower of Jesus Christ knows that the Lord came into the world *to die for us*. What is not so well known and appreciated is that He came also *to live in us*.

We live in a culture in which excellence and success and victory are drilled into us from the time we are old enough to take part in society. Words like *submission* and *surrender* are almost foreign to our way of life. But, in fact, submission is absolutely necessary if we are to be happy; surrender is vital if we are to be at peace. Christ invites His disciples to submit to Him, to have an eye single to His glory (Matthew 6:22; Doctrine and Covenants 88:67), and to yield their hearts unto Him (Helaman 3:35). Christ invites His disciples to surrender, to lay down their mortal weapons and acknowledge His Lordship. As we are able to trust in the Master—to trust in His way of life, His vision of what is best for us, His timetable—we begin to mature in our faith.

Without such trust in the Lord, without relinquishing our own stranglehold on life, we will probably either work ourselves into a frenzy of spiritual and physical exhaustion, or else find ourselves doing all the right things but feeling little pleasure in doing so. In short, we may find ourselves "going through the motions"—performing the appropriate labors but not enjoying them, doing the right things but having to force ourselves to do them—because we are trying to do good works against a will that has not been fully surrendered or spiritually transformed. Now it's always better to do the right thing, even for the wrong reason, than to do the wrong thing. There is a better and higher motivation, however—one that is above and beyond self-discipline, well beyond sheer willpower and dogged determination. It is a motivation borne of the Spirit, one that comes to us as a result of a change of heart.

Through the Atonement of Christ we can do more than enjoy a

change of behavior; we can have our *nature* changed. One Christian theologian, John Stott, explained:

> We may be quite sure that Christ-centeredness and Christ-likeness will never be attained by our own unaided efforts. How can self drive out self? As well expect Satan to drive out Satan! For *we are not interested in skin-deep holiness, in a merely external resemblance to Jesus Christ.* We are not satisfied by a superficial modification of behavior patterns in conformity to some Christian sub-culture which expects this, commands that and prohibits the other. No, *what we long for is a deep inward change of character, resulting from a change of nature and leading to a radical change of conduct.* In a word we want to be like Christ, and that thoroughly, profoundly, entirely. Nothing less than this will do.[14]

"I do not frustrate [i.e., nullify] the grace of God: for if righteousness come by the law, then Christ is dead in vain" (verse 21). It's as if Paul had written: "There's no way that I will treat lightly or ignore the grace of God—the divine strength and encouragement that come through accepting and striving to live the gospel of Jesus Christ. To treat lightly the gift we have been given is to act as though there was no Atonement made for me and all the children of God."

TRUE FOLLOWERS OF ABRAHAM (3:7–14)

Many of the Jews in Jesus's day prided themselves in being descendants of Abraham. They perceived their lineal descent from the Father of the Faithful as placing them above the Gentiles, the non-Israelite nations. Matthew recorded the following:

> Then went out to him [i.e., John the Baptist] Jerusalem, and all Judea, and all the region round about Jordan, and many

---

14. Stott, *Life in Christ*, 109.

were baptized of him in Jordan, confessing their sins. But when he saw many of the Pharisees and Sadducees come to his baptism, he said unto them, O, generation of vipers [i.e., crop of serpents]! Who hath warned you to flee from the wrath to come? . . . Repent, therefore, and bring forth fruits meet for repentance; and think not to say within yourselves, We are the children of Abraham, and we only have power to bring seed unto our father Abraham; for I say unto you that God is able of these stones to raise up children unto Abraham. (Matthew 3:31–33, 35–36, JST)

Referring to the words of John the Baptist, the Prophet Joseph Smith declared on one occasion: "Of these stony Gentiles," God is able to "raise up children of Abraham."[15]

"Know ye therefore," Paul teaches, "that *they which are of faith*"—meaning faith in the Lord Jesus Christ—"*the same are the children of Abraham*" (verse 7). I am reminded of the words of Nephi: "And now behold, my beloved brethren, I would speak unto you; for I, Nephi, would not suffer that ye should suppose that ye are more righteous than the Gentiles shall be. For behold, except ye shall keep the commandments of God ye shall all likewise perish; and because of the words which have been spoken ye need not suppose that the Gentiles are utterly destroyed. For behold, I say that unto you that *as many of the Gentiles as will repent are the covenant people of the Lord; and as many of the Jews as will not repent shall be cast off*." Now note this vital truth: "For *the Lord covenanteth with none save it be with them that repent and believe in his Son, who is the Holy One of Israel*" (2 Nephi 30:1–2). In other words, the children of Christ, those who have been born again and for whom Christ becomes the Father of their salvation (see Mosiah 5:7), are the true children of Abraham. As Paul declared to the Roman Saints, "They are not all Israel, which are of Israel" (Romans 9:6).

---

15. Joseph Smith, Journal, July 23, 1843; punctuation and spelling standardized.

Paul writes in verse 8, "And the scripture, foreseeing that God would justify the heathen through faith, preached before the gospel unto Abraham, saying, In thee shall all nations be blessed." Or as rendered in the New International Version, "*Scripture* foresaw that God would justify the Gentiles by faith, and *announced the gospel in advance to Abraham*: 'All nations will be blessed through you.'" Here we stumble upon a pearl of great price, a truth that is little understood in the Christian world. One of the brilliant gems of the Restoration, delivered through the Prophet Joseph Smith, is what might be called "Christ's eternal gospel": Christian prophets have declared Christian doctrine and administered Christian ordinances since the beginning of time.

We know from modern revelation that the gospel was first taught to Adam and Eve (Moses 5:4–8; 6:51–67); to Enoch (Moses 7:10–11, 45–56, 62, 65); to Noah (Moses 8:23–24); and to all the patriarchs and prophets who lived before the Son of Man came to earth. Joseph Smith taught that all the prophets held the Melchizedek Priesthood.[16] He also observed that "we cannot believe that the ancients in all ages were so ignorant of the system of heaven as many suppose, since all that were ever saved, were saved through the power of this great plan of redemption, as much before the coming of Christ as since; if not, God has had different plans in operation (if we may so express it), to bring men back to dwell with Himself; and this we cannot believe, since there has been no change in the constitution of man since he fell."[17]

Brother Joseph also pointed out that "according to Paul, the gospel was preached to Abraham. We would like to be informed in what name the gospel was then preached, whether it was in the name of Christ or some other name. If in any other name, was it the gospel? And if it was

---

16. Joseph Smith, in "Discourse, 5 January 1841, as Reported by William Clayton."
17. *Teachings of Presidents of the Church: Joseph Smith*, 48–49.

the gospel, and that preached in the name of Christ, had it any ordinances? If not, was it the gospel?"[18]

In scolding the Pharisees and Sadducees who gloried in their lineage, Jesus said: "Your father Abraham rejoiced to see my day: and he saw it, and was glad" (John 8:56). While there is no biblical source for this statement, we find the following in the Prophet's Bible translation: "And Abram said, Lord God, how wilt thou give me this land for an everlasting inheritance? And the Lord said, Though thou wast dead, yet am I not able to give it thee? And if thou shalt die, yet thou shalt possess it, for the day cometh, that the Son of Man shall live; but how can he live if he be not dead? he must first be quickened. And it came to pass, that *Abram looked forth and saw the days of the Son of Man, and was glad, and his soul found rest,* and he believed in the Lord; and the Lord counted it unto him for righteousness" (Genesis 15:9–12, JST).

Verse 13 of Galatians 3 sounds very much like 2 Corinthians 5:21: the Savior, who had never transgressed God's law Himself, became "sin for us." In Gethsemane and on Golgotha, He bowed beneath the unfathomable load of the sins and iniquities of all God's children. Verse 13 reads: "Christ hath redeemed us from the curse of the law, being made a curse for us: for it is written, Cursed is every one that hangeth on a tree [Deuteronomy 21:23]." Mormon taught that each person brings upon himself or herself the "curse" of unrighteousness (Alma 3:19), thereby forfeiting the sweet influence of God's sustaining Spirit. Because Jesus assumed our burdens during His passion, He thereby was "made a curse for us."

JESUS CHRIST: A FULFILLMENT OF THE ABRAHAMIC PROMISE (3:16–18)

The Abrahamic covenant consists of Jehovah's promises made to Abraham and his seed (posterity), contingent on their faithfulness.

---

18. Joseph Smith, in "Letter to the Church, circa March 1834"; punctuation standardized.

Abraham and his posterity were promised (1) the gospel; (2) the priesthood; (3) eternal life, and the continuation of his family into eternity; and (4) a land inheritance (Abraham 2:8–11, 19). These blessings are what scripture call "the promises made to the fathers," the fathers being Abraham, Isaac, and Jacob (Doctrine and Covenants 2:2; 27:10).

In verse 16, Paul suggests a slightly different application of the Abrahamic promises than that to which we are accustomed. He draws to our attention the fact that the promise God made to Abraham pertained to his *seed* (singular), not *seeds* (plural). He then explains that the "seed" to whom and through whom the promised blessings are to come is Jesus Christ. Jesus was a descendant of Judah, one of the twelve sons of Jacob of old. Jesus was entitled to those same blessings. And it is not difficult to recognize how all the nations of this earth are and will be blessed through the birth, life, teachings, ministry, atoning sufferings, and Resurrection of the principal descendant of Abraham—namely, the Son of Almighty God.

A SCHOOLMASTER TO BRING US TO CHRIST (3:19–25)

From the days of Adam until the time of Moses, a period of some 2,600 years, the only priesthood that existed was the Melchizedek Priesthood, or higher priesthood, which administers *the everlasting gospel* of Jesus Christ. Joseph Smith taught that all the ancient prophets held the Melchizedek Priesthood.[19] In the days of Moses, however, the children of Israel failed to live up to their spiritual privileges and fulfill their covenantal obligations. They chose not to enjoy the power of godliness in their midst (see Doctrine and Covenants 84:19–21) and refused to prepare themselves to come into the divine presence and thereby see the face of God (see Exodus 20:19). Therefore, Jehovah "took Moses out of their midst, and the Holy Priesthood also; and the lesser [or Aaronic] priesthood continued, which priesthood holdeth

---

19. Joseph Smith, in "Discourse, 5 January 1841, as Reported by William Clayton."

the key of the ministering of angels and *the preparatory gospel*; which gospel is the gospel of repentance and of baptism, and the remission of sins, and the law of carnal commandments, which the Lord in his wrath caused to continue with the house of Aaron among the children of Israel until John [the Baptist]" and the coming of the Savior to the earth (Doctrine and Covenants 84:25–27).

"When the Lord took Moses out of Israel," President Joseph Fielding Smith explained,

> he took the higher priesthood also and left Israel with the lesser priesthood which holds the keys to the temporal salvation of mankind—the temporal gospel—that which deals with repentance and baptism particularly, but does not have to do with the higher ordinances which have been revealed in the dispensation in which we live.
>
> Therefore, in Israel, the common people, the people generally, did not exercise the functions of priesthood in its fulness, but were confined in their labors and ministrations very largely to the Aaronic Priesthood. The withdrawal of the higher priesthood was from the people as a body, but the Lord still left among them men holding the Melchizedek Priesthood, with power to officiate in all its ordinances, so far as he determined that these ordinances should be granted unto the people.[20]

We all know the story of Moses ascending Mount Sinai and receiving the Ten Commandments. When, after forty days, the Lawgiver descended the mountain and found his people immersed in wickedness, he broke the set of tablets. From Joseph Smith's inspired translation of the Bible, we gain deeper insight into what the Lord had intended to give the Israelites but was prevented from doing when they proved unworthy of such transcendent blessings:

---

20. Joseph Fielding Smith, *Doctrines of Salvation*, 3:85.

And the Lord said unto Moses, Hew thee *two other tables of stone*, like unto the first, and I will write upon them also, the words of the law, according as they were written at the first on the tables which thou brakest; but *it shall not be according to the first, for I will take away the priesthood out of their midst; therefore my holy order, and the ordinances thereof, shall not go before them*; for my presence shall not go up in their midst, lest I destroy them.

But I will give unto them the law as at the first, but *it shall be after the law of a carnal commandment*; for I have sworn in my wrath, that *they shall not enter into my presence, into my rest*, in the days of their pilgrimage. (Exodus 34:1–2, JST; compare Deuteronomy 10:1–2, JST)

The law of Moses consisted of strict dietary laws, health laws, and laws of reparation, equity, and justice. Abinadi taught the wicked priests of King Noah that "it was expedient that there should be a law given to the children of Israel, yea, even a very strict law; for they were a stiffnecked people, quick to do iniquity, and slow to remember the Lord their God; therefore there was a law given them, yea, a law of performances and of ordinances, a law which they were to observe strictly from day to day, to keep them in remembrance of God and their duty towards him" (Mosiah 13:29–30; compare 2 Nephi 25:30).

Professor Andrew C. Skinner has written that the law of Moses

> was a comprehensive religious and legal system revealed to the prophet-lawgiver-deliverer on Mount Sinai. It replaced, for a time, the higher law and fulness of the gospel that had operated from Adam to Moses and that the Lord had intended to reconfirm to Israel after their Egyptian sojourn had ended. But because Israel kept rebelling against sacred things, including the requirements of the higher law, the law of Moses, or

lesser law, was "added because of transgressions," as Paul taught (Galatians 3:19). . . .

Besides prescribing moral, ethical, and physical behavior, the law of Moses contained an elaborate system of sacrifices that included animals, grains, and other commodities (Leviticus 1–7). These were to remind the Israelites of their duties to God and to point them to the great and last sacrifice of Jesus Christ, which ended sacrifice by the shedding of blood.[21]

Paul wrote that the law was a "schoolmaster to bring us unto Christ, that we might be justified by faith. But after that faith is come [i.e., after Christ had come], we are no longer under a schoolmaster" (verses 24–25). The word translated here as "schoolmaster" is *pedagogue*, which means director or supervisor of children, perhaps even a babysitter. One of the many qualities of our Father in Heaven is that He never gives to individuals or whole nations what they are not prepared to receive. Isaiah and Nephi described this as learning line upon line, precept upon precept, here a little and there a little (Isaiah 28:13; 2 Nephi 28:30). He who is omnipotent is also omniscient; He knows all things, including what we have the capacity to bear and what we are prepared to receive. Had the ancient Israelites been given the fullness of the blessings of the priesthood and the everlasting gospel in the days of Moses, it would have proven far more harmful to them than helpful.

It is important to understand that the law of Moses "was a higher and more perfect order of worship than any system of worship other than the fulness of the everlasting gospel. . . . *Those who lived the law of Moses had revelation, were led by prophets, held the priesthood, and did the things that started them in the direction of the celestial kingdom.* . . . Theologically speaking, *those who received and lived the law of Moses might be said to have been walking in a celestial course, to have*

---

21. "Law of Moses," in Millet, Olson, Skinner, and Top, *LDS Beliefs*, 378, 380.

been taking some of the initial steps leading to eternal life, to have been preparing themselves for that eternal fulness out of which eternal life comes."[22]

TRUE CHILDREN OF GOD PUT ON CHRIST (3:26–29)

In the opening chapter of His Gospel, John the Beloved wrote of the Lamb of God: "He came unto his own [i.e., the Jews], and his own received him not. But as many as received him, to them gave he power to become the [children] of God, even to them that believe on his name" (John 1:11–12). The spirit children of God become the children of God by redemption, by the transforming power of the gospel. They become part of the royal family of God. This is why Paul writes to the Galatians that "ye are all the children of God by faith in Christ Jesus" (verse 26). Paul adds that "as many of you as have been baptized into Christ have put on Christ" (verse 27). An angel explained to King Benjamin that "the natural man is an enemy of God, and has been from the fall of Adam, and will be, forever and ever, unless he yields to the enticings of the Holy Spirit, and *putteth off the natural man* and becometh a saint through the atonement of Christ the Lord" (Mosiah 3:19).

When we put off the natural man or the natural woman, we put on Christ—we take His name, we seek to live worthy of that holy name, and we strive to emulate Him. King Benjamin commended his people who had covenanted to keep the commandments the remainder of their days: "And now, because of the covenant which ye have made ye shall be called the children of Christ, his sons, and his daughters; for behold, this day he hath spiritually begotten you; for ye say that your hearts are changed through faith on his name; therefore, ye are born of him and have become his sons and his daughters" (Mosiah 5:7). Paul also alluded to putting on Christ in Romans 6:3–6; 13:14.

---

22. McConkie, *Mortal Messiah* 1:71–72.

In verse 28, Paul writes of the leveling effect of the gospel of Jesus Christ—it breaks down barriers between people and dissolves walls that society has erected on the basis of gender, wealth, education level, popularity, and all other worldly measures of success or prominence. "There is neither Jew nor Greek, there is neither bond nor free, there is neither male nor female: for ye are all one in Christ Jesus." And then Paul repeats that true children of Abraham are children of Christ (verse 29).

SONS, DAUGHTERS, AND HEIRS (4:1–7)

Robert Matthews related to me an experience he once had as a young man during the summer. He went to work for a rancher and soon learned, more than he had understood before, that successful ranches require long and exhausting hours of work. He noted that during the day all of the hired hands and sons of the owner worked together, side by side, and there was no difference in the intensity of the workload between the hirelings and the sons of the rancher. Brother Matthews then spoke, however, of what happened at dinnertime. The members of the family went into the home to have a large, many-course meal and rested for a time in comfortable chairs or took a power nap on their beds. The hirelings, on the other hand, found a place in the shade and ate the meager sandwiches that had been provided by the mother of the house. After dinner the family workers showered and enjoyed a pleasant evening sitting around the fireplace. The hirelings, however, found their way to the barn, where they slept on thin and uncomfortable mattresses. This story dramatizes the difference between the treatment of the family members and that of the hired laborers.

In the opening verses of chapter 4, Paul teaches by contrast. He points out that there is a genuine difference between the lives of those who live without the gospel fullness—who are not members of the family of God and thus live "without God in the world" (Alma 41:11)—and the lives of those who have been adopted into the divine family through the atoning work of Jesus Christ, the cleansing powers of the Holy Spirit, and the covenants and ordinances of the gospel. Those who lived their lives under the law of Moses were like children who needed to be carefully watched over, kept busy, and babysat. But when Christ came and offered Himself as a ransom for our sins, the law was fulfilled in Him. He "redeem[ed] them that were under the law, that we might receive the adoption of sons [and daughters]. And because ye are sons [and daughters], God hath sent forth the Spirit of his Son into your hearts, crying, Abba, Father. Wherefore thou art no more a servant, but a son [and daughter]; and if a son [or daughter], then an heir of God through Christ" (verses 5–7).

Those who are born again, who are born from above or undergo what the scriptures call "a mighty change" of heart (Mosiah 5:2; Alma 5:14), draw closer to the Father and Son. As they strive to cultivate and maintain the constant companionship of the Holy Ghost in their daily walk and talk, they are gradually "transformed by the renewing of [their] mind" (Romans 12:2). They gain what Paul referred to as "the mind of Christ" (1 Corinthians 2:16). They are close with the members of the Godhead, such that they can cry out to the Father of their spirits, "Abba." *Abba* is the Aramaic word for "Father," a word that implies the adoption of these individuals as sons or daughters. *Abba* implies an intimacy like that enjoyed by family members who love each other. Some New Testament scholars agree that while *Abba* does mean "Father," the word could imply something even more intimate, like "Papa" or "Daddy."[23]

KNOWING GOD AND BEING KNOWN BY HIM (4:9)

One of the imposing challenges we face in this enlightened age is to get the gospel from our minds to our hearts, to seek for and allow the power of the blood of Christ to transform us into men and women

---

23. See Freedman, *Anchor Bible Dictionary*, 1:3.

who *do* what we say and, more important, who *are* what we say. For far too many, the gospel of Jesus Christ has yet to begin the arduous journey from the head to the heart. To be sure, each of us lives well beneath our spiritual privileges; every one of us finds some gap between our ideals and our actions. We are not speaking, however, of striving and then falling short; rather, we are addressing the far more serious concern of hypocrisy, of being purveyors but not practitioners of the word.

Only those who do the will of the Father will enter the kingdom of God (Matthew 7:21); we learn something of the context from the Joseph Smith Translation: "For the day soon cometh, that men shall come before me to judgment, to be judged according to their works" (Matthew 7:31, JST). Continuing from the King James Version: "Many will say to me in that day [i.e., the Day of Judgment], Lord, Lord, have we not prophesied in thy name? and in thy name have cast out devils? and in thy name done many wonderful works? And then will I profess unto them, I never knew you: depart from me, ye that work iniquity" (Matthew 7:22–23). It is almost as though our Lord is addressing two sides of the same coin. On the one side, only those who do the works of the Father have any hope of salvation in His kingdom (Matthew 7:21). On the other side, clearly the performance of works alone will not open the gates of heaven (Matthew 7:22). Why? Because even though certain persons—*many* persons, in the language of Christ—prophesy, exorcise demons, and otherwise perform "many wonderful works"—the Lord and Redeemer, serving in His capacity as the ultimate judge and the Keeper of the Gate (John 3:35; 5:22; 2 Nephi 9:41)—*does not know them.*

Is this a matter of visual or cognitive recognition? Hardly. Has Jesus simply forgotten their identity? Surely not. He remembers only too well. In fact, what He remembers is what many will wish He would forget. Notably, the Joseph Smith Translation of this passage alters the King James Version: "And then will I say, *Ye never knew me*; depart from me ye that work iniquity" (Matthew 7:33, JST).

Returning to the epistle to the Galatians, in verse 9 of chapter 4, Paul writes, "But now, after that ye have known God, or rather are known of God, how turn ye again to the weak and beggarly elements, whereunto ye desire again to be in bondage?" Another translation reads, "But now that you've come to know God—or, better, to be known by God—how can you turn back again to that weak and poverty-stricken lineup of elements that you want to serve all over again?" (KNT). In other words, "How is it possible that you have received the gospel of Jesus Christ and have come to know God (and He has come to know you) and yet you can forsake the liberty found in the gospel of Christ and return to the burdensome focus and tiresome emphasis on the ceremonial ordinances within the Mosaic law?"

PAUL'S INFIRMITY OF THE FLESH (4:13–15)

Paul here references his "infirmity of the flesh" and expresses appreciation to the Galatian Saints that they did not find him to be off-putting. "And my temptation which was in my flesh ye despised not" (verse 14). The word translated here as "temptation" could also be rendered as "weakness" or "feebleness." As mentioned in our consideration of 2 Corinthians 12:7, no one knows for certain what Paul's infirmity, his "messenger of Satan to buffet me," really was. A growing number of scholars believe that Paul had serious problems with his eyes or that there was something about his appearance that led listeners to remark that "his letters . . . are weighty and powerful; but *his bodily presence is weak*, and his speech contemptible" (2 Corinthians 10:10).

Paul expresses how consoling it was that the Galatians "received [him] as an angel of God, even as Christ Jesus" (verse 14). Or, "Even though my illness was a trial to you, you did not treat me with contempt or scorn. Instead, you welcomed me as if I were an angel of God, as if I were Christ Jesus himself" (NIV). Notice what follows in verse 15: "I bear you record, that, if it had been possible, *ye would have plucked out your own eyes, and have given them to me.*"

As Paul draws near the close of his letter, he states: "Ye see *how large a letter I have written* unto you with mine own hand" (Galatians 6:11). A cursory reading of Galatians might cause a person unfamiliar with the Pauline epistles to conclude it was a very long letter. But we can see, by comparing it with Romans, 1 Corinthians, or Hebrews, that it is extremely short. Well then, what would Paul mean? Here are a couple of alternate translations:

> See what large letters I make when I am writing in my own hand. (NRSV)

> Look how big the letters are, now that I am writing to you in my own hand. (REB)

Those who subscribe to the idea that Paul had serious challenges with his eyes might conclude that he is writing with large letters simply because he has poor eyesight. It would seem reasonable to suppose that up to now a scribe had been doing the writing, but at this point Paul assumes the scribal responsibility.

CHRIST IS FORMED IN US (4:19)

President Howard W. Hunter said in a Christmas message:

> Paul expressed himself as suffering pain and anxiety until Christ "formed" in them. *This is another way of saying "in Christ,"* as that expression is used by Paul repeatedly in his writings.
>
> It is possible for Christ to be born in men's lives, and when such an experience actually happens, a man is "in Christ"—Christ is "formed" in him. *This presupposes that we take Christ into our hearts and make him the living contemporary of our lives. He is not just a general truth or a fact in history but also the Savior of men everywhere and at all times.* When we strive to be Christlike, he is "formed" in us; if we open the door, he will

enter; if we seek his counsel, he will counsel us. For Christ to be "formed" in us, we must have a belief in him and his atonement. Such a belief in Christ, and the keeping of his commandments, are not restraints upon us. By these, men are set free. This Prince of Peace wants to give peace of mind which may make each of us a channel of that peace.

The real Christmas comes to him who has taken Christ into his life as a moving, dynamic, vitalizing force. The real spirit of Christmas lies in the life and mission of the Master.[24]

"CHILDREN OF PROMISE" (4:21–31)

Continuing to focus on the liberty to be found in Jesus versus the bondage to be found under the law of Moses, Paul develops an analogy. He mentions that Abraham had two sons, Ishmael and Isaac. The first was born of a bondwoman (Hagar, Sarah's handmaiden), and the second was born of a freewoman (Sarah). The one born to a bondwoman, Ishmael, was born "after the flesh," meaning born to be a slave, which brought no special status for Ishmael. The one born to a freewoman, Isaac, was the son of promise, the one through whom the supernal covenant made with Father Abraham would be perpetuated. Paul then likens the two women to two covenants—Hagar (or Ishmael) is linked with Mount Sinai in Arabia, while Sarah (or Isaac) is linked with the heavenly Jerusalem. Paul then reminds his Christian followers that "we are not children of the bondwoman [i.e., a slave], but of the free [i.e., of Sarah]" (verse 31).

CIRCUMCISION PROFITS NOTHING (5:1–12)

Having had the covenant explained to him, Abraham was instructed that male infants were to be circumcised on the eighth day after their birth. The Joseph Smith Translation adds important insight

---

24. Hunter, *"Real Christmas,"* 4–5.

regarding circumcision: male infants were to be circumcised on the eighth day following their birth to remind parents that children are not accountable for their sins until they are eight years old (Genesis 17:11–12, JST). This significant teaching regarding children and accountability is confirmed in modern revelation (see Doctrine and Covenants 68:25–26, 28).

Abraham received the directive to circumcise male children in about 1800 BC, while the law of Moses was given to the Israelites some four hundred years later, during the time of Moses. Faithful Christians understood, however, that in addition to the law of Moses, the law of circumcision was done away with after the Savior made His atoning sacrifice and later rose from the dead. In the Western Hemisphere, some four centuries after the Savior's mortal ministry, a falsehood arose among some of the Nephites—that infants needed to be baptized. Mormon, the great prophet and military leader at the time, inquired of the Lord concerning the matter. The word came to Mormon as follows: "Listen to the words of Christ, your Redeemer, your Lord and your God. Behold, I came into the world not to call the righteous but sinners to repentance; the whole need no physician, but they that are sick; wherefore, little children are whole, for they are not capable of committing sin; wherefore the curse of Adam is taken from them in me, that it hath no power over them; and *the law of circumcision is done away in me*" (Moroni 8:8; compare Doctrine and Covenants 74:1–7).

In the Old World, Paul understood that circumcision, like the law of Moses, was to come to an end after the great and last sacrifice was offered by the Lamb of God. This is why he labored and preached so tirelessly that circumcision was no longer required of Christian converts, whether they be Jews or Gentiles: "For in Jesus Christ neither circumcision availeth any thing, nor uncircumcision; but faith which worketh by love" (verse 6).

Paul then writes, no doubt, with much emotion and with great weariness from teaching these things to the people: "I would they were even cut off which trouble you" (verse 12). Most Latter-day Saints would be prone to read this verse and suppose that Paul is recommending that the Judaizers or agitators be excommunicated from the Church, which would be perfectly appropriate since they had for some time been spreading false doctrine among members of the Church. Actually, however, Paul's language is even stronger. What he is really proposing is that the Judaizers should all castrate or emasculate themselves! (see ESV, NRSV, REB, NIV).

Paul writes in verse 2 that "if ye be circumcised, Christ shall profit you nothing." That is, "If you still feel compelled to focus on who is circumcised and who is not, or to cling to the law of Moses, then the atoning mission of Jesus Christ can do you little good." Paul then adds: "For I testify again to every man that is circumcised, that he is a debtor to do the whole law" (verse 3). It's as though Paul is teaching, "If you choose to hold to one practice that has, like the law of Moses, been done away, you might as well accept and abide by all of the law, including the dietary laws, the laws of purification, the extensive system of sacrifices and offerings, and, of course, the 613 commandments, together with the heavy burden and frustration that come with seeking to do the impossible." This sentiment is similar to the teaching of James, the Lord's brother (see James 2:10; compare Galatians 3:10).

LOVE: THE FULFILLMENT OF THE LAW (5:14)

A lawyer once approached Jesus and asked, "Master, which is the great commandment in the law?" Our Lord then replied that the first and great commandment is to love God with all our heart, soul, and mind. He then added, "And the second is like unto it, Thou shalt love thy neighbour as thyself." Christ then summarized the matter: "On these two commandments hang all the law and the prophets" (Matthew 22:35–40). Paul will later write to the Romans that the commands against adultery, murder, theft, lying, and coveting are "comprehended in this saying, namely, Thou shalt love thy neighbour as thyself" (Romans 13:9; compare Leviticus 19:18). James, the brother of Jesus, wrote: "If ye fulfil *the royal law* according to the scripture, Thou shalt love thy neighbour as thyself, ye do well" (James 2:8).

Indeed, one can only imagine the kind of world we would live in if all people truly loved God and their fellow mortals. The absence of this love is why many in today's world long for the Savior's Second Coming, since that advent will initiate a thousand years of peace and joy. In a modern revelation the Lord declared: "Wherefore, labor ye, labor ye in my vineyard for the last time—for the last time call upon the inhabitants of the earth. For in mine own due time will I come upon the earth in judgment, and my people shall be redeemed and shall reign with me on earth. For the great Millennium, of which I have spoken by the mouth of my servants, shall come. For Satan shall be bound" (Doctrine and Covenants 43:28–31).

WORKS OF THE FLESH, FRUIT OF THE SPIRIT (5:19–25)

Paul begins to teach by contrast. He first refers to what he calls "the works of the flesh" (verse 19). The works of the flesh are those character traits and attributes that characterize a man or a woman who has not been changed by the cleansing power of the blood of Christ and the work of the Holy Spirit. These kinds of attitudes and behaviors simply flow naturally from an unredeemed soul. They are what most natural men and women reflect and do. Paul adds that "they which do such things shall not inherit the kingdom of God" (verses 19–21). He then speaks of the "fruit of the Spirit"—namely, those character traits and attributes that flow from the heart of a person who has enjoyed the redeeming and refining power of the Savior's Atonement.

Paul does not refer to the *fruits* of the Spirit (plural) but rather the *fruit* of the Spirit (singular). One Pauline scholar offered a possible explanation: Paul

> speaks of *fruit* singular, not "fruits." This suggests the unity and unifying nature of these qualities, as opposed to the division

and discord produced by works of the flesh. The singular also suggests that all these qualities should be manifest in any Christian's life. The term *fruit* also suggests that *we are not talking about natural virtues or personal attainments but character traits wrought in the believer's life by the work of the Spirit.* Believers must work out these qualities in their social interactions, but the Spirit is their source.

Love is the signature Christian quality to which Paul refers here, as in 1 Corinthians 13. Romans 5:5 makes abundantly clear he is not talking about natural human feelings but rather about *love poured into the hearts of believers by the Spirit.*[25]

Verse 25 is a summarizing sermon of its own: "If we live in the Spirit, let us also walk in the Spirit." To put this another way, we as Christians need to walk the walk and not just talk the talk. We need to be what we claim to be. If we were to be arrested for being a follower of Jesus Christ, there needs to be enough evidence, in the way we live, to convict us.

LIFTING THOSE WHO HAVE FALLEN (6:1–2)

The first verse of chapter 6 reads: "Brethren [and sisters], if a [person] be overtaken in a fault [i.e., transgression, trespass], ye which are spiritual, restore such an one in the spirit of meekness; considering thyself, lest thou also be tempted." The Revised English Bible renders the verse this way: "If anyone is caught doing something wrong, you, my friends, who live by the Spirit must gently set him right. Look to yourself, each one of you: you also may be tempted." Underlying this charge to the Christian disciple is the implied idea that we must be in a spiritual condition to be able to lift another person. "*You cannot lift another soul,*" President Harold B. Lee taught, "*until you are standing on higher ground than he is.* You must be sure, if you would rescue the

---

25. Witherington, *Paul Quest*, 85.

man, that you yourself are setting the example of what you would have him be. *You cannot light a fire in another soul unless it is burning in your own soul.*"[26]

When I read the second part of verse 1—"considering thyself, lest thou also be tempted"—there comes to mind two closely related ideas. The first is the need of the lifter to be careful, cautious, and safe, for we are not invulnerable; we can fall just as quickly as the man or woman who needs lifting. No mortal ever reaches the point in life where he or she does not need to be vigilant, ever aware of temptation, always on guard against that insane insomniac whose mission is to destroy the souls of men and women and thwart the plan of God our Father. The second idea that comes to my mind is that we need to be charitable to the one who has fallen, both in our feelings as well as our actions. We dare not be judgmental of the fallen one. Why? Because "there but by the grace of God go I." This is but one of many ways followers of the Prince of Peace can "bear . . . one another's burdens, and so fulfil the law of Christ" (verse 2; compare Mosiah 18:8–9).

THE LAW OF THE HARVEST (6:7–8)

Few New Testament passages are as well known and oft quoted as verses 7 and 8. "Be not deceived," Paul writes. "God is not mocked: for whatsoever a man soweth, that shall he also reap. For he that soweth to his flesh shall of the flesh reap corruption; but he that soweth to the Spirit shall of the Spirit reap life everlasting." The farmer cannot reasonably expect to sow slightly and reap bountifully. The student cannot expect to ignore assignments or skip exams and continually receive A's. And the member of the Church of Jesus Christ cannot expect to sleep in on the Sabbath, consistently miss church meetings, avoid scripture study, and, at the same time, grow spiritually. No one of us can live a worldly, telestial life and expect to be rewarded with celestial glory in

---

26. Lee, "Stand Ye in Holy Places."

the Resurrection. This potent principle is taught also in the Book of Mormon, but there it is called the law of restoration (see Alma 41:3–4, 10–11).

A similar principle is taught in a modern revelation that Joseph Smith called the "Olive Leaf." Here we are told that those who are quickened, or made alive by a portion of celestial glory in this life, will in the Resurrection receive a fullness of that glory. Those who are quickened by a portion of terrestrial or telestial glory in this life—that is, who lived either a terrestrial or telestial life—will receive a fullness of the same glory in the Resurrection (Doctrine and Covenants 88:28–31).

"BE NOT WEARY IN WELL DOING"
(6:9–10; COMPARE 2 THESSALONIANS 3:13)

Sometimes it's hard to keep going. Once in a while we feel as if we're spinning our wheels and going nowhere. The Saints of God are not spared moments of discouragement, periods of disillusionment, or seasons of deep frustration. We often try so hard to do what's right and live our religion, but things are definitely not always what they need to be. There are Latter-day Saint parents who have always tried their best to be faithful to their temple covenants; to have regular family prayer, home evening, and scripture study; and to be valiant in their testimony of Jesus and dependable in their service in the kingdom—but whose children have strayed from the faith and even chosen to break their ties with religion in any form. There are husbands and wives whose partners have been unfaithful and sinned against their covenants and left the faith. These faithful parents often must rear children all on their own, work long hours at a job that does not quite cover the bills, and sit in sacrament meeting alone, amid happy families who seem to have it all together. In summary, we live in a fallen, telestial world in which bad things happen to very good people all the time. The expression "and they lived happily ever after" generally does not pertain to mortality; that blessing will not be fully enjoyed until the next life.

Jesus Christ came to bring beauty for ashes (Isaiah 61:1–3)—to replace distress with comfort, worry with peace, turmoil with rest. Things do not always turn out as we expect, and today is often not the day we bargained for. "Every one of us," Elder Jeffrey R. Holland pointed out,

> has times when we need to know things will get better. The Book of Mormon speaks of this as "hope for a better world" (Ether 12:4). For emotional health and spiritual stamina, everyone needs to be able to look forward to some respite, to do something pleasant and renewing and hopeful, whether that blessing be near at hand or still some distance ahead. . . .
>
> My declaration is that this is precisely what the gospel of Jesus Christ offers us, especially in times of need. There *is* help. There *is* happiness. There really *is* light at the end of the tunnel. It is the Light of the World. . . . I say: Hold on. Keep trying. God loves you. Things will improve. Christ comes to you in his "more excellent ministry" with a future of "better promises."[27]

During times of extreme stress and distress or days of worry and deep anxiety—many disciples of Christ have found great comfort, peace, and perspective through singing or reflecting on the words of sacred music. For example,

> *Be still, my soul: The Lord is on thy side;*
> *With patience bear thy cross of grief or pain.*
> *Leave to thy God to order and provide;*
> *In ev'ry change he faithful will remain.*
> *Be still my soul: Thy best, thy heav'nly Friend*
> *Thru thorny ways leads to a joyful end.*

---

27. Holland, "High Priest of Good Things to Come."

> *Be still my soul: Thy God doth undertake*
> *To guide the future as he has the past.*
> *Thy hope, thy confidence let nothing shake;*
> *All now mysterious shall be bright at last.*
> *Be still, my soul: The waves and winds still know*
> *His voice who ruled them while he dwelt below.*
>
> *Be still, my soul: The hour is hast'ning on*
> *When we shall be forever with the Lord,*
> *When disappointment, grief, and fear are gone,*
> *Sorrow forgot, love's purest joys restored.*
> *Be still, my soul: When change and tears are past,*
> *All safe and blessed we shall meet at last.*[28]

We need not be free from turmoil or sorrow in order to be at rest in today's world. Like Nephi, we need not know the meaning of all things to know that the Savior loves us (see 1 Nephi 11:17) and that He can strengthen us to bear heavy burdens with relative ease. God may not always remove our burdensome and toilsome circumstances, but He will empower us to deal responsibly with and even change the circumstances. President Russell M. Nelson taught a profound truth: "The joy we feel has little to do with the circumstances of our lives and everything to do with the focus of our lives. When the focus of our lives is on God's plan of salvation . . . and Jesus Christ and His gospel, we can feel joy regardless of what is happening—or not happening—in our lives. Joy comes from and because of Him. . . . For Latter-day Saints, Jesus Christ is joy."[29]

Revelation 7:13–17 reads:

> And one of the elders answered, saying unto me, What are these [people who] are arrayed in white robes? and whence

---

28. "Be Still, My Soul," *Hymns*, no. 124.
29. Nelson, "Joy and Spiritual Survival."

came they? And I said unto him, Sir, thou knowest. And he said to me, *These are they which came out of great tribulation, and have washed their robes, and made them white in the blood of the Lamb*. Therefore are they before the throne of God, and serve him day and night in his temple: and he that sitteth on the throne shall dwell among them. *They shall hunger no more, neither thirst any more*; neither shall the sun light on them, nor any heat. For the Lamb which is in the midst of the throne shall feed them, and shall lead them unto living fountains of waters: and God shall wipe away all tears from their eyes.

DOING GOOD TO ALL (6:10)

The Galatians are counseled to "do good unto all men, especially unto them who are of the household of faith." It has wisely been said that service to all of our brothers and sisters is the price we pay to live on this earth. We are all children of the same God. People throughout the earth are our spirit brothers and sisters. In a significant address delivered at the University of Southern California, Elder Dieter F. Uchtdorf stated: "The effort to throw off traditions of distrust and pettiness and truly see one another with new eyes—to see each other not as aliens or adversaries but as fellow travelers, brothers and sisters, and children of God—is one of the most challenging while at the same time most rewarding and ennobling experiences of our human existence."[30]

This should especially be the case when we interact with those who have accepted the message of the restored gospel and come into The Church of Jesus Christ of Latter-day Saints. We have things in common with each other that those not of our faith do not understand. We have the same perspective toward God, our Eternal Father; His Son, Jesus Christ; and the Father's plan of salvation. We know where we were before we were born, why we are here on the earth, and where we

---

30. Uchtdorf, "Fellow Travelers, Brothers and Sisters, Children of God."

will go after we die. And we delight in the words of the Prophet of the Restoration, who taught, "When the Savior shall appear we shall see him as he is. We shall see that he is a man like ourselves. And that same sociality which exists among us here will exist among us there, only it will be coupled with eternal glory, which glory we do not now enjoy" (Doctrine and Covenants 130:1–2).

Brother Joseph wrote from Liberty Jail: "There is a love from God that should be exercised toward those of our faith, who walk uprightly, which is peculiar to itself, but *it is without prejudice; it gives scope to the mind, which enables us to conduct ourselves with greater liberality towards all that are not of our faith, than what they exercise towards one another.* These principles approximate nearer to the mind of God, because [they are] like God, or Godlike."[31]

GLORYING IN THE CROSS (6:14–17)

In these verses we get a glimpse into the heart of perhaps the greatest missionary in Christian history, a person who had every right to feel proud of his accomplishments, perhaps even to boast now and then. Saul of Tarsus had come so very far. He had undergone a major transformation—from persecutor to prophet, from enemy of the Saints to beloved "father" of those whom he had "begotten . . . through the gospel" (1 Corinthians 4:15). Paul the Apostle had accomplished so much, and yet even the idea of boasting of his spiritual achievements was repugnant to his soul.

Indeed, there was only one matter about which Paul felt motivated, compelled, even driven, to boast. "God forbid that I should glory, *save in the cross of our Lord Jesus Christ,* by whom the world is crucified unto me, and I unto the world" (verse 14). Paul boasts of the cross of Christ in the sense that he rejoices and glories in the atoning sacrifice and Resurrection of the Son of God. For the Apostle to write that the

---

31. Joseph Smith, in "Letter to Edward Partridge and the Church, circa 22 March 1839"; punctuation and spelling standardized.

world is "crucified unto him" is to declare boldly that, as far as he is concerned, the sin, corruption, and gross evil in the world were "dead to him"; they had no pull or influence over him. To say that he was crucified unto the world is to repeat what he said earlier in this epistle: "I am crucified with Christ: nevertheless I live; yet not I, but Christ liveth in me" (Galatians 2:20). Paul has died as to the things of the world and been born anew—"born of God, changed from [his] carnal and fallen state, to a state of righteousness, being redeemed of God, becoming his [son]." He has become a "new creature" in Christ (Mosiah 27:25–26; compare 2 Corinthians 5:16–17).

Isaac Watts (1674–1748) penned one of the most beautiful and soul-stirring hymns ever written, no doubt with Galatians 6:14 in mind:

> *When I survey the wond'rous Cross*
> *On which the Prince of Glory died,*
> *My richest gain I count but Loss,*
> *And pour contempt on all my Pride.*
>
> *Forbid it, Lord, that I should boast,*
> *Save in the death of Christ my God:*
> *All the vain things that charm me most,*
> *I sacrifice them to his Blood.*
>
> *See from his Head, his Hands, his Feet,*
> *Sorrow and love flow mingled down!*
> *Did ever such love and sorrow meet?*
> *Or thorns compose so rich a crown?*
>
> *His dying crimson, like a robe,*
> *Spreads o'er his body on the tree;*
> *Then am I dead to all the globe,*
> *And all the globe is dead to me.*
>
> *Were the whole realm of nature mine,*

> *That were a present far too small;*
> *Love so amazing, so divine,*
> *Demands my soul, my life, my all.*[32]

Paul then makes it clear that in the long run, from the perspective of eternity, neither circumcision nor uncircumcision matters one iota. What truly matters, he says, is "a new creature" (verse 15). People within the Christian fold should cease wrangling over whether a person has or has not been circumcised. It doesn't matter! What really matters is whether women and men are accepting the message of the gospel of Jesus Christ; taking full advantage of the Savior's cleansing blood; seeking for, cultivating, and maintaining the constant companionship of the Holy Spirit; and being changed, born again, and renewed, thereby becoming a son or daughter of the Lord Jesus Christ, who is the Father of our salvation (see Mosiah 5:7–8; 27:25–26).

Paul closes his testimony by writing that "I bear in my body the marks of the Lord Jesus" (verse 17). "The scars in Paul's flesh . . . testified of his steadfastness in the face of persecution (2 Corinthians 11:23–27)." Truly, the scars in his flesh were "the holy symbols typifying faith in Christ and his gospel, which are borne by all the faithful."[33]

---

32. *Cokesbury Worship Hymnal*, no. 32.
33. McConkie, *Doctrinal New Testament Commentary*, 2:487.

THE EPISTLE TO THE EPHESIANS

This epistle was written from Rome during Paul's first Roman imprisonment, around AD 60–62. "The cities on the western coast of Asia Minor," Richard Lloyd Anderson wrote, "were heavily Greek because of earlier migrations across the Aegean, and they were wealthy both in money and religious tradition. On his third mission, Paul picked populous Ephesus as the hub for spreading the gospel through the province of Asia. . . . The population of Ephesus at that time was as large as a quarter of a million."[1]

CALLED AND ELECTED IN HEAVENLY PLACES (1:3–8)

In our first estate, our premortal existence, all of the spirit children of God were taught the plan of salvation, the Father's great plan of happiness. We understood then that each of us would have the opportunity to come to earth and take upon us a wondrous physical body. In doing so, our spirits would be added upon (Abraham 3:26), and we would take a step in our eternal quest to become like our exalted Heavenly Father, a Man of Holiness (Moses 6:57), who is possessed of a glorified body of flesh and bones (Doctrine and Covenants 130:22).

Just as it is inconceivable that a person comes to earth at a given

---

1. Anderson, *Understanding Paul*, 259–60.

place and in a given time by chance alone (see Acts 17:26), when it comes to the organization of humankind into lineages and families, nothing was left to chance. Our Father in Heaven is a God of order, and His house is a house of order (Doctrine and Covenants 132:8). There is purpose and design in all He does, in all He brings to pass. Joseph Smith taught, "Spirits are eternal. At the first organization in heaven, we were all present and saw the Savior chosen and appointed and the plan of salvation made, and we sanctioned it."[2]

After his death, the Prophet Joseph appeared to Brigham Young and beckoned: "Tell the people to be humble and faithful, and be sure to keep the Spirit of the Lord and it will lead them right. . . . Tell the [people] if they will follow the Spirit of the Lord, they will go right. Be sure to tell the people to keep the Spirit of the Lord; and *if they will they will find themselves just as they were organized by our Father in Heaven before they came into the world. Our Father in Heaven organized the human family*, but they are [now] all disorganized and in great confusion."[3]

Following our birth as spirit sons and daughters of God, and being endowed with agency, we grew and progressed according to our desires for truth and righteousness. Many were called and elected, foreordained, to assume specific responsibilities on earth and to receive special blessings in their second estate, if they proved worthy. Here in the opening verses of his letter to the Ephesian Saints, the Apostle Paul speaks of noble people being (1) "chosen . . . before the foundation of the world . . . [to] be holy" (verse 4); and (2) "predestinated . . . unto the adoption of children by Jesus Christ" (verse 5). That is, many were foreordained to receive the gospel of Jesus Christ, cultivate the gift of the Holy Ghost, and be born again, thereby becoming the children of Christ (Mosiah 5:7; 27:25). And finally noble people are (3) recipients

---

2. Joseph Smith, in "Discourse, 5 January 1841, as Reported by William Clayton"; punctuation standardized.
3. Young, vision, February 17, 1847; punctuation and spelling standardized.

of "redemption through his blood, the forgiveness of sins, according to the riches of his grace" (verse 7).

THE FINAL DISPENSATION (1:9–12)

In the spiritual sense, a *dispensation* is a period when the gospel of Jesus Christ, the new and everlasting covenant (Doctrine and Covenants 66:2), is on the earth. Various prophets through the ages have been called to serve as a dispensation head, to be (1) the pre-eminent prophetic revealer of Christ and the Father's plan of salvation and (2) the principal legal administrator, the recipient and dispenser of divine priesthood authority and its keys. We do not know how many dispensations there have been since the beginning of time, although we often speak of seven major dispensations: the dispensations of Adam, Enoch, Noah, Abraham, Moses, Jesus Christ, and Joseph Smith.

Joseph Smith occupies a significant place in the Father's plan, for he was called to preside over the last dispensation, the dispensation of the fullness of times. Throughout the ages it was not uncommon for a period of apostasy to take place between dispensations, but we understand that in the present dispensation there will never again be an apostasy of the Lord's gospel and His Church. While some individuals will unfortunately apostatize from the faith, the fullness of the gospel and the priesthood of Almighty God are here to stay.

Paul informs us that in the dispensation of the fullness of times, the Lord will "gather together in one all things in Christ, both which are in heaven, and which are on earth; even in him" (verse 10). This is what Jehovah referred to when He spoke through Isaiah the prophet: "Forasmuch as this people draw near me with their mouth, and with their lips do honour me, but have removed their heart far from me, and their fear [i.e., regard, reverence, respect] toward me is taught by the precept of men [see Joseph Smith—History 1:19]: Therefore, behold, I will proceed to do *a marvellous work among this people, even a marvellous work and a wonder*" (Isaiah 29:13–14). This marvelous wonder is what the Apostle Peter referred to when he spoke of the Savior's coming in glory: "And he [i.e., God the Father] shall send Jesus Christ, [who] before was preached unto you: whom the heaven must receive [i.e., hold, detain, cause to wait] until *the times of restitution of all things*, which God hath spoken by the mouth of all his holy prophets since the world began" (Acts 3:20–21).

The Prophet Joseph Smith once remarked:

> It is in the order of heavenly things that God should always send a new dispensation into the world, when men have apostatized from the truth and lost the priesthood, but when men come out and build upon other men's foundation, they do it on their own responsibility, without authority from God; and when the floods come and the winds blow, their foundations will be found to be sand, and their whole fabric will crumble to dust. Did I build on any other man's foundation? I have got all the truth which the Christian world possessed, and an independent revelation in the bargain, and God will bear me off triumphant.[4]

In regard to gathering all things together in Christ in the final dispensation, the Prophet wrote a letter to the Saints in which he taught that "it is necessary in the ushering in of the dispensation of the fulness of times, which dispensation is now beginning to usher in, that *a whole and complete and perfect union, and welding together of dispensations, and keys, and powers, and glories should take place, and be revealed from the days of Adam even to the present time. And not only this, but those things which never have been revealed from the foundation of the world*, but have been kept hid from the wise and prudent, shall be revealed unto babes and sucklings in this, the dispensation of the fulness of times" (Doctrine and Covenants 128:18).

---

4. Joseph Smith, in "History, 1838–1856, volume F-1," 105; punctuation and spelling standardized.

"Truly, this is a day long to be remembered by the Saints of the last days," the Prophet commented, "a day in which the God of heaven has begun to restore the ancient order of his kingdom unto his servants and his people, a day in which all things are concurring together *to bring about the completion of the fulness of the gospel, a fulness of the dispensation of dispensations, even the fulness of times* . . . to prepare the earth for the return of his glory, even a celestial glory, and a kingdom of priests and kings to God and the Lamb forever, on Mount Zion."[5]

"THE EARNEST OF OUR INHERITANCE"
(1:12–14; 2 CORINTHIANS 1:21–22; 5:5)

This topic is covered more thoroughly in our discussion of 2 Corinthians 1:21–22 and 5:5. There we pointed out the great importance of the Saints' striving with all their might to receive and maintain the Spirit of God in their lives. When the Holy Ghost dwells in us, we are in covenant; we are "in Christ"; we are in harmony with the will of God; we are gaining an actual knowledge that our course in life is pleasing to the Lord;[6] and we are in line to receive the greatest of all the gifts of God, eternal life (Doctrine and Covenants 14:7). Our Heavenly Father and His Son, Jesus Christ, send the Spirit to us so that we may know that They are pleased with us.

Whereas the verses in 2 Corinthians speak of "the earnest of the Spirit," Paul writes to the Ephesians of "the earnest of our inheritance" (verse 14), meaning the hope and assurance of eternal life in the celestial kingdom of God.

"THE GOD OF OUR LORD JESUS CHRIST" (1:15–19)

The New Testament, particularly the Gospel of John, clearly teaches that Jesus Christ, the Son, is subordinate to Elohim, the Eternal

---

5. Joseph Smith, Journal, January 6, 1842; punctuation and spelling standardized.
6. *Lectures on Faith*, 3:5; p. 38; and 6:1–10; pp. 67–70.

Father. There is an abundance of passages, which we will not enumerate here, that state that the Father and the Son are one; that Christ received a fullness of the glory and power of the Father in the Resurrection;[7] and that Jesus possesses in perfection every divine quality, attribute, and endowment—just as His Father does.

The point to be made here, however, is that there is in fact a hierarchy among the members of the Godhead. "Our Father in heaven . . . is the Father of all spirits," wrote President John Taylor, "and who, with Jesus Christ, his first begotten Son, and the Holy Ghost, are one in power, one in dominion, and one in glory, *constituting the first presidency of this system, and this eternity.*"[8] Of that royal presidency, Brother Joseph explained that it is "the province of the Father to preside as the Chief or President, Jesus as the Mediator, and the Holy Ghost as the Testator or Witness."[9]

Paul's prayer is that God will "give you, in your spirit, the gift of being wise, of seeing things people can't normally see, because you are coming to know him and to have the eyes of your inmost self opened to God's light. Then you will know what the hope is that goes with God's call; you will know the wealth of the glory of his inheritance in his holy people; and you will know the outstanding greatness of his power toward us who are loyal to him in faith, according to the working of his strength and power" (verses 17–19, KNT).

SAVED BY GRACE, THROUGH FAITH (2:4–10)

In our dispensation the Savior said: "For what doth it profit a man if a gift is bestowed upon him, and he receive not the gift? Behold, he rejoices not in that which is given unto him, neither rejoices in him who is the giver of the gift" (Doctrine and Covenants 88:33). Thus,

---

7. Joseph Fielding Smith, *Doctrines of Salvation,* 2:269; see also Matthew 28:18; Doctrine and Covenants 93:16–17.
8. Taylor, "Living God," 809.
9. *Teachings of Presidents of the Church: Joseph Smith,* 42.

while Latter-day Saints speak of being justified (forgiven, pardoned, pronounced innocent) and sanctified (cleansed and purified from the effects, pull, or lure of sin) through the mercy of God, we believe that such gifts must be received, must be accessed. Receiving these gifts comes through the first principles and ordinances of the gospel—faith in Jesus Christ, repentance, baptism, and the receipt of the Holy Ghost by the laying on of hands (Articles of Faith 1:4). Joseph Smith also called these the "articles of adoption," the means by which men and women are adopted into the family of the Lord Jesus Christ.[10] In a very real sense, all that is needed is to have faith in the Lord Jesus Christ, since repentance, baptism, and confirmation are the fruits of faith—effects that flow from saving faith. Some have called this "the faith package."

In commenting on the Apostle Paul's teaching that "by grace are [we] saved" in Ephesians 2:8–10, Elder Orson Pratt explained:

> We are to understand from these passages, that the grace and faith by which man is saved, are the gifts of God, having been purchased for him not by his own works, [for] . . . the exertions on his part would have been entirely unavailing and fruitless. Whatever course man might have pursued, he could not have atoned for one sin; it required the sacrifice of a sinless and pure Being in order to purchase the gifts of faith, repentance, and salvation for a fallen man. Grace, Faith, Repentance, and Salvation, when considered in their origin, are not of man, neither by his works; man did not devise, originate, nor adopt them; superior Beings in Celestial abodes, provided these gifts, and revealed the conditions to man by which he might become a partaker of them. Therefore all boasting on the part of man is excluded. He is saved by a plan which his works did not originate—a plan of heaven and not of earth.[11]

---

10. Joseph Smith, Journal, October 15, 1843.
11. Pratt, *True Faith*, 3–9.

In short, when we have faith, repent, and are baptized, we become justified before God. That is, by virtue of the Lord's Atonement and our baptism (an outward symbol of our ready acceptance of Christ's atoning work), we receive from God a remission of sins. We readily acknowledge, as Elder D. Todd Christofferson has taught, that "none of us, of course, is perfectly obedient, and thus we rely on our baptismal covenant to bring a remission of sins after baptism just as it has been done for our lives before baptism. We rely on repentance to reinvigorate that covenant [or renew it], to bring the Holy Spirit and, with it, atoning grace. The process of cleansing and sanctifying through the baptisms of water and of the Holy Ghost can be continued weekly as we worthily partake of the sacrament of the Lord's Supper."[12] Strictly speaking, the ordinance of baptism does not forgive sins or save us, nor does partaking of the emblems of the Savior's broken body and spilt blood, because salvation is in *Christ the person*. Forgiveness and cleansing come from Him, not a rite or ceremony. Rather, baptism and the sacrament of the Lord's Supper are channels of divine power that help to activate the powers of godliness in our lives (Doctrine and Covenants 84:19–22).

Note Paul's words in verse 8: "For by grace are ye saved through faith; and that [faith] not of yourselves: it is the gift of God." We must acknowledge that faith itself is a gift of the Spirit (see 1 Corinthians 12:9; Moroni 10:11; Doctrine and Covenants 46:19–20), not something we conjure up ourselves. No mortal could ever take credit for his or her salvation. Why? Because salvation or eternal life is "the greatest of all the *gifts of God*" (Doctrine and Covenants 6:13; 14:7).

Verse 10 gets at the matter of good works. Paul writes: "For we are his workmanship, created in Christ Jesus unto good works, which God hath before ordained that we should walk in them." That is, when God's Holy Spirit is with us, that Spirit prompts and motivates charitable actions, the works of righteousness. The Revised English Bible

---

12. Christofferson, "Justification and Sanctification."

renders "workmanship" as "handiwork," since the original Greek word often has the connotation of a "work of art." It's as if we are God's poem, His painting, His precious work of art.

FROM ALIENS TO FELLOW CITIZENS (2:11–19)

Many of the Ephesian Saints had been Gentiles before their conversion to Christianity. That is, they did not descend from the twelve tribes of Israel. Thus the blessings of Abraham, the promises made to the fathers, were out of their reach. In that sense, they were "aliens from the commonwealth of Israel" (verse 12). In other words, they were "separate from Christ, excluded from citizenship in Israel and foreigners to the covenant of promise" (NIV). Because they were brought up in a pagan environment, they were "without God in the world" (verse 12). Few of them knew anything about Jehovah—the God of Abraham, Isaac, and Jacob—and so obviously they knew nothing about how salvation comes through the atoning ministry and Resurrection of the Son of God. However, because Paul and his missionary associates had brought the gospel of Jesus Christ to them, and because they had accepted the message and received the saving covenants and ordinances, those who were "sometimes . . . far off [were] made nigh by the blood of Christ" (verses 11–13).

Paul writes that Christ "is our peace, who hath made both"—Israelites and Gentiles—"and hath broken down the middle wall of partition between us" (verse 14). This reminds us of what Paul wrote to the Galatians: "For ye are all the children of God by faith in Christ Jesus. . . . There is neither Jew nor Greek, there is neither bond nor free, there is neither male nor female: for ye are all one in Christ Jesus." Now note what follows, a message that surely contained glad tidings to those who had previously been Gentiles: "And *if ye be Christ's, then are ye Abraham's seed, and heirs according to the promise*" (Galatians 3:26, 28–29; see also 2 Nephi 30:1–2).

Those Gentiles who received the gospel of Christ accepted both the new covenant and the Mediator of that covenant (Jesus Christ) and were thereby adopted into the family of Abraham, Isaac, and Jacob. They were now members of the royal family of God, as though they had been born Israelites. The law of Moses—along with its "outward performances" (Alma 25:15), its dietary or kosher laws, and its intricate system of sacrifices—had separated the Israelites from the nations (the Gentiles) for a millennium and a half, had basically built a wall between the two groups. This law was now done away in the Savior's Atonement. Jesus thereby reconciled "both unto God in one body by the cross, having slain the enmity [i.e., friction, ill will] thereby; and came and preached peace to you which were afar off [i.e., the Gentiles], and to them that were nigh [i.e., members of the house of Israel]. For through [Christ] we both have access by one Spirit unto the Father" (verses 16–18). Both groups, now one in Christ, are invited to "come boldly unto the throne of grace, that [they] may obtain mercy, and find grace to help in time of need" (Hebrews 4:16).

THE FOUNDATION OF APOSTLES AND PROPHETS (2:19–22)

As "fellowcitizens with the saints, and of the household of God"—that is, as members of the Church of Jesus Christ—those who had been Gentiles are now "built upon the foundation of the apostles and prophets, Jesus Christ himself being the chief corner stone" (verses 19–20). Apostles and prophets convey the mind and will of God to the people of the Church. They have been given the responsibility to declare and interpret doctrine, to rightly divide between that which is true and uplifting and that which is false and deceptive. Most important, the keys of the kingdom of God are vested in the First Presidency and the Quorum of the Twelve Apostles. These keys allow them to oversee the covenants and ordinances, directing the power to bind and seal on earth and to have those actions certified and approved in heaven. In modern revelation we read that the Apostles are called to be "special witnesses of the name of Christ in all the world," charged to "build up the church, and regulate all the affairs of the same in all nations" (Doctrine and Covenants 107:23, 33).

Eugene Peterson's paraphrase of Paul's words is plainly and beautifully expressed: "You're no longer wandering exiles. This kingdom of faith is now your home country. You're no longer strangers or outsiders. You *belong* here, with as much right to the name Christian as anyone. God is building a home. He's using us all—irrespective of how we got here—in what he is building. He used the apostles and prophets for the foundation. Now he's using you, fitting you in brick by brick, stone by stone, with Christ Jesus as the cornerstone that holds all the parts together. We see it taking shape day after day—a holy temple built by God, all of us built into it, a temple in which God is quite at home" (*The Message*).

GOD'S MYSTERY CONCERNING THE GENTILES (3:1–8)

Paul begins chapter 3 by referring to a revelation that God gave to him about a great mystery. This mystery was not understood for generations but "is now revealed unto his holy apostles and prophets by the Spirit" (verses 1–5). Students of the Book of Mormon may recall the language of Jacob, son of Lehi, regarding this mystery. Having spoken of the blindness that came upon the Jews by "looking beyond the mark," Jacob continued: "And now I, Jacob, am led on by the Spirit unto prophesying; for I perceive by the workings of the Spirit which is in me, that by the stumbling of the Jews they will reject the stone upon which they might build and have safe foundation" (Jacob 4:14–15). Jesus Christ is the stone upon which they should have built (see Matthew 21:42; Acts 4:11).

And yet Jacob is well aware that eventually Christ will "become the great, and the last, and the only sure foundation, upon which the Jews can build." Jacob's question is simply this: How is it that the Jews will reject their Messiah when He comes to earth and yet, in the long run, build their foundation of faith upon Him? He then speaks of this doctrinal dilemma: "Behold, my beloved brethren, *I will unfold this mystery unto you*; if I do not, by any means, get shaken from my firmness in the Spirit, and stumble because of my over anxiety for you" (Jacob 4:16–18). Jacob then proceeds to unfold the allegory of Zenos—seventy-seven verses in the fifth chapter of Jacob that focus on the scattering and gathering of Israel. The allegory is a panoramic view of God's tender regard for His chosen people and His infinite patience with the house of Israel, in spite of their spiritual wanderings over centuries of time. And of course linked with the destiny of Israel is the destiny of the Gentiles and God's dealings with them (see 3 Nephi 23:1–3; Mormon 5:10).

What then is the great mystery? It is that, despite the innumerable times that the people of Israel have forsaken their Lord and rejected the message of salvation, God, the Lord of the vineyard, together with His servants, the prophets, will continue to labor in their behalf. He will evermore call upon the people of Israel to repent, forsake their sins, return to Him, and take their place as children of the covenant and heirs of the blessings God promised Abraham. *God simply will not let Israel go*!

Returning to the third chapter of Ephesians, the mystery is that "the Gentiles should be fellowheirs, and of the same body, and partakers of his promise in Christ by the gospel." Paul continues, "Whereof I was made a minister [i.e, the Apostle to the Gentiles], according to the gift of the grace of God given unto me." He then humbly acknowledges that "unto me, who am less than the least of all saints, is this grace given, that I should preach among the Gentiles the unsearchable riches of Christ" (verses 6–8).

CHRIST DWELLS IN US BY FAITH (3:14–19)

In verse 14, Paul states, "I bow my knees unto the Father of our Lord Jesus Christ." The God of whom the Apostle speaks here is Elohim—God, the Eternal Father. We worship the Father; indeed, He is *"the only living and true God, . . . the only being whom [we] should worship"* (Doctrine and Covenants 20:19). What is meant here? Do we not worship the Lord Jesus Christ? Yes, of course we do (see 2 Nephi 25:16, 29). But God the Father is the ultimate object of our worship. Christ loved, served, and worshipped the Father, and so must we. Jesus sought to carry out the will of the Father (John 5:30; 6:38), and so must we. Jesus came to teach the doctrine of the Father (John 7:16), and so must we. Jesus taught only what He heard from God the Father (John 8:26, 40), and so must we listen to and teach what the Father makes known to us through the power of the Holy Ghost. Jesus explained to the woman at the well that "the hour cometh, and now is, when the true worshippers shall worship the Father in spirit and in truth: for the Father seeketh such to worship him" (John 4:23).

It is in this spirit that Paul bows in humble reverence before the Father and prays "that [God] would grant [the Ephesians], according to the riches of his glory, to be strengthened with might by his Spirit in the inner man" (verse 16). Another translation states this differently: "I kneel in prayer to the Father, from whom every family in heaven and on earth takes its name, that out of the treasures of his glory he may grant you inward strength and power through his Spirit" (verses 14–16, REB).

It is thus by means of the Holy Spirit that "Christ may dwell in your hearts by faith; that ye, being rooted and grounded in love, may be able to comprehend with all saints what is the breadth, and length, and depth, and height; and to know the love of Christ, which passeth knowledge, that ye might be filled with all the fulness of God" (verses 17–19).

Christ Himself, a physical being, cannot dwell in another person; "the idea that the Father and the Son dwell in a man's heart is an old sectarian notion, and is false" (Doctrine and Covenants 130:3). Christ dwells in our hearts when He sends the Holy Spirit to convey the light and truth and understanding of the Father and the Son to us. Jesus Himself taught His disciples at the Last Supper that "when he, the Spirit of truth, is come, he will guide you into all truth: for he shall not speak of himself; but whatsoever he shall hear [presumably from the Father], that shall he speak" (John 16:13). Christ dwells in our hearts by the power of the Spirit when we always remember Him (see Doctrine and Covenants 20:77, 79). Christ dwells in our hearts when, on those special occasions, the gift of charity, the pure love of Christ, is bestowed upon us (see Moroni 7:47–48). Christ dwells in our hearts when, by means of the Holy Spirit, we begin to think and act and speak as He would—that is, when we have "the mind of Christ" (1 Corinthians 2:16). And of course, as Paul teaches here, Christ dwells in our hearts as we gradually grow in faith—as we develop total trust and complete confidence in Him and as we always rely upon Him. Indeed, the depth and breadth and length and height of the love of Christ—what Paul here calls the "fulness of God"—is grander and more glorious than mere mortals can comprehend (see Romans 8:35, 38–39).

"ONE LORD, ONE FAITH, ONE BAPTISM" (4:1–7)

Chapter 4 begins with Paul's plea for the Saints to look after and care for one another. There is and should be a love that members of the Church of Jesus Christ have for one another that is unique. This love centers on the shared knowledge, understanding, and conviction of the truthfulness of the gospel of Jesus Christ; it is an elevated perspective on life here and hereafter that welds together human minds and hearts. Paul counsels the Saints to "walk worthy of the vocation [i.e., calling] wherewith ye are called" (verse 1).

Paul writes simply of "one Lord, one faith, one baptism, one God and Father of all, who is above all, and through all, and in you all" (verses 5–6). Many years ago, President Boyd K. Packer spoke of why Latter-day Saints must hold to a belief that the restored Church of Jesus Christ is "the only true and living church upon the face of the whole earth" (Doctrine and Covenants 1:30). He asked:

> Could we not use the words *better* or *best*? The word *only* really isn't the most appealing way to begin a discussion of the gospel. . . .

We know there are decent, respectable, humble people in many churches, Christian and otherwise. In turn, sadly enough, there are so-called Latter-day Saints who by comparison are not as worthy, for they do not keep their covenants. But it is not a matter of comparing individuals. We are not baptized collectively, nor will we be judged collectively. . . .

We Latter-day Saints did not invent the doctrine of the only true church. It came from the Lord. Whatever perception others may have of us, however presumptuous we appear to be, whatever criticism is directed to us, we must teach it to all who will listen. . . .

As I grow in age and experience, I grow ever *less* concerned over whether others agree with us. I grow ever *more* concerned that they understand us. If they do understand, they have their agency and can accept or reject the gospel as they please.[13]

THE SAVIOR'S POSTMORTAL DESCENT (4:8–10)

Paul here quotes from Psalm 68:18: "Thou hast ascended on high, thou hast led captivity captive: thou hast received gifts for men; yea, for the rebellious also, that the Lord God might dwell among them." In a latter-day revelation we read that Jesus Christ "ascended up on high, as also he descended below all things, in that he comprehended all things, that he might be in all and through all things, the light of truth" (Doctrine and Covenants 88:6). What does it mean that our Lord "led captivity captive"? It means that through His atoning suffering in the Garden of Gethsemane and on the cross of Calvary, He made it possible for women and men, boys and girls, to repent of their sins, to turn away from evil and turn toward God, to thereby be delivered from the "chains of hell" or the "bonds of iniquity" (Alma 5:7, 9–10; Mosiah 27:29).

---

13. Packer, "Only True Church"; emphasis in original.

Thus the Redeemer's Atonement loosed the bands of wickedness, undid the heavy burdens, and let the oppressed go free (Isaiah 58:6).

We also know from President Joseph F. Smith's vision of the redemption of the dead that, following His death on the cross, the disembodied Christ led captivity captive in that He entered paradise in the postmortal world of spirits. There He preached the doctrine of redemption from the Fall, including the glorious Resurrection from the dead that every man and woman who comes into mortality will experience. He organized His missionary forces in paradise and sent these representatives into the realm of darkness—what we know variously as spirit prison, hell, or outer darkness (see 1 Peter 3:18–20; 4:6; 2 Nephi 9:10–12; Alma 40:13–14)—to preach to the inhabitants of that sphere of existence. In other words, "the Son of God appeared, declaring liberty to the captives who had been faithful" (Doctrine and Covenants 138:18–19, 29–36). This is what the early Christians, as well as some in our day, have referred to as "Christ's descent into hell."

THE NEED FOR A CHURCH ORGANIZATION (4:11–15)

Christianity entails more than praying, fasting, and searching the scriptures—more than an individual effort to live the principles of the gospel of Jesus Christ. As vital as personal devotion and individual effort are, Christianity is fully lived out only *in community*. The Greek term used to describe those who congregate in the name of Jesus Christ refers to those who are or have been "called out" and are "elect." In a day like our own, when millions of persons throughout the world have walked away from any form of organized religion, we are blessed to know that God called Joseph Smith to set in motion the Restoration, a very significant part of which is *the restored Church of Jesus Christ*. Without the Church, one cannot receive the requisite ordinances of salvation or exaltation; cannot develop those Christlike qualities and attributes that come only through association and affiliation with others who are striving for basically the same things; cannot participate in the ongoing service and "organized sacrifice" that come only through working with others. Without the Church and Church affiliation and involvement, one simply cannot cultivate the gospel light that emanates freely and enticingly from striving and stretching members of the Church.

President Henry B. Eyring spoke of one person's attempt to go it on his own. "I have heard the boast of a man," President Eyring said,

> who walked away from the Church slowly, at first just ceasing to teach his Sunday School class and then staying away from church and then forgetting tithing now and then. Along the way he would say to me: "I feel just as spiritual as I did before I stopped those things and just as much at peace. Besides, I enjoy Sundays more than I did; it's more a day of rest." Or, "I think I've been blessed temporally as much or more as I was when I was paying tithing." *He could not sense the difference, but I could. The light in his eyes and even the shine in his countenance were dimming.* He could not tell, since one of the effects of disobeying God seems to be the creation of just enough spiritual anesthetic to block any sensation as the ties to God are being cut. Not only did the testimony of truth slowly erode, but even the memories of what it was like to be in the light began to seem to him like a delusion.[14]

Paul indicates that the various officers and callings of the Church were established for "the perfecting of the saints, for the work of the ministry, for the edifying of the body of Christ" (verses 11–12). Reminding ourselves that the Greek word translated as "perfect" means finished, complete, whole, and mature, Paul seems to be saying that the Church of Jesus Christ isn't quite whole until certain offices and callings are in place. Having a Church built upon the foundation of the apostles and prophets—together with evangelists (patriarchs), pastors

---

14. Eyring, *Because He First Loved Us*, 7–8.

(bishops and branch presidents), teachers (those charged to know the doctrine and declare it by the power of the Holy Spirit), and other callings and assignments as they are needed—contributes to the edification of the members of the body of Christ.

When the gospel of Jesus Christ, as contained in holy scripture, is taught in its plainness and simplicity, unity of the faith is the result. The Saints speak the same language and teach the same eternal truths. This manner of learning and proclaiming the message of salvation results in "mature [personhood], measured by nothing less than the full stature of Christ." Thus, the members of Christ's Church "are no longer to be children, tossed about the waves and whirled around by every fresh gust of teaching, dupes of cunning rogues and their deceitful schemes. Rather we are to maintain the truth in a spirit of love; so shall we fully grow up unto Christ" (verses 13–15, REB).

PUTTING OFF THE "OLD MAN" (4:20–32)

Paul counsels the members of the Ephesian branch to "*put off* concerning the former conversation [i.e., conduct] *the old man, which is corrupt* according to the deceitful lusts; and *be renewed* in the spirit of your mind; and that ye *put on the new man,* which after God is created in righteousness and true holiness" (verses 22–24). Several verses later, he warns against behavior of the "natural man," such as lying, anger, stealing, corrupt communication or unwholesome talk, bitterness, wrath, and evil speaking (verses 25–29, 31; see 1 Corinthians 2:14).

Fallen men and women are transformed by virtue of the precious blood of Jesus Christ; indeed, there is power in the blood (see Leviticus 17:11)! The spiritual metamorphosis is accomplished through the sanctifying work of the Holy Spirit. Attend carefully to the language of the risen Lord to His American Hebrews: "And no unclean thing can enter into [God's] kingdom; therefore nothing entereth into his rest save it be those who have *washed their garments in my blood,* because of their faith, and the repentance of all their sins, and their faithfulness unto the end. Now this is the commandment: Repent, all ye ends of the earth, and come unto me and be baptized in my name, that *ye may be sanctified by the reception of the Holy Ghost*, that ye may stand spotless before me at the last day. Verily, verily, I say unto you, this is my gospel" (3 Nephi 27:19–21).

The renewal of the mind is discussed in our consideration of Romans 12:2. Paul is basically teaching the same doctrine that King Benjamin put forth when, quoting an angel, he declared that "the natural man is an enemy of God" (Mosiah 3:19). Indeed, we cannot *put on* the "new man"—the reborn man or woman of Christ—until we *put off* the natural man. C. S. Lewis once asked a very pertinent question:

> If Christianity is true why are not all Christians obviously nicer than all non-Christians? . . . If conversion to Christianity makes no improvement in a man's outward actions—if he continues to be just as snobbish or spiteful or ambitious as he was before—then I think we must suspect that his "conversion" was largely imaginary. . . . Fine feelings, new insights, greater interest in "religion" mean nothing unless they make our actual behavior better; just as in an illness "feeling better" is not much good if the thermometer shows that your temperature is still going up. . . . Christ told us to judge by results. A tree is known by its fruit; or, as we say, the proof of the pudding is in the eating. When we Christians behave badly, or fail to behave well, we are making Christianity unbelievable to the outside world.[15]

Paul implores, "Grieve not the holy Spirit of God, whereby ye are sealed unto the day of redemption" (verse 30). The Holy Ghost, or Holy Spirit, is also known as the Holy Spirit of Promise. It is through the power of God's Spirit that individuals and couples are "sealed by the Holy Spirit of Promise." "Those saints who keep the commandments,"

---

15. Lewis, *Mere Christianity*, 177–78 (book 4, chap. 10).

Elder Bruce R. McConkie wrote, "who overcome the world, who are faithful in all things, who are married in the temple, who live by every word that proceedeth forth from the mouth of God, have their calling and election made sure. 'They are sealed by the Holy Spirit of Promise . . . unto the day of redemption' [Doctrine and Covenants 132:26]."[16]

"WALK AS CHILDREN OF LIGHT" (5:1–14)

Paul begins this chapter by encouraging the members of Christ's Church to "be ye therefore followers of God" (verse 1), meaning *imitators* of God. How does one seek to imitate God, meaning, presumably, God the Father? Because God's Beloved Son is one with His Heavenly Father (see John 10:30; 3 Nephi 11:27), the way to imitate the Father is to strive to imitate the Son, to live as Jesus did.

Paul mentions numerous evil and unclean acts that true Saints must avoid, including covetousness, foolish talking, sexual immorality, and idolatry: "For ye were sometimes darkness, but now are ye light in the Lord: walk as children of light (for the fruit of the Spirit is in all goodness and righteousness and truth); proving what is acceptable [pleasing] unto the Lord" (verses 8-10). The Apostle Peter put it this way: "But ye are a chosen generation, a royal priesthood, an holy nation, a peculiar [i.e., purchased] people; that ye should shew forth *the praises of him who hath called you out of darkness into his marvelous light*" (1 Peter 2:9).

"REDEEMING THE TIME" (5:15–17)

"See then that ye walk circumspectly, not as fools, but as wise, redeeming the time, because the days are evil" (verses 15–16). To be circumspect is to be watchful and discrete, to be vigilant and ever aware that Satan is alive and well on earth. Some of the best ways to be circumspect are to use our time wisely, to take every opportunity to do good, and to stand up and speak out against evil. To "redeem the time"

---

16. McConkie, *Doctrinal New Testament Commentary*, 2:513.

is to make righteous use of our time. Amulek warned the Zoramites that because this life is "given us to prepare for eternity, behold, if we do not *improve our time* while in this life, then cometh the night of darkness wherein there can be no labor performed" (Alma 34:33).

A beloved hymn calls upon the children of God to

> *Improve the shining moments;*
> *Don't let them pass you by.*
> *Work while the sun is radiant;*
> *Work, for the night draws nigh.*
> *We cannot bid the sunbeams*
> *To lengthen out their stay,*
> *Nor can we ask the shadow*
> *To ever stay away.*
>
> *Time flies on wings of lightning;*
> *We cannot call it back.*
> *It comes, then passes forward*
> *Along its onward track.*
> *And if we are not mindful,*
> *The chance will fade away,*
> *For life is quick in passing,*
> *'Tis as a single day.*[17]

PSALMS, HYMNS, AND SPIRITUAL SONGS (5:18–20)

Paul here cautions against drunkenness, "wherein is excess," and encourages us instead to "be filled with the Spirit" (verse 18). In other words, "If you must binge on something, then binge on the Holy Spirit." The Apostle then instructs his readers to speak "to yourselves in psalms and hymns and spiritual songs, singing and making melody in your heart to the Lord; giving thanks always for all things unto God and

---

17. "Improve the Shining Moments," *Hymns*, no. 226.

the Father in the name of our Lord Jesus Christ" (verses 19–20). One of the most powerful ways to purify our lives is to purify our thoughts, to see to it that we are always reflecting on things that really matter.

Decades ago President Boyd K. Packer taught:

> Probably the greatest challenge to people of any age, particularly young people, and the most difficult thing you will face in mortal life is to learn to control your thoughts. As a man "thinketh in his heart, so is he" (Proverbs 23:7). One who can control his thoughts has conquered himself. . . .
>
> This is what I would teach you. Choose from among the sacred music of the Church a favorite hymn, one with words that are uplifting and music that is reverent, one that makes you feel something akin to inspiration. . . . Go over it in your mind carefully. Memorize it. Even though you have had no musical training, you can think through a hymn.
>
> Now, use this hymn as the place for your thoughts to go. Make it your emergency channel. Whenever you find these shady actors have slipped from the sidelines of your thinking onto the stage of your mind, put on this record, as it were.
>
> As the music begins and as the words form in your thoughts, the unworthy ones will slip shamefully away. It will change the whole mood of the stage of your mind. Because it is uplifting and clean, the baser thoughts will disappear. For while virtue, by choice, *will not* associate with filth, evil *cannot* tolerate the presence of light.
>
> In due time you will find yourself humming the music inwardly. As you retrace your thoughts, you discover some influence from the world about you encouraged an unworthy thought to move onto the stage in your mind, and the music almost automatically began. . . .
>
> Once you learn to clear the stage of your mind from

unworthy thoughts, keep it busy with learning worthwhile things. Change your environment so that you have things about you that will inspire good and uplifting thoughts. Keep busy with things that are righteous.[18]

HUSBANDS AND WIVES SUBMIT TO ONE ANOTHER (5:21–33)

Over the generations, few verses of scripture have been more misunderstood and misused than the following: "Wives, submit yourselves unto your own husbands, as unto the Lord. For the husband is the head of the wife, even as Christ is the head of the church: and he is the saviour of the body. Therefore as the church is subject unto Christ, so let the wives be to their own husbands in every thing" (verses 22–24). In the first century, including in the first-century Christian Church, the home was operated in a patriarchal manner, with the father presiding over the wife and children. In principle, Latter-day Saints have been given the same counsel that Paul gave to the former-day Saints. From the proclamation on the family we read: "By divine design, fathers are to preside over their families in love and righteousness and are responsible to provide the necessities of life and protection for their families. Mothers are primarily responsible for the nurture of their children. In these sacred responsibilities, fathers and mothers are obligated to help one another as equal partners. Disability, death, or other circumstances may necessitate individual adaptation."[19]

Too often, one parent or another (generally the father) has used this direction to justify exercising unrighteous dominion. A man exercises unrighteous dominion in his home when he makes all of the decisions for the family, when he fails to involve his wife and even the children in family decisions, when he rules the home "with an iron hand," when he

---

18. Packer, "Inspiring Music—Worthy Thoughts."
19. "The Family: A Proclamation to the World."

bullies or pressures family members, and especially when his approach to motivation borders on abuse. Moral agency is a precious, God-given gift, which we fought for in the War in Heaven. God will not violate it, and a parent who misuses agency operates on his own and without the authority or power of the priesthood (Doctrine and Covenants 121:34–38).

Regarding the kind of union and partnership that ought to exist between a husband and wife, President Spencer W. Kimball taught: "When we speak of marriage as a partnership, let us speak of marriage as a *full* partnership. We do not want our LDS women to be *silent* partners or *limited* partners in that eternal assignment! Please be a *contributing* and *full* partner."[20] Similarly, President Howard W. Hunter, in speaking to the men of the Church, was very direct: "Presiding in righteousness necessitates a shared responsibility between husband and wife; together you act with knowledge and participation in all family matters. For a man to operate independently of or without regard to the feelings and counsel of his wife in governing the family is to exercise unrighteous dominion."[21]

Paul's statement that "the husband is the head of his wife, even as Christ is the head of the church" places a sobering responsibility upon the shoulders of husbands—to lead as Jesus did, to lift and strengthen as Jesus did, and in general, to love as He did. In Paul's words, "Husbands, love your wives, even as Christ also loved the church, and gave himself for it" (verse 25).

HARMONY AND LOVE IN THE HOME (6:1–9)

In the opening verses of chapter 6, the Apostle counsels children to obey their parents and thus live in a manner that would entitle them to the blessing pronounced by Jehovah on Mount Sinai: "Honour thy father and thy mother: that thy days may be long upon the land which the Lord thy God giveth thee" (Exodus 20:12). Paul then directs

---

20. Kimball, "Privileges and Responsibilities of Sisters"; emphasis in original.
21. Hunter, "Being a Righteous Husband and Father."

fathers to "provoke not your children to wrath." Instead, "bring them up in the nurture and admonition of the Lord" (verse 4). This is rendered slightly different in the Revised English Bible: "Fathers, do not goad your children to resentment, but bring them up in the discipline and instruction of the Lord."

"I can imagine few if any things more objectionable in the home than the absence of unity and harmony," President David O. McKay said. "On the other hand, I know that a home in which unity, mutual helpfulness, and love abide is just a bit of heaven on earth. I surmise that nearly all of you can testify of the sweetness of life in homes in which these virtues predominate. . . . Unity, harmony, good will are virtues to be fostered and cherished in every home."[22]

Paul also offers advice to slaves to be obedient to those who are their earthly masters, with respect and devotion, just as they would serve Christ. (Because slavery was allowed in Roman society, the Apostle Paul chooses not to undermine the existing cultural institution.) At the same time, he counsels masters to avoid, if possible, threats to the slave, knowing that God is no respecter of persons; He loves slaves just as He loves free men (verse 5–9).

WIELDING THE WHOLE ARMOR OF GOD (6:10–18)

Paul charges the members of the Ephesian branch to "be strong in the Lord, and in the power of his might. Put on the whole armour of God, that ye may be able to stand against the wiles of the devil" (verses 10–11). As it was in the first century, so it is in the twenty-first century: the war for the souls of women and men is well underway. It is a battle to be fought, not with bullets or grenades or bombs, but rather with wisdom, discernment, good judgment, vigilance, personal revelation, power in the priesthood, and eternal perspective. "For we wrestle not against flesh and blood, but against principalities [i.e., rulers], against

---

22. McKay, *Gospel Ideals*, 477–78.

powers [i.e., authorities], against the rulers of the darkness of this world, against spiritual wickedness in high places" (verse 12).

The Apostle then instructs us to put on the whole armor of God, "that ye may be able to withstand in the evil day, and having done all, to stand" (verse 13). Let's consider each of the weapons of spiritual warfare mentioned by Paul:

"Stand therefore, having your loins girt about with truth" (verse 14). Another way to render this is "the belt of truth buckled around your waist" (NIV). President Harold B. Lee, at the time a member of the Quorum of the Twelve Apostles, explained: "*Truth is to be the substance of which the girdle about your loins is to be formed if your virtue and vital strength are to be safeguarded.* How can truth protect you from one of the deadliest of all evils, unchastity? Remember that the Lord tells us that truth is knowledge—'knowledge of things as they are, and as they were, and as they are to come' (Doctrine and Covenants 93:24)."

President Lee continued:

> Those who make themselves worthy and enter into the new and everlasting covenant of marriage in the temple, for time and all eternity, will be laying the first cornerstone for an eternal family home in the celestial kingdom, which will be forever. Their reward is to have "glory added upon their heads for ever and ever" [Abraham 3:26]. These eternal truths, if you believe them with all your soul, will be *as a girdle or armor about your loins to safeguard your virtue as you would protect your life*. But if you allow the vain theories of men to cause you to doubt your relationship to God, the divine purpose of marriage, and your future prospects for eternity, you are being victimized by the master of lies, because all such is contrary to truth, which saves you from these perils.[23]

---

23. Lee, "Put on the Whole Armor of God."

The next piece of battle attire is **"the breastplate of righteousness"** (verse 14). Righteousness is and forever will be linked inextricably with an individual's integrity, her singlemindedness, his quest to remain free from sin. President Russell M. Nelson explained that when the Lord calls upon the members of the Church of Jesus Christ to repent, He is "inviting us to change our mind, our knowledge, our spirit—even the way we breathe. He is asking us to change the way we love, think, serve, spend our time, treat our [spouses], teach our children, and even care for our bodies."[24]

Next, Paul instructs us that our feet must be **"shod with the preparation of the gospel of peace"** (verse 15). An alternate translation reads, "Let the shoes on your feet be the gospel of peace, to give you firm footing" (REB). Few things dissipate our spiritual energies and weaken our righteous resolve more than being spiritually unsettled, divided, ill at ease, and in some cases even double-minded. James taught that "a double minded man is unstable in all his ways" (James 1:8). On the other hand, nothing can enable a person to face challenges and regular roadblocks quite like peace. In His closing moments with His beloved Apostles, Jesus said: "Peace I leave with you, my peace I give unto you: not as the world giveth, give I unto you. Let not your heart be troubled, neither let it be afraid" (John 14:27). A person who is at peace is one who is not distracted by either a guilty conscience or by turmoil and trauma in society.

In verse 16, Paul charges the Saints to go to battle with **"the shield of faith."** One who has taken up the shield of faith is a person who is buoyed up by the assurance that he or she is not alone in this battle for the souls of men and women. The Christian soldier who wields the shield of faith is one who draws upon divine strength and courage to "quench all the fiery darts of the wicked"—to put out the flames of burning arrows and spears.

Next is the **"helmet of salvation"** (verse 17). How is this a weapon?

---

24. Nelson, "We Can Do Better and Be Better."

In his letter to the Thessalonians, Paul sheds some light on this matter: "Therefore let us not sleep, as do others; but let us watch and be sober. For they that sleep sleep in the night; and they that be drunken are drunken in the night. But let us, who are of the day, be sober, putting on the breastplate of faith and love; and *for an helmet, the hope of salvation*" (1 Thessalonians 5:6–8). There it is: we are to put on "the hope of the helmet of salvation." Gospel hope is not worldly wishing. Hope in scripture is assurance, expectation, and anticipation.

Notice Mormon's words in his marvelous sermon on faith, hope, and charity: "And again, my beloved brethren, I would speak unto you concerning hope. How is it that ye can attain unto faith, save ye shall [then] have hope?" Faith produces and results in hope. Once we have true faith in Jesus Christ, we gain the assurance that, through the saving work of our Lord, we will qualify for eternal life. We're on course. We're going to make it, and we know it. Mormon asked: "And what is it that ye shall hope for? Behold I say unto you that ye shall have hope through the atonement of Christ and the power of his resurrection, to be raised unto life eternal, and this because of your faith in him according to the promise. Wherefore, if a man have faith he must needs have hope; for without faith there cannot be any hope" (Moroni 7:40–42).

It is fascinating that all of the parts of the armor of the Christian soldier we have mentioned so far are *defensive* weapons. The only *offensive* weapon mentioned in Paul's letter to the Ephesians is **"the sword of the Spirit, which is the word of God"** (verse 17). Mormon wrote that "the Lord is merciful unto all who will, in the sincerity of their hearts, call upon his holy name. Yea, thus we see that the gate of heaven is open unto all, even to those who will believe on the name of Jesus Christ, who is the Son of God." Now notice the sword imagery that follows: "Yea, we see that *whosoever will may lay hold upon the word of God, which is quick and powerful, which shall divide asunder all the cunning and the snares and the wiles of the devil*, and lead the man [and woman] of Christ in a strait and narrow course across that everlasting gulf of misery which is prepared to engulf the wicked—and land their souls, yea, their immortal souls, at the right hand of God in the kingdom of heaven" (Helaman 3:27–30).

Paul's discussion of the whole armor of God is deeply significant and terribly relevant in these last days, as evidenced in the fact that the Lord chose to repeat these vital principles of truth in a revelation given to the Prophet Joseph Smith in August 1830 (Doctrine and Covenants 27:15–18).

THE EPISTLE TO THE PHILIPPIANS

This epistle was written from Rome during Paul's first Roman imprisonment in about AD 60–62. Philippi was a city in Macedonia (northern Greece) that had been "founded by Philip, father of Alexander the Great. . . . It is described as a Roman 'colony,' i.e., it contained a body of Roman citizens, placed there for military purposes, governed directly from Rome and independent of provincial governors and local magistrates. The church there was mainly gentile, there being no Jewish synagogue."[1]

GOD WORKING WITHIN US (1:1–6)

Paul begins his letter to the Saints at Philippi by indicating that his beloved companion, Timothy, is with him while Paul is a prisoner in Rome (his first Roman imprisonment). He writes to "all the saints in Christ Jesus which are at Philippi, with the bishops and deacons" (verse 1). The Greek word here translated as "bishop" is *episkopos*, meaning an "overseer," one who has spiritual oversight or responsibility for a group of the Saints. The Greek word here translated as "deacon" is *diakona*, meaning "helper" or "assistant." Later, in his epistle to Timothy, Paul sets forth the requirements or standards that should characterize a man

---

1. Bible Dictionary, "Philippi," 750.

called to be a bishop, as well as those called as deacons (1 Timothy 3:1–14; see also Titus 1:4–9). Latter-day Saints "believe in the same organization that existed in the Primitive Church, namely, apostles, prophets, pastors [i.e., bishops or branch presidents], teachers, evangelists [i.e., patriarchs], and so forth" (Articles of Faith 1:6).

Paul expresses gratitude and joy in the progress and spiritual growth of the Saints in Philippi, "for [their] fellowship in the gospel from the first day until now" (verse 5). He then adds: "Being confident of this very thing, that he which hath begun a good work in you will perform it until the day of Jesus Christ" (verse 6). After members of this branch first accepted the gospel of Jesus Christ, were baptized, received the gift of the Holy Ghost, and sought to live worthily as members of the Savior's Church, God continued to work on their hearts and minds—maturing them in the faith, strengthening their conscience, educating their desires, purifying their hearts, shaping their judgment, and empowering them in their convictions. As we will see in our consideration of verse 13 of chapter 2, our Father in Heaven performs a mighty work within each follower of Christ who lives in a manner that allows the companionship of the Holy Spirit. And He will continue to do so "until the day of Jesus Christ" (verse 6), meaning the Savior's Second Coming—His coming in glory, when He will destroy the wicked and initiate the Millennium.

PAUL'S AFFLICTIONS BLESS THE SAINTS (1:12–14)

For those who are striving to be true to their calling as Christian disciples, God can, in His infinite knowledge and power, work His wonders, even to the point that good comes from what might normally be considered unfortunate or even tragic. Let's consider the case of a father who has, for the last year, lapsed in his Church involvement and neglected his responsibilities as a holder of the Melchizedek Priesthood. Now let's suppose that his oldest son, a sixteen-year-old, is involved in a tragic automobile accident. In a moment of consciousness, the boy pleads for his father to give him a priesthood blessing. Dad does not, however, feel worthy to do so. But the son insists, and so Dad gives in and invites a neighbor to join him, and they lay their hands upon the head of a young man who needs more than anything for his father to step up and assume his duty. The son is healed and made well, and all of the family members, including Dad, sense the hand of the Lord in what has taken place. Dad puts aside his pride, repents of his slothfulness, and once again becomes a righteous priesthood man. God did not cause the accident to take place, but He can orchestrate matters so that the unfortunate incident becomes an opportunity to rescue one of His straying sheep.

In verses 12–14, Paul observes that his imprisonment in Rome has not only captured the compassion of the Saints but also motivated them to be bolder, more dynamic in the faith, fearless in their discipleship, and valiant in their testimony of Jesus. Thus, "many of the brethren in the Lord, waxing confident by my bonds," Paul explains, "are much more bold to speak the word without fear" (verse 14).

THE WORK OF GOD, HERE AND HEREAFTER (1:21–26)

The work of the Lord, including the gathering of Israel, goes forward on both sides of the veil, and according to Paul, it may not matter a great deal which side we are working on. Paul feels that, on the one hand, if he were to die, he would be with his Lord and rejoice in that more immediate and sweet reassociation. On the other hand, Paul loves being with his beloved converts to the faith, strengthening and encouraging them; these marvelous and generous Saints mean more to him than his own life. Paul thus says, "I am in a strait betwixt two [i.e., hard pressed to choose one or the other option], having a desire to depart, and to be with Christ; . . . Nevertheless to abide in the flesh is more needful for you" (verses 23–24).

OUR LORD "EMPTIED" HIMSELF (2:5–11)

The God of Abraham, Isaac, and Jacob (see 1 Nephi 19:10) was required to descend below all things in order to ascend to celestial heights and, further, in order for the sons and daughters of Adam and Eve to do the same. Here in chapter 2, the Apostle Paul describes Christ's descent below all things as follows: "Let this mind be in you, which was also in Christ Jesus: who, being in the form of God, thought it not robbery to be equal with God: but *made himself of no reputation, and took upon him the form of a servant, and was made in the likeness of men: and being found in fashion as a man, he humbled himself, and became obedient unto death, even the death of the cross*" (verses 5–8). A different translation of verse 7 states that Jesus "*emptied himself*, taking the form of a slave, being born in human likeness" (NRSV).

"Emptied himself" comes from the Greek word *kenosis*. The word *kenosis* is a "theological term for the 'self-emptying' of Jesus Christ in which he took the form of a slave or servant . . . to accomplish the work of salvation by his death and resurrection."[2] That is, Jesus Christ elected to come to a telestial world and "be like man almost."[3]

Jesus was more than familiar with pain and distress. During His mortal life, He was exposed to suffering, loneliness, sickness, weakness, and alienation; because of this, His empathy for all men and women is perfect (see Alma 7:11–13). In Gethsemane and on Golgotha, He truly descended below all things, that He might comprehend all things (Doctrine and Covenants 88:6). During His atoning hours, Jesus trod the winepress alone and was thus subject to "the fierceness of the wrath of Almighty God"—that is, the withdrawal of the Father's strengthening Spirit (Doctrine and Covenants 76:107; 88:106; see also 133:50; Isaiah 63:3).[4]

Elder Jeffrey R. Holland taught that "for His Atonement to be infinite and eternal, He had to feel what it was like to die not only physically but spiritually, to sense what it was like to have the divine Spirit

---

2. McKim, *Westminster Dictionary of Theological Terms*, 153.
3. "O God, the Eternal Father," *Hymns*, no. 175.
4. See Brigham Young, in *Journal of Discourses*, 3:205–6.

withdraw, leaving one feeling totally, abjectly, hopelessly alone."[5] He suffered more than a mortal man—unaided by divine influence—can suffer (Mosiah 3:7). As teachings to the early elders of this dispensation confirm, Jesus Christ "descended in suffering below that which man can suffer; or, in other words, suffered greater sufferings, and was exposed to more powerful contradictions than any man can be."[6]

It's worth pointing out that most other translations of verses 5–6 are rendered differently than the King James Version. In fact, they state just the opposite:

> In your relationships with one another, have the same mindset as Christ Jesus: who, being in very nature God, did not consider equality with God something to be used to his own advantage. (NIV)

> Have this mind among yourselves, which is yours in Christ Jesus, who, though he was in the form of God, did not count equality with God a thing to be grasped. (ESV)

> This is how you should think among yourselves—with the mind that you have because you belong to the Messiah, Jesus: Who though in God's form did not regard his equality with God as something he ought to exploit. (KNT)

> Take to heart among yourselves what you find in Christ Jesus: he was in the form of God; yet he laid no claim to equality with God. (REB)

I choose to hold to the King James Version: "Let this mind be in you, which was also in Christ Jesus: who, being in the form of God, *thought it not robbery to be equal with God.*" I do so, not just because of my love and reverence for the King James Version, but rather for

---

5. Holland, "None Were with Him."
6. *Lectures on Faith*, 5:2; p. 59; compare Hebrews 12:3.

doctrinal reasons. To say that Jesus "did not count equality with God a thing to be grasped" or "made no claim to equality with God" is not doctrinally consistent with what we read in the New Testament. Consider the following statements:

In the beginning was the Word, and the Word was with God, and *the Word was God*. (John 1:1)

Therefore the Jews sought the more to kill him, because he not only had broken the sabbath, but said also that God was his Father, *making himself equal with God*. (John 5:18)

For the Father judgeth no man, but hath committed all judgment unto the Son: that *all men should honour the Son, even as they honour the Father*. He that honoureth not the Son honoureth not the Father which hath sent him. (John 5:22–23)

For as the Father hath life in himself; so hath he given to the Son to have life in himself. (John 5:26)

I and my Father are one. (John 10:30)

The Jews answered him, saying, For a good work we stone thee not; but for blasphemy; and because that *thou, being a man, makest thyself God*. (John 10:33)

Jesus cried and said, He that believeth on me, believeth not on me, but on him that sent me. (John 12:44)

If ye had known me, ye should have known my Father also: and from henceforth ye know him, and have seen him. (John 14:7)

All things that the Father hath are mine. (John 16:15)

And now, O Father, glorify thou me with thine own self with *the glory which I had with thee before the world was*. (John 17:5)

> Neither pray I for these alone, but for them also which shall believe on me through their word; that they all may be *one; as thou, Father, art in me, and I in thee*, that they also may be one in us. . . . And the glory which thou gavest me I have given them; *that they may be one, even as we are one.* (John 17:20–22)

> And Thomas answered and said unto [Jesus], *My Lord and my God.* (John 20:28)

Regarding Philippians 2:5–6, President Lorenzo Snow wrote the following poem:

> *Dear Brother:*
>
> *Hast thou not been unwisely bold,*
> *Man's destiny to thus unfold?*
> *To raise, promote such high desire,*
> *Such vast ambition thus inspire?*
>
> *Still, 'tis no phantom that we trace*
> *Man's ultimatum in life's race;*
> *This royal path has long been trod*
> *By righteous men, each now a God.*
>
> *As Abram, Isaac, Jacob, too,*
> *First babes, then men—to gods they grew.*
> *As man now is our God once was;*
> *As now God is, so man may be,—*
> *Which doth unfold man's destiny.*
>
> *. . .*
>
> *The boy, like to his father grown,*
> *Has but attained to his own;*
> *To grow to sire from state of son,*
> *Is not 'gainst Nature's course to run.*

A son of God, like God to be,
Would not be robbing Deity;
And he who has this hope within,
Will purify himself from sin.

You're right, St. John, supremely right:
Who'er essays to climb this height,
Will cleanse himself of sin entire—
Or else 'twere needless to aspire.[7]

"WORK OUT YOUR OWN SALVATION" (2:12–13)

Latter-day Saints often quote verses 12–13 to point out the need for good works: "Wherefore, my beloved, as ye have always obeyed, not as in my presence only, but now much more in my absence, *work out your own salvation* with fear and trembling." We are called upon to "work out our own salvation," but how do we do that? Is it even possible? We all understand that men and women cannot save themselves; they simply do not have the power to do so. But note the next verse: "For *it is God which worketh in you* both to will and to do of his good pleasure." We have an obligation to cooperate with God in the salvation of our souls. While the ultimate power of change is in Christ, we can do our part and choose to be changed.

The grace of God is not just a final divine boost into celestial glory that a gracious Father and benevolent Savior provide at the time of judgment. We, to be sure, require all the help we can get to be prepared to go and feel comfortable where God, Christ, and angels are; at the same time, grace is something we have access to every hour of every day of every year. We have been taught that it is through the grace of God "that individuals, through faith in the atonement of Jesus Christ and repentance of their sins, *receive strength and assistance to do good*

---

7. Snow, "Man's Destiny."

works that they otherwise would not be able to maintain if left to their own means."[8] The Lord provides to His followers a strength, an energy, a living power. By this means, by this new life in Christ, we do what we could not do on our own.

In reality, the work of salvation of the human soul is a product of divine grace, coupled with true faith and its attendant actions. C. S. Lewis explained:

> Christians have often disputed as to whether what leads the Christian home is good actions, or Faith in Christ. I have no right really to speak on such a difficult question, but it does seem to me like asking which blade in a pair of scissors is most necessary. A serious moral effort is the only thing that will bring you to the point where you throw up the sponge [i.e., throw in the towel]. Faith in Christ is the only thing to save you from despair at that point: and out of that Faith in Him good actions must inevitably come. . . .
>
> The Bible really seems to clinch the matter when it puts the two things together into one amazing sentence. The first half is, "Work out your own salvation with fear and trembling"—which looks as if everything depended on us and our good actions: but the second half goes on, "For it is God who worketh in you" [Philippians 2:12–13]—which looks as if God did everything and we nothing. . . . You see, *we are now trying to understand, and to separate into water-tight compartments, what exactly God does and what man does when God and man are working together.*"[9]

Indeed, saving human souls comes through a synergistic relationship with our Savior.

---

8. Bible Dictionary, "Grace," 697.
9. Lewis, *Mere Christianity*, 131–32 (book 3, chap. 12).

HOW OUR GAINS BECOME LOSSES (3:1–11)

Chapter 3 begins with a warning to the Philippians. Paul writes: "Beware of dogs, beware of the evil workers, beware of the concision" (verse 2). As explained by one study Bible, "Dogs" is certainly "a harsh word for Paul's opponents, showing their aggressive opposition to the gospel and the seriousness of their error and its destructive 'devouring' results (compare Galatians 5:15). Their teaching was probably similar to what Paul had to oppose in the Galatian churches." Paul uses *concision*, which is again "a strong, painfully vivid term; the false teachers have so distorted the meaning of circumcision that it has become nothing more than a useless cutting of the body."[10]

In verse 3, Paul goes on to say that "we are the [true] circumcision, which worship God in the spirit, and rejoice in Christ Jesus, and have no confidence in the flesh." As discussed in Galatians, it is the circumcision of the heart, the inner cleansing and purification of the human soul, that matters to God and thus to Paul. "For in Christ Jesus neither circumcision availeth any thing, nor uncircumcision, but a new creature" (Galatians 6:15).

No one, Paul declares, was as devoted and consumed with keeping the law of Moses so meticulously as he was before his conversion. He was circumcised on the eighth day, was of the tribe of Benjamin, and was, as he puts it, "an Hebrew of the Hebrews"—as Jewish as one could be. And, of course, he was a strict Pharisee. His zeal toward Judaism was manifest plainly in his efforts to stamp out the "way" of Christianity (see Acts 19:9; 22:4; 24:22). In retrospect, Paul now realizes that "what things were gain [i.e., profit] to me" before my conversion, "those I [now count as] loss for Christ." In fact, "I count all things but loss for the excellency of the knowledge of Christ Jesus my Lord: for whom I have suffered the loss of all things, and do count them but dung, that I may win Christ" (verses 4–8). Other translations render

---

10. *Zondervan New American Standard Study Bible*, 1734.

"dung" as "garbage" or "rubbish" (NRSV, REB, NASB, NIV) or "trash" (KNT, *The Message*).

In *Lectures on Faith*, we read:

> Nothing short of an actual knowledge of their being the favorites of heaven, and of their having embraced that order of things which God has established for the redemption of man, will enable [the Saints] to exercise that confidence in him, necessary for them to overcome the world, and obtain that crown of glory which is laid up for them that fear God.
>
> For a man to lay down his all, his character and reputation, his honor, and applause, his good name among men, his houses, his lands, his brothers and sisters, his wife and children, and even his own life also—counting all things but filth and dross for the excellency of the knowledge of Jesus Christ—requires more than mere belief or supposition that he is doing the will of God; but actual knowledge [that his course in life is pleasing to God], realizing that, when these sufferings are ended, he will enter into eternal rest, and be a partaker of the glory of God.[11]

Paul continues, saying that "I have suffered the loss of all things . . . that I may win Christ, and *be found in him*, not having mine own righteousness, which is of the law, but that which is through the faith of Christ, the righteousness which is of God by faith" (verses 8–9). Once again, for Paul to be "in Christ" is for him to be united, in covenant, and in harmony with his Lord and Savior, by means of that indwelling Spirit we know as the Holy Ghost. Like Jacob, the son of Lehi, Paul was redeemed "because of the righteousness of [his] Redeemer" (2 Nephi 2:3).

Paul's "losses," however, mean nothing to him. Why? Because of what he has to gain: "That I may know him, and the power of his

---

11. *Lectures on Faith*, 6:4–5; p. 68.

resurrection, and the fellowship of his sufferings, being made conformable to his death; if by any means I might attain unto the resurrection of the dead." The Joseph Smith Translation changes this to "if by any means I might attain unto *the resurrection of the just*," meaning the First Resurrection (verses 10–11).

THE FORGIVEN MUST NEVER LOOK BACK (3:12–14)

Verses 12–14 in the Revised English Bible are as follows: "It is not that I have already achieved this [i.e., the resurrection of the just]. *I have not yet reached perfection, but I press on*, hoping to take hold of that for which Christ once took hold of me. My friends, I do not claim to have hold of it yet. What I do say is this: *forgetting what is behind and straining towards what lies ahead, I press toward the finishing line*, to win the heavenly prize to which God has called me in Christ Jesus."

Far too often, members of the Church of Jesus Christ who have committed serious sin and then repented find that they cannot forget what they have done. They are troubled even after they have confessed their offenses properly; worked closely with their priesthood leader; and fasted, prayed, and pleaded for forgiveness for a substantial period of time. Even when they have returned to church, remained active and involved, and reached the point where they know that God has forgiven them and they can once again feel the Spirit of the Lord, they simply cannot move on. This is tragic.

The story is told of a woman who visited President Joseph Fielding Smith. She had been guilty of immoral conduct but had fully repented and now just wanted to find her way. She had great difficulty forgiving herself, even though she had complied with the laws and principles of repentance. President Smith asked her to read to him from Genesis 19 the story of the destruction of Sodom and Gomorrah and of Lot's wife being turned to a pillar of salt. He asked her what lesson was to be learned. She answered, tearfully: "The message of that story is that God will destroy the wicked." "Not so," President Smith told this repentant woman. "The message for you is: *'Don't look back!'*"[12]

OUR BODIES WILL BE CHANGED (3:17–21)

Paul calls upon the Philippians to follow the examples of Christlike living that he and the other Saints have set. He warns them also to be vigilant, ever aware of the fact that not everyone sees things through the lenses of the gospel of Jesus Christ. Many look upon life in the world through glasses that are tainted, smeared, even encrusted with sin. And some individuals are what Paul calls "enemies of the cross of Christ" (verses 17–18). That is, they do not acknowledge their sinful plight, do not feel they need divine assistance, refuse to accept Jesus as the Messiah, and do not utilize the blessings of the cross of Christ. They refuse to apply the atoning blood of Jesus Christ shed in Gethsemane and on Golgotha, for they do not feel it is necessary. Some even choose not only to deny but also to defy the Lord and His Church. These people's "end [i.e., destiny] is destruction, whose God is their belly." They have given themselves up to the indulgences of the flesh and "glory in their shame." They "mind earthly things"—that is, their minds are obsessed with carnal and worldly matters (verse 19, JST). "For our conversation [i.e., citizenship] is in heaven; from whence also we look for *the Saviour*, the Lord Jesus Christ: who *shall change our vile body, that it may be fashioned like unto his glorious body*, according to the working whereby he is able even to subdue all things unto himself" (verses 20–21).

"What Paul is asking us to imagine," N. T. Wright explained,

> is that there will be a new mode of physicality, which stands in relation to our present body as our present body does to a ghost. It will be as much more real, more firmed up, more *bodily*, than our present body is more substantial, more touchable, than a disembodied spirit. We sometimes speak of

---

12. Cited in Packer, "Fountain of Life."

someone who's been very ill as being a shadow of their former self. If Paul is right, a Christian in the present life is a mere shadow of his or her future self. . . . Paul declares that "flesh and blood cannot inherit God's kingdom." He doesn't mean that physicality will be abolished. "Flesh and blood" is a technical term for that which is corruptible, transient, heading for death. . . . Belief in the bodily resurrection includes the belief that what is done in the present in the body, by the power of the Spirit, will be reaffirmed in the eventual future, in ways at which we can presently only guess.[13]

TRUE SAINTS LOOK TO THE NEEDS OF OTHERS (4:1–5)

Paul charges his beloved Philippian Saints to "stand fast in the Lord" (verse 1). In other words, the Apostle encourages them to hold their ground, to be true to their convictions, to be, as the scriptures teach, "steadfast and immovable, always abounding in good works, that Christ, the Lord God Omnipotent, may seal you his" (Mosiah 5:15; see also Alma 1:25; 1 Corinthians 15:58). In encouraging members of the Church to deal wisely and responsibly with hard questions or doubts, Elder Jeffrey R. Holland counseled: "In moments of fear or doubt or troubling times, hold the ground you have already won, even if that ground is limited. . . . When those moments come and issues surface, the resolution of which is not immediately forthcoming, *hold fast to what you already know and stand strong until additional knowledge comes*. . . . The size of your faith or the degree of your knowledge is not the issue—it is the integrity you demonstrate toward the faith you do have and the truth you already know."[14]

Paul also pleads with his "yokefellows," or associates, his companions in spreading the gospel and strengthening the Saints, to "help

---

13. Wright, *Surprised by Hope*, 154, 156.
14. Holland, "Lord, I Believe"; emphasis in original.

those women which laboured with me in the gospel, with Clement also, and with other my fellowlabourers, whose names are in the book of life" (verse 3). These may be the women Paul encountered as he and his fellow missionaries first entered Philippi (see Acts 16:12–15). He refers here to these faithful souls having their names written in the book of life. It reminds us of John the Revelator's vision of the resurrection and judgment: "And I saw the dead, small and great, stand before God; and the books were opened: and another book was opened, which is the book of life: and the dead were judged out of those things which were written in the books, according to their works. . . . And whosoever was not found written in the book of life was cast into the lake of fire" (Revelation 20:12, 15).

In an epistle written by the Prophet Joseph Smith to the Saints in Nauvoo, Brother Joseph explained that "the books spoken of must be the books which contained the record of their works, and refer to the records which are kept on the earth. And the book which was the book of life is the record which is kept in heaven" (Doctrine and Covenants 128:6–7). According to the Guide to the Scriptures, "In one sense the Book of Life is the total of a person's thoughts and actions—the record of his life. However, the scriptures also indicate that a heavenly record is kept of the faithful, including their names and accounts of their righteous deeds."[15]

The Apostle then writes simply, "Rejoice in the Lord alway: and again I say, Rejoice" (verse 4). Charles Wesley no doubt had this verse in mind when he penned the great anthem, "Rejoice, the Lord Is King," a beloved hymn sung often in Latter-day Saint congregations.[16] (The need for the Saints to rejoice is discussed further in our commentary of verse 8 of this chapter.)

The Philippians are invited in verse 5 to "let [their] moderation [i.e., gentleness] be known unto all men." Of all the people in this wide

---

15. Guide to the Scriptures, "Book of Life," 33; see also Bible Dictionary, "Book of Life," 626–27.
16. "Rejoice, the Lord Is King," *Hymns*, no. 66.

world, it is the Christians, the followers of the Lord Jesus, who ought regularly to demonstrate kindness and gentleness. Far too many persons who claim to be Christian have concerning attitudes and behaviors, which are anything but Christian, toward others—especially those who believe differently than they do. Their insistence that those who believe differently are bound for the lowest pits of hell have contributed substantially to the mass exodus of hundreds of millions throughout the world from organized religion. These so-called Christians have, sadly, given Christianity a very bad name. The words of John Stackhouse Jr. express my sentiments well: "God cares about people more than he cares about 'truth' in the abstract. Jesus didn't die on the cross to make a point. He died on the cross to save people whom he loves. We, too, must represent our love to God and our neighbor always foremost in our concerns."[17]

Paul then adds, "The Lord is at hand" (verse 5). Elder Bruce R. McConkie wrote that "one of the great incentives which encourages and entices men to live lives of personal righteousness, is the doctrine of the Second Coming of the Messiah. . . . Deliberately and advisedly the actual time of his coming has been left uncertain and unspecified, so that men of each succeeding age shall be led to prepare for it as though it would be in their mortal lives. And for those who pass on before the promised day, none of their preparation will be wasted, for both the living and the dead, speaking in the eternal sense, must prepare to abide the day."[18]

THE PEACE THAT PASSES UNDERSTANDING (4:6–7)

Paul's counsel to the Philippians to "be careful for nothing" (verse 6) is basically the same direction Jesus gave in His Sermon on the Mount: "Wherefore, if God so clothe the grass of the field, which to day is, and to morrow is cast into the oven, how much more will he not provide for you, if ye are not of little faith? Therefore take no thought"—that

---

17. Stackhouse, *Humble Apologetics*, 142.
18. McConkie, *Doctrinal New Testament Commentary*, 1:674–75.

is, don't be anxious or unduly concerned—"saying, What shall we eat? or, What shall we drink? or, Wherewithal shall we be clothed? . . . For your heavenly Father knoweth that ye have need of all these things. Wherefore, seek not the things of this world but seek ye first to build up the kingdom of God, and to establish his righteousness, and all these things shall be added unto you" (Matthew 6:34–35, 37–38, JST). Indeed, persons who seek first the kingdom of God are far more prone to enjoy the "peace of God, which passeth all understanding, [which] shall keep [their] hearts and minds through Christ Jesus" (verse 7).

There is a peace that comes to those who choose to keep the commandments, do things the Lord's way, surrender their will to the Almighty, and dedicate their hearts and minds to the building of Zion and the establishment of the kingdom of God on earth. Jesus made it very clear that the peace He offers is not at all what the world has to offer (John 14:27). His peace comes from above, and it may surface at times of great distress, even in times of trauma or tragedy. His peace is not dependent upon circumstances in the environment. In our dispensation, the Saints are taught that "he who doeth the works of righteousness shall receive his reward, even peace *in this world*, and eternal life in the world to come" (Doctrine and Covenants 59:23).

"THINK ON THESE THINGS" (4:8)

"Whatsoever things are true," Paul writes to the Philippian Saints, "whatsoever things are honest, whatsoever things are just, whatsoever things are pure, whatsoever things are lovely, whatsoever things are of good report; if there be any virtue, and if there be any praise, *think on these things*" (verse 8).

While we must, on the one hand, be fully aware of the evils of our time and ever vigilant to the creeping corruption and raging relativism of the day, we must not allow ourselves to become prey to that cynicism that is an enemy to spirituality. Just after the Watergate scandal was uncovered, at a time when the morale of the people of the United

States was extremely low, Elder Bruce R. McConkie lifted his voice to the members of the Church:

> There is an eternal law, ordained by God himself before the foundations of the world, that every man shall reap as he sows. If we think evil thoughts, our tongues will utter unclean sayings. If we speak words of wickedness, we shall end up doing the works of wickedness. If our minds are centered on the carnality and evil of the world, then worldliness and unrighteousness will seem to us to be the normal way of life. If we ponder things related to sex immorality in our minds, we will soon think everybody is immoral and unclean and it will break down the barrier between us and the world. . . . On the other hand, if we are pondering in our hearts the things of righteousness, we shall become righteous.[19]

Paul states that we are to think—that is, focus—on things that are true, honest, just, pure, lovely, of good report, virtuous, and praiseworthy. This statement is, of course, the basis of Article of Faith 13. While we are not to be naïve of the unholy influences about us, we must not fixate on them, focus unduly on them, or conclude that all is lost. There is too much good to be seen and acknowledged, too much good to be enjoyed and appreciated and celebrated, and too much good to be accomplished by those bent on the salvation of souls. We have no time for despair, no time to feel sorry for ourselves; we only have time to be about our Father's business.

DOING ALL THINGS THROUGH CHRIST (4:11–13)

In verse 11, Paul writes, "I have learned, in whatsoever state I am, therewith to be content." Men and women who are restless, constantly grasping for more or for something different, novel, or

---

19. McConkie, "Think on These Things."

sensational—these are people who will never, unless they have their perspective changed, be happy in this life. The world offers nothing, no telestial toys, that will bring peace and satisfaction to an individual's heart.

We recall that Alma the Younger wanted to be an angel so that he could "declare unto every soul, as with the voice of thunder, repentance and the plan of redemption." There is nothing wicked about Alma's desires, for he yearned to spread the gospel message far and wide. Yet in the midst of his longing, he was brought back to reality: "But behold, I am a man, and do sin in my wish; for *I ought to be content with the things which the Lord hath allotted unto me.*" In fact, what came to Alma at that moment was a sweet realization that our Almighty God will see to it that every one of His children has the opportunity to hear and receive the glad tidings found in the great plan of happiness. In fact, "the Lord doth grant unto all nations, of their own nation and tongue, [messengers] to teach his word, yea, in wisdom, all that he seeth fit that they should have" (Alma 29:1–8). Our omniscient and omnipotent Father in Heaven knows when and under what circumstances individuals and whole nations are prepared to receive the gospel of Jesus Christ. He knows what we can bear and what our minds and hearts are prepared to digest.

Following the remarkably successful fourteen-year mission to the Lamanites, Ammon began to rejoice in the fruits of their labors. "I do not boast in my own strength, nor in my own wisdom," he said, "but behold, my joy is full, yea, my heart is brim with joy, and I will rejoice in my God." Then from Ammon's lips came words akin to those of the Apostle Paul: "Yea, I know that I am nothing; as to my strength I am weak; therefore I will not boast of myself, but I will boast of my God, for *in his strength I can do all things*" (Alma 26:11–12).

THE EPISTLE TO THE COLOSSIANS

THIS LETTER WAS WRITTEN from Rome to the Colossians during Paul's first Roman imprisonment in about AD 60–62. One work of scholarship provides helpful background on Colossae: "Colossae, one of the older cities in the Lycus valley (going back to at least the fifth century B.C.), was set within southwestern Phrygia in the western interior of Asia Minor. Colossae was then, however, dwarfed by the larger cities of Hierapolis and Laodicea, . . . each with a population of around 10,000. The three cities are within a day's walk of each other."[1] Further, "Colossae lay in a high valley with mountain scenery resembling the arid west of the United States." Colossae was a "hundred miles east of Ephesus."[2]

GOSPEL HOPE WILL GO TO ALL NATIONS (1:1–11)

In his letter, Paul greets the members of the meridian Church of Jesus Christ in Colossae with expressions of love and appreciation for how they have accepted the gospel, applied the principles and practices in their individual lives, and grown in love for one another as people of the everlasting covenant. He glories in "the hope which is laid up for [them] in heaven," since they first heard and accepted the glad tidings

---

1. Wright and Bird, *New Testament in Its World*, 456.
2. Anderson, *Understanding Paul*, 244.

that salvation is to be found alone in Jesus Christ the Redeemer (verses 1–5). Indeed, the word that has "come unto [them]" is the same word that has been dispensed "in all generations of the world" (verse 6, JST).

The gospel is called "the new and everlasting covenant" since it is (1) *new* to those who first receive it and (2) *everlasting* in that it has been delivered to men and women on earth since the days of Adam and Eve. In fact, the gospel extends back to even before the time our first parents had it delivered to them. This new and everlasting covenant "is the sum total of all gospel covenants and obligations."[3]

One of the earnest desires of the Apostle is "that ye might be filled with the knowledge of [God's] will in all wisdom and spiritual understanding" (verse 9). Knowing the will of God is obviously prerequisite to carrying out that will. After persons hear of or read the divine message, ponder upon it, pray to know of its truthfulness, and gain the heaven-sent assurance that it is true and of God, they are baptized by water and then by fire as they receive the Holy Ghost. Receiving the gift of the Holy Ghost entitles them to seek after and acquire divine direction, personal revelation to know the will of the Almighty. Thereafter, members of the household of faith are expected to "walk worthy of the Lord," or live in a manner that pleases the Father—being "fruitful in every good work, and increasing in the knowledge of God" and being "strengthened with all might, according to [God's] glorious power." They are thereby equipped to face life's struggles joyfully, with patience and long-suffering (verses 10–11).

TRANSLATED INTO THE KINGDOM OF GOD (1:12–14)

Members of the Church of Jesus Christ must always give thanks to God the Father, who qualifies them to receive the inheritance promised true believers. Thereafter they are able to walk in the light of the Lord (verse 12; compare 1 John 1:7). In this way, "He has rescued us

---

3. Joseph Fielding Smith, *Doctrines of Salvation*, 1:156.

from the powers of darkness and *transferred* us into the kingdom of his beloved Son, in whom we have redemption, the forgiveness of sins" (verses 13–14, NRSV).

When persons become embroiled in sin, they essentially sell their souls to Lucifer (see Isaiah 50:1; 52:3). But along comes one who loves us infinitely, who desires to reclaim us—that is, redeem us. To be redeemed is to be purchased, bought back, paid for, and freed. This is why, as Paul explained to the Corinthians, we are not our own; we have been bought with a price (1 Corinthians 6:19–20; 7:23), and that price is "the precious blood of Christ, as of a lamb without blemish and without spot" (1 Peter 1:19). Indeed, there is power in the blood of the Lamb: power to purify, power to energize, and power to help us become sons and daughters of God, new creatures in Christ (see 2 Corinthians 5:17; Galatians 6:15; Mosiah 27:25–26).

CHRIST: THE FIRSTBORN OF EVERY CREATURE (1:15–19)

Paul writes that Jesus Christ "is the image of the invisible God, the firstborn of every creature" (verse 15). In a revelation given to the Prophet Joseph Smith, the Savior explained, "I was in the beginning with the Father, and am the Firstborn. . . . Ye were also in the beginning with the Father; that which is Spirit, even the Spirit of truth" (Doctrine and Covenants 93:21, 23). We are all the spirit sons and daughters of our Father in Heaven; He is the Father of our spirits (see Numbers 16:22; 27:16; Hebrews 12:9).

In November of 1909, the First Presidency issued a statement entitled "The Origin of Man," in which they taught: "The Father of Jesus is our Father also. Jesus Himself taught this truth, when He instructed His disciples how to pray: 'Our Father which art in heaven,' etc. *Jesus, however, is the first-born among all the sons [and daughters] of God—the first begotten in the spirit,* and the only begotten in the flesh. He is our elder brother, and we, like him, are in the image of God. All men and women are in the similitude of the universal Father and Mother, and are literally the sons and daughters of Deity."[4]

A few years later, the First Presidency and Quorum of the Twelve Apostles released an official declaration on June 30, 1916, entitled "The Father and the Son: A Doctrinal Exposition." In that document we read the following: "God, whom we designate by the exalted name-title 'Elohim,' is the literal parent of our Lord and Savior Jesus Christ, and of the spirits of the human race. Elohim is . . . the Father of spirits."[5]

Christ is also called the Firstborn of the Father since He was the first person to rise from the dead, His "spirit and the body . . . united never again to be divided, that [He] might receive a fulness of joy" (Doctrine and Covenants 138:17). This seems to be the meaning of "firstborn" in verse 18 of this chapter in Colossians, where Jesus is referred to as "the firstborn from the dead" (see also Romans 8:29).

Paul adds that by Christ "were all things created, that are in heaven, and that are in earth, visible and invisible . . . : all things were created by him, and for him" (verse 16). We understand that, under the direction of our Heavenly Father, Jehovah, who would be born on earth as Jesus of Nazareth, was the executive in the Creation. This is taught by Paul in Ephesians 3:9 and in Hebrews 1:1–2. This doctrine is also taught repeatedly in the Book of Mormon (see Mosiah 4:2; 3 Nephi 9:15).

IN CHRIST DWELLS THE FULLNESS (1:19)

"For it pleased the Father that in him [i.e., Christ] should all fulness dwell" (verse 19). Turning to the Gospel of John, we find John the Baptist bearing witness of the divine Sonship of his cousin, the Lord Jesus: "For he whom God hath sent speaketh the words of God: for God giveth not the Spirit by measure unto him" (John 3:34). In his inspired revision of the Bible, Joseph Smith rendered this verse

---

4. Clark, *Messages of the First Presidency*, 4:203.
5. Clark, *Messages of the First Presidency*, 5:26.

differently: "For he whom God hath sent speaketh the words of God: for *God giveth him not the Spirit by measure, for he dwelleth in him, even the fullness*" (John 3:34, JST).

We can say of our Savior what can be said of no other person on earth: He was totally and completely innocent—never took a backward step or a moral detour and never committed sin. He also has an inheritance that no other mortal does. In speaking to students at a Brigham Young University devotional, Elder Bruce R. McConkie stated: "We have to become perfect to be saved in the celestial kingdom. But nobody becomes perfect in this life. Only the Lord Jesus attained that state, and *he had an advantage that none of us has.* He was the Son of God, and *he came into this life with a spiritual capacity and a talent and an inheritance that exceeded beyond all comprehension what any of the rest of us was born with.*"[6] As Joseph Smith taught: "Where is the man that is free from vanity? None ever were perfect but Jesus; and why was He perfect? Because *He was the Son of God, and had the fullness of the Spirit,* and greater power than any man."[7]

Even though Jesus had within Him the fullness of the Spirit, He did not receive the fullness of the power and glory of the Father until the Resurrection. Following His Resurrection, just as He was about to ascend to the Father, Jesus declared: "All power is given unto me in heaven and in earth" (Matthew 28:18). It is in that context, following the Savior's rise from the tomb, that John wrote: "And I, John, bear record that he received a fulness of the glory of the Father; and he received all power, both in heaven and on earth, and the glory of the Father was with him, for he dwelt in him" (Doctrine and Covenants 93:16–17).[8]

---

6. McConkie, "Jesus Christ and Him Crucified," 399.
7. *Teachings of Presidents of the Church: Joseph Smith,* 53.
8. See Joseph Fielding Smith, *Doctrines of Salvation,* 2:269.

RECONCILED TO THE FATHER (1:20–22)

See the discussion of reconciliation in the commentary herein on Romans 5:11 and 2 Corinthians 5:17–21.

GROUNDED AND SETTLED IN THE LORD (1:23–29; 2:6–7)

Paul encourages the Colossians to "continue in the faith grounded and settled, and be not moved away from the hope of the gospel, which ye have heard, and which was preached to every creature which is under heaven; whereof I Paul am made a minister" (verse 23).

A life that is described as "grounded and settled" in Paul's writings is referred to as "steadfast and immovable" in the Book of Mormon (Mosiah 5:15; Alma 1:25). Such a life is solid, secure in the faith, unshaken by happenings in society or individual trials. "How vital it is to be rooted and grounded," Elder Neal A. Maxwell stated,

> in order to take the scorching heat that will be a part of that special summer of circumstances which precedes the second coming of the Son of Man in power and glory and majesty. . . .
>
> The undernourished and the shallow will not endure, because they cannot stand the heat. They are not likely to acknowledge that as the real reason, however, preferring to find a convenient cause over which to become offended, or wishing to cover behavioral lapses by a supposed grievance. These are they who, among other things, will end up . . . "preaching what they practice"! . . .
>
> People who are grounded in the Lord and His gospel have a deep and extensive root system. Having applied the various principles and truths of the gospel, they have specific faith from and experience with each principle in its turn. Their faith is not a generalized feeling, but reflects specific experience with interlocking principles.[9]

---

9. Maxwell, *We Will Prove Them Herewith*, 17–18.

Paul goes on to explain his specific calling as a minister of the gospel and his "dispensation," meaning his charge to dispense the "mystery" of God's making available the gospel of Jesus Christ to the Gentiles (see the commentary on Ephesians 3:1–8). Through this divinely ordained gift to those who are not lineal descendants of Abraham, Isaac, and Jacob, Paul indicates that [God] is able to "present every man perfect [i.e., whole, complete] in Christ Jesus" (verses 25–28).

BEWARE THE PHILOSOPHIES OF MEN (2:1–8)

The Apostle counsels the Colossians that since they have "received Christ Jesus the Lord, so walk [they] in him" (verse 6). That is, since they have accepted the gospel of Jesus Christ, they should live in such a manner that others might "see [their] good works, and glorify [their] Father which is in heaven" (Matthew 5:16). Here we see again Paul's emphasis on being "in Christ," which means enjoying the gift of the Holy Ghost, becoming linked with Jesus Christ, being one in mind and heart with the Savior, having an eye single to His divine glory, and walking the path of a Christian. The aged John the Beloved explained that "hereby know we that we dwell in him, and he in us, because he hath given us of his Spirit" (1 John 4:13; compare Doctrine and Covenants 50:43).

Paul writes, "Beware lest any man spoil you through philosophy and vain deceit, after the tradition of men, after the rudiments of the world, and not after Christ" (verse 8). N. T. Wright rendered this verse as follows: "Watch out that nobody uses philosophy and hollow trickery to take you captive! These are in line with human tradition, and with the 'elements of the world'—not the king [i.e., Christ]" (KNT).

Argument and reason are extremely important, but one must always be aware and conscious of their limitations—what they cannot do or explain. Paul taught the Corinthians that the things of God are known only by the power of the Spirit of God (1 Corinthians 2:11–14). No one comes to know God or understand His plan of salvation by scientific investigation. No one can explain the truth of where we came from, why we are here, and where we will go after death through rational argument. God and His gospel must be revealed or they remain forever unknown. Indeed, the answers to life's most vital and crucial questions can only come by revelation.

Consider the message of the following scriptural passages:

> By the Spirit are *all things made known*. (1 Nephi 22:2)

> And by the power of the Holy Ghost *ye may know* the truth of all things. (Moroni 10:5)

> Verily, verily, I say unto you, *I will impart unto you of my Spirit*, which shall enlighten your mind, which shall fill your soul with joy; and *then shall ye know, or by this shall you know*, all things whatsoever you desire of me. (Doctrine and Covenants 11:13–14)

One of the greatest defenders of the restored gospel in the twentieth century was the late Hugh W. Nibley, professor of ancient studies at Brigham Young University. Decades ago he explained:

> *The words of the prophets cannot be held to the tentative and defective tests that men have devised for them.* Science, philosophy, and common sense all have a right to their day in court. But the last word does not lie with them. Every time men in their wisdom have come forth with the last word, other words have promptly followed. *The last word is a testimony of the gospel that comes only by direct revelation.* Our Father in heaven speaks it, and if it were in perfect agreement with the science of today, it would surely be out of line with the science of tomorrow. Let us not, therefore, seek to hold God to the learned opinions of the moment when he speaks the language of eternity.[10]

---

10. Nibley, *World and the Prophets*, 134.

IN CHRIST DWELLS THE FULLNESS OF THE GODHEAD (2:9)

We now come to one of the deepest and most beautifully expressed doctrinal principles in all of scripture regarding the relationship of the Savior to the other two members of the Godhead. This passage is also one of the most challenging to understand. Paul writes, "For in him dwelleth all the fulness of the Godhead bodily" (verse 9). We begin by establishing that the members of the Godhead are truly one. Each possesses all godly attributes and qualities in perfection. The love and unity that exists among these three persons is of such magnitude that the prophets can properly and accurately speak of them as "one God," meaning one supreme Godhead (see 2 Nephi 31:21; Alma 11:44; 3 Nephi 11:27, 36; Mormon 7:7; Doctrine and Covenants 20:28). Thus to perform an action in the name of one member of the Godhead is to also perform it in the names of the other two.

In speaking of the Resurrection to the wicked people of Ammonihah, Amulek declared: "Now, this restoration shall come to all . . . ; and even there shall not so much as a hair of their heads be lost; but every thing shall be restored to its perfect frame, as it is now, or in the body, and shall be brought and be *arraigned before the bar of Christ the Son, and God the Father, and the Holy Spirit, which is one Eternal God, to be judged according to their works,* whether they be good or whether they be evil" (Alma 11:44). Notice that to be judged by Jesus Christ, the Holy One of Israel (see 2 Nephi 9:41), is also to be judged by the Father and the Holy Ghost.

In giving instructions to the Nephite Apostles, the risen Lord said: "Verily I say unto you, that whoso repenteth of his sins through your words, and desireth to be *baptized in my name,* on this wise shall ye baptize them—behold, ye shall go down and stand in the water, and *in my name shall ye baptize them.* And now behold, these are the words which ye shall say, calling them by name, saying: Having authority given me of Jesus Christ, *I baptize you in the name of the Father, and of the Son, and of the Holy Ghost*. Amen. And then shall ye immerse them in the water, and come forth again out of the water" (3 Nephi 11:23–26). Again, to be baptized in the name of Jesus Christ is also to be baptized in the names of God the Father and the Holy Ghost. Truly, "in [Christ] dwelleth all the fulness of the Godhead bodily."

WE ARE COMPLETE IN HIM (2:10)

Paul then writes, "And ye are complete in him, [who] is the head of all principality and power" (verse 10). "My people have committed two evils," declared Jehovah to Jeremiah. "They have forsaken me the fountain of living waters, and hewed them out cisterns, broken cisterns, that can hold no water" (Jeremiah 2:13). Forsaking the Lord—ignoring or rejecting His counsel, turning a deaf ear to His divine direction—is a very serious matter. *The Lord is the Way*, and those who refuse His message enter the broad road that leads to destruction. *The Lord is the Truth*, and those who spurn His teachings and authority wander in ignorance. *The Lord is the Life*, and those who feel no need to align themselves with His will enter into league with him who seeks our spiritual death. *The Lord is the Light*, and those who forsake Him choose to walk in darkness.

To forsake the Fountain of Living Waters is to deny oneself access to the only sure antidote to the world's desperate thirst. And, unfortunately, there is no relief to be found in digging our own cisterns or even in using those of others, especially those cisterns that are, at best, deficient and, at worst, perverse. Those, in the language of Jehovah, can hold no water (Jeremiah 2:13), provide no deliverance from this world's woes.

The devil doesn't need to get us to steal or lie or commit adultery; he just needs us to undersell, understate, and underestimate the powers and relevance of the gospel of Jesus Christ. One challenge we face in a world that is expanding dramatically in information, discovery, and technology is holding fast to that which is fundamental, riveting ourselves to the simple. In many ways, new discoveries have and will yet ameliorate human suffering and remove many of life's struggles. There are, however, some things that never change, some problems and challenges for which only divine intervention can bring resolution.

In our complex world, we find people on every corner eager to provide solutions to modern men's and women's troubles. Radio, television, podcasts, newspaper columns, magazine articles, and individual and group seminars abound. Some focus on the importance of self-discovery, of coming to know who we are and what marvelous possibilities exist for us. Others have an inordinate concern with being on a type of emotional high, fearing that if one is not giddy and blissful during every waking moment, then something must be wrong. Too many of our own people have concluded that scripture study, prayer, temple attendance, forgiveness, repentance, and the ordinances of the priesthood are overly simplistic and thus inadequate to deal with today's difficult challenges.

BURIED WITH THE LORD IN BAPTISM (2:12–13)

See the commentary herein on Romans 6:3–10.

AVOID THE WORSHIP OF ANGELS (2:18–23)

The meaning of verses 18–19 in the King James Version is unclear: "Let no man beguile you of your reward in a voluntary humility and worshipping of angels, intruding into those things which he hath not seen, vainly puffed up by his fleshly mind, and not holding [fast to] the Head, from which all the body by joints and bands having nourishment ministered, and knit together, increaseth with the increase of God." Perhaps another translation of this passage will help: "Do not let anyone who delights in false humility and the worship of angels disqualify you. They have lost connection with the head, from whom the whole body, supported and held together by its ligaments and sinews, grows as God causes it to grow" (NIV).

What angels are certain people in Colossae worshiping? This may be another reference to very early Gnostic influences, which is discussed briefly in our commentary on Paul's first letter to the Corinthians.

One study Bible offers the following explanation: "Second-century Gnosticism conceived of a list of spirit beings who had emanated from God and through whom God may be approached."[11] Becoming involved in this kind of false worship lessens the reverence and worship of Church members toward the one who is the true head of all principality and power, Jesus Christ.

Verses 20–23 essentially pose this question: if, in fact, Jesus has truly risen from the dead, has fulfilled the law of Moses, and now stands supreme above all false systems of religion, why do some members still follow needless directives to avoid eating or touching some foods, or choose to believe in will worship and asceticism?

PUTTING ON THE NEW MAN (3:1–4, 9–11)

Verses 1–2 are Paul's plea to focus more on things above—celestial, heavenly, eternal matters—than on things below—telestial, earth-bound, temporary matters. In a revelation given to the Church in August 1831, the Lord Jesus Christ stated: "*I am from above*, and my power lieth beneath [i.e., on the earth]. I am over all, and in all, and through all, and search all things, and the day cometh that all things shall be subject unto me. . . . Remember that *that which cometh from above is sacred*, and must be spoken with care, and by constraint of the Spirit; and in this there is no condemnation . . . ; wherefore, without this there remaineth condemnation" (Doctrine and Covenants 63:59–64).

Paul then writes, "For ye are dead, and your life is hid with Christ in God. When Christ, who is our life, shall appear, then shall ye also appear with him in glory" (verses 3–4). These individuals are dead in the sense that they have put off the natural man, the old man or woman of sin; the carnal person has been put to death. The expression "Your life is hid with Christ in God" is a fascinating remark. It reminds us of passages from the Old Testament:

---

11. *New International Version Study Bible*, 2014.

The Lord hath called me from the womb; from the bowels of my mother hath he made mention of my name. And he hath made my mouth like a sharp sword; *in the shadow of his hand hath he hid me*, and made me a polished shaft; *in his quiver hath he hid me*; and said unto me, Thou art my servant, O Israel, in whom I will be glorified. (Isaiah 49:1–3)

For *in the time of trouble he shall hide me* in his pavilion: *in the secret of his tabernacle shall he hide*; he shall set me up upon a rock. (Psalm 27:5)

Oh how great is thy goodness, which thou hast laid up for them that fear thee; which thou hast wrought for them that trust in thee before the sons of men! *Thou shalt hide them in the secret of thy presence* from the pride of man: *thou shalt keep them secretly in a pavilion* from the strife of tongues. (Psalm 31:19–20)

Now notice the words of Christ in this dispensation: "Therefore, thus saith the Lord unto you, with whom the priesthood hath continued through the lineage of your fathers—for ye are lawful heirs, according to the flesh, and *have been hid from the world with Christ in God*" (Doctrine and Covenants 86:8–9).

Can God eventually hide His faithful children from a wicked world and from the degrading influence of perverse people? Is there a way for those who strive to remain on the covenant path to stay safe until the day they pass through the veil of death? The Lord can, in fact, preserve those who hunger and thirst after righteousness, who seek to live by every word of God, who conduct their lives in a manner that enables the Holy Ghost to be their constant companion, and who trust in God. This preservation and safety come through passing the tests of mortality and receiving from God the assurance of eternal life; it is to have made one's calling and election sure.[12]

---

12. See Joseph Smith, "Discourse, between circa 26 June and circa 2 July 1839, as Reported by Wilford Woodruff."

The Prophet Joseph Smith's history, under the date May 16, 1843, records the following experience in the home of Benjamin F. Johnson in Ramus, Illinois: "Before retiring, I gave Brother and Sister Johnson some instructions on the priesthood; and putting my hand on the knee of William [Clayton], I said: '*Your life is hid with Christ in God, and so are many others. Nothing but the unpardonable sin can prevent you from inheriting eternal life* for you are sealed up by the power of the priesthood unto eternal life, having taken the step necessary for that purpose.'"[13]

In verse 4 of Colossians 3, Paul writes, "When Christ, who is our life, shall appear, then shall ye also appear with him in glory." John the Beloved stated this same truth beautifully: "Behold, what manner of love the Father hath bestowed upon us, that we should be called the [children] of God. . . . Beloved, now are we the sons [and daughters] of God, and it doth not yet appear what we shall be [in the glorious Resurrection]: but we know that, *when he shall appear, we shall be like him;* for we shall see him as he is" (1 John 3:1–2; compare Moroni 7:48).

THE CHRISTLIKE LIFE (3:12–22)

In verses 12–16, Paul describes the Spirit-filled, Christlike life. True followers of the Son of Man are, to follow the list in the text, merciful, kind, humble, meek, long-suffering, filled with forbearance, forgiving, peaceful, thankful, wise, and lovers of sacred music. And the capstone virtue, the supreme quality of the soul, is charity, the pure love of Christ—what Paul calls in verse 14 "the bond of perfectness," or as the Savior described in modern revelation, "the bond of perfectness and peace" (Doctrine and Covenants 88:125). These virtues and qualities are very similar to what Paul called elsewhere the "fruit of the Spirit" (Galatians 5:22–25); to King Benjamin's description of the Sainted life (Mosiah 3:19); and to Alma's call to higher righteousness (Alma 7:23–24).

Paul encapsules the life surrendered to and graced by the only

---

13. Joseph Smith, in "History, 1838–1856, volume D-1," 1551; punctuation and spelling standardized.

perfect human being to walk the earth: "And whatsoever ye do in word or deed, do all in the name of the Lord Jesus, giving thanks to God and the Father [i.e., God the Father] by him" (verse 17; compare Doctrine and Covenants 46:31; Moses 5:8). Finally, Paul offers sound advice to the Saints in Colossae regarding how to maintain harmony in the home between family members (verses 18–22). The counsel is almost identical to that which he delivered to the Ephesians (Ephesians 5:21–28).

CONVERSING WITH THOSE OF OTHER FAITHS (4:5–6)

In chapter 4, Paul begins by recommending that the Colossians be wise in how they converse and interact with those who are outside the Christian faith. He counsels the Colossians to "walk in wisdom toward them that are without [i.e., outside], redeeming the time," meaning making good and wise use of their time (see the discussion herein of Ephesians 5:16). He continues: "Let your speech be alway with grace, seasoned with salt, that ye may know how ye ought to answer every man" (verses 5–6).

Most of us know what it means to be gracious with those of other faiths or no faith, but what does it mean to have our speech "seasoned with salt"? We recall that our Lord has called upon us to be the "salt of the earth" (Matthew 5:13; 3 Nephi 12:13). Salt may serve many functions—to add flavor, preserve, or heal. For Paul to say that our speech should be "seasoned with salt" implies that we should speak and act in a manner that makes a difference for good, that adds something worthwhile to the conversation or that serves to heal or edify other people.

As to how we should respond to people's questions, the Apostle Peter wrote that the Saints should "be ready always to give an answer to every man that asketh you a reason [for] the hope that is in you with meekness and fear" (1 Peter 3:15). That is, members of the Lord's Church need to be competent witnesses of the gospel, capable member missionaries, and knowledgeable enough to satisfy curiosity and maybe even correct misunderstanding. Another way of putting this is that members of the Church of Jesus Christ ought to know enough about the gospel of Jesus Christ to provide answers that are as solid and stimulating to the mind as they are settling and soothing to the heart. Regarding how we should answer another's queries, other translations render "with meekness and fear" as "with courtesy and respect" (REB), "with gentleness and respect" (ESV, KNT, NIV), or "with gentleness and reverence" (NASB, NRSV).

We cannot make our influence felt if we completely avoid the troublesome issues in society and insulate ourselves and our families from today's challenges. President Howard W. Hunter explained that "the gospel of Jesus Christ, which gospel we teach and the ordinances of which we perform, is a global faith with an all-embracing message. It is neither confined nor partial nor subject to history or fashion. Its essence is universally and eternally true. Its message is for all the world, restored in these latter days to meet the fundamental needs of every nation, kindred, tongue, and people on the earth. It has been established again as it was in the beginning—to build brotherhood, to preserve truth, and to save souls."[14]

As members of The Church of Jesus Christ of Latter-day Saints, we have a responsibility to love and care for our neighbors and make a difference for good in their lives. Perhaps they will join our Church, but perhaps they will not. Regardless, we have been charged by our Lord and Master to love them, to serve them, and to treat them with the same respect and kindness that we would extend to a person of our own faith. Given the challenges we face in our society—fatherless homes, child and spouse abuse, divorce, poverty, spreading crime and delinquency, ethical relativism, and so on—it seems foolish to allow doctrinal differences to prevent us from working together.

President Gordon B. Hinckley beckoned to the Saints: "We must not become disagreeable as we talk of doctrinal differences. There is no

---

14. Hunter, "The Gospel, a Global Faith."

place for acrimony. . . . We can respect other religions and must do so. We must recognize the great good they accomplish. *We must teach our children to be tolerant and friendly toward those not of our faith.* We can and do work with those of other religions in the defense of those values which have made our civilization great and our society distinctive."[15]

PAUL SENDS HIS LOVE TO BELOVED FRIENDS (4:7–18)

In the closing verses of Paul's epistle to the Colossians, he passes along the well-wishes of Saints who are with him in Rome:

- Tychicus, a native of Asia Minor who traveled and taught with Paul and one of those who will deliver this letter (verses 7–8; see also Acts 20:4).
- Onesimus, a runaway slave who was converted to the gospel and another of the letter carriers (verse 9). (Onesimus is discussed more in our commentary on Paul's epistle to Philemon.)
- Aristarchus, one who labored with Paul earlier in the ministry (verse 10; see also Acts 19:29; 20:4; 27:2).
- John Mark, the cousin of Barnabas and former missionary companion of Paul (verse 10; see also Acts 13:13; 15:36–40).
- Jesus, also called Justus, about whom we know nothing (verse 11).
- Epaphras (short for Epaphroditus), who was from Colossae and would also deliver the epistle (verses 12–13).
- Luke, the author of the Gospel of Luke and the Acts of the Apostles, as well as a missionary companion of Paul (verse 14; see also 2 Timothy 4:11; Philemon 1:24).

Paul adds a couple of requests: (1) that when the letter to the Colossians is read, it also be taken and read to the church of the Laodiceans; and (2) that the letter from the Laodiceans be read to the Colossians (verse 16). Paul's last words are simply, "Remember my bonds. Grace be with you" (verse 18).

---

15. Hinckley, "We Bear Witness of Him."

THE FIRST EPISTLE TO THE THESSALONIANS

THESSALONICA, OR WHAT IS NOW Saloniki, was named after Thessalonica, sister of Alexander the Great. Thessalonica "is located on . . . the northeastern coast of Greece. The Romans annexed Macedonia in 168 BC; Thessalonica became the capital of the region in 146 BC. In Paul's day, Thessalonica was a free city with tax exemptions. It was predominantly Greek, but with significant numbers of Italians, Thracians [i.e., Indo-European people], and Jews. The city was in an important location . . . , connecting the Balkans to Asia Minor, facilitating Paul's Macedonian travels. The Jewish community in the city was large enough (unlike the small numbers in Philippi) to support a synagogue building."[1] This epistle was written from Corinth in about AD 50–51. Many believe that this was Paul's first epistle.

THE GOSPEL COMES BY POWER (1:1–6)

As this epistle begins, Paul, Silas, and Timothy remember the people's faith, hope, and love and address the Saints in Thessalonica with Paul's customary greeting: "Grace be unto you, and peace, from God our Father, and the Lord Jesus Christ" (verses 1–3). Verse 4 continues, "Knowing, brethren beloved, your election of God," or, in other words, knowing that you have been called by God.

---

1. Wright and Bird, *New Testament in Its World*, 417.

Paul goes on to say, "For our gospel came not unto you in word only, but also in power, and in the Holy Ghost, and in much assurance" (verse 5). To put it another way, "Your choice to become Christians was not built on sophistry or oratory, not grounded in reason alone or in philosophical arguments. You were not persuaded by our eloquence, but rather felt and experienced the power of the Holy Spirit bearing witness that our message was true and from God." President Brigham Young once spoke of how he became persuaded that the message of the restored gospel was true:

> If all the talent, tact, wisdom, and refinement of the world had been sent to me with the Book of Mormon, and had declared, in the most exalted of earthly eloquence, the truth of it, undertaking to prove it by learning and worldly wisdom, they would have been to me like the smoke which arises only to vanish away. But when I saw a man without eloquence or talents for public speaking, who could only say, "I know, by the power of the Holy Ghost, that the Book of Mormon is true, that Joseph Smith is a prophet of the Lord," *the Holy Ghost proceeding forth from that individual illuminated my understanding . . . and I knew for myself that the testimony of the man was true.* . . . My own judgment, natural endowments, and education bowed to this simple, but mighty testimony.[2]

WALKING WORTHY OF GOD (2:7–13)

In verses 1–6, Paul repeats how he and his associates had preached in Thessalonica and how those who accepted the gospel were converted. He goes on to explain that the messengers of salvation were gentle, affectionate, and prepared to give their all to the people there. "So being affectionately desirous of you, we were willing to have imparted unto

---

2. Young, in *Journal of Discourses*, 1:90.

you, not the gospel of God [see commentary on Romans 1:1] only, but also our own souls, because ye were dear unto us" (verse 8). The missionaries not only shared the glorious and glad tidings that salvation is in Christ, but they also fell in love with the people. *They shared themselves.* It is rare indeed for a full-time missionary to return home and *not* be fully convinced that the men and women in the part of the world where they served are the greatest people on earth. Why? Because the gospel of Jesus Christ is a gospel of love, of caring, of sharing—a gospel of service and a message that is manifest in the loving-kindness and tender regard of the messengers themselves.

Paul explains further that he and his associates are determined not to be a burden on the people in Thessalonica; for that reason, they undertook manual labor and toiled to provide for themselves (verse 9). In fact, Paul frequently drew upon his skills as a tentmaker or leather worker to put food on the table (see Acts 18:3). In general, as Paul puts it, the Thessalonian Saints "are witnesses, and God also, how holily and justly and unblameably we behaved ourselves among you that believe." The missionaries "exhorted and comforted and charged every one of you, as a father doth his children" (verses 10–11). In other words, the missionaries taught, testified, and worked patiently and lovingly with the new converts, "that [they] would walk worthy of God, who hath called [them] unto his kingdom and glory" (verse 12).

Eugene Peterson's paraphrase of these verses ties it all together nicely:

> Even though we had some standing as Christ's apostles, we never threw our weight around, or tried to come across as important, with you or anyone else. We weren't aloof with you. We took you just as you were. We were never patronizing, never condescending, but we cared for you the way a mother cares for her children. We loved you dearly. Not content to just

pass on the Message, we wanted to give you our hearts. And we did.

You remember us in those days, friends, working our fingers to the bone, up half the night, moonlighting so that you wouldn't have the burden of supporting us while we proclaimed God's Message to you. You saw with your own eyes how discreet and courteous we were among you, with keen sensitivity to you as fellow believers. And God knows we weren't freeloaders! You experienced it all firsthand. With each of you we were like a father with his child, holding your hand, whispering encouragement, showing you step-by-step how to live well before God, who called us into his own kingdom, into this delightful life. (*The Message*)

STANDING FAST IN THE LORD (3:7–13)

"Therefore, brethren, we were comforted over you in all our affliction and distress by your faith: for now we live, if we stand fast in the Lord" (verses 7–8). Paul and his colleagues were able to face the challenges and difficulties that came their way by learning of the Thessalonian Saints' faithfulness and spiritual progress. Members of the Church of Jesus Christ who are steadfast; who do their duties joyfully; who overcome temptation through their faith in Jesus Christ (Alma 37:33); and who remain unshaken in the midst of denials, defiance, and accusations come alive to the things of the Spirit. Their waters have begun to run deep, and their Christian character shines the light of Jesus Christ wherever they go.

"For what thanks can we render to God again for you," Paul asks, "for all the joy wherewith we joy for your sakes before our God" (verse 9). In other words, "How could we ever thank you enough for the joy you have brought into our lives by receiving and then faithfully living the gospel of Jesus Christ?" Truly, "there is joy in the presence of the angels of God over one sinner that repenteth" (Luke 15:10).

290   BECOMING NEW

Paul and his associates in the ministry prayed night and day "that we might see your face, and might perfect that which is lacking in your faith" (verse 10). To be perfect is to be whole, complete, fully integrated, and spiritually mature. Their concern about the Saints' lack of faith reflects the reality that persons who come into the Lord's Church through conversion grow in faith, understanding, and devotion incrementally, bit by bit (see 2 Nephi 28:30); thus it is crucial for them to be properly fellowshipped. They need to be taught the pure gospel and thereby nourished by the good word of God, and to develop friendships with other members of the faith (see Moroni 6:4).

THE CALL TO HOLINESS (4:3–7)

To be holy is to be "sacred, having a Godly character, or spiritually and morally pure. The opposite of holy is common or profane."[3] Paul writes to the Thessalonians that "this is the will of God, even your sanctification, that ye should abstain from fornication: that every one of you should know how to possess his vessel [i.e., physical body] in sanctification and honour; not in the lust of concupiscence, even as the Gentiles which know not God" (verses 3–5).

We recall that to be *justified* is to be pardoned and pronounced innocent, blameless, and forgiven of *sin*. The work of *sanctification*, on the other hand, is a lifelong process by which God's Holy Spirit works upon an individual's soul, cleansing and purifying him or her from *the effects of sin,* including the pull of sin itself. In speaking of the ancient high priests and the priesthood that they held, Alma states that "they were called after this holy order [of God], and were *sanctified*, and *their garments were washed white through the blood of the Lamb.* Now they, after being sanctified by the Holy Ghost, having their garments made white, *being pure and spotless before God, could not look upon sin save it be with abhorrence*; and there were many, exceedingly great many, who

---

3. Guide to the Scriptures, "Holy," 112.

were made pure and entered into the rest of the Lord their God" (Alma 13:11–12).

The Greek word translated as "fornication" is *porneia*, the root from which we derive the word *pornography*. Paul warns the Thessalonians not to yield to "the lust of concupiscence [i.e., passionate lust], even as the Gentiles which know not God" (verse 5). "Sexual union is lawful in wedlock," President Joseph F. Smith declared, "and if participated in with right intent is honorable and sanctifying. But without the bonds of marriage, sexual indulgence is a debasing sin, abominable in the sight of Deity."[4] Paul then states the obvious: "God hath not called us unto uncleanness, but unto holiness" (verse 7).

In all ages of time, whenever the gospel of Jesus Christ has been on earth, the God of heaven (who is holy) has called and commissioned His children to "be a special people unto himself, above all people that are upon the face of the earth" (Deuteronomy 7:6). To do this, it has always been necessary to "put [a] difference between holy and unholy, and between unclean and clean" (Leviticus 10:10)—to draw the line between righteousness and unrighteousness.

"STUDY TO BE QUIET" (4:8–12)

Paul cautions that the Saints should not reject or set aside the Savior's law of love. To spurn or reject a man or woman is to despise or reject God Himself, for the mortals that occupy this earth are all spirit sons and daughters of our Heavenly Father and thus our brothers and sisters. We all belong to the family of God. Paul's apostolic colleague, John the Beloved, wrote: "My little children, let us not love in word, neither in tongue; but in deed and in truth" (1 John 3:18). Paul encourages the Saints to "increase more and more" in their love for God and their fellow man to "*study to be quiet*, and to do your own business, and to work with your own hands, as we commanded you" (verses 10–11).

---

4. Joseph F. Smith, *Gospel Doctrine*, 309.

What does the expression "study to be quiet" mean? Another translation may help clarify: "Make it your ambition to lead a quiet life, to mind your own business and to work with your hands, just as we told you, so that your daily life may win the respect of outsiders and so that you will not be dependent on anybody" (NIV).

THE FATE OF THE RIGHTEOUS DEAD (4:13–18)

Paul has learned that the Thessalonians are deeply concerned about loved ones who have passed away—namely, about what their status will be in the Resurrection and when they will rise from the dead (verse 13). The Apostle teaches beautifully that the Thessalonians have no reason to be concerned, for when the Lord Jesus returns, He will bring with Him the faithful dead, who will be resurrected; thus the First Resurrection, which began with Jesus's rise from the tomb, will resume when He returns in glory. Paul delivers to the Thessalonians "the word of the Lord" on the matter, that "they who are alive at the coming of the Lord, shall not prevent [i.e., precede] them *who remain unto the coming of the Lord, who* are asleep"—that is, who have died (1 Thessalonians 4:15, JST). The Revised English Bible reads, "Those of us who are still alive when the Lord comes will have no advantage over those who have died."

In verse 16 we read, "For the Lord himself shall descend from heaven with a shout." Other translations render "shout" as "a cry of command" (NRSV), "a loud command" (NIV), or "a shouted order" (KNT). The archangel, who is Michael, or Adam (see Doctrine and Covenants 27:11; 107:54; 128:21), "shall sound his trump, and then shall all the dead awake, for their graves shall be opened, and they shall come forth—yea, even all" (Doctrine and Covenants 29:26; see also 88:98).

Why does Michael, or Adam, sound the trump that will call the dead to come forth? We find an answer in Joseph Smith's teaching that Adam "is the father of the human family and presides over the spirits of all men." Further, Adam "delivers up his stewardship to Christ [at the council of Adam-ondi-Ahman] that which was delivered to him as holding the keys of the universe but retains his standing as head of the human family."[5] And Christ delivered to Adam "the keys of salvation under the counsel and direction of the Holy One, who is without beginning of days or end of life" (Doctrine and Covenants 78:16). Returning to verse 16, the voice of the archangel and the trump of God will be heard, "and the dead in Christ shall rise first."

In both verses 15 and 17 of the King James Version, we see the words "*we* which are alive and remain" until the Lord's Second Coming. The reader will notice that the Joseph Smith Translation changes the word *we* in both verses to *they*. Scholars for generations have concluded that this use of "we" is one evidence that Paul and the early Saints believed that the Savior's Second Coming, and thus the return of the righteous dead to the earth, was imminent. The Joseph Smith Translation alterations suggest, however, that Paul understood that the Second Advent of the Savior was well in the future.

Let's return to verse 13 for a moment: "But I would not have you to be ignorant, brethren, concerning them which are asleep, that ye sorrow not, even as others which have no hope." Paul is not saying we shouldn't feel sorrow at the passing of loved ones or friends, for the revelations teach otherwise (see Doctrine and Covenants 42:45). "Irrespective of age," President Russell M. Nelson expressed, "we mourn for those loved and lost. It is a natural response in complete accord with divine commandment. Moreover, we can't fully appreciate joyful reunions later without tearful separations now." Then this modern prophet put forward a profound truth: "*The only way to take sorrow out of death is to take love out of life.*"[6]

In verse 13, Paul is really saying that we should not sorrow *without*

---

5. Joseph Smith, "Discourse, between circa 26 June and circa 4 August 1839–A, as Reported by Willard Richards"; punctuation and spelling standardized.
6. Nelson, "Doors of Death"; see also *Teachings of Russell M. Nelson*, 79–80.

the hope of the immortality of the soul and the resurrection of the body. "Let us not sorrow as those without hope," the Prophet Joseph Smith counseled the Saints. "The time is fast approaching when we shall see [those who are absent from us for a season] again and rejoice together, without being afraid of wicked men. Yes, those who have slept in Christ shall he bring with him when he shall come to be glorified in his Saints and admired by all those who believe, but to take vengeance on his enemies and all those who obey not the gospel. At that time, the hearts of the widow and fatherless shall be comforted, and every tear shall be wiped from off their faces."[7]

"AS A THIEF IN THE NIGHT" (5:1–4)

Paul explains to his beloved Thessalonian Saints that Jesus Christ will come "as a thief in the night" (verse 2). Seldom does a homeowner know that there is a thief in his or her neighborhood or the exact time when the thief will break into the home and steal things of value. Paul also likens the specific time of the Savior's return in glory to a pregnant woman. Let's suppose that a woman's pregnancy has passed full term by two weeks and is terribly uncomfortable; she is impatiently eager to bring this baby into the world. If a person were to walk up to her and ask, "Well, when do you think the baby will come?" we can be assured that her answer *will not be* something like the following: "Oh, I don't know. You know how these things are. It may be today or next week, or perhaps even a year from now!"

In reality, her reply to the question would probably sound something like this: "Look, I don't know exactly when the birth will take place, but I know this much: it will be soon!" If asked how she knows that it will be soon, her reply might be: "The signs in my body, the birth pangs I am experiencing, the discomfort I feel—all of these things tell me that the time is near."

---

7. "Extract from the Private Journal of Joseph Smith Jr.," 8.

As it is with a pregnant mother, so it will be with the coming of the Bridegroom (Jesus Christ) to His bride (the Church). In fact, modern revelation attests that Jesus will *not* come as a thief in the night to His faithful followers, but rather to the world. Note the language of a revelation given to Warren Cowdery: "And again, verily I say unto you, the coming of the Lord draweth nigh, and *it overtaketh the world as a thief in the night*—therefore, *gird up your loins, that you may be the children of light, and that day shall not overtake you as a thief*" (Doctrine and Covenants 106:4–5).

To brethren who would be called to serve as members of the Quorum of the Twelve Apostles in this dispensation, the Lord issued the great commission: "Go ye into all the world, preach the gospel to every creature, acting in the authority which I have given you, baptizing in the name of the Father, and of the Son, and of the Holy Ghost. And he that believeth and is baptized shall be saved, and he that believeth not shall be damned. And he that believeth shall be blest with signs following, even as it is written." Now look carefully at what the Savior said to these men: "And *unto you it shall be given to know the signs of the times, and the signs of the coming of the Son of Man*" (Doctrine and Covenants 68:8–11).

"When the Spirit teaches prophets the truth of things as they really are," Elder Neal A. Maxwell observed, "this includes sensitizing these special men to *the implications of what is just beginning*, implications that are imperceptible to others. Prophets are *alerted to tiny trends that bode ill for mankind*. Prophets, therefore, are *the Lord's early-warning system*: they both detect and decry at his direction. What may seem to be a premature expression of prophetic concern is actually the early discovery of a difficulty that will later plague the people."[8]

Elder M. Russell Ballard of the Quorum of the Twelve Apostles

---

8. Maxwell, *Things as They Really Are*, 77–78.

offered the following timely advice to Brigham Young University students:

> I am called as one of the Apostles to be a special witness of Christ in these exciting, trying times, and I do not know when [Jesus Christ] is going to come again. As far as I know, none of my brethren in the Council of the Twelve or even in the First Presidency knows. And I would humbly suggest to you, my young brothers and sisters, that *if we do not know, then nobody knows*, no matter how compelling their arguments or how reasonable their calculations. . . . I believe when the Lord says "no man" knows, it really means that no man knows. You should be extremely wary of anyone who claims to be an exception to divine decree.[9]

As we move closer and closer to our Lord's Second Advent, wise members of the Church of Jesus Christ will keep their eyes riveted upon and their ears attuned to those we sustain as prophets, seers, and revelators. Seers are divinely called to behold "things which [are] not visible to the natural eye" (Moses 6:36).

WALKING AS CHILDREN OF LIGHT (5:5–11)

John, son of Zebedee and brother of James, wrote that "if we walk in the light, as he [i.e., God the Father] is in the light, we have fellowship one with another, and the blood of Jesus Christ his Son cleanseth us from all sin" (1 John 1:7). The Saints of God, those who have come out of a darkened world by covenant, have been charged to be the light of the world (Matthew 5:14; 3 Nephi 12:14). They are to hold up the Light, who is the Lord Jesus Christ (3 Nephi 18:24), and to have an eye single to the glory of God, thereby becoming vessels of light themselves (Doctrine and Covenants 88:67). And as those who are both

---

9. Ballard, "When Shall These Things Be?" 2.

called and chosen, they are never to be guilty of "walking in darkness at noon-day" (Doctrine and Covenants 95:6).

"Therefore let us not sleep, as do others," Paul writes, "but let us watch and be sober [i.e., vigilant, circumspect]. . . . But let us, who are of the day, be sober, putting on the breastplate of faith and love; and for an helmet, the hope of salvation" (see commentary on Ephesians 6:10–18). "For God hath not appointed us to wrath [i.e., to merit the wrath of God], but to obtain salvation by our Lord Jesus Christ, who died for us, that, whether we wake or sleep, we should live together with him" (verses 6–10). This message seems similar to that contained in several revelations received by the Prophet Joseph Smith: "But blessed are they who are faithful and endure, whether in life or in death, for they shall inherit eternal life" (Doctrine and Covenants 50:5; compare 5:22; 58:2; 61:39).

BRIEF BUT WEIGHTY COUNSEL (5:16–22)

The Apostle closes the final chapter of his first epistle to the Thessalonians with several simple requests, which have consequences that are anything but simple; members of the Lord's Church who take these bits of divine wisdom seriously will live a happy life and enjoy the companionship of God's Holy Spirit all the days of their lives.

"Rejoice evermore" (verse 16). If any people throughout the world have a reason to live in a constant state of gratitude, it is the Saints of God in all ages and dispensations. Elder Bruce R. McConkie recommended that the Latter-day Saints lift up their hearts in joy and appreciation often and regularly. "I think the Lord's people should rejoice in him and shout praises to his holy name. Cries of hosannah should ascend from our lips continually. . . . When I think that the Lord has a living oracle guiding his earthly kingdom, and that there are apostles and prophets who walk the earth again; when I think that the Lord has given us the gift and power of the Holy Ghost so that we have the revelations of heaven and the power to sanctify our souls; when I think of the unnumbered blessings . . . my desire to praise the Lord and proclaim his goodness and grace knows no bounds."[10]

"Pray without ceasing" (verse 17). The Saints of God are expected to pray often and intently. We pray to express gratitude and love. We pray to hold communion with Deity. We pray in times of tragedy, and we pray in times of joy and delight. "Yea, and when you do not cry unto the Lord, let your hearts be full, drawn out in prayer unto him continually" (see Alma 34:18–27).

"In every thing give thanks" (verse 18). The Nephites were instructed to "pray without ceasing, and . . . give thanks in all things" (Mosiah 26:39). In this dispensation, the Lord revealed this simple directive: "Thou shalt thank the Lord thy God in all things." Later in that same revelation, the Savior declared that "in nothing doth man offend God, or against none is his wrath kindled, save those who confess not his hand in all things, and obey not his commandments" (Doctrine and Covenants 59:7, 21; compare 50:34; 78:19).

"Quench not the Spirit" (verse 19). While the gift of the Holy Ghost is given to us when we are confirmed members of the Church, that gift can only be had and enjoyed if we are striving to do what is right. We quench (that is, extinguish, hinder, or suppress) the Spirit when we live beneath our spiritual privileges or when we harbor evil or bitter feelings in our minds and hearts. We quench the Spirit when we are purposely cruel or unkind to a son or daughter of God, when we regularly entertain lustful thoughts, or when we are dishonest in our dealings with our fellow men and women. And we quench the Spirit when we live on the edge of evil and violate the commandments of God, knowing full well what we are doing.

"Despise not prophesyings" (verse 20). Those who have come into the Church of Jesus Christ are charged to "live by every word that proceedeth forth from the mouth of God" (Doctrine and Covenants

---

10. McConkie, "Think on These Things."

84:44; see also Deuteronomy 8:3; Matthew 4:4). To despise prophesyings is to take lightly the word of God, to ignore it, to refuse it, or to condemn it—whether that word be in holy scripture or from the mouths of living apostles and prophets.

"Prove all things; hold fast that which is good" (verse 21). True disciples of the Lord Jesus Christ have learned to be discerning—to test and examine ideas and concepts and to evaluate whether a teaching or a practice is of the Lord or of Lucifer. In our day of growing secularism and expanding cynicism, the continual challenge of followers of Christ is to discern carefully between absolute truths and values and those sounded loudly by a relativistic society. It is through attending carefully and regularly to the Light, or Spirit, of Jesus Christ that such judgments are made (see Moroni 7:12–16, 19).

"Abstain from all appearance of evil" (verse 22). This is an expression that has, over the years, come to mean that it isn't enough to refrain from doing evil; we shouldn't do anything that even resembles evil. Alternate translations of this verse include "If something looks evil, keep well away" (KNT), and "Abstain from every form of evil" (ESV).

Paul offers a summary of his pithy counsel this way: "And [may] the very God of peace sanctify you wholly [i.e., make you holy, through and through]; and I pray God your whole spirit and soul and body be preserved blameless unto the coming of our Lord Jesus Christ" (verse 23).

THE SECOND EPISTLE TO THE THESSALONIANS

THE SECOND EPISTLE TO the Saints in Thessalonica was written from Corinth in about AD 50–51. In this letter, Paul picks up where he left off in his first missive—he continues to address matters pertaining to the Lord's return in glory, including the "flaming fire" and "everlasting destruction" that await the unworthy and unprepared (2 Thessalonians 1:8–9). Paul explains further that Jesus will not come until an apostasy, or falling away, has taken place. He denounces idleness among the people and counsels them not to be busybodies and to never grow weary in well-doing.

VENGEANCE UPON THOSE WHO KNOW NOT GOD (1:7–10)

After commending the members of the Church at Thessalonica for their growing faith, charitable manner, and patient endurance of trials, Paul mentions that "it is a righteous thing with God to recompense [i.e., pay back] tribulation to them that trouble you" (verses 1–6). Since the epistles to the Thessalonians were among Paul's first letters, we would presume that one source of trouble would have been the Judaizers—those Jewish Christians who continued to hold to the law of Moses and to insist that all other members of the Church of Jesus Christ do the same.

This was borne out during Paul's second missionary journey, as told in Acts 17. After coming into Thessalonica, Paul and his associates entered the local Jewish synagogue and there preached from the scriptures, "opening and alleging, that Christ must needs have suffered, and risen again from the dead; and that this Jesus, whom I preach unto you, is Christ [the Messiah]. And some of them believed, and consorted with Paul and Silas; and of the devout Greeks a great multitude, and of the chief [i.e., prominent] women not a few. But *the Jews which believed not, moved with envy*, took unto themselves certain lewd [i.e., wicked, evil] fellows of the baser sort, and *gathered a company, and set all the city on an uproar*" (Acts 17:1–5).

The Apostle describes that great and dreadful day when a divine recompense will be answered upon the heads of those who defy God and fight against the gospel of Jesus Christ. Paul writes that "the Lord Jesus shall be revealed from heaven with his mighty angels, in flaming fire taking vengeance on them that know not God, and that obey not the gospel of our Lord Jesus Christ: who shall be punished with everlasting destruction from the presence of the Lord, and from the glory of his power; when he shall come to be glorified in his saints" (verses 7–10).

When Jesus Christ returns to the earth in glory and majesty, He will come to greet and reward the faithful, as well as to confront those who "know not God." It seems there are two categories of persons who know not God. We know from latter-day revelation that those who never had the opportunity to hear the message of salvation and thereby receive the requisite covenants and ordinances will eventually have that opportunity, if not in this life then in the postmortal spirit world (see Doctrine and Covenants 137–138). As Joseph the Prophet wrote from Liberty Jail, "there are many yet on the earth among all sects, parties, and denominations . . . who are only kept from the truth because they know not where to find it" (Doctrine and Covenants 123:12). These are not the ones who will be burned at the coming of Christ. They "know not God" because they have yet to hear the glad tidings.

Jacob, son of Lehi, explained that God "has given a law; and where there is no law given there is no punishment; and where there is no punishment there is no condemnation; and where there is no condemnation the mercies of the Holy One of Israel have claim upon them, because of the [Savior's] atonement; for they are delivered by the power of him" (2 Nephi 9:25; compare Doctrine and Covenants 137:7–9).

The second category of those who "know not God" are those who refuse to know Him. They have the opportunity to bask in the light of revealed religion and its accompanying covenants and ordinances but shun that opportunity. These are the ones who are described in scripture as "natural" men and women, who because of their dispositions and unwise choices, are enemies of God, perpetual foes, unless they yield "to the enticings of the Holy Spirit, and [put] off the natural man and [become] a saint through the atonement of Christ the Lord" (Mosiah 3:19). Alma the Younger explained to his son Corianton that "all men that are in a state of nature, or I would say, in a carnal state, are in the gall of bitterness and in the bonds of iniquity; *they are without God in the world, and they have gone contrary to the nature of God*; therefore, they are in a state contrary to the nature of happiness" (Alma 41:11). This latter group are the ones who will be burned at the time of the Savior's Second Advent (see 1 Nephi 22:15–17).

AN APOSTASY MUST FIRST COME (2:1–15)

Paul's epistle continues: "Now we beseech you, brethren, [concerning] the coming of our Lord Jesus Christ, and by our gathering together unto him, that ye be not soon shaken in mind, or be troubled by letter, except ye receive it from us; neither by spirit, nor by word, as that the day of Christ is at hand. Let no man deceive you by any means; for *there shall come a falling away first*, and that man of sin be revealed, the son of perdition; who opposeth and exalteth himself above all that is called God, or that is worshipped; so that he as God sitteth in the temple of God, shewing himself that he is God" (verses 1–4, JST).

It appears that some unauthorized person or persons had been communicating to the Thessalonian Saints that the Messiah's coming was imminent. Professor Sidney B. Sperry has written that "some person might have forged a letter purporting to come from Paul, which gave faulty information to the Thessalonians and caused them to be shaken in mind and considerably troubled."[1] Paul did not believe the Lord would come within a short time, and he sought to persuade the members of Christ's Church to believe the same. He also adds an important detail: an apostasy or falling away will precede the Lord's coming in glory. Presumably the "man of sin" is Satan, Lucifer, the father of all lies. Among many other things, the apostasy of the Christian Church would entail Satan's manifesting himself or his evil influence within the "temple of God," which seems to refer to the Church itself.

What happened to bring about this apostasy from the Christian Church? President David O. McKay explained that "inner weakness is more dangerous and more fatal than outward opposition. The Church is little if at all injured by persecution and calumnies from ignorant, misinformed, or malicious enemies; a greater hindrance to its progress comes from faultfinders, shirkers, commandment-breakers, and apostate cliques within."[2]

The Great Apostasy occurred when, first, people from within the faith whose commitment to the gospel had waned fought against the Church. In many ways, a mutiny took place. Paul spoke often of this very concern (see Acts 20:29–30; 1 Timothy 4:1–3).

Second, the Melchizedek Priesthood and the keys associated with that priesthood were taken from the earth.

Third, the ordinances of the early Church were altered, modified,

---

1. Sperry, *Paul's Life and Letters*, 102.
2. McKay, "Unity in the Home—the Church—the Nation," 77.

twisted, and, in some cases, jettisoned. This was especially the case with the mode of baptism in general, infant baptism in particular, and the sacrament of the Lord's Supper. Isaiah had prophesied of just such a time (Isaiah 24:5; compare Doctrine and Covenants 1:14–16). Joseph Smith taught, "Ordinances instituted in the heavens before the foundation of the world, in the priesthood, for the salvation of men, are not to be altered or changed. All must be saved on the same principles."[3]

Fourth, plain and precious truths were taken away or kept back from the Bible (see 1 Nephi 13:20–40; Doctrine and Covenants 76, preface; Moses 1:40–41). The Prophet Joseph thus stated, "I believe the Bible as it read when it came from the pen of the original writers. Ignorant translators, careless transcribers, or designing or corrupt priests have committed many errors."[4]

Fifth, Christian theology began to blend with Greek philosophy, resulting in the loss or corruption of significant doctrine (for example, the nature of God and the Godhead, the nature of humanity, and the gospel of Jesus Christ as an everlasting gospel that was first revealed in the days of Adam and Eve).

"We know the Apostasy occurred in part because the philosophies of men were elevated over Christ's basic, essential doctrine," Elder Quentin L. Cook taught. "Instead of the simplicity of the Savior's message being taught, many plain and precious truths were changed or lost. In fact, Christianity adopted some Greek philosophical traditions to reconcile people's beliefs with their existing culture. The historian Will Durant wrote: '*Christianity did not destroy paganism; it adopted it.*' . . . Historically, and in our own day, some people reject the gospel of Jesus Christ because, in their view, it does not have adequate intellectual sophistication."[5]

---

3. Joseph Smith, in "History, 1838–1856, volume D-1," 1572; spelling and punctuation standardized; see also Joseph Smith, Journal, June 11, 1843.
4. *Teachings of Presidents of the Church: Joseph Smith*, 207.
5. Cook, "Valiant in the Testimony of Jesus," 41; citing Durant, *Story of Civilization*, 3:595.

In speaking of this apostasy, Paul writes: "For the mystery of iniquity doth already work, and he it is who now worketh, and Christ suffereth him [i.e., Satan] to work, until the time is fulfilled that he shall be taken out of the way. And then shall that wicked one be revealed, whom the Lord shall consume with the spirit of his mouth, and shall destroy with the brightness of his coming. Yea, the Lord, even Jesus, whose coming is not until after there cometh a falling away, by the working of Satan with all power, and signs and lying wonders" (verses 7–9, JST).

To say that "God shall send them [i.e., members of the Church] strong delusion, that they should believe a lie" (verse 11) really means that our Father in Heaven will not force any person to heaven and will allow people to face the bitter consequences of their wicked or unwise choices. We must be clear that no person is predestined to be evil, do evil, or spread evil,[6] but when men and women choose darkness and find delight in wickedness and falsehood, God allows them to continue on the path to their own destruction.

On the other hand, women or men who desire to know God and to please Him, who accept the doctrine and ordinances of the Savior's gospel, and who then live as true Saints are the ones who were chosen and foreordained before the foundation of the earth to gain eternal life, contingent on their continued faithfulness and endurance to the end. "Therefore, brethren [and sisters], stand fast, and hold [to] the traditions which ye have been taught, whether by word, or our epistle" (verses 13–15).

WITHDRAWING FROM THE IDLE (3:6–13)

The Saints of God have always been commanded to be out among the people and to be an influence for good, holding up that light which is Jesus Christ (see 3 Nephi 18:24). It is particularly difficult,

---

6. Joseph Fielding Smith, *Doctrines of Salvation*, 1:61.

however, to be the salt of the earth and the light of the world (see Matthew 5:13–14; 3 Nephi 12:13–14) if we choose to leave the world behind, hunker down, and await with impatience the Second Coming of Christ. It is almost impossible to be a leavening influence to those living in a darkening world if we forsake society and avoid contact with other individuals. Our Lord has commissioned His followers to be *in the world*.

At the same time, members of the Church of Jesus Christ who are striving to build Zion and establish the kingdom of God on earth must never yield to the enticings of those who chant and ridicule from the great and spacious building (see 1 Nephi 8:26–27; 11:34–36); true disciples never permit themselves to be *of the world*. It is in that spirit that the Apostle Paul writes: "Now we command you, brethren, in the name of our Lord Jesus Christ, that ye withdraw yourselves from every brother that walketh disorderly [i.e., is living in idleness], and not after the tradition which he received of us. For yourselves know how ye ought to follow [i.e., imitate] us: for we behaved not ourselves disorderly [i.e., were not idle] among you; neither did we eat any man's bread for nought [i.e., undeservedly]; but wrought [i.e., worked] with labour and travail night and day, that we might not be chargeable to any of you" (verses 6–8). Paul goes on to explain that as an Apostle of the Lord Jesus Christ, he has every right to expect to be cared for and supported by the members of the Church, but he and his associates did not exercise that authority. "For even when we were with you, this we commanded you, that if any would not work, neither should he eat" (verses 9–10).

The Lord revealed to His Latter-day Saints the same guiding principle He delivered through Paul to the former-day Saints: "Thou shalt not be idle; for *he that is idle shall not eat the bread nor wear the garments of the laborer*" (Doctrine and Covenants 42:42; compare 60:13). He further instructed "that every man who is obliged to provide for his own family, let him provide, and he shall in nowise lose his crown; and let him labor in the church. Let every man be diligent in all things. And *the idler shall not have place in the church, except he repent and mend his ways*" (Doctrine and Covenants 75:28–29; see also 68:30–31; 75:3, 29; 88:124).

The Apostle also warns the Thessalonians about those in their midst who refuse to work but rather spend their time as "busybodies" (verse 11). The Revised English Bible renders verse 11 as follows: "We mention this because we hear that some of you are idling their time away, minding everybody's business but their own."

"BE NOT WEARY IN WELL DOING"
(3:13; COMPARE GALATIANS 6:9–10)

Here Paul writes, "But ye, brethren, be not weary in well doing" (verse 13). Prophets and apostles through the ages have encouraged members of the Lord's Church to remain at their duty stations, to continue their earnest efforts, to stay with it, even and especially when it appears that no progress is being made.

Just as the Latter-day Saints began to arrive in Independence, Missouri, the Savior offered this sweet reassurance: "Ye cannot behold with your natural eyes, for the present time, the design of your God concerning those things which shall come hereafter, and the glory which shall follow after much tribulation. For after much tribulation come the blessings" (Doctrine and Covenants 58:3–4). Another modern revelation beautifully states, "Wherefore, be not weary in well-doing, for ye are laying the foundation of a great work. And out of small things proceedeth that which is great. Behold, the Lord requireth the heart and a willing mind; and the willing and obedient shall eat the good of the land of Zion in these last days" (Doctrine and Covenants 64:33–34).

Many a missionary of the restored Church has received a spiritual lift, a renewed energy, from such scriptural passages. How many elders or sisters or senior couples have labored for scores if not hundreds of hours with little or no visible success, seeking only to find one interested person to whom they can teach the gospel? Our Father in Heaven and His Beloved Son see and know the end from the beginning; They look forward through the corridors of time and recognize what marvelous fruits will come as a result of one missionary's persistence, steadfastness, and obedience.

Likely many bishops in the Church leave their church office late on a Sunday evening, exhausted and wrung out, shaking their head and wondering if they have really done any good, discouraged because they simply couldn't get to everything that needed their attention. At the same time, how many rank-and-file members of the Church kneel in prayer that same evening and express to their Heavenly Father their undying gratitude for a sensitive and inspired bishop, whose small but charitable acts and wise counsel have literally changed the lives of many, many people? Regardless of our role or calling, we should all strive not to be "weary in well-doing."

THE FIRST EPISTLE TO TIMOTHY

PAUL HEAPED MORE PRAISE on and demonstrated more affection for Timothy than any of his other missionary companions, referring to him as "my beloved son" (1 Corinthians 4:17). He also said of his young companion that "he worketh the work of the Lord, as I also do" (1 Corinthians 16:10). Timothy apparently lived in Lystra before joining Paul in his labors in about AD 51. Of Timothy, Robert J. Matthews wrote: "He often travelled with Paul and was frequently sent by him on confidential errands to various branches of the church. In the mid-sixties, while Paul was imprisoned in Rome, Timothy seems to have been an officer in the Church at Ephesus."[1]

The epistles of 1 Timothy, 2 Timothy, and Titus are known as the "pastoral epistles." Titus, like Timothy, apparently served at this time in a pastoral capacity, presumably as what we know today as a branch president or bishop. The first epistle to Timothy was written in about AD 64–65, but exactly where Paul was when he sent this letter is uncertain. Many scholars believe it was written from Macedonia.

BEWARE THOSE WHO SPREAD FALSE DOCTRINE (1:1–7)

In communicating with Timothy, his beloved "son in the faith" (verse 2), Paul writes, "As I besought thee to abide still at Ephesus,

---

1. Matthews, *Unto All Nations*, 32.

when I went into Macedonia, that thou mightest charge some that they teach no other doctrine, neither give heed to fables and endless genealogies, which minister [i.e., offer, present] questions, rather than godly edifying which is in faith: so do" (verses 3–4). These "endless genealogies" may refer to early manifestations of Gnostic teachings, including the idea of a lineage or line of gods, down to Jehovah. Gnosticism's false cosmology—it's view of the origin and structure of the universe—resulted in false teachings and polluted doctrine.

"I have spoken before about the importance of keeping the doctrine of the Church pure," President Gordon B. Hinckley explained, "and seeing that it is taught in all our meetings. I worry about this. Small aberrations in doctrinal teaching can lead to large and evil falsehoods."[2] "I do not get very troubled about an honest and sincere person who makes a mistake in doctrine," Elder Bruce R. McConkie echoed, "provided that it is a mistake of the intellect or a mistake of understanding, and provided that it is not on a great basic and fundamental principle.... If you err in some doctrines, and I have, and all of us have, what we want to do is get the further light and knowledge that we ought to receive and get our souls in tune and clarify our thinking."[3]

Because what we believe affects strongly what we do, it is crucial for all members of the Lord's Church to learn and teach the doctrine of the gospel in a way that is accurate, true, and faith affirming. All can be spiritually enlightened and edified when we teach what is true under the influence of the Holy Spirit and if the listeners receive the message by that same Spirit (see Doctrine and Covenants 50:13–14, 17–22).

WHAT THE LAW OF MOSES ACCOMPLISHES (1:8–13)

Paul declares that "the law [of Moses] is good, if a man use it lawfully; knowing this, that the law is not made for a righteous man, but for the lawless and disobedient, for the ungodly and for sinners" (verses

---

2. *Teachings of Gordon B. Hinckley*, 620.
3. McConkie, *Doctrines of the Restoration*, 338–39.

8–9). Truly righteous women or men do not require a great deal of structure in their lives, nor do they need to have every sin and misdeed spelled out in the minutest detail. Such people strive to love God with all their hearts and to love and serve their brothers and sisters on earth. As Jesus said, on these two commandments "hang all the law and the prophets" (Matthew 22:36–40).

Paul then provides a detailed list of people for whom the law was given: the lawless, disobedient, ungodly, sinners, persons who were unholy and profane, murderers, the sexually immoral, kidnappers, liars, and "any other thing that is contrary to sound doctrine" (verses 9–10). That's quite a comprehensive list.

Paul then speaks of the fullness of the everlasting gospel, which he calls "the glorious gospel of the blessed God, which was committed to [his] trust" (verse 11). He then expresses gratitude to the Lord Jesus, "who hath enabled [him]"—that is, who hath cleansed, purified, fortified, strengthened, empowered, and reoriented him and counted him faithful. The Lord put Paul "into the ministry; who was before a blasphemer, and a persecutor, and injurious: but [he] obtained mercy, because [he] did it ignorantly in unbelief" (verses 12–13). If the God of heaven can take a zealous Pharisee whose bitterness toward the Christians knew no bounds and make him into "a new creature" in Christ (2 Corinthians 5:17) and a powerful witness of the divine Sonship of Jesus Christ, what can He do for you and me?

"And it is requisite with the justice of God," Alma clarified for Corianton, "that men should be judged according to their works; and if their works were good in this life, *and the desires of their hearts were good*, that they should also, at the last day, be restored unto that which is good" (Alma 41:3; see also Doctrine and Covenants 137:9). So far as we can discern from the scriptural record, Saul of Tarsus was fully persuaded that he was serving God in seeking to put an end to the "blasphemy" that came to be known as Christianity. For a broader look at the law of Moses, see the commentary on Galatians 3:19–25.

JESUS CAME TO SAVE SINNERS (1:15–16)

Verses 15 and 16 contain one of the finest distillations of the mission and ministry of the Lord Jesus Christ and the Father's plan of salvation in scripture: "This is a faithful saying, and worthy of all acceptation [i.e., this is a message that every reasonable and submissive person should accept], that Christ Jesus came into the world to save sinners; of whom I am chief. Howbeit for this cause I obtained mercy, that in me first Jesus Christ might shew forth all longsuffering, for a pattern to them which should hereafter believe on him to life everlasting." How plainly this is stated—Jesus the Messiah came into the world to save sinners. And how could such a miracle be more graphically demonstrated than through the transformed life of Saul of Tarsus, the persecutor who became Paul, the Apostle to the Gentiles?

GOD DESIRES TO SAVE ALL OF HIS CHILDREN (2:3–4)

What earthly parents who believe in God would not want every one of their children to look to God and live? To be successful in life? To have happiness and fulfillment? To be productive and to make a contribution to society? If frail, fallen mortals can feel this way, how much more does God, the Eternal Father, the Father of our spirits, desire that each of His children on earth be true to the Light of Christ within them, recognize and accept the gospel of Jesus Christ when it is presented to them, and go on to eternal glory and exaltation hereafter? Our Heavenly Father and His Son, Jesus Christ, possess all of the attributes of godliness in perfection—certainly including an infinite and eternal love for each of us—and thus it is the work and glory of the members of the Godhead to "bring to pass the immortality and eternal life of man" (Moses 1:39). Or, as Paul here states the matter, "This is good and acceptable in the sight of *God* our Saviour; *who will have all men to be saved, and to come unto the knowledge of the truth*" (verses 3–4).

Simon Peter, the senior Apostle and, following the death of Jesus

Christ, the president of the meridian Church, penned the same overarching truth in his second epistle: "The Lord is not slack [i.e., slow] concerning his promise and [Second] coming, as some men count slackness; but long-suffering toward us, not willing that any should perish, but that all should come to repentance" (2 Peter 3:9, JST; compare 2 Nephi 33:12; Helaman 12:24–25). Put another way, "The Lord is not delaying his promise, in the way that some reckon delay, but he is very patient toward you. He does not want anyone to be destroyed. Rather, he wants everyone to arrive at repentance" (KNT).

ONE MEDIATOR BETWEEN GOD AND MAN (2:5–6)

"For there is one God," Paul writes, "and one mediator between God and men, the man Christ Jesus; who gave himself a ransom for all, to be testified in due time" (verses 5–6). All mortals desperately need help. Those who are lost need to be found. Those who are fallen need to be lifted up. President Boyd K. Packer reminded us soberly that "each of us, without exception, one day will settle [our spiritual] account. We will, that day, face a judgment for our doings in mortal life and face a foreclosure of sorts. . . . Each of us lives on a kind of spiritual credit. One day the account will be closed, a settlement demanded. However casually we may view it now, when that day comes and the foreclosure is imminent, we will look around in restless agony for someone, anyone, to help us."[4]

Jesus was sent by the Father to help us, to show us the way back home. He is able to do so because He *knows* the way; indeed, He *is* the way (John 14:6). We can have total trust and confidence in Him and rely completely upon His merits, mercy, and grace. This is what it means to have faith in Christ. We simply cannot be saved *in* our sins, nor can we merit anything of ourselves (Alma 11:37; 22:14). In the words of the Apostle Paul, "By the deeds of the law there shall no

---

4. Packer, "Mediator."

flesh be justified" (Romans 3:20; see also 2 Nephi 2:5). Because of our fallen nature, we must be justified—forgiven, pardoned, and placed once again in a proper relationship with God, our Heavenly Father. We cannot fix the damaged relationship on our own, but Jesus can. Through His advocacy and mediation, He is able to effect a reconciliation with God. In short, God reconciles fallen men and women to Himself through Jesus Christ (2 Corinthians 5:18).

A mediator is a go-between, an intermediary between two parties, an arbitrator who intervenes to resolve a conflict or, in some cases, ratify a covenant. In the Old Testament, Abraham was a mediator between God and the corrupt people of Sodom and Gomorrah. In spite of their gross wickedness, he pleaded for divine mercy in their behalf—to spare them from destruction if he could identify but ten righteous people in those wicked cities (see Genesis 18:22–32). Moses, the Lawgiver, mediated in behalf of the children of Israel. Jehovah declared that because of their wandering rebellion, He would destroy the people and basically start over.

After Moses discovered that the Israelites had built and worshipped a golden calf, he said to the people: "Ye have sinned a great sin: and now I will go up unto the Lord; peradventure [i.e., perhaps] *I shall make an atonement for your sin.*" Other translations render this passage as "secure pardon for your sin" (REB) or "clear you of your sin" (*The Message*). Then, speaking to the Lord, Moses declared: "Oh, this people have sinned a great sin, and have made them gods of gold." Now note this tender plea, a touching act of mediation: "Yet now, if thou wilt forgive their sin—; and *if not, blot me, I pray thee, out of thy book which thou hast written*" (Exodus 32:30–32).

"Truth, glorious truth, proclaims there is . . . a Mediator," President Packer testified. "Through him mercy can be fully extended to each of us without offending the eternal law of justice." Then President Packer powerfully stated that this doctrine is central to our faith: "*This truth is the very root of Christian doctrine.* You may know much about the gospel as it branches out from there, but if you only know the branches and those branches do not touch that root, if they have been cut free from that truth, *there will be no life nor substance nor redemption in them.*"[5]

Paul then states that Christ "gave himself a ransom for all" (verse 6). The word *ransom* is not used many times in the New Testament. In teaching His disciples the importance of servant leadership, Jesus explained that "whosoever will be chief among you, let him be your servant: even as the Son of man came not to be ministered unto, but to minister, and *to give his life [as] a ransom for many*" (Matthew 20:27–28; see also Mark 10:45). And the only other place the word appears is here in 1 Timothy 2:6. To ransom is "to redeem from captivity, bondage, detention, etc., by paying a demanded price."[6]

CAUTIONS TO MEN AND WOMEN IN THE CHURCH (2:8–15)

As pertaining to worship, Paul expresses concern and offers counsel to both Christian men and women. "I will therefore that men pray every where, lifting up holy hands, without wrath [i.e., anger] and doubting [i.e., disputes]" (verse 8). It appears some of the men of the Church were expressing anger and encouraging arguments or disputations in their local worship, and Paul is here condemning it. Women were instructed to be modest in their dress and appearance (verses 9–10). This was not "a total ban on the wearing of jewelry or braided hair. Rather, Paul was expressing caution in a society where such things were signs of extravagant luxury and proud personal display."[7]

Paul continues: "Let the woman learn in silence with all subjection. But I suffer not a woman to teach, nor to usurp authority [i.e., exercise dominion, be autocratic, domineer] over the man, but to be in silence

---

5. Packer, "Mediator."
6. *Random House College Dictionary*, s.v. "ransom."
7. *New International Version Study Bible*, 2039.

[i.e., quiet, tranquility]" (verses 11–12). Regarding women speaking or teaching in the Church, see the commentary herein on 1 Corinthians 14:34–35. Paul's rationale for the female being subject to the male is that man was created before woman, and woman was the first to partake of the forbidden fruit in the Garden of Eden (verses 13–14). He concludes the chapter with this observation: "Notwithstanding they [i.e., women] shall be saved in childbearing, if they continue in faith and charity and holiness with sobriety [i.e., modesty]" (verse 15, JST).

One study Bible offers three possible interpretations of Paul's statement that women will be saved in childbearing: "(1) This speaks of the godly woman finding fulfillment in her role of wife and mother in the home; (2) it refers to women being saved spiritually through the most significant birth of all, the incarnation of Christ; or (3) it refers to women being kept physically safe in childbirth."[8]

In a fascinating book, Professor Elaine Pagels chronicles the various interpretations and implications of the Fall of Adam and Eve.[9] She shows how, historically and theologically, beginning with St. Augustine, woman became the goat of Genesis 1–3, responsible for the disaster of Eden and sin itself, human depravity, and the Edenic curse that has been inherited by all humankind.

Restoration scripture, linked with temple instruction, teaches otherwise—the Fall was as much a part of God's foreordained plan as was the Savior's Atonement (see 2 Nephi 2:22–26; Moses 5:10–11; Articles of Faith 1:2). If there had been no Fall, there would have been no Atonement. In the marvelous words of Elder Orson F. Whitney, "The Fall had a two-fold direction—downward, yet forward. It brought man into the world and set his feet upon progression's highway."[10] Latter-day Saints feel to cry out, "Thank God for Eve!"

"It was Eve who first transgressed the limits of Eden in order to

---

8. *New International Version Study Bible*, 2040.
9. Pagels, *Adam, Eve, and the Serpent*.
10. Cowley and Whitney, *Cowley and Whitney on Doctrine*, 287.

initiate the conditions of mortality," President Dallin H. Oaks declared. "Her act, whatever its nature, was formally a transgression but eternally a glorious necessity to open the doorway toward eternal life. Adam showed his wisdom by doing the same. And thus Eve and 'Adam fell that men might be' (2 Nephi 2:25). Some Christians condemn Eve for her act, concluding that she and her daughters are somehow flawed by it. Not the Latter-day Saints! Informed by revelation, we celebrate Eve's act and honor her wisdom and courage in the great episode called the Fall."[11]

President Joseph Fielding Smith expressed his optimistic view as follows:

> I am very, very grateful for Mother Eve. If I ever get to see her, I want to thank her for what she did, and she did the most wonderful thing that ever happened in this world, and that was to place herself where Adam had to do the same thing that she did or they would have been separated forever. . . . They had to partake of that fruit or you wouldn't be here. I wouldn't be here. No one would have been here except Adam and Eve; and they would have stayed there and been there today and been there forever. . . . Adam and Eve did the very thing they had to. I tell you, I take my hat off to Mother Eve.[12]

QUALIFICATIONS FOR BISHOPS AND DEACONS
(3:1–13; COMPARE TITUS 1:6–14)

In his instructions to Timothy, Paul sets out the qualifications or requirements for a man to be called as a bishop, or overseer, of the Christian Church. This person must be blameless, the husband of one wife, vigilant, sober, of good behavior, hospitable, apt [i.e., prone] to teach, not given to wine, not abusive, not in love with money, not

---

11. Oaks, "Great Plan of Happiness."
12. Joseph Fielding Smith, *Take Heed to Yourselves*, 291–92.

covetous, not a brawler, patient, one who rules his house well, not a novice [i.e., recent convert], and a man who has a good reputation among those outside the faith (verses 1–7). Further, deacons [i.e., assistants, helpers] must be grave [i.e., honorable, dignified], not double-tongued [i.e., deceitful], not heavy drinkers, not in love with money, and husbands of one wife. And their wives should also be grave, not slanderers, sober, and faithful in all things (verses 8–12). Paul set a very high standard for those called to sacred and serious positions of responsibility.

"THE MYSTERY OF GODLINESS" (3:16)

Verse 16 of chapter 3 quickly captures our attention: "And without controversy [i.e., beyond all question, without any doubt] great is the mystery of godliness: God was manifest in the flesh, justified in the Spirit, seen of angels, preached unto the Gentiles, believed on in the world, received up into glory." In other words, the central mystery of all mysteries is the condescension of God the Son (see 1 Nephi 11:16–33)—His divine birth, His loving ministry, and, of greatest importance, His mediatorial Atonement and Resurrection.

In general, a mystery is that which is beyond human comprehension. From a gospel or doctrinal perspective, a mystery is "a truth which cannot be known except by revelation."[13] We are often told that we must "leave the mysteries alone." It is true that extremely deep and ponderous matters should probably not be discussed in sacrament meeting, Sunday School, Relief Society, or priesthood quorum meetings. In addition, it is seldom wise to wade into deep water if we are not properly prepared to swim. Jesus certainly taught a system of gospel prerequisites (see Matthew 7:9–11, JST).

And yet, the revelations teach us that we should seek to understand the mysteries of God. Consider the following:

---

13. *Teachings of Harold B. Lee*, 575.

> I, Nephi, . . . having great desires to know of the mysteries of God, wherefore, I did cry unto the Lord; and behold he did visit me, and did soften my heart. (1 Nephi 2:16)

> Hearken unto me, and open your ears that ye may hear, and your hearts that ye may understand, and your minds that the mysteries of God may be unfolded to your view. (Mosiah 2:9)

> Seek not for riches but for wisdom, and behold, the mysteries of God shall be unfolded unto you. (Doctrine and Covenants 6:7)

> If thou shalt ask, thou shalt receive revelation upon revelation, knowledge upon knowledge, that thou mayest know the mysteries and peaceable things—that which bringeth joy, that which bringeth life eternal. (Doctrine and Covenants 42:61)

> But unto him that keepeth my commandments I will give the mysteries of my kingdom, and the same shall be in him a well of living water, springing up unto everlasting life. (Doctrine and Covenants 63:23)

Finally, in speaking of those who love, serve, and honor God, the Lord declared:

> Great shall be their reward and eternal shall be their glory. And *to them will I reveal all mysteries*, yea, all the hidden mysteries of my kingdom from days of old, and for ages to come. (Doctrine and Covenants 76:6–7)

In a revelation given to Martin Harris, the Savior proclaimed: "For, behold, *the mystery of godliness, how great is it!* For, behold, I am endless, and the punishment which is given from my hand is endless punishment, for Endless is my name. Wherefore—eternal punishment is God's punishment. Endless punishment is God's punishment" (Doctrine and Covenants 19:10–12).

In his last address to Brigham Young University students, only three months before his death, Elder Bruce R. McConkie said, "It is true that finite man cannot comprehend his infinite Maker in the full sense of the word. We cannot tell how gods began to be or from whence existent matter came. But we are duty-bound to learn all that God has revealed about himself and his everlasting gospel. . . . *The saints are in a position to comprehend all mysteries, to understand all doctrine, and eventually to know all things.* These high levels of intelligence are reached only through faith and obedience and righteousness. A person who relies on the intellect alone and who does not keep the commandments can never, worlds without end, comprehend the mystery of godliness."[14]

WARNINGS OF APOSTASY (4:1–6)

Paul begins what we know as chapter 4 with another warning that an apostasy, or falling away from the faith, lies ahead. He states that "the Spirit speaketh expressly, that in the latter times some shall depart from the faith, giving heed to seducing [i.e., deceitful] spirits, and doctrines of devils" (verse 1). The phrase "the Spirit speaketh expressly" implies that what came to the Apostle by prophetic revelation was a message that was crystal clear, unambiguous, and specific, leaving no doubt as to what he was to understand and pass along to the Saints through Timothy.

"Seducing spirits" refers to evil or distracting doctrines, principles, or guidelines. This is not a reference to a faithful member of the Church innocently teaching a mistaken concept or belief, but rather to premediated, carefully planned, and intended false teaching or instruction, serious enough to be classified as devilish and destructive. Those who propagate these errors are guilty of hypocrisy. The root of the word *hypocrite* refers to one who wears a mask or falsely and knowingly

---

14. McConkie, "Mystery of Godliness," 49–50.

pretends to be something he or she is not. Such persons have had their "conscience seared with a hot iron" (verse 2). They have sinned against light with such fervor for so long that (1) they have quenched or silenced the Light of Christ within them, that inborn light that signals right from wrong, good from bad, significant from insignificant. They have spoken or acted in evil ways to such an extent that (2) they have, like Korihor the anti-Christ, begun to believe what they preach (see Alma 30:53).

Paul continues, saying that some who leave the faith will also be guilty of "forbidding to marry, and commanding to abstain from meats" that God intended for His children to eat (verse 3). These are prophetic words, and they point to very specific beliefs and practices that were introduced and implemented throughout the history of the Christian Church. The notion that refusing to marry would help one become closer to God, and was thus a sign of spiritual maturity, was taught very early in Christendom. It is important to note that this practice was confined to Western Christianity. Eastern Orthodoxy did not and does not require their priests or other officers to be celibate. Some of the early Christian writers used synonyms for celibacy such as "chastity" or "sanctity." Here are a few examples:

> "You would find many among us, both men and women, growing old and unmarried, in hope of living in closer communion with God."[15]

> "There are many who do so [i.e., abstain from marriage] and seal themselves up to being eunuchs for the sake of the kingdom of God, spontaneously relinquishing a pleasure. So honorable and committed."[16]

---

15. Athenagoras, about AD 175; in Roberts and Donaldson, *Ante-Nicene Fathers*, 2:146.
16. Tertullian, about AD 198; in Roberts and Donaldson, *Ante-Nicene Fathers*, 4:23.

"We do not reject marriage, but simply refrain from it [voluntarily]. Nor do we prescribe celibacy as the rule, but only recommend it. We observe it as a good state—yes, even as the better state—if each man uses it carefully according to his ability."[17]

"Certain ones among them—from a desire of exceeding chastity and a wish to worship God with greater purity—abstain even from the permitted indulgences of love [in marriage]."[18]

"Now that the world is filled [with people] and the earth is cultivated, those who can receive celibacy—*living after the manner of eunuchs*—are made eunuchs unto the kingdom. The *Lord does not* command this, but he *exhorts* it."[19]

The first written declaration that priests should be chaste came in AD 304, when bishops, priests, and other clerical officers were instructed not to have sexual relations with their wives and not to have children. The practice of priestly celibacy spread during the Middle Ages, and in the eleventh century, Pope Gregory VII decreed that priests should not marry. A definitive stand against the marriage of priests was taken at the Second Lateran Council in 1139. This decree was reaffirmed at the Council of Trent in 1563.[20]

Regarding the command "to abstain from meats," the Roman Catholic Church has for centuries called upon their members to abstain from meat on Friday, especially the Friday before Easter (Good

---

17. Tertullian, about AD 207; in Roberts and Donaldson, *Ante-Nicene Fathers*, 3:294.
18. Origen, about AD 248; in Roberts and Donaldson, *Ante-Nicene Fathers*, 4:407.
19. Cyprian, about AD 250; in Roberts and Donaldson, *Ante-Nicene Fathers*, 5:436.
20. For a brief discussion of this practice, see Callister, *Inevitable Apostasy and the Promised Restoration*, 205–7; see also Wilken, *First Thousand Years*, 227–28, 298–99.

Friday) and throughout the year. The choice not to do so is considered a sin that should be repented of.

Section 49 of the Doctrine and Covenants is a revelation given through the Prophet Joseph Smith, intended for the Shakers, the United Society of Believers in Christ's Second Appearing. We are told in the preface to this revelation that the Shakers "rejected marriage and believed in a life of total celibacy. Some Shakers also forbade the eating of meat." The Lord condemned these practices as follows: "And again, verily I say unto you, that whoso forbiddeth to marry is not ordained of God, for marriage is ordained of God unto man. . . . And whoso forbiddeth to abstain from meats, that man should not eat the same, is not ordained of God; for, behold, the beasts of the field and the fowls of the air, and that which cometh of the earth, is ordained for the use of man for food and for raiment, that he might have in abundance" (Doctrine and Covenants 49:15, 18–19; compare 59:16–20).

"AN EXAMPLE OF THE BELIEVERS" (4:12–16)

One of the most memorable statements by the Apostle Paul is the sweet counsel he offers to his beloved companion in the faith, Timothy: "Be thou an example of the believers, in word, in conversation, in charity, in spirit, in faith, in purity" (verse 12). We are called upon as followers of Jesus Christ to act in a Christlike manner.

In word. How we speak and what we say as disciples of our Lord is crucial; so very often people (and the organization they represent) are judged by what they say and the manner in which those words are spoken. Saints of God must speak in a way that is dramatically different from the sounds that echo from the mouths of uninspired, ungodly, and profane people. We want what we say and how we say it to bless, not to curse; to edify, not to embarrass; to inspire, not to offend.

In conversation. Here the word *conversation* refers to our conduct, behavior, or actions. Paul's words to the Galatian Saints are priceless: "If we live in the Spirit, let us also walk in the Spirit" (Galatians 5:25).

Spiritually mature persons strive constantly to not only talk the talk but also walk the walk. If we claim to be true Christians, followers of the Prince of Peace, how we act ought to bear witness of that fact. Some people profess with all their hearts that they are disciples of Christ, but they deal with people who disagree with them or interpret the Bible differently in a way that is judgmental, critical, accusing, and angry. The way they treat people is anything but Christian. The Savior Himself put it this way: "Out of the abundance of the heart the mouth speaketh" (Matthew 12:34). Without question, the best way to assess to what extent I am a Christian is to look at how I speak of and to others, and in general how I treat my fellow brothers and sisters.

In charity. In the early decades of the Christian era, following the Ascension of the Savior, those who disliked the Saints looked for ways to criticize, embarrass, and persecute them and even put them to death. It was not uncommon, however, that following a lengthy negative assessment of the followers of Jesus, someone would remark something like, "But oh, how they loved one another!" This was a manifestation of the Savior's specific charge to His disciples at the Last Supper to "love one another. By this shall all men know that ye are my disciples, if ye have love one to another" (John 13:34–35). True charity spreads itself well beyond the household of faith; as we love one another, so we are called to love those not of the faith.

In faith. Those who strive to be an example of the believers have faith in Christ, the Son of God. They have faith in our Heavenly Father's plan of salvation and see their place within that plan. They have faith in the future, a trust that what lies ahead, though challenging, will prove to be deeply rewarding. And they have faith in the Lord's timetable, confident and assured that God knows best what and when they are prepared to receive (see Doctrine and Covenants 88:68).

In purity. Firm believers strive to have both clean hands and a pure heart. They have developed the kind of discernment and judgment that allow them to perceive the cheap and the tawdry, the fleeting and the ephemeral. They also recognize the good and the beautiful that is in the world, and they are drawn to it (see Articles of Faith 1:13). Because they have an eye single to the glory of God, their greatest desire is to build the kingdom of God on earth and establish Zion.

The Apostle then offers simple advice that has profound and lasting impact on human souls and greatly affects our behavior: read and study holy scripture; exhort, or proclaim, the word of truth; and continue to focus on true doctrine (verse 13). Further, Timothy is charged to remember and magnify the spiritual gift that was given him when the hands of the elders of the Church were placed upon his head—that is, when he was ordained and set apart (verse 14).

ATTENDING TO VARIOUS RESPONSIBILITIES (5:1–25)

Chapter 5 is basically a to-do list for Timothy, including various and sundry matters he needs to attend to as a Church officer. These matters include

- being respectful to older persons, both men and women (verses 1–2);
- using care in how he serves those who are widows; encouraging the families of widows to see to the welfare of their own (verses 3–16);
- seeing to it that the men of the Church assume their responsibilities as providers for their families (verse 8);
- cautioning the members against being idle "busybodies" (verse 13);
- rewarding those elders who govern their homes faithfully, particularly those who teach the doctrine of the Church (verse 17);
- understanding that when an elder of the Church is accused of misbehavior, two or three witnesses are needed in order to establish the veracity of the claim (verse 19);
- being careful about prematurely ordaining or setting apart someone who is not prepared for such a responsibility (verse 22);

- and drinking a little wine to help with digestion due to Timothy's sickness and because clean drinking water was often difficult to find (verse 23).

SLAVES SHOULD HONOR THEIR FAITHFUL MASTERS (6:1–2)

Because slavery was allowed in Roman society, the Apostle Paul chooses not to undermine the existing cultural institution. Paul often communicated to slaves who had joined the Church of Jesus Christ of the need to be respectful of their masters, especially those who were brothers in the gospel, fellow Saints.

"THE ROOT OF ALL EVIL" (6:5–11)

Paul begins here by referring to "perverse disput[es] of men of corrupt minds" who are "destitute of the truth" and who suppose (and no doubt teach) that "gain is godliness." "From such withdraw thyself," writes Paul. "But godliness with contentment is great gain" (verses 5–6). The Revised English Bible renders this passage as follows: wicked men "whose minds are corrupted and who have lost their grip of the truth . . . think religion should yield dividends; and of course religion does yield high dividends, but only to those who are content with what they have."

"For we brought nothing into this world," the Apostle continues, "and it is certain we can carry nothing out" (verse 7). The children of God are born into this world as the most helpless of all creatures, utterly dependent upon loving parents and others who care. They bring no money with them; they convey no dowry that can be used to provide for their food, clothing, or shelter. It has wisely been said that most earthly valuables—whether they be money, stocks and bonds, certificates of achievement, or earthly prominence—simply cannot make it through celestial customs. When someone asks how much the billionaire left behind after passing away, the only answer that can be given is "all of it."

One historian of religion in America wrote of what has been called the Protestant, or Puritan, or Calvinist, work ethic—titles created by sociologist Max Weber. "According to Weber," historian Peter Williams explained, "the desire for assurance that one was indeed one of God's elect could receive an indirect satisfaction from external evidences of worldly success, which could be interpreted as signs of divine favor."[21] Or, stated simply, if an individual is highly successful in business, resulting in great wealth, for example, it is an indication that the person is elect, approved of God, destined for salvation in God's kingdom.

A Latter-day Saint might ask, "But doesn't the Book of Mormon teach that if we keep the commandments of God, we will prosper? Doesn't that mean if we prosper financially, we are clearly approved of God?" No, not necessarily. There are certainly instances in Nephite history where, because of their faithfulness, the children of Lehi were prospered in terms of their crops, herds, and monetary possessions. But it is vitally important to remember the second part of the Lord's promise—if we *do not* keep the commandments, we will be *cut off from his presence* (1 Nephi 2:20–21; Alma 36:1, 30). Being cut off from the presence of God is a statement of one's *spiritual* plight.

The same is true of Jehovah's promise to ancient Israel, delivered through the prophet Malachi: "Bring ye all the tithes into the storehouse, that there may be meat in mine house, and prove me now herewith, saith the Lord of hosts, if I will not open [to] you the windows of heaven, and pour you out a blessing, that there shall not be room enough to receive it" (Malachi 3:10). Of this promise, President Harold B. Lee taught: "The opening of the windows of heaven, of course, means revelation of God to him who is willing thus to sacrifice."[22]

Paul points out that "they that will be rich [i.e., those who desire

---

21. Williams, *America's Religions*, 114.
22. *Teachings of Harold B. Lee*, 206; see also 613.

to be rich] fall into temptation and a snare, and into many foolish and hurtful lusts, which drown men in destruction and perdition [i.e., ruin]." He continues with one of the great truths of eternity, a lesson that has been ignored by millions through the years, many of whom sold their birthright for a mess of pottage: "For the love of money is the root of all evil" (verses 9–10). Notice that Paul does not say that "*money* is the root of all evil." Rather, it is "the *love of money*" that dooms souls. Hugh Nibley has written poignantly that "wealth is a jealous master who will not be served half-heartedly, and will suffer no rivals, not even God."[23]

THE LIGHT OF IMMORTALITY (6:12–16)

Paul calls upon his beloved Timothy to "fight the good fight of faith" so that he might eventually "lay hold on eternal life" until the return of the Savior, who will manifest "the blessed and only Potentate, the King of kings, and Lord of lords; *who only hath immortality*, dwelling in the light which no man can approach unto; whom no man hath seen, nor can see: to whom be honour and power everlasting" (verses 12, 14–16). There are two issues to consider in this passage: (1) Who is, according to Paul, the Potentate, the King of kings, and the Lord of lords? Is it God the Father or His Only Begotten Son? and (2) How are we to understand Paul's statement that God is the only one who possesses immortality? Other translations conclude that Paul is speaking of God the Father as the King of kings and Lord of lords (NIV, REB, KNT).

Note the Joseph Smith Translation: "I give thee charge in the sight of God, who quickeneth all things, and before Christ Jesus, who before Pontius Pilate witnessed a good confession; that thou keep this commandment without spot, unrebukable, until the appearing of our Lord Jesus Christ; which in his times he [i.e., Christ] shall show, who is the

---

23. Nibley, *Since Cumorah*, 356–57.

blessed and only Potentate, the King of kings, and Lord of lords, to whom be honor and power everlasting; *whom no man hath seen, nor can see, unto whom no man can approach, only he who hath the light and the hope of immortality dwelling in him"* (verses 13–16, JST).

After studying the Joseph Smith Translation, I am prone to believe that it is God the Father who, in this instance, is the great Potentate and King of kings, largely because of what follows—the statement that no one has ever seen Him or can see Him. This cannot refer to Jesus because obviously He came to earth, lived a mortal life, and was seen by thousands—as attested by the New Testament and Book of Mormon. Besides, other scriptures that reference no person ever seeing God refer to our Heavenly Father (see Exodus 33:11; John 1:18; 1 John 4:12; 3 John 1:11).

Now as to the matter of immortality. Verse 16 is one of the reasons that most Christians believe that only God and Christ are immortal beings. They believe that immortality, the power to live forever, comes to us as a gift of Jesus Christ in the Resurrection. Fellow Christians feel that our Latter-day Saint beliefs about our premortal existence— that we have always lived, that we had no beginning—all contradict this verse. We know from modern revelation that we are immortal beings (see Doctrine and Covenants 29:36; 49:17; 93:21–23, 29; Moses 3:5; 6:36; Abraham 3:22–23). "We say that God himself is a self-existent being," the Prophet Joseph Smith remarked in his King Follett discourse.

> Who told you so? It is correct enough; but how did it get into your heads? Who told you that man did not exist in like manner upon the same principles? Man does exist upon the same principles. . . .
>
> The mind or the intelligence which man possesses is co-equal [i.e., coeternal] with God himself. . . . I am dwelling on the immortality of the spirit of man. Is it logical to say that the

intelligence of spirits is immortal, and yet that it had a beginning? The intelligence of spirits had no beginning, neither will it have an end. That is good logic. That which has a beginning may have an end. There never was a time when there were not spirits; for they are co-equal [i.e., coeternal] with our Father in heaven.[24]

Each one of us, every child of God, is an immortal being; we have always lived, and we will live forever. So when it is said that Christ "brought life and immortality to light through the gospel" (2 Timothy 1:10), we need to understand that what the Savior made available to us is *resurrected and glorified immortality*.

"RICH IN GOOD WORKS" (6:17–21)

As the Apostle nears the end of his first epistle to Timothy, he counsels his colleague in the faith to "charge them that are rich in this world, that they be not highminded [i.e., arrogant, proud], nor trust in uncertain riches, but in the living God, who giveth us richly all things to enjoy" (verse 17). This stern warning brings to mind Jesus's parable of the rich fool. He taught, "Take heed, and beware of covetousness: for a man's life consisteth not in the abundance of the things which he possesseth."

The Lord then spoke of a rich man who simply couldn't decide what to do with his bulging granaries, how to care for his ever-accumulating wealth. Finally, the rich man determines to tear down his old barns and build new and grander buildings to store his earnings. "And I will say to my soul, Soul, thou hast much goods laid up for many years; take thine ease, eat, drink, and be merry." Then follows this chilling verse: "But God said unto him, Thou fool, this night thy soul shall be required of thee: then whose shall those things be, which thou hast provided?" Then

---

24. Joseph Smith, in "Discourse, 7 April 1844, as Reported by *Times and Seasons*."

comes the ever timely and forever timeless lesson: "So is he that layeth up treasure for himself, and is not rich toward God" (Luke 12:15–21).

Jacob, the son of Lehi, presented timeless truths when he charged his people to "think of your brethren like unto yourselves, and *be familiar with all and free with your substance*, that they may be rich like unto you. But *before ye seek for riches, seek ye for the kingdom of God*. And after ye have obtained a hope in Christ ye shall obtain riches, if ye seek them; and *ye will seek them for the intent to do good*—to clothe the naked, and to feed the hungry, and to liberate the captive, and administer relief to the sick and the afflicted" (Jacob 2:17–19).

In our dispensation, the Savior offered this significant counsel to Joseph Smith and Oliver Cowdery: "Seek not for riches but for wisdom, and behold, the mysteries of God shall be unfolded unto you, and then shall you be made rich. Behold, *he that hath eternal life is rich*" (Doctrine and Covenants 6:7). Some seven months later, the Lord similarly said, "And if ye seek the riches which it is the will of the Father to give unto you, ye shall be the richest of all people, for ye shall have the riches of eternity" (Doctrine and Covenants 38:39).

Paul then goes on to explain that those who are rich in good works are "laying up in store for themselves a good foundation against the time to come, that they may lay hold on eternal life" (verse 19). He then beckons to Timothy to "keep that which is committed to thy trust"—namely, the gospel of Jesus Christ in its purity and simplicity—"avoiding profane and vain babblings, and oppositions of science falsely so called" (verse 20). Or, as translated elsewhere: "Timothy, guard what has been entrusted to your care. Turn away from godless chatter and the opposing ideas of what is falsely called knowledge, which some have professed and in so doing have departed from the faith" (NIV).

This verse seems to refer once again to some early forms of Gnosticism, a heretical version of Christianity that blossomed and spread in the second and third centuries AD. Gnosticism emphasized that salvation is to be had through the acquisition of knowledge—not just any knowledge, but secret, sacred, saving, and esoteric knowledge that Jesus had presumably conveyed to His disciples in private gatherings. Gnosticism proved to be one of the most spiritually destructive variants of Christianity, a movement away from "the simplicity that is in Christ" (2 Corinthians 11:3). Perhaps more than any other philosophy or way of life, Gnosticism led many naïve Christians away from the true gospel and into what we know as the Great Apostasy.

THE SECOND EPISTLE TO TIMOTHY

PAUL'S SECOND EPISTLE TO Timothy was written from Rome, where the Apostle was being held captive. It was written in about AD 65–67 and has the distinction of being Paul's last letter to his beloved Saints. He was put to death not long after he wrote this precious letter.

TRANSMITTING TRUTH THROUGH THE GENERATIONS (1:5–6)

Paul writes in this epistle that whenever he reflects on the unfeigned [i.e., genuine, real] faith of Timothy, he is reminded of those responsible for helping to plant that faith within him early on—namely, Timothy's grandmother and his mother (verse 5). "Although the first mention of Timothy is when he joined Paul's second mission tour at Lystra," explained one scholar, "Paul probably had met and converted Timothy during his first mission at Lystra two or three years earlier. Timothy's father was a Greek and, so far as we are informed, was not a Christian. However, his mother, Eunice, and his grandmother, Lois, were both members of the church and were of strong faith."[1]

How often have faithful parents or loved ones had a deeply significant effect on the rising generation? In our day and time, perhaps

---

1. Matthews, *Unto All Nations*, 32.

the influence happens when parents teach children during home evening or at the dinner table or in family scripture study. Or maybe it comes through the kind of lives the parents live. Their devotion and commitment to the Lord, His gospel, and His Church may move the younger generation to seek after the kind of testimony and conviction that they hear or witness so often. As the early elders of this dispensation were taught, "It was human testimony . . . that excited the inquiry, in the first instance, in [the children's] minds. It was the credence they gave to the testimony of the [parents or loved ones], this testimony having aroused their minds to inquire after the knowledge of God; the inquiry frequently terminated, indeed always terminated when rightly pursued, in the most glorious discoveries and eternal certainty."[2]

Paul charges Timothy to "stir up [i.e., rekindle or revive] the gift of God, which is in thee by the putting on of my hands" (verse 6). Paul was apparently involved in either the confirmation, ordination, or setting apart of Timothy. The gift of God could be (1) the gift of the Holy Ghost, so essential to spreading the gospel message, or (2) the power of the priesthood, the power to act in the name of the Almighty. The phrase probably refers to both. Every member of the Lord's Church and kingdom needs to be involved in ongoing, regular spiritual experiences in order to keep the flame of faith burning brightly (see Jacob 7:4–5; Enos 1:4–11).

"Testimony isn't something that you have today and you keep always," President Harold B. Lee taught. "Testimony is either going to grow and grow to the brightness of certainty, or it is going to diminish to nothingness, depending upon what we do about it. I say, the testimony that we recapture day by day is the thing that saves us from the pitfalls of the adversary." Using analogies, President Lee continued: "Testimony is as elusive as a moonbeam; it's as fragile as an orchid; you

---

2. *Lectures on Faith*, 2:56; p. 24.

have to recapture it every morning of your life. You have to hold on by study, and by faith, and by prayer."³

GOD HAS NOT GIVEN US THE SPIRIT OF FEAR (1:7–8)

Paul writes, "God hath not given us the spirit of fear" (verse 7). How very often the Lord Jesus Christ pleads with His people to "fear not." Consider just a small sample of scriptural passages:

> Behold, I speak with boldness, having authority from God; and I fear not what man can do; for perfect love casteth out all fear. (Moroni 8:16)

> Fear not, little flock; do good; let earth and hell combine against you, for if ye are built upon my rock, they cannot prevail. . . . Look unto me in every thought; doubt not, fear not. (Doctrine and Covenants 6:34, 36)

> You shall ever open your mouth in my cause, not fearing what man can do, for I am with you. (Doctrine and Covenants 30:11)

> If ye are prepared ye shall not fear. (Doctrine and Covenants 38:30)

> Fear not, little children, for you are mine, and I have overcome the world, and you are of them that my Father hath given me. (Doctrine and Covenants 50:41)

> Inasmuch as you strip yourselves from jealousies and fears, and humble yourselves before me, . . . the veil shall be rent and you shall see me and know that I am. (Doctrine and Covenants 67:10)

Fear can cloud our judgment and prevent us from carrying out the

---

3. *Teachings of Harold B. Lee*, 139.

will of God; it can block us from enjoying the peace of the Holy Spirit and make us spiritually dysfunctional. Hence, we do not take counsel from our fears. President Boyd K. Packer declared: "This is a great time to live. When times are unsettled, when the dangers persist, the Lord pours out His blessings upon His church and kingdom. I have been associated now in the councils of the Church for [many] years. During that time I have seen, from the sidelines at least, many a crisis. Among the leaders I have at times seen great disappointment, some concern, maybe some anxiety. *One thing I have never seen is fear. Fear is the antithesis of faith.* In this Church and in this kingdom there is faith."[4]

Truly, as Paul teaches in his letter, God has given members of the Church of Jesus Christ power, love, and sound minds. "Be not thou therefore ashamed of the testimony of our Lord" (verses 7–8). As Paul explained to the Roman Saints: "I am not ashamed of the gospel of Christ: for it is the power of God unto salvation to every one that believeth" (Romans 1:16). Very often those who are ashamed of the gospel of Jesus Christ are those who have placed too much stock in what people of the world think about God, Christ, the gospel, and the Lord's Church. Much too often those who have received the glad tidings of the gospel and come into the Church of Jesus Christ allow themselves to be distracted by the loud and raucous voices of those who have less than noble motives—by the pride and vain imaginations of worldly people (see 1 Nephi 8:24–28; 11:32–36; 12:18).

In offering sound but sober counsel to Brigham Young University students, Elder Neal A. Maxwell spoke prophetically: "Make no mistake about it, brothers and sisters; in the months and years ahead, events will require of each member that he or she decide whether or not he or she will follow the First Presidency. Members will find it more difficult to halt [i.e., hesitate, stumble, falter] longer between two opinions. . . . In short, brothers and sisters, not being ashamed of the

---

4. Packer, *Mine Errand from the Lord*, 405.

gospel of Jesus Christ includes *not being ashamed of the prophets of Jesus Christ.*"[5]

CHRIST HAS ABOLISHED DEATH (1:9–11)

Paul testifies that God "hath saved us, and called us with an holy calling, not according to our works, but according to his own purpose and grace, which was given us in Christ Jesus before the world began" (verse 9). These early Christians were saved from physical death by virtue of the Resurrection and saved from spiritual death because they had been forgiven of their sins by means of the Atonement of Jesus Christ; they were also saved in the sense that those who enjoy the gifts and fruit of the Spirit live in a saved condition—they receive what Paul calls the "earnest of the Spirit" (2 Corinthians 1:21–22; 5:5) or "the earnest of [their] inheritance" (Ephesians 1:13–14). That is, they receive God's "earnest money" to His Saints—His sign or token that He fully intends to save them—which is the Holy Spirit. When the Spirit dwells in them or with them, the Saints are on course, in Christ, in line to receive eternal life (see 1 John 3:24; 4:13).

What peace and assurance must have filled the hearts of the Saints who lived in the meridian of time to know that "our Saviour Jesus Christ [has] abolished death, and . . . brought life and immortality to light through the gospel," a gospel whereunto Paul has been "appointed a preacher, and an apostle, and a teacher of the Gentiles" (verses 10–11).

THE SAINTS ARE PERSECUTED FOR THEIR TESTIMONY (2:8–13)

There is a cost associated with following the Lord Jesus Christ, a very real cost of discipleship. Sometimes being counted among the believers will cost us friends, while at other times it may cost us opportunities or deny us privileges. And, in some cases, discipleship may bring

---

5. Maxwell, "Meeting the Challenges of Today," 149.

with it rejection, unemployment, assaults, or even death. "Behold, I send you forth as sheep in the midst of wolves," Jesus warned His original Apostles. "Be ye therefore wise as serpents, and harmless as doves. But beware of men: for they will deliver you up to the councils, and they will scourge you in their synagogues. . . . And the brother shall deliver up the brother to death, and the father the child: and the children shall rise up against their parents, and cause them to be put to death. And ye shall be hated of all men for my name's sake: but he that endureth to the end shall be saved" (Matthew 10:16–17, 21–22).

Paul writes to Timothy, "Remember that Jesus Christ of the seed of David was raised from the dead according to my gospel: wherein I suffer trouble, as an evil doer, even unto bonds [i.e., chains, imprisonment]; but the word of God is not bound," meaning, you cannot block the good news of salvation in Christ, for it is destined to spread throughout the earth. "Therefore I endure all things for the elect's sakes, that they may also obtain the salvation which is in Christ Jesus with eternal glory," for if a disciple is called upon to die for their testimony of Jesus, they have this assurance: "We shall also live with him." In addition, those who serve Him faithfully will one day reign with the King of kings and Lord of lords (verses 8–12; compare Revelation 5:10; 20:4; 22:5).

STUDY TO BE APPROVED (2:14–19)

In verse 14, Paul calls upon Timothy to warn the Saints to "strive not about words to no profit, but to the subverting of the hearers." In other words, time is precious. Members of the Lord's Church simply do not have the time to sit around debating trivialities—arguing about topics that matter precious little or speculating about the inane and the unimportant.

Paul counsels Timothy to "study [i.e., try hard] to shew thyself approved unto God, a workman that needeth not to be ashamed, rightly dividing the word of truth," or setting forth the truth without perversion or distortion. "But shun profane and vain babblings [i.e., irreverent or irreligious chatter] for they will increase unto more ungodliness. And their word will eat as doth a canker [i.e., spread like gangrene]" (verses 15–17).

Two of these deceivers are named: Hymenaeus and Philetus, "who concerning the truth have erred, saying that the resurrection is past already; and overthrow the faith of some" (verses 17–18). While we have no information in the text regarding Philetus, Hymenaeus is identified as a false teacher in 1 Timothy 1:20. Perhaps Philetus was a replacement for Alexander, mentioned in 1 Timothy 1:20. Why would Hymenaeus and Philetus teach that the Resurrection is past? A couple of possibilities come to mind. Perhaps these two men are believers in an early form of Gnosticism, mentioned in our commentary on Paul's writings to the Corinthians. If so, believing that physical matter is evil and the spirit is good, they may have concluded that the physical Resurrection of Jesus was actually a kind of spiritual resurrection, an ascent into higher, saving knowledge.

N. T. Wright has written of how vastly different the Christian concept of resurrection was from that of first-century Jews. "No first century Jew prior to Easter," Wright explained, "expected the resurrection to be *anything other than a large-scale event happening to all of God's people, or perhaps to the entire human race*, as part of the sudden event in which God's kingdom would finally come on earth as in heaven. *There is no suggestion that one person [i.e., Jesus Christ] would rise from the dead in advance of all the rest.*" He went on to restate that "we never find outside Christianity what becomes a central feature within it: the belief that the mode of this inauguration consisted in the resurrection itself happening to one person in the middle of history in advance of its great, final occurrence, anticipating and guaranteeing the final resurrection of God's people at the end of history."[6]

---

6. Wright, *Surprised by Hope*, 44–45.

AVOIDING FOOLISH SPECULATIONS (2:23–26)

For commentary on verses 23–26, see our discussion of 2 Timothy 2:14–19.

PERILOUS TIMES AHEAD (3:1–9)

From our twenty-first-century perspective, reading Paul's prophecy and warning in verses 1–7 can be a haunting experience. His words are as real, pertinent, and applicable to our time as they would have been to the former-day Saints of his time. One has only to watch or read the news to recognize the frightening cavalcade of evil actions described here by Paul:

- Self-centered and selfish people who are covetous of what others have, self-promoters, prideful people, those who blaspheme, those who disobey their parents, and the unthankful—in general, an unholy people (verse 2)
- Unnatural or perverse expressions of affection, people who do not keep their promises, those who perjure themselves, people guilty of slander, those who have no self-control, and those who despise good people (verse 3)
- Those who betray other persons, causes, or countries; those who are rash or reckless; those dripping with conceit; those who have chosen to bow beneath the gods of this world rather than the true and living God (verse 4)
- People who claim to be holy and God-ordained but who do not have, and do not desire to have, divine authorization; those who talk the talk but do not walk the walk. Paul mentions specifically that we should "turn away" from such people (verse 5).
- Lustful men who frequent dens of iniquity devoted to prostitution or other forms of sexual perversion (verse 6)
- Those who constantly fill their minds with information but are unable to recognize or acquire truth (verse 7)

Paul uses Pharaoh's magicians and sorcerers who contended with Moses (Exodus 7:11), here named Jannes and Jambres, as an analogy. His point is that men and women who resist the truth, have corrupt minds, and in general are reprobates (depraved and unprincipled individuals) are like those false priests who sought to win a victory over Moses, the Lawgiver, a prophet of God and the head of a gospel dispensation. As Jannes and Jambres were defeated and humiliated by Moses and the power of Jehovah, so will the God-fearing and faithful of the last days be protected and victorious over the powers of Satan (verses 8–9).

THE SCRIPTURES: A GODSEND (3:10–17)

The Apostle pays tribute to Timothy as an example of one who knew Paul's teachings, faithfulness to his sacred apostolic calling, and persecutions and afflictions—which all obedient and godly people may be called upon to pass through. He then acknowledges, sadly, that "evil men and seducers" will descend into even deeper depravity and deception, but God has provided a medication for the maladies of a troubled world (verses 10–14). Paul then reminds Timothy, "From a child thou hast known the holy scriptures, which are able to make thee wise unto salvation through faith which is in Christ Jesus" (verse 15).

Those disciples of Christ who devote themselves to a serious, daily, and lifelong study of holy scripture place themselves on a pathway to holy and sacred experience. Repeated, ongoing, and daily searching of the word of the Lord stamps upon the mind and the human soul the language, learning, and logic of the words of God and His divinely called prophets.

Paul continues: "All scripture is given by inspiration of God, and is profitable for doctrine, for reproof, for correction, for instruction in righteousness: that the man [or woman] of God may be perfect [i.e., complete, whole, finished], throughly furnished unto all good works" (verses 16–17). The Joseph Smith Translation of these verses reads as follows: "And all scripture *given by inspiration of God*, is profitable for doctrine, for reproof, for correction, for instruction in righteousness: that the man [or woman] of God may be perfect, thoroughly furnished unto all good works." This is an interesting revision—not everything that wears the label of "scripture" in the Bible is inspired. As one example, the following is written on the manuscript of the Joseph Smith Translation, following the book of Ecclesiastes: "The Songs of Solomon are not inspired writings."

Notice the areas of the life of the disciple of Christ that are enriched, edified, and strengthened by serious scripture study:

- **Doctrine.** The scriptures, together with the words and warnings of latter-day prophets, contain the doctrine of the gospel, those matters that are of greatest worth.
- **Reproof.** A careful and sincere study of the scriptures can result in the reader feeling chastened by the Holy Spirit, who can reveal to the individual a specific attitude or behavior that needs to be repented of. A person may be reading the four Gospels, for example, looking carefully at the tender and ever-loving way the Savior treated other people, especially those who were needy or heartbroken, and feel uncomfortable or ill at ease about the way he or she often treats people.
- **Correction.** Not only do the scriptures teach us what we should *not* do, but through the searching of those sacred pages, God's Holy Spirit can also make known to His children what they *should* do. For example, someone may read 3 Nephi, particularly of the ministry of the risen Lord to the Nephites, and come away feeling the need to be more consistent and more focused in their individual prayers. Or someone may read about the ancient tabernacle in the days of Moses and come away sensing the need to spend more time in temple worship.
- **Instruction.** Let us suppose a newly called bishop of a ward finds himself, not long after his call, facing some very serious cases of transgression among the members of his congregation.

He feels overwhelmed and, like Alma the Elder, is deeply worried "that he should do wrong in the sight of God" (Mosiah 26:13). He picks up his copy of the Book of Mormon and finds himself reading the instructions of Jesus Christ to Alma concerning how priesthood leaders should deal properly and lovingly with members of the Church who have fallen into serious sin (see Mosiah 26:13–32). He is both comforted and instructed as he identifies significant principles taught in that specific chapter.

The Apostle Paul's words help us appreciate how vital our standard works, our divine curriculum—the Bible, Book of Mormon, Doctrine and Covenants, and Pearl of Great Price—are to the formation of a Christian character. These holy words are fundamental in our continuing quest to become perfect—that is, suited, ready, mature, and complete—as our Exemplar Jesus Christ has called us to be (see Matthew 5:48; 3 Nephi 12:48).

MORE PROPHECY OF THE COMING APOSTASY (4:1–5)

The message within verse 2 of chapter 4 in the King James Version will not be clear to many readers: "Preach the word; be instant in season, out of season; reprove, rebuke, exhort with all longsuffering and doctrine." Let's look at another translation of this verse: "I solemnly urge you: proclaim the message; be persistent whether the time is favorable or unfavorable; convince, rebuke, and encourage, with the utmost patience in teaching" (NRSV).

"For the time will come," Paul continues, "when they will not endure sound doctrine; but after their own lusts shall they heap to themselves teachers, having itching ears; and they shall turn away their ears from the truth, and shall be turned unto fables" (verses 3–4). N. T. Wright's translation renders these verses as follows: "The time is coming, you see, when people won't tolerate healthy teaching. Their ears will start to itch, and they will collect for themselves teachers who will tell them what they want to hear. They will turn away from listening to the truth and will go after myths instead" (KNT).

In verse 5, Paul encourages Timothy to be patient in afflictions and to "do the work of an evangelist" and fulfill his ministry. Other Christian denominations define "evangelist" as a preacher of the gospel of Jesus Christ, particularly one who declares the word to those outside the Christian faith. Joseph Smith explained that "an Evangelist is a Patriarch, even the oldest man of the blood of Joseph or of the seed of Abraham. Wherever the Church of Christ is established in the earth, there should be a Patriarch for the benefit of the posterity of the Saints, as it was with Jacob in giving his patriarchal blessing unto his sons, etc."[7]

According to the Bible Dictionary, "A patriarch is called an evangelist in D&C 107:39–52. As such, patriarch is an ordained office in the Melchizedek Priesthood. The fathers from Adam to Jacob were all patriarchs of this kind. The word as used in the Bible seems to denote also a title of honor to early leaders of the Israelites, such as David (Acts 2:29) and the 12 sons of Jacob (Acts 7:8–9)."[8] Paul lists evangelists as one of the offices within the Church of Jesus Christ (Ephesians 4:11). Philip, one of the seven men chosen to serve the Apostles (Acts 6:5), was later in his life, called to be an evangelist or patriarch (Acts 21:8).

PAUL IS PREPARED TO FACE THE END (4:6–8)

Paul's thirty-year ministry as the Apostle to the Gentiles was filled with suspicion, dismissal, rejection, persecution, arrests, confinement, loneliness, and discouragement. He suffered an unremovable thorn in the flesh and, finally, a martyr's death. On the other hand, those three decades were filled also with extensive travel, discovery, enlightenment,

---

7. Joseph Smith, in "Discourse, between circa 26 June and circa 2 July 1839, as Reported by Wilford Woodruff"; spelling and punctuation standardized.
8. Bible Dictionary, "Patriarch, patriarchs," 742.

enrichment, visions and revelations, powerful preaching, hundreds of conversions, sweet associations, and joy in the fruit of his labors.

As mentioned in the introduction of this epistle, 2 Timothy is the last of Paul's letters, written just prior to his death by beheading at the hands of Nero Caesar in about AD 64–65. "For I am now ready," the Apostle writes, "to be offered, and the time of my departure is at hand. I have fought a good fight, I have finished my course, I have kept the faith" (verses 6–7). Saul of Tarsus—at one time the great enemy of the followers of Jesus of Nazareth, and the one who was marvelously and miraculously transformed into Paul the Apostle—did indeed fight the good fight of faith.

He battled against Satan and his emissaries, both seen and unseen. He proclaimed against falsehood by declaring sound doctrine, which he spoke or wrote by the power of God's Holy Spirit. He dealt Lucifer, the father of all lies, a major blow again and again as he gave all he had to defend the name and ministry and divine Sonship of Jesus the Messiah. He finished his course. He was true and faithful to his apostolic calling. He was a chosen vessel (Acts 9:15), a special witness of the name of Christ in all the world, constantly building up and regulating the affairs of the Church of Jesus Christ in all nations that he visited (see Doctrine and Covenants 107:23, 33).

In short, Paul endured to the very end. He wrote, "Henceforth there is laid up for me a crown of righteousness, which the Lord, the righteous judge, shall give me at that [judgment] day: and not to me only, but unto all them also that love his [second] appearing" (verse 8). "Blessed are they who are faithful and endure," a modern revelation declares, "whether in life or in death, for they shall inherit eternal life" (Doctrine and Covenants 50:5; compare 5:22; 58:2; 61:39). A modern Apostle put it this way: "If we die in the faith, that is the same thing as saying that our calling and election has been made sure and that we will go on to eternal reward hereafter. . . . As far as faithful people are concerned, if they are in the line of their duty, if they are doing what they ought to do, although they may not have been perfect in this sphere, their probation is ended."⁹

PAUL'S FINAL INSTRUCTIONS (4:11–13)

Writing from his imprisonment (house arrest), Paul mentions that "only Luke is with me" (verse 11). Luke, the author of the two-part work, the Gospel of Luke and the Acts of the Apostles, seems to have joined Paul on the Apostle's second missionary journey. In Acts 16, Luke begins speaking of "we" in verses 10 and 13. He becomes a beloved traveling companion with Paul thereafter.

John-Mark—or as he is better known, Mark, the author of the second Gospel—traveled and ministered for a time with Paul and Barnabas on the Apostle's first missionary journey. For some unstated reason, Mark decided to leave the brethren in Perga of Pamphilia and return home to Jerusalem (Acts 13:13). Later, as Paul and Barnabas were preparing to begin their second missionary journey, Barnabas suggested that they include Mark, a relative of his. Paul objected because of Mark's previous departure from the mission. There was then what is described by Luke as sharp contention, resulting in Paul taking Silas with him and returning to the sites of the first missionary journey to confirm the faith of the converts there. Barnabas took Mark and traveled to Cyprus, Barnabas's homeland (Acts 4:36; 15:36–41). The magnanimity of Paul, his willingness to forgive and forget, is seen in his instruction to Timothy to "take Mark, and bring him with thee [to Rome]: for he is profitable to me for the ministry" (verse 11).

That Paul's circumstances as a prisoner were not ideal is evident in Paul's next request: "The cloak that I left at Troas with Carpus, when thou comest, bring with thee, *and the books, but especially the parchments*" (verse 13). A highly respected and beloved New Testament scholar, F. F. Bruce, wrote many years ago of this verse:

---

9. McConkie, address delivered at the funeral of S. Dilworth Young, 5.

It has been suggested that the word translated as "cloak" in Paul's message was not really a cloak. The Greek word is *phailones*, borrowed from the Latin *paenula*; and sometimes it means a piece of cloth to wrap around books to protect them against the weather. And it is suggested that Paul was more concerned about protecting his books than about protecting his body. Perhaps we can have it both ways. . . .

In New Testament times, parchment, being more durable and more costly than papyrus, was used chiefly for documents of greater value, or for such as were constantly in use and were, therefore, exposed to greater wear and tear. What the parchments were that Paul so particularly desired Timothy to bring we cannot be sure, but *it is a reasonable guess that they contained portions of Holy Scripture.*[10]

---

10. Bruce, *Books and the Parchments*, 10, 12.

THE EPISTLE TO TITUS

❖

The epistle of the Apostle Paul to Titus was also written late in the Apostle's ministry, in about AD 64–65. Titus served as a missionary companion and accompanied Paul to the Jerusalem conference, where important decisions were made by the leaders of the Church regarding what was and was not required of Gentile converts (see Acts 15). Titus apparently directed the Church of Jesus Christ on the isle of Crete.

THE PREMORTAL PROMISE OF ETERNAL LIFE (1:1–5)

The letter to Paul's missionary companion Titus begins, "Paul, a servant of God, and an apostle of Jesus Christ, according to the faith of God's elect [i.e., for the sake of God's elect], and the acknowledging of the truth which is after [i.e., which leads to] godliness; in hope of eternal life, which God, that cannot lie, promised before the world began; but hath in due times manifested his word through preaching, which is committed unto me according to the commandment of God our Saviour" (verses 1–3).

Paul is teaching that many of the children of God were foreordained in the premortal world to receive on earth marvelous opportunities and supernal blessings, including eternal life. In that first estate, no person was predestined to inherit either eternal life or damnation. All spirit sons and daughters of God have within them the capacity to come to earth, accept the gospel of Jesus Christ, enter into sacred covenants and receive saving ordinances, and endure faithfully to the end, thus qualifying for the greatest of all blessings—salvation or eternal life (Doctrine and Covenants 6:13; 14:7). God's premortal promises regarding receiving salvation or eternal life are conditional; inheriting the highest of heavenly rewards is contingent on the faithfulness of each person to the end of mortality. The principle of promised blessings being conditional is perhaps best illustrated by patriarchal blessings. Frequently, a person is prophetically promised, through an ordained patriarch, blessings such as spiritual gifts, a deeper understanding of the gospel, missionary service, or eternal marriage, but these privileges are based upon the obedience of the person receiving the blessing.

Paul was one among many who was commissioned to take these glad tidings to the people of the earth. The Apostle left Titus in Crete and commissioned him to "set in order the things that are wanting [i.e., matters that still needed attention]" and to "ordain elders in every city" (verses 4–5).

QUALIFICATIONS FOR AND DUTIES OF A BISHOP (1:6–14)

The qualifications listed here for a person to be called as a bishop are almost identical to those set forth in 1 Timothy 3:1–7. Paul describes an effective bishop as one who "[holds] fast the faithful word as he hath been taught, that he may be able by sound doctrine both to exhort and to convince the gainsayers [i.e., those who deny or contradict]. For there are many unruly and vain talkers [i.e., idle speakers or disputers] and deceivers, specially they of the circumcision," meaning Jewish converts to Christianity who encourage other Jewish or Gentile converts to hold to the teachings and practices of the law of Moses (verses 9–10). Paul mentions specifically the need to ignore and shun those who seek to perpetuate Jewish fables or myths (verse 14). What specific myths he is referring to here is unclear, but, whatever they are, they tend to lead people away from the salvation that comes only through the atoning sacrifice of the Lord Jesus Christ.

"UNTO THE PURE ALL THINGS ARE PURE" (1:15–16)

Paul then expresses a marvelous truth—unto persons who are pure, all things are pure, while to those who have become defiled and unbelieving, nothing (and presumably no one) is pure. The minds and consciences of the latter group are also defiled; further, "they profess that they know God; but in works they deny him, being abominable, and disobedient, and unto every good work reprobate [i.e., unfit, worthless]" (verses 15–16). The Joseph Smith Translation changes this verse to a directive, a duty: "unto the pure, *let all things be pure.*"

So often we as flawed humans do not see things as they really are—that is, we do not see truthfully (Doctrine and Covenants 93:24); rather, we tend to see things *as we are.* The Savior declared that "he that *doeth truth* cometh to the light, that his deeds may be made manifest, that they are wrought in God" (John 3:21). Or, "If we say that we have fellowship with [God], and walk in darkness, we lie, and *do not the truth*" (1 John 1:6).

Jesus the Messiah was and forevermore will be the purest human being to walk the earth. Although Jesus was and is "touched with the feeling of our infirmities"—our weaknesses or even our failings—and "was in all points tempted like as we are, yet [He remained] without sin" (Hebrews 4:15). Simon Peter taught that our Lord "did no sin, neither was guile found in his mouth" (1 Peter 2:22; see also 1 John 3:5). There was no telestial film over the eyes of the Savior's understanding as a result of His sins and misdeeds. Consequently the Son of God was able to see into the hearts and minds of people, to feel sorrow with them, to delight with them, to empathize with them, and to look beyond their sinful actions or attitudes and recognize their potential and possibilities. He saw goodness while others were fixated on flaws. Obviously, He was able to witness, recognize, and identify sins and sinfulness, but He did not dwell on these matters endlessly (see Philippians 4:8). Jesus came to earth to transform ashes into beauty, "the oil of joy for mourning, the garment of praise for the spirit of heaviness" (Isaiah 61:3).

TEACH SOUND DOCTRINE TO EVERYONE (2:1–10)

Titus is charged to teach sound doctrine—doctrine that inspires, lifts, edifies, enriches, chastens, corrects, and strengthens individuals and congregations. He was to teach sound doctrine so that

- older men may be and remain sober or circumspect (verse 2);
- older women may strive for holiness (verse 3);
- older women may teach younger women to love and care for their families and their husbands and to be pure and dedicated homemakers (verses 4–5);
- young men may be sober minded or self-controlled, prone to good works, dignified, respectful, sincere, and willing to offer sound instruction, so as to always maintain a good reputation (verses 6–8);
- and slaves may be obedient and respectful to their masters, never arguing or contradicting, robbing or misappropriating, and may always adore or honor "the doctrine of God our Savior in all things" (verses 9–10).

LIVING SOBERLY, RIGHTEOUSLY, AND GODLY (2:11–15)

The King James Version of Titus 2:11–12 reads as follows: "For the grace of God that bringeth salvation hath appeared to all men, teaching us that, denying ungodliness and worldly lusts, we should live soberly, righteously, and godly, in this present world." The Revised English Bible of verse 11 reads, "For the grace of God has dawned upon the world with healing for all mankind." Note the subtle but significant change in the Joseph Smith Translation of verse 11: "For the grace of God *which bringeth salvation to all men*, hath appeared."

The King James Version states that the grace of God that brings salvation has been made available to everyone, to all women and men. Examples of that grace would be (1) the Light, or Spirit, of Jesus Christ, which is given to every person who comes into this second estate; (2) moral agency, or the right to choose (2 Nephi 2:26–27); and (3) the Resurrection of the dead.

The Joseph Smith Translation emphasizes that the grace of God brings *salvation to all persons*. If we read carefully the vision of the degrees of glory received by Joseph Smith and Sidney Rigdon in February of 1832 (see Doctrine and Covenants 76), we discover that all men and women (with the exception of the sons of perdition) will hereafter enjoy some degree of salvation, for they will inherit a kingdom of glory, whether it be the telestial, terrestrial, or celestial. In that sense, The Church of Jesus Christ of Latter-day Saints teaches a kind of universal salvation for all of God's children. Even in the telestial kingdom, which is the lowest of the three kingdoms, inheritors will be glorified. Notice the language of the revelation: "And thus we saw, in the heavenly vision, the glory of *the telestial*, which *surpasses all understanding*" (Doctrine and Covenants 76:89).

Paul continues by saying we should "[look] for that blessed hope, and the glorious appearing of the great God and our Saviour Jesus Christ" (verse 13). The "blessed hope" is the anticipated Second Coming of Jesus Christ. Christ is God, just as is the Almighty Elohim, our Heavenly Father. Paul adds that Jesus "gave himself for us, that he might redeem us from all iniquity, and purify unto himself a peculiar people, zealous of good works" (verse 14). Indeed, Christ was the glorious offering and the consummate sacrifice; the son of Mary "gave himself for us"—He stood in for us, substituted for us, and assumed the infinite burden of our sinfulness, as though He was the guilty and sinful one (see 2 Corinthians 5:21; Galatians 3:13; Hebrews 2:9). Through the blessings of His atoning sacrifice, we can become "a peculiar people" (1 Peter 2:9), meaning a *purchased* and *distinctive* people.

"THE WASHING OF REGENERATION" (3:4–8)

According to the Apostle, it was the kindness and love of Jesus Christ, and not our works of righteousness, that brought about the centerpiece of the Father's plan of salvation, or great plan of happiness (verses 4–5). If there had been no Atonement of Christ, no amount of good works on our part could ever make up for its absence. "No matter how hard we work," President M. Russell Ballard stated, "no matter how much we obey, no matter how many good things we do in this life, it would not be enough were it not for Jesus Christ and His loving grace. On our own we cannot earn the kingdom of God, no matter what we do. Unfortunately, there are some within the Church who have become so preoccupied with performing good works that they forget that those works—as good as they may be—are hollow unless they are accompanied by a complete dependence on Christ."[1]

Jesus is not only central to the plan of salvation; He is vital and indispensable. We cannot save ourselves. We cannot *earn* our exaltation. We cannot exercise sufficient grit and willpower to resist the pull of evil, do the works of righteousness, and battle against Satan on our own. Christ is our Lord, our Savior, our Redeemer, and our King. He is the Lord of Hosts, meaning the Lord of armies and the Captain of our salvation. He is God, and if it were not so, He could not save us. Without Him, we have nothing. With Him, we have everything.

There is a troublesome tendency for weak, and often myopic, mortals to be so consumed with our own problems, our own setbacks, our own sins, that we allow our gaze upon God and the ways of God to be deflected and riveted onto ourselves. In other words, too often we tend to assume that what took place is the following: God the Father put forward His marvelous, merciful plan of salvation. Being omniscient, He knew all things from beginning to end. With that elevated perspective He was able to look ahead to the mortal experience and recognize that all

---

1. Ballard, "Building Bridges of Understanding."

would fall into sin and thus be alienated from Him and be in desperate need of a Savior. Hence Jesus was called up, forgiveness was made available, and divine grace was extended to the faltering family of God.

Latter-day Saint philosopher Adam Miller stated the problem with this line of thinking poignantly when he wrote: "We have to stop pretending that the world revolves around us. *We have to let God be the center of the universe.* We have to stop looking at God's grace from the perspective of our sin and, instead, let sin appear in light of grace. . . . Sin likes to think that it came first and that grace, then, is God's stopgap response." Miller insists that "this is exactly backwards. *Grace is not God's backup plan. Jesus is not plan B.* God's boundless grace comes first and sin is what follows. Grace is not God's response to sin. Sin is our embarrassed, improvised, rebellious rejection of God's original grace."[2]

Paul reminds us that it is by mercy that God has "saved us, by the washing of regeneration, and renewing of the Holy Ghost; which he shed on us abundantly through Jesus Christ our Saviour" (verses 5–6). The "washing of regeneration" refers to and begins with the Christian baptism by water. We are immersed into the watery grave (reminiscent of the Savior's descent into the tomb of Joseph of Arimathea) as the first phase of baptism. Ananias asked the blinded Saul of Tarsus: "And now why tarriest thou? *arise, and be baptized, and wash away thy sins,* calling on the name of the Lord" (Acts 22:16). Christ explained to James Covel, a Methodist minister, that "the days of thy deliverance are come, if thou wilt hearken to my voice, which sayeth unto thee: *Arise and be baptized, and wash away your sins,* calling on my name, and you shall receive my Spirit, and a blessing so great as you never have known" (Doctrine and Covenants 39:10; compare Alma 7:14).

"The baptism of water, without the baptism of fire and the Holy Ghost attending it, is of no use," the Prophet Joseph taught. "They are necessarily and inseparably connected. An individual must be born of

---

2. Miller, *Grace Is Not God's Backup Plan,* 2–4.

water and the Spirit in order to get into the kingdom of God."[3] On another occasion he added, "You might as well baptize a bag of sand as a man, if not done in view of the remission of sins and getting of the Holy Ghost. Baptism by water is but half a baptism, and is good for nothing without the other half—that is, the baptism of the Holy Ghost."[4]

The complete washing, then—what Paul calls the "washing of regeneration"—is not accomplished until the second phase of baptism takes place—the confirmation and conferral of the gift of the Holy Ghost. "Sins are remitted not in the waters of baptism, as we say in speaking figuratively," Elder Bruce R. McConkie wrote, "but when we receive the Holy Ghost. It is the Holy Spirit of God that erases carnality and brings us into a state of righteousness. *We become clean when we actually receive the fellowship and companionship of the Holy Ghost.*"[5]

"That being justified by his grace," the Apostle Paul continues, "we should be made heirs according to the hope of eternal life" (verse 7). By being justified—forgiven, pardoned, exonerated, pronounced innocent, and placed in a proper standing before God—we begin to be led more and more by the Holy Spirit. Having been born again and having taken upon us the name of Christ, we become heirs of God and joint heirs with Jesus Christ, coinheritors with the Only Begotten to all the Father has (see Romans 8:14–17; Doctrine and Covenants 76:95; 84:38; 88:107).

Continued companionship with the third member of the Godhead always results in the reborn individual becoming "careful to maintain good works. These things are good and profitable unto men" (verse 8; see also verse 14). Works of righteousness, including charitable acts, demonstrate our love for the Father and Son and our appreciation for all They have done for us. Good works are the least we can do, given the gracious gifts of God that are extended to us.

---

3. *Teachings of Presidents of the Church: Joseph Smith*, 90.
4. *Teachings of Presidents of the Church: Joseph Smith*, 95.
5. McConkie, *New Witness for the Articles of Faith*, 290.

THE EPISTLE TO PHILEMON

T HE EPISTLE TO PHILEMON was written from Rome during Paul's first Roman imprisonment, in about AD 60–62. This is, of course, the shortest of the fourteen epistles. It is also a beautiful story of love, wherein Paul pleads to Philemon to be forgiving to the latter's servant (slave), Onesimus, who deserted his post and then became converted to the gospel of Jesus Christ. Philemon is gently counseled to receive Onesimus back as a brother in Christ.

One study Bible provides context for slavery during Paul's time:

> It is estimated that slaves composed about one-third of the population of a city like Ephesus. They were considered an integral part of a family, so Paul's instructions for slaves were a natural part of his dealing with family relationships. In both Greek and Roman culture, slaves had limited rights and were subject to exploitation and abuse. Paul does not condone the system of slavery but instead provides instructions to believing masters and slaves regarding their relationship to each other in the Lord, and how this should be lived out in the bounds of their social and legal culture. The result, as is often observed, is that slavery slowly died out in antiquity through the influence of Christianity.[1]

---

1. *English Standard Version Study Bible*, 2273.

RECEIVING THE PENITENT PRODIGAL (1:1–25)

Paul identifies himself in verses 1 and 9 as "a prisoner of Jesus Christ." This label is true in two ways: (1) Paul was literally imprisoned (under house arrest) in Rome, and (2) Paul was the ever obedient and faithful servant of the Savior and realized his own powerlessness without the saving and sanctifying grace of God. The Apostle to the Gentiles knew only too well that, at best, he walked in the shadow of the Lord Jesus Christ. Paul describes himself in verse 9 as "Paul the aged." At this point, Paul would have been at least sixty years old, in contrast to the much younger man who was involved in the stoning of Stephen some three decades earlier (see Acts 7:58).

Verses 2–7 are almost identical to what is found at the beginning of many of Paul's epistles: his prayer that God's grace or unmerited divine assistance will continue to strengthen and fortify the Saints in that area; his acknowledgement of the love and faith that Philemon demonstrated toward the Redeemer and the members of the Church of Jesus Christ; his hope that the works of righteousness, including sacred charitable service, might abound among the members of the Church in Colossae.

From verse 8 to the end of this rather short letter, Paul pleads with Philemon to exercise magnanimity, forgiveness, and Christian love toward his slave, Onesimus. It seems that Onesimus was once a dedicated and obedient slave who respected and appreciated his master, Philemon (verse 11). Of late, however, Onesimus converted to Christianity, ran away and deserted his responsibilities, and even stole from his master (verses 15, 18). Onesimus then traveled to Rome and became a great boon to Paul and the Saints.

Paul indicates that he sent Onesimus back to Colossae and back to Philemon's home (verse 12), and he calls upon his friend to receive the deserter back, not as a slave but rather as a brother in the gospel (verse 16)—one who has shifted his allegiance to Jesus Christ, thereby becoming, like Paul, a servant of the Savior. As one New Testament scholar explained, "The letter . . . appears to contain a veiled request for Onesimus's emancipation [i.e., his freedom]. Philemon should be able to grant physical freedom and liberation to Onesimus, given what both Philemon and Onesimus have spiritually experienced that now makes them brothers in the Lord (v. 16). The spiritual transformation of all three men proves foundational for Paul's request."[2]

Paul then draws on his close relationship and past association with Philemon: "If thou count me therefore a partner, receive him as [though he was] myself. If he hath wronged thee, or owed thee ought [i.e., something], put that on mine account" (verses 17–18). Paul explains that in time he will repay whatever is owed to Philemon, but then adds, "Albeit I do not say to thee how thou owest unto me even thine own self besides" (verse 19). Paul introduced Philemon to the gospel of Jesus Christ and received him into that sacred fellowship known only by those who have entered joyfully into the gospel and onto the covenant path.

Paul then reiterates, "Yes, brother, I am asking this favor of you as a fellow-Christian; set my mind at rest. I write to you confident that you will meet my wishes; I know that you in fact will do more than I ask" (verses 20–21, REB). Paul makes one more request: that Philemon keep a room available for when Paul returns to Colossae, which he earnestly hopes to be able to do in the future.

Many points within this brief letter turn our attention to the redeeming work of the Savior. In some ways, Paul is acting as a mediator, an advocate between Onesimus and Philemon, just as Jesus serves as our Mediator with God the Father. Paul pleads for the mercy of God to be extended to Onesimus, just as Christ pleads our cause on the basis of His sufferings and death (see Doctrine and Covenants 45:3–5). In many ways, Onesimus will return to his master's residence in deep humility, trusting in the tender mercy of his master, just as the prodigal son

---

2. Blomberg, *New Testament Theology*, 190.

returned and was welcomed back by the ever-solicitous, ever-waiting, and ever-patient father (see Luke 15:11–32). Likewise, all are invited to come unto Christ "and partake of his goodness; and he denieth none that come unto him, black and white, bond and free, male and female; and he remembereth the heathen; and all are alike unto God, both Jew and Gentile" (2 Nephi 26:33).

THE EPISTLE TO THE HEBREWS

The epistle to the Hebrew Saints—Jewish members of the Church of Jesus Christ—was likely written from Rome between Paul's two Roman imprisonments, about AD 60–62. In this letter, Paul seeks

> to persuade them that significant aspects of the law of Moses, as a forerunner, had been fulfilled in Christ, and that the higher gospel law of Christ had replaced it. When Paul returned to Jerusalem at the end of his third mission (about AD 60), he found that many thousands of Jewish members of the Church were still "zealous of the law" of Moses (Acts 21:20). This was at least ten years after the conference at Jerusalem had determined that certain ordinances of the law of Moses were not necessary for the salvation of Gentile Christians, but had not settled the matter for Jewish Christians. It appears that soon thereafter, Paul wrote the epistle to the Hebrews to show them by their own scripture and by sound reason why they should no longer practice the law of Moses.[1]

The Epistle to the Hebrews contains many names or titles of Jesus

---

1. Bible Dictionary, "Pauline Epistles," 746.

Christ, including God (1:8); the Captain of our salvation (2:10); the merciful and faithful High Priest (2:17); the Apostle and High Priest of our profession (3:1); the Author of eternal salvation (5:8); a High Priest after the order of Melchizedek (5:10); a High Priest of good things to come (9:11); the Mediator of the new testament, or covenant (9:15); and, the Testator (9:16).

"If you proceed to learn all you can about Jesus Christ," President Russell M. Nelson testified, "I promise you that your love for Him, and for God's laws, will grow beyond what you currently imagine. I promise you also that your ability to turn away from sin will increase. Your desire to keep the commandments will soar. You will find yourself better able to walk away from the entertainment and entanglements of those who mock the followers of Jesus Christ. . . . Study everything Jesus Christ *is* by prayerfully and vigorously seeking to understand what each of His various titles and names means *personally* for you."[2]

GOD MANIFESTS HIS WILL THROUGH HIS SON (1:1–2)

Paul begins his epistle to the Hebrews by reminding us that God has revealed Himself, His mind and will, through prophets from the beginning (verse 1). Jesus is obviously not a prophet in the same way that Abraham, Moses, Nephi, and Moroni were; rather, He is the fulfillment of the prophetic word—the Prototype, the one toward whom all the Lord's anointed spokesmen have pointed. As John the Revelator taught, the testimony of Jesus is the spirit of prophecy (Revelation 19:10). All of God's prophets have borne witness of Jesus Christ (see Acts 3:24; 10:43; 2 Nephi 11:4; Jacob 4:4; 7:11; Moses 6:63). The Apostle Paul goes on to say that God "hath in these last days spoken unto us by his Son, whom he hath appointed heir of all things, by whom also he made the worlds" (verse 2). Jesus the Christ is the principal and preeminent heir of God the Father.

---

2. Nelson, "Prophets, Leadership, and Divine Law."

Paul points out that by and through Jehovah-Christ, the worlds were created (verse 2; compare Ephesians 3:9). We know from latter-day scripture that worlds without number have been created (Moses 1:33). While viewing the days of Noah in vision, Enoch remarked to God that "were it possible that man could number the particles of the earth, yea, millions of earths like this, it would not be a beginning to the number of thy creations" (Moses 7:30).

President Russell M. Nelson declared that Christ's "Atonement is infinite—without an end. It was . . . infinite in that all humankind would be saved from never-ending death. It was infinite in terms of his immense suffering. It was infinite in time, putting an end to the preceding prototype of animal sacrifice. It was infinite in scope—it was to be done once for all. And *the mercy of the Atonement extends not only to an infinite number of people, but also to an infinite number of worlds created by Him*."[3]

"We surely do not worship a one-planet God!" Elder Neal A. Maxwell similarly observed. However, he continued, "The vastness of the Lord's creations is matched by the personalness of His purposes."[4] Indeed, the ministry of Jesus is galactic in scope; He is the Cosmic Christ.

JESUS CHRIST: IN THE LIKENESS OF HIS FATHER (1:3–5)

Paul mentions in verse 3 that Jesus is in "the express image of his person." In recounting what Joseph Smith had taught him about the First Vision, Orson Pratt wrote that as the Father and the Son descended in the midst of glory, the boy prophet "was caught away from the natural objects with which he was surrounded, and he was enwrapped in a heavenly vision, and saw *two glorious personages, who exactly resembled each other in their features or likeness*."[5]

---

3. Nelson, *Perfection Pending*, 167.
4. Maxwell, *Moving in His Majesty and Power*, 24.
5. See Millet, *I Saw a Pillar of Light*, 136.

In his 1842 account of the same vision, Orson Hyde mentioned that "two glorious heavenly personages stood before him, *resembling each other exactly in features and stature*."⁶ And in writing of the first two members of the Godhead, Elder Parley P. Pratt explained: "Here, then, we have a sample of an immortal God [i.e., Christ]—a God who is often declared in the scriptures to be like his Father, 'being the brightness of his glory, and the express image of his person' (Hebrews 1:3), and possessing the same attributes as his Father, in all their fulness. . . . He differs in nothing from his Father except in age and authority, the Father having the seniority and, consequently, the right, according to the patriarchal laws of eternal priesthood, to preside over him and over all his dominions, for ever and ever."⁷

We are also told that Jesus Christ upholds all things by the word of His power (verse 3), meaning by the power of His Spirit (see Doctrine and Covenants 29:30). Further, "when he had *by himself purged our sins*, [He] sat down on the right hand of the Majesty on high" (verse 3). Jesus was indeed "by himself" during the hours of His greatest suffering in Gethsemane and on Golgotha. Because Jesus stood in our place, as our substitute, He assumed the unimaginable weight of the pain and anguish associated with the burden of our sins. When we continue in sin, the Father withdraws His Spirit from us (see Mosiah 2:36; Alma 34:35; Helaman 13:8; Doctrine and Covenants 20). So it was with the one who was made "to be sin" for us (2 Corinthians 5:21; see also Galatians 3:13)—for a time our Heavenly Father withdrew His Spirit from the sinless Son of Man, as though He, Christ, was the greatest of all sinners. It was that withdrawal of divine strength and support from God, something Jesus had never experienced before (having never been guilty of sin), that caused Him to bleed from every pore.⁸

---

6. Millet, *I Saw a Pillar of Light*, 137.
7. Pratt, *Key to the Science of Theology*, 20–21.
8. See Brigham Young, in *Journal of Discourses*, 3:205–6; Holland, "None Were with Him"; see also Mosiah 3:7; Doctrine and Covenants 19:16–18.

When the Savior declared from the cruel cross of Calvary, "It is finished" (John 19:30) and "Into thy hands I commend my spirit" (Luke 23:46), He was announcing that His atoning suffering was done, complete, and that His mortal ministry on earth had now come to an end. The debt was paid. At the very moment of death, Christ's spirit left His body and entered into that realm of postmortality we know as paradise (see Alma 40:11–12). There He preached the gospel and the plan of salvation to the faithful. In addition, He organized His forces and sent representatives into the realm we know variously as spirit prison (1 Peter 3:18–20),[9] hell (2 Nephi 9:12), or outer darkness (Alma 40:13–14). These commissioned spirits were sent to declare His glad tidings to those in the spirit world (Doctrine and Covenants 138:29–34). Then, following His glorious Resurrection from the dead and His forty-day ministry in the Old World (see Acts 1:1–3), Jesus returned to the presence of His Father and "sat down on the right hand of the Majesty on high" (verse 3; see also Hebrews 10:12; 1 Peter 3:22).

HIGHER THAN THE ANGELS (1:4–14)

Paul writes that Jesus Christ occupies a higher spiritual station than that of angels and thus has "a more excellent name" than the angels (verse 4). Paul taught the Saints "that at the name of Jesus every knee should bow" and "every tongue should confess that Jesus Christ is Lord, to the glory of God the Father" (Philippians 2:10–11).

In verses 4–6 and 13, the Apostle highlights the supreme status and standing enjoyed by the Son of God. He refers to three messianic passages from the Old Testament to indicate the superior status of the Son of God:

> For unto which of the angels said he [i.e., God the Father]

---

9. "Spirit prison is a term that may seem too harsh, too graphic, and too simplistic. Yet it deserves unmistakably a restraining barrier that actually exists. Only further revelation will supply details." Maxwell, *Moving in His Majesty and Power*, 90.

at any time, Thou art my Son, this day have I begotten thee? (verse 5; see Psalm 2:7)

And again, I will be to him a Father, and he shall be to me a Son? (verse 5; see 2 Samuel 7:14)

And again, when [God] bringeth in the firstbegotten into the world, he saith, And let all the angels of God worship him. . . . But to which of the angels said he at any time, Sit on my right hand, until I make thine enemies thy footstool? (verses 6, 13; see Psalm 110:1)

"SO GREAT SALVATION" (2:1–3)

Paul begins what is now Hebrews 2 as follows: "Therefore we ought to give the more earnest heed to the things which we have heard, lest at any time we should let them slip. For if the word spoken by angels was steadfast, and every transgression and disobedience received a just recompence of reward; how shall we escape, if we neglect so great salvation; which at the first began to be spoken by the Lord, and was confirmed unto us by them that heard him"? (Hebrews 2:1–3).

This is Paul's way of encouraging the Hebrew Saints to remember, ponder upon, and rehearse with other members of the Christian community all that the Savior taught when He ministered on earth, as well as the fundamental teachings they had received from the Lord's anointed servants. Many points of doctrine and Christian practice must never be allowed to slip or drift away from our hearts and minds. To allow that to happen is to risk falling short of "so great salvation"—the exaltation and glorification of individuals and families in the highest degree of the celestial kingdom.

MAN: A LITTLE LOWER THAN THE GODS (2:6–8)

Paul returns to a Messianic psalm: "What is man, that thou art mindful of him? or the son of man, that thou visitest him? Thou madest him a little lower than the angels; thou crownedst him with glory and honour, and didst set him over the works of thy hands" (verses 6–7; see also Psalm 8:4–6). The Greek word translated in verse 7 as "angels" is in the Hebrew—the language in which the Psalms were originally written—"Elohim," meaning "gods." Commenting on verses 6 and 7, Elder Bruce R. McConkie wrote: "The marginal reading of this quotation from Psalm 8:4–6 recites that man is made, not a little lower than the angels, but a little lower than Elohim, which means that all God's offspring, Jesus included, as children in his family, are created subject to him, with the power to advance until all things are 'in subjection to them.' Of those who gain eternal life, it is written: 'Then shall they be above all, because all things are subject unto them. Then shall they be gods, because they have all power, and the angels are subject to them' [Doctrine and Covenants 132:20]."[10]

JESUS WILL BE CROWNED WITH GLORY AND HONOR (2:9–11)

In verse 9, the Apostle points out that Jesus was made a little lower than the angels [i.e., gods] through His atoning suffering. In treading the winepress alone, He was subject to "the fierceness of the wrath of Almighty God" (Doctrine and Covenants 76:107; 88:106). In another revelation, the Savior declared that "I have trodden the wine-press alone, . . . and none were with me" (Doctrine and Covenants 133:50). Having tasted death for every person (see the commentary herein for 2 Corinthians 5:21), Jesus "descended below all things" (Doctrine and Covenants 88:6; 122:8). And as He descended to the depths, so also will He ascend above and beyond all earthly things, crowned with glory and honor (Psalm 68:18).

Paul adds that "it became him, for whom are all things, and by whom are all things, in bringing many sons [and daughters] unto glory,

---

10. McConkie, *Doctrinal New Testament Commentary*, 3:143.

to make *the captain of their salvation* perfect through sufferings" (verse 10; compare Hebrews 5:8). What an apt title for Jesus the Christ—the Captain of our salvation. He is indeed our Commander-in-Chief in the battle for the souls of men and women; our leader who guides us through this world of strife and wickedness; the Alpha and Omega, the beginning and the end; and the one for whom "the past, the present, and the future were and are 'one eternal now.'"[11] He, knowing the end from the beginning, will follow implicitly and undauntingly the plan of His superior, even God, the Eternal Father.

Paul continues, "Both he that sanctifieth [i.e., the Savior through the Holy Spirit] and they who are sanctified [i.e., those who continue to be cleansed and renewed by the blood of the Lamb] are all of one: for which cause [Christ] is not ashamed to call them brethren [and sisters]" (verse 11). We are all, including the Redeemer Himself, the spirit sons and daughters of our Almighty Father in Heaven (see Numbers 16:22; 27:16; Hebrews 12:9). Jehovah, who was the firstborn spirit child of God (Doctrine and Covenants 93:21; see also Colossians 1:15), is our Elder Brother. In mortality and resurrected immortality, He is the Lord of Hosts (armies), the Lion of the tribe of Judah, the King of Zion, the King of kings, the Holy One of Israel, and the Lord God Omnipotent.

CHRIST IDENTIFIES WITH AND SUCCORS US (2:14–18)

Jesus of Nazareth came into this fallen, mortal world just as we do. In spite of what we sing at Christmastime ("Little Lord Jesus, no crying he makes"[12]), when He was an infant, there must have been occasions when Mary and Joseph slept very little during the night because of their inability to quiet their baby boy. We would suppose that the boy Jesus of Nazareth lived a fairly normal existence. One precious morsel of divine truth concerning our Lord's early years has come to us

---

11. Joseph Smith, "Baptism for the Dead," 760.
12. "Away in a Manger," *Children's Songbook*, 42.

through the Prophet Joseph's inspired translation of the Bible: "And it came to pass that Jesus grew up with his brethren, and waxed strong, and waited upon the Lord for the time of his ministry to come. And he served under his father [presumably Joseph], and he spake not as other men, neither could he be taught; for he needed not that any man should teach him. And after many years, the hour of his ministry drew nigh" (Matthew 3:24–26, JST).

The scriptures are relatively silent regarding His years between birth and the age of twelve, and again between twelve and the beginning of His formal ministry at age thirty. When Luke tells us that He "increased in wisdom and stature, and in favour with God and man" (Luke 2:52), it is implied that as the years passed, He grew cognitively, in intellect and understanding, and He grew in physical strength, no doubt due largely to the strenuous physical labor of being a carpenter. He likely also developed spiritually, as He drew close to that holy being who was in reality His true Father, and grew socially; He was probably congenial, happy and even playful, and got along well with His friends.

On the other hand, His years of preparation must have been somewhat unusual. We know nothing about His relationship with His brothers and sisters, except for the names of His brothers—James, Joseph, Simon, and Judah. In Matthew, Jesus is called "the carpenter's son," while in Mark He is spoken of as "the carpenter" (Matthew 13:55–56; Mark 6:3). We do know that by the time Jesus's ministry began, His brothers did not believe in Him (John 7:5) and that some of His friends spoke of Him as being "beside himself" (Mark 3:21), which is translated elsewhere as "He has lost his senses" (NASB) or "He is out of his mind" (ESV).

In a revelation received in May of 1833, we are told that Jesus "received not of the fulness [of the glory and power of the Father] at first, but received grace for grace; and he received not of the fulness at first, but continued from grace to grace, until he received a fulness" in the Resurrection.[13] "And thus he was called the Son of God, because he received not of the fulness at the first" (Doctrine and Covenants 93:12–14).

Paul states that Jesus sacrificed His flesh and blood "that through death he might destroy him that had the power of death, that is, the devil; and *deliver them who through fear of death were all their lifetime subject to bondage*" (verses 14–15). Jesus faced death straight on so that, as N. T. Wright's translation renders it, He "might destroy the one who has the power of death—that is, the devil—and *set free the people who all their lives long were under the power of slavery because of the fear of death*" (KNT). Paul adds the detail that Jesus "took not on him the nature of angels; but he took on him the seed of Abraham" (verse 16). In other words, Jesus did not come to earth principally to help or support the angels, but rather the mortal descendants of Abraham.

Paul continues, "Wherefore in all things it behoved [Jesus] to be made like unto his brethren, that he might be a merciful and faithful high priest in things pertaining to God, to make reconciliation for the sins of the people" (verse 17). The ancient high priest went into the Holy of Holies once each year on Yom Kippur, the Day of Atonement, to offer a sacrifice or sin offering, seeking a reconciliation of the people of Israel with Jehovah, the God of Israel. Even so did the Promised Messiah (He toward whom all sacrifices pointed) take His place as the great High Priest of our profession (see Hebrews 3:1) and sprinkle His atoning blood upon all those who receive Him and repent of their sins.

"For in that he himself hath suffered being tempted, he is able to succor them that are tempted" (verse 18; compare Doctrine and Covenants 62:1). Surely no scriptural passage does more to describe why Jesus faced all of the challenges and pain of this mortal world than Alma's words:

---

13. See Joseph Fielding Smith, *Doctrines of Salvation*, 2:269; see also Millet, *Whole in Christ*, chap. 4.

And he shall go forth, suffering pains and afflictions and temptations of every kind; and this that the word might be fulfilled which saith he will take upon him the pains and the sicknesses of his people [see Isaiah 53:3–4, 7].

And he will take upon him death, that he may loose the bands of death which bind his people; and he will take upon him their infirmities, that his bowels may be filled with mercy, according to the flesh, that he may know according to the flesh how to succor his people according to their infirmities.

Now the Spirit knoweth all things; nevertheless the Son of God suffereth according to the flesh that he might take upon him the sins of his people, that he might blot out their transgressions according to the power of his deliverance; and now behold, this is the testimony which is in me. (Alma 7:11–13)

Note that Alma's prophecy speaks of the Savior's mortal experience, His walk and talk each day of His thirty-three years in this life. Alma prophesied that Jesus would suffer pains, afflictions, temptations, sicknesses, infirmities (weaknesses), and, of course, death itself—just as each and every mortal being will. The Lord Jehovah—the great I Am, the Creator of worlds without number—was not spared the aches, pains, and burdens of our second estate. Indeed, He faced all that we face and more so that He may comprehend what we go through. Thus, He that loves each of us perfectly and completely is also able to feel and empathize with us perfectly as we cry out for mercy and deliverance.

In addition, Alma prophesied that the Son of God would in Gethsemane and on Golgotha become, as it were, the great sinner, or as Paul put it, He became "sin for us" (2 Corinthians 5:21). He, in all the awful and agonizing ways possible, took upon Him the burden of the sins of the world. He experienced in the Garden of Gethsemane and on the cross of Calvary something utterly unknown to Him at that point of His existence—the loss of the Father's Spirit and thus the poignant sense of divine alienation. He experienced spiritual death, which is the separation of a person from God and from things of righteousness (see Alma 12:16, 32). Thus by personal experience, Jesus knows how best to run to us, to help and lift us, or as Paul puts it, to succor us.

OUR APOSTLE AND HIGH PRIEST (3:1)

An *Apostle* is literally "one who is sent." If anyone in the history of worlds without number is worthy of being called an Apostle, it is Jesus Christ, the Only Begotten Son of God. "God sent not his Son into the world to condemn the world; but that the world through him might be saved" (John 3:17). Of Jesus, John the Baptist testified that "he whom God hath sent speaketh the words of God" (John 3:34). "I seek not mine own will," the Lord proclaimed, "but the will of the Father which hath sent me" (John 5:30). Christ also testified, "My doctrine is not mine, but his that sent me" (John 7:16). John the Beloved summed up the matter this way: "In this was manifested the love of God toward us, because that God sent his only begotten Son into the world, that we might live through him" (1 John 4:9).

As we mentioned elsewhere, once each year, on the Day of Atonement, the ancient high priest officiated in the temple, entered the Holy of Holies, and spilt animal blood on the altar in behalf of the people of Israel. All of this was in similitude of the one after whom the higher priesthood is named (Doctrine and Covenants 107:3) and the one who would in time's meridian spill His own blood in a garden and on a cross in behalf of all the children of God.

The Prophet Joseph Smith instructed the Saints that "John [the Baptist] was a priest after the order of Aaron, and had the keys of that priesthood, and came forth preaching repentance and baptism for the remission of sins, but at the same time cries out, 'There cometh one after me more mightier than I.' . . . Christ came according to the words of John, and he was greater than John, because he held the keys of the

Melchisedec Priesthood, and Kingdom of God."[14] The Prophet also taught: "The Priesthood is everlasting—without beginning of days or end of years. . . . Christ is the Great High priest."[15] Elder Bruce R. McConkie pointed out that "Christ is the chief minister of salvation for men on earth, in that through his atoning sacrifice salvation itself comes."[16]

EVEN GREATER THAN MOSES (3:2–6)

Paul writes in verses 3–4 that "[Christ] was counted worthy of more glory than Moses, inasmuch as he who hath builded the house hath more honour than the house. For every house is builded by some man; but he that built all things is God." Moses was certainly a faithful and obedient servant of God the Father, but Christ is the Son of God and, in reality, God the Son. Moses may have been the mediator for the people of Israel under the covenant of Sinai, but Jesus Christ is the Mediator of the new covenant—the covenant of which Jeremiah prophesied (Jeremiah 31:31–34), the covenant associated with the fullness of the gospel. And it is by means of the Mediator of the new covenant that men and women are "made perfect" and thereby qualify for life in the celestial kingdom (Doctrine and Covenants 76:69).

ENTERING THE REST OF THE LORD (3:8–14; 4:9)

In verses 8–11 of chapter 3, the Apostle issues a charge and a warning to the Hebrew Saints: "Harden not your hearts, as in the provocation, in the day of temptation in the wilderness: when your fathers tempted me, proved me, and saw my works forty years." Jehovah thus decreed that "they shall not enter into my rest." This refers, of course, to the hardheartedness of the children of Israel as Moses sought to lead them through the deserts of Sinai to a land of promise.

---

14. Joseph Smith, in "History 1838–1856, volume D-1," 6, addenda.
15. Joseph Smith, in "Discourse, between circa 26 June and circa 4 August 1839–A, as Reported by Willard Richards"; punctuation standardized.
16. McConkie, *Doctrinal New Testament Commentary*, 3:147.

We learn from modern revelation that it is in and through the ordinances of the Melchizedek Priesthood, the ordinances of salvation and exaltation, that the power of godliness is manifest. That is, priesthood ordinances—baptism, confirmation, ordination to the priesthood, the temple endowment, and the new and everlasting covenant of marriage—become channels for receiving divine grace and God's power. "And without the ordinances thereof, and the authority of the priesthood, the power of godliness is not manifest unto men in the flesh; for without this"—the power of godliness—"no man can see the face of God, even the Father, and live" (Doctrine and Covenants 84:19–22).

The revelation continues: "Now this Moses plainly taught to the children of Israel in the wilderness, and sought diligently to sanctify his people that they might behold the face of God; but they hardened their hearts and could not endure his presence; therefore, *the Lord* in his wrath, for his anger was kindled against them, *swore that they should not enter into his rest* while in the wilderness, *which rest is the fulness of his glory.* Therefore, he took Moses out of their midst, and the Holy Priesthood also" (Doctrine and Covenants 84:23–25).

The expression "rest of the Lord" or "rest of God" can have a number of meanings. First, people enter the rest of the Lord when they live so as to enjoy the comfort, peace, perspective, and spiritual assurance that come through the power of the Holy Spirit.[17] In his powerful epistle to his son Moroni on faith, hope, and charity, Mormon addressed himself to "you that are of the church, that are *the peaceable followers of Christ,* and *that have obtained a sufficient hope by which ye can enter into the rest of the Lord*" (Moroni 7:3).

Second, people enter into the rest of the Lord as they live true to their covenants and die in the faith. They then enter paradise in the postmortal spirit world, where they "rest from all their troubles and from all care, and sorrow" (Alma 40:12). This is what Mormon meant when

---

17. See Joseph F. Smith, *Gospel Doctrine,* 58, 126.

he spoke of "the peaceable followers of Christ [who] have obtained a sufficient hope" by which they can "enter into the rest of the Lord, from this time henceforth *until ye shall rest with him in heaven*" (Moroni 7:3).

Third, there is the rest which consists of the fullness of God's glory (Doctrine and Covenants 84:24). We enter into this ultimate rest as we qualify for eternal life and exaltation—life in the highest degree of the celestial kingdom. Those who enter this rest have overcome by faith and are sealed by the Holy Spirit of Promise. They become members of the Church of the Firstborn, kings and queens, priests and priestesses, who receive all that the Father has and who have attained unto godhood, becoming truly the sons and daughters of God (Doctrine and Covenants 76:53–58; see also 132:19–20).

Paul then calls upon the members of Christ's Church to "exhort one another daily, while it is called To day; lest any of you be hardened through the deceitfulness of sin." He adds that we are made partakers of Christ "if we hold the beginning of our confidence steadfast unto the end" (verses 13–14). How vital it is to maintain and continually nourish the testimony we received when we first came to faith in Christ and acquired an assurance of the truthfulness of His gospel. It is tragic that many of those who once rejoiced in their convictions have somehow become prey to a kind of spiritual amnesia—a tendency to forget what they once felt, to ignore what they once rejoiced in, and to deny and treat lightly what they once knew through the power of God's Spirit. This is why Paul pleads with the body of believers to "exhort one another daily" (verse 13).

THE GOSPEL PREACHED FROM THE BEGINNING (4:1–2)

Referring to the ancient Israelites and their wilderness wanderings, Paul writes, "For unto us was the gospel preached, *as well as unto them*: but the word preached did not profit them, not being mixed with faith in them that heard it" (verse 2). This is a second witness of Paul's statement to the Galatians that the gospel was preached to Abraham

(Galatians 3:8). "We find . . . that *when the Israelites came out of Egypt,*" Joseph Smith taught, "*they had the gospel preached to them,* according to Paul in his letter to the Hebrews."[18] Surely no truth is of greater worth, no insight from the Restoration of more precious value, than the idea of an eternal gospel. Because of the supplementary scriptures of the Restoration, we know that Christian prophets have declared Christian doctrine and administered Christian ordinances since the dawn of time.

"Now taking it for granted that the scriptures say what they mean and mean what they say," the Prophet Joseph pointed out, "we have sufficient grounds to go on and prove from the Bible that *the gospel has always been the same; the ordinances to fulfill its requirements, the same, and the officers to officiate, the same*; and the signs and fruits resulting from the promises, the same." The Prophet then supplied a specific illustration of this principle: "Therefore, as Noah was a preacher of righteousness he must have been baptized and ordained to the priesthood by the laying on of the hands."[19]

SHARPER THAN A TWO-EDGED SWORD (4:12)

The Apostle writes that "the word of God is quick, and powerful, and sharper than any twoedged sword, piercing even to the dividing asunder of soul and spirit, and of the joints and marrow, and is a discerner of the thoughts and intents of the heart" (verse 12). The scriptures, words of the living prophets, and the inspiration of the Holy Spirit constitute the word of God. These precious gifts of God can eliminate the "cunning and the snares and the wiles of the devil" and direct the man or woman of Christ in the path that leads to exaltation (Helaman 3:29). The word of God is "quick" in that it is alive, active, and powerful. Indeed, as Alma taught, "the preaching of the word [has] a great tendency to lead the people to do that which [is] just—yea, it

---

18. Joseph Smith, in "Letter to the Church, circa March 1834."
19. Joseph Smith, "Baptism," 904.

[has a] more powerful effect upon the minds of the people than the sword, or anything else" (Alma 31:5).

How is the word of God "a discerner of the thoughts and intents of the heart"? This distinctive power lies in the fact that people of all types, races, genders, or religious beliefs can read the word of God and be transformed by His power. In a fascinating and figurative way, the words of life found in holy scripture can read our minds and hearts and discern our thoughts and intents. This touches upon a matter discussed in our commentary on 2 Timothy 3:16—that scripture is "profitable for doctrine, for *reproof,* for *correction,* for *instruction* in righteousness." Holy writ tends to cut through the shallow and vain lifestyles and beliefs of the worldly, to expose false doctrines and the persons who propagate them, and to make known the profane and unholy matters that true seekers after light and truth discern and dismiss.

CHRIST IS TOUCHED WITH THE FEELING OF OUR INFIRMITIES (4:14–15)

Jesus the Christ is not a distant Deity, nor is His Eternal Father. They are not absentee Masters. Many philosophers and theologians through the centuries of Christianity have concluded that God is *impassible.* One modern theologian explained that the expression "divine impassibility" is "a reference to the idea that God is unaffected by whatever happens in the world; in particular, he does not experience suffering or pain."[20] Another professor of theology indicated that the impassibility of God is a belief that "God is active, rather than passive or acted upon by other agents."[21]

Clearly the Apostle Paul teaches otherwise. Since we have a High Priest, the Lord Jesus Christ, who has gone into heaven, Paul declares, we should "hold fast our profession." That is, members of the Church of Jesus Christ need to cultivate, expand upon, and deepen the witness

---

20. Erickson, *Concise Dictionary of Christian Theology,* 97–98.
21. McKim, *Westminster Dictionary of Theological Terms,* 116.

of the Spirit or profession of our faith that Jesus is the Christ and the Father of our salvation. "For we have not an high priest which cannot be touched with the feeling of our infirmities; but was in all points tempted like as we are, yet without sin" (verses 14–15).

Our Savior's everyday encounters with the challenges and vicissitudes of being human all contribute to His understanding of what His mortal brothers and sisters face each and every day of their lives—including the disappointments, tragedies, traumas, betrayal, and pain they must endure. All of these experiences collectively ministered to His compassion and His empathy, precious attributes that enabled him to "be with" and "feel for" every son and daughter of Adam and Eve.

Surely no one has come to this marvelous discovery more powerfully than the ancient prophet Enoch. Witnessing God's sorrow for the sins and pain of the world, particularly in the days of Noah, Enoch "said unto the Lord: How is it that thou canst weep, seeing thou art holy, and from all eternity to all eternity? And were it possible that man could number the particles of the earth, yea, millions of earths like this, it would not be a beginning to the number of thy creations; . . . and yet *thou art there, and thy bosom is there*; and also thou art just; thou art merciful and kind forever" (Moses 7:29–30). The principle here is powerful and profound: God's infinity does not preclude either His immediacy or His intimacy.

"COME BOLDLY UNTO THE THRONE OF GRACE" (4:16)

Verse 16 is one of the most beloved passages in the New Testament: "Let us therefore come boldly unto the throne of grace, that we may obtain mercy, and find grace to help in time of need." What does Paul mean that we can come "boldly" before the throne of God? It isn't that we should come before the Almighty with pride or cockiness or brashness; such would be absolutely inappropriate and certainly irreverent. No, when Paul speaks of boldness he means quiet assurance, *confidence* in Jesus Christ. This boldness has nothing to do with self-esteem; it has everything to do with Christ-esteem.

God spoke to Enoch some three millennia before the Lord Jesus came to earth: "That which I have chosen"—that is, He whom God has chosen to redeem humankind—"*hath pled before my face. Wherefore, he suffereth for their sins*" (Moses 7:39). In our dispensation, the Redeemer spoke through Joseph Smith: "Listen to him who is the advocate with the Father, *who is pleading your cause before him*—saying: Father, behold the sufferings and death of him who did no sin, in whom thou wast well pleased; behold the blood of thy Son which was shed, the blood of him whom thou gavest that thyself might be glorified; wherefore, Father, *spare these my brethren [and sisters] that believe on my name, that they may come unto me and have everlasting life*" (Doctrine and Covenants 45:3–5). This is why we can go before our Heavenly Father confidently—not because of all the wonderful things we have done while on earth, but because of the Savior's singular offering, His unspeakable gift to those who believe on His name and follow Him faithfully.

The words *mercy* and *grace* are often used interchangeably. There is, however, a slight but important difference between the two. Christ's suffering and death extend mercy to the penitent believer. To receive *mercy* is *to not get what you deserve*—in this case, punishment, pain, suffering, and spiritual alienation. To find *grace*, on the other hand, is to discover and open ourselves to receive *what we don't deserve*. Each one of us needs all of the mercy and grace we can receive in order to qualify for eternal life in the highest heaven. We are now and forevermore will be absolutely dependent on the merits, mercy, and grace of the Holy Messiah (see 2 Nephi 2:8). It is the knowledge and understanding of *who Jesus Christ is* and *what He has done* that will allow His true disciples to feel confidence in the presence of our Heavenly Father.

THE SAVIOR'S AUTHORITY IS FROM GOD (5:4–6)

In writing to the Hebrew Saints about the holy priesthood, the Apostle emphasizes that "no man taketh this honour unto himself, but he that is called of God, as was Aaron" (verse 4). Moses wrote of the occasion when Aaron received divine authority. Jehovah instructed the Lawgiver to "take thou unto thee Aaron thy brother, and his sons with him, from among the children of Israel, that he may minister unto me in the priest's office, even Aaron, Nadab and Abihu, Eleazar and Ithamar, Aaron's sons. And thou shalt make holy garments for Aaron thy brother for glory and for beauty" (Exodus 28:1–2).

Later Jehovah instructed Moses: "And thou shalt bring Aaron and his sons unto the door of the tabernacle of the congregation, and wash them with water. And thou shalt put upon Aaron the holy garments, and anoint him, and sanctify him; that he may minister unto me in the priest's office. And thou shalt bring his sons, and clothe them with coats: And thou shalt anoint them, as thou didst anoint their father, that they may minister unto me in the priest's office: for their anointing shall surely be an everlasting priesthood throughout their generations. Thus did Moses: according to all that the Lord commanded him, so did he" (Exodus 40:12–16). Joseph Smith affirmed that "no man can administer salvation through the gospel to the souls of men in the name of Jesus Christ except he is authorized from God by revelation or by being ordained by someone whom God hath sent by revelation. And I would ask, *how was Aaron called, but by revelation?*"[22]

In our dispensation the Lord spoke on this matter through the Prophet Joseph Smith in August 1831: "Behold, *I am from above*, and my power lieth beneath. I am over all, and in all, and through all, and search all things, and *the day cometh that all things shall be subject unto me*. Behold, I am Alpha and Omega, even Jesus Christ. Wherefore, let all men *beware how they take my name in their lips*." Christ went

---

22. Joseph Smith, in "Copy of a Letter from J. Smith Jr. to Mr. Galland," 54.

on to explain that there are many "who are under this condemnation, who use the name of the Lord, and *use it in vain, having not authority*" (Doctrine and Covenants 63:59–62).

It is fairly common for people throughout the world to proclaim that God has spoken to them and called them to the ministry, as pastors, preachers, evangelists, or priests. And far be it from us to suggest that such calls to minister to God's children are either fictitious or in some way evil. Our Heavenly Father loves all of His children and is no respecter of persons (Acts 10:34; Ephesians 6:9; 1 Peter 1:17; Alma 29:8). We do believe, however, "that a man must be called of God, by prophecy, and by the laying on of hands by those who are in authority, to preach the Gospel and administer in the ordinances thereof" (Articles of Faith 1:5).

In fact, one of Christ's denunciations in the Sacred Grove had to do with local ministers or pastors: "They draw near to me with their lips, but their hearts are far from me, they teach for doctrines the commandments of men, *having a form of godliness, but they deny the power thereof*" (Joseph Smith—History 1:19). To *deny* is to contradict or contravene, to say something is not true or is not what it seems or purports to be. To deny can also mean to stand in opposition to something. From one perspective, to deny the power of God is to say or act as though it does not exist or is not necessary. To deny the power of God is to contend that no priesthood or divine authority, which comes through the laying on of hands, is required in order to officiate in the Lord's kingdom. To deny the power of God is to attempt to silence Him, to resist any and all additional divine communication. Nephi warned of a time when people would cry out "All is well!" and "We have . . . the word of God, and we need no more" (2 Nephi 28:24–30).

Paul points out that even Jesus, God the Son, the second member of the Godhead, did not presume that He could serve and minister without divine authority. Note verses 5–6: "Christ glorified not himself to be made an high priest; but he [i.e., God the Father] that said unto him, Thou art my Son, to day have I begotten thee [Psalm 2:7]. As he saith also in another place, Thou art a priest for ever after the order of Melchisedec [Psalm 110:4]." Elder Bruce R. McConkie wrote:

> Christ and others held the priesthood in pre-existence. But as pertaining to his mortal ministry, Christ our Lord received the Melchizedek Priesthood here on earth, and was ordained to the office of a high priest therein, thus setting an example for others and being in all things the Prototype of salvation. With reference to the mortal receipt of that holy order which is his, and which he had afore used to create this and an infinite number of other worlds, and which he had in fact given to Melchizedek in the first instance, the Prophet says: "If a man gets a fulness of the priesthood of God he has to get it in the same way that Jesus Christ obtained it, and that was by keeping all the commandments and obeying all the ordinances of the house of the Lord."[23]

LIKE CHRIST, MELCHIZEDEK LEARNED OBEDIENCE (5:7–11)

Paul continues, "Who in the days of his flesh, when he had offered up prayers and supplications with strong crying and tears unto him that was able to save him from death, and was heard in that he feared; though he were a Son, yet learned he obedience by the things which he suffered" (verses 7–8). The antecedent and identity of "Who" in this passage is ambiguous. Is it Jesus Christ? Is it Melchizedek? Based on the context of verse 5, one may suppose that Paul is referring to Christ. However, on the original manuscript of the Joseph Smith Translation of the Bible, the following note is written near these verses: "The 7th and 8th verses allude to Melchizedek and not to Christ." Of this fascinating

---

23. McConkie, *Doctrinal New Testament Commentary*, 3:156–57; see also Joseph Smith, in "History, 1838–1856, volume D-1," 1572.

note, Robert J. Matthews wrote, "This seems a bit strange in its declaration, but I have examined the original manuscript and confirmed that the note is assuredly found therein." Brother Matthews then adds, "Perhaps it was awkwardly recorded, and the meaning was intended to be that the verses could allude to both Melchizedek and Christ."[24]

This seems to be a reasonable conclusion, especially given that the man Melchizedek was in fact a type of Christ. Melchizedek is referred to as both the king of Salem (Genesis 14:18; Alma 13:18) and the prince of peace (Alma 13:18); this latter title almost always refers to Christ, the Prince of Peace (Isaiah 9:6). Further, the word *Melchizedek* is made up of two Hebrew words: *Melchi* and *Tzedek*. *Melekh* is the Hebrew word for "king," while *Tzedek* means "righteous" or "righteousness." Thus the name of this great high priest who ordained Abraham to the priesthood (Doctrine and Covenants 84:14) means either "king of righteousness" or "my king is righteous."

Verse 7 may refer specifically to Jesus's agony and suffering in Gethsemane: "In the days of his flesh, when he had offered up prayers and supplications with strong crying [i.e., mighty, powerful supplication] and tears unto him that was able to save him from death [i.e., God the Father], and was heard in that he feared," or was heard because of His piety or reverence.

As pertaining to the Savior, one study Bible says of verse 8: "Jesus, though fully divine, was also fully human. Though always without sin and thus always obedient, Jesus nevertheless acquired knowledge and experience by living as a human being, and he especially came to know firsthand what it cost to maintain obedience in the midst of suffering. As Jesus increased in wisdom and stature (Luke 2:52), successive temptations were no doubt more difficult to deal with, and as he obeyed his Father in the face of each temptation, he 'learned obedience,' so that

---

24. Matthews, *"Plainer Translation,"* 383–84.

his human moral ability was strengthened."[25] Jesus is the Author of our salvation in the sense that He is "the author and finisher of our faith" (Hebrews 12:2; Moroni 6:4). He is the Alpha and Omega, the First and the Last (Doctrine and Covenants 110:4).

We are unaware of what specific circumstances in Melchizedek's life may have caused him to pray and weep with intensity and thereby become perfect—whole, complete, fully formed, single-minded, full of integrity. In verse 11, the Apostle writes that "we have many things to say" about Melchizedek, but there is much that remains unexplained (compare Alma 13:19).

One stirring account of Melchizedek is found in the Joseph Smith Translation of the Bible.

> And Melchizedek lifted up his voice and blessed Abram.
>
> Now Melchizedek was a man of faith, who wrought righteousness; and when a child he feared God, and stopped the mouths of lions, and quenched the violence of fire.
>
> And thus, having been approved of God, he was ordained an high priest after the order of the covenant which God made with Enoch. . . . For God having sworn unto Enoch and unto his seed with an oath by himself; that every one being ordained after this order and calling should have power, by faith, to break mountains, to divide the seas, to dry up waters, to turn them out of their course;
>
> To put at defiance the armies of nations, to divide the earth, to break every band, to stand in the presence of God. . . .
>
> And men having this faith, coming up unto this order of God, were translated and taken up into heaven.
>
> *And now, Melchizedek was a priest of this order;* therefore he obtained peace in Salem, and was called the Prince of peace.
>
> *And his people wrought righteousness, and obtained heaven,*

---

25. *English Standard Version Study Bible*, 2368.

and sought for the city of Enoch which God had before taken, separating it from the earth, having reserved it unto the latter days, or the end of the world. (Genesis 14:25–27, 30–34, JST)

MILK BEFORE MEAT, BUT MEAT (5:12–14)

For a discussion of how we need milk before meat, see the commentary herein for 1 Corinthians 3:1–4.

BUILDING ON THE FIRST PRINCIPLES (6:1–3)

The sixth chapter of the Epistle to the Hebrews begins: "Therefore leaving the principles of the doctrine of Christ, let us go on unto perfection; not laying again the foundation of repentance from dead works, and of faith toward God. Of the doctrine of baptisms, and of laying on of hands, and of resurrection of the dead, and of eternal judgment. And this will we do, if God permit" (verses 1–3). The fact is that we *never* leave behind the first principles, never reach a point in our spiritual progression and gospel understanding where we no longer stand in need of foundational principles, sacred covenants, and the ordinances of salvation and exaltation. Consequently, it is no surprise that the Prophet Joseph Smith altered verse 1 in his inspired translation of the Bible: "Therefore *not leaving* the principles of the doctrine of Christ. . . ."

The gospel of Jesus Christ is the good news, the glad tidings that the Son of God has come to earth, offered Himself as a ransom for the sins of the world, and made eternal life a reality for all who will receive His teachings by faith and apply His atoning blood (3 Nephi 27:13–16; Doctrine and Covenants 76:40–42). In modern revelation, we learn that faith, repentance, baptism, and the gift of the Holy Ghost—the means by which we utilize the Savior's Atonement—is also called the gospel (Doctrine and Covenants 33:10–13; 39:5–6). These principles and ordinances are vital.

THE UNPARDONABLE SIN (6:4–6)

In his counsel to his errant son Corianton, Alma condemns sexual immorality as "an abomination in the sight of the Lord; yea, most abominable above all sins save it be the shedding of innocent blood [i.e., premeditated murder] or denying the Holy Ghost." He then speaks of the most abominable action one can perform: "For behold, if ye deny the Holy Ghost when it once has had place in you, and ye know that ye deny it"—that is, it is not done accidentally or unknowingly—"behold, this is a sin which is unpardonable" (Alma 39:5–6).

Paul writes to the Hebrews of this most grievous of all offenses against God and against light and truth: "For it is impossible for those who were once enlightened, and have tasted of the heavenly gift, and were made partakers of the Holy Ghost, and have tasted the good word of God, and the powers of the world to come, if they shall fall away, to renew them again unto repentance; seeing they crucify to themselves the Son of God afresh, and put him to an open shame" (verses 4–6).

Denying the Holy Ghost is an offense about which the Prophet Joseph Smith spoke often. The following are just a couple examples of his teachings on this sobering topic:

> "Say to the brothers Hulet and to all others, that the Lord never authorized them to say that the devil, his angels, or the sons of perdition, should ever be restored; for their state of destiny was not revealed to man, is not revealed, nor ever shall be revealed, save to those who are made partakers thereof; consequently those who teach this doctrine have not received it of the Spirit of the Lord. Truly Brother Oliver declared it to be the doctrine of devils."[26]
>
> "All sins shall be forgiven, except the sin against the Holy

---

26. Joseph Smith, in "Letter to Church Leaders in Jackson County, Missouri, 25 June 1833," [2]; punctuation and spelling standardized.

Ghost; for Jesus will save all except the sons of perdition. What must a man do to commit the unpardonable sin? He must receive the Holy Ghost, have the heavens opened unto him, and know God, and then sin against Him. After a man has sinned against the Holy Ghost, there is no repentance for him. He has got to say that the sun does not shine while he sees it; he has got to deny Jesus Christ when the heavens have been opened unto him, and to deny the plan of salvation with his eyes open to the truth of it; and from that time he begins to be an enemy. This is the case with many apostates of the Church of Jesus Christ of Latter-day Saints.

"When a man begins to be an enemy to this work, he hunts me, he seeks to kill me, and never ceases to thirst for my blood. He gets the spirit of the devil—the same spirit that they had who crucified the Lord of Life—the same spirit that sins against the Holy Ghost. You cannot save such persons; you cannot bring them to repentance; they make open war, like the devil, and awful is the consequence."[27]

GOD'S COVENANT WITH ABRAHAM (6:13–20)

As discussed elsewhere in this work, if Abraham and his posterity remain faithful and obedient to the mind and will of Jehovah, they will be blessed with (1) the gospel of Jesus Christ; (2) the powers and privileges of the holy priesthood, including its saving and exalting ordinances; (3) eternal increase, the continuation of the family unit into eternity; and (4) a land inheritance (Abraham 2:8–11, 19). This is the Abrahamic covenant.

As modern children of Abraham, Isaac, and Jacob, we are entitled to those same blessings, which we receive through faith in Christ,

---

27. Joseph Smith, in "Discourse, 7 April 1844, as Reported by *Times and Seasons*."

repentance, baptism by proper authority, the gift of the Holy Ghost, and enduring faithfully to the end of our lives. These are the *saving* ordinances and principles, and salvation is an *individual* affair. As we continue to righteously traverse the covenant path, we prepare to receive the higher covenants and ordinances of the holy temple, including the temple endowment as well as eternal sealings. These are *exalting* ordinances, and exaltation is a *family* affair.[28]

In verse 16, Paul refers to God swearing an oath to Abraham to assure the Father of the Faithful that He fully intends to keep His covenant with the human family. Let's consider first what an oath is. Anciently, men and women relied on oaths as outward evidences of the efficacy of some fact or matter. The oath was a solemn attestation, and "to swear with an oath [was] the most solemn and binding form of speech known to the human tongue."[29] The power of an oath in antiquity is seen in Nephi's words: "when Zoram had made an oath unto us, our fears did cease concerning him" (1 Nephi 4:37). Even wicked men in ancient times did not swear oaths that they knew they would break (see Alma 44:8).

Wickedly using oaths to bring about unholy ends began early in human history. Cain swore unto Satan by an oath that he would not reveal the nature of the "great secret"—namely, that there was advantage to be gained in wanton murder (Moses 5:31). From these beginnings came myriads of secret combinations, bound by unholy oaths, in which the wicked have vowed to destroy the works of God.

In His magnificent Sermon on the Mount, the Savior called His people to a higher righteousness. People were no longer to swear by anything—their word was to be their bond; saying *yes* or *no* was sufficient. Under the law of Moses, if people did not swear by an oath, there was always the possibility that they might not keep their promises

---

28. See *Teachings of Russell M. Nelson*, 100.
29. Joseph Fielding Smith, in Conference Report, April 1970, 92.

(Numbers 30:2). Under the law of Christ, however, men and women were to possess integrity and be trustworthy enough so that oaths were no longer necessary (Matthew 5:33–37).

To be sure, there are times in the scriptures when the words *covenant* and *oath* are used interchangeably (see, for example, Mosiah 5:5; 6:3). But in regard to the oath and covenant of the Melchizedek Priesthood, they are not the same. The covenant consists of what we promise God and what He promises us (Doctrine and Covenants 84:33–44). But the oath is another thing entirely. "There is an oath and covenant of the priesthood," President Boyd K. Packer explained. "The covenant rests with man; the *oath* with God. The Melchizedek Priesthood is received by covenant. A man's covenant with God is: to be faithful and magnify his callings in the priesthood; to give heed to the words of eternal life; and to live by every word that proceedeth forth from the mouth of God."[30]

Elder Bruce R. McConkie taught that when a couple is married for eternity in the house of the Lord,

> the Lord admits them to his eternal patriarchal order, an order that prevails in the highest heaven of the celestial world, an order that assures its members of eternal increase, or in other words of spirit children in the resurrection (see Doctrine and Covenants 131:1–4).
>
> These are the most glorious promises given to men [and women]. There neither is nor can be anything as wondrous and great. And so the Lord uses the most powerful and emphatic language known to the human tongue to show their importance and immutability. That is to say, *the Lord swears with an oath in his own name*, because he can swear by no greater, that everyone who keeps the covenant made in connection with the Melchizedek Priesthood shall inherit, receive, and possess all

---

30. Packer, "What Every Elder Should Know—and Every Sister as Well."

things in his everlasting kingdom, and shall be a joint-heir with that Lord who is his Only Begotten. . . . Thus *we make the covenant with Deity; and God swears the oath to us all, to show the importance and eternal worth of the covenant.*[31]

This is what Paul is discussing in verses 15–17: "And so, after [Abraham] had patiently endured [the promise of an endless posterity], he obtained the promise. For men verily swear by the greater [i.e., by God]: and an oath for confirmation is to them an end to all strife. Wherein God, willing more abundantly to shew unto the heirs of promise the immutability of his counsel, confirmed it by an oath."

The Apostle goes on to explain that because it is impossible for God to lie, the oath extends to those of us "who have fled [to the Lord Jesus Christ] for refuge to lay hold upon the hope set before us: which hope we have as an anchor of the soul, both sure and steadfast, and which entereth into that within the veil" (verses 18–19). Latter-day Saint professors Richard D. Draper and Michael D. Rhodes offered this comment: "The context of Hebrews suggests the flight is from a spiritually dangerous and physically hostile world. The shelter or protection from the world is the gospel in general and the promises of God in particular. The author's admonitions that readers stay faithful 'unto the end' (6:11) remind them that although they have found refuge, they must continue to press toward the final rest of the Lord (4:1, 11), the ultimate place of refuge."[32]

THE HIGHER PRIESTHOOD: WITHOUT BEGINNING OR END (7:1–10)

Two of the most enigmatic biblical figures, persons who would remain a mystery were it not for modern revelation, are Enoch and Melchizedek. Many in both the Jewish and Christian worlds are not

---

31. McConkie, "Doctrine of the Priesthood."
32. Draper and Rhodes, *Epistle to the Hebrews*, 348.

quite sure what to do with the ancient leaders, given that so few biblical verses are devoted to them (for Enoch, see Genesis 5:18–24; Hebrews 11:5; for Melchizedek, see Genesis 14:18–20; Hebrews 7:1–7, 10–11, 15–17, 21). Enoch is the scriptural prototype for how to establish Zion, a society of the pure in heart. Such insights, which came as the Prophet Joseph worked on his inspired translation of the Bible (see Moses 6–7), may well have prompted him to seek to create a city of God, where the people would be of one heart and one mind and dwell in righteousness, with no poor among them (Moses 7:18).

As for Melchizedek, we know from both ancient and modern scripture that he was a contemporary of Abraham and the king of Salem (Genesis 14:18; Alma 13:17). He conferred upon Abraham the higher priesthood (Doctrine and Covenants 84:14), and Abraham paid tithes to him (Genesis 14:20; Alma 13:15). We also know that Melchizedek was a high priest and, more specifically, a "priest of the most high God" (Genesis 14:18; Alma 13:14). He conducted a meeting in which he administered bread and wine, presumably an ancient foreshadowing of what the Savior would institute at the Last Supper (Genesis 14:17, JST).[33] And according to Joseph Smith, Melchizedek "had power and authority over that of Abraham, holding the key of the power of endless life." As Joseph Smith explained, the power of Melchizedek was not "the priesthood of Aaron, which administers in outward ordinances, and the offering of sacrifices," and "those holding the fulness of the Melchizedek Priesthood are kings and priests [and queens and priestesses] of the most high God, holding the keys of power and blessings."[34]

Verse 3 of Hebrews 7 describes Melchizedek as a person who was "without father, without mother, without descent, having neither

---

33. See also McConkie, *Promised Messiah*, 384.
34. Joseph Smith, Journal, August 27, 1843; punctuation and spelling standardized; Joseph Smith, in "History, 1838–1856, volume E-1," 1708; punctuation and spelling standardized.

beginning of days, nor end of life; but made like unto the Son of God; [abiding] a priest continually." The Joseph Smith Translation assists our understanding of this verse: "For this Melchizedek was ordained a priest after the order of the Son of God [i.e., held the fullness of the priesthood], *which order was without father, without mother, without descent, having neither beginning of days, nor end of life*" (compare Alma 13:7–8). The higher order of the priesthood is without beginning or end.

The Melchizedek Priesthood does not continue in lineal descent, as did the Aaronic Priesthood, given only to those who were descendants of Aaron. Further, Abraham paid his tithes to Melchizedek (who held the higher priesthood), not to Aaronic priests (who held the lesser priesthood). The Prophet Joseph explained that "the priesthood is an everlasting principle and existed with God from eternity and will to eternity, without beginning of days or end of years. The keys have to be brought from heaven whenever the gospel is sent."[35]

The meaning of verses 6 and 7 is not especially clear: "But he whose descent is not counted from them [i.e., Melchizedek] received tithes of Abraham, and blessed him [i.e., Abraham] that had the promises [made to the fathers; Abraham 2:8–11]. And without all contradiction the less is blessed of the better." The English Standard Version reads as follows: "But this man [i.e., Melchizedek] who does not have his descent from them [i.e., the Levites] received tithes from Abraham and blessed him [i.e., Abraham] who had the promises [made to the fathers]. It is beyond dispute that the inferior [i.e., Abraham] is blessed by the superior [i.e., Melchizedek]." Paul then makes a rather fascinating comment: "One might even say that Levi himself, who receives tithes, paid tithes through Abraham, for he was still in the loins of his ancestor when Melchizedek met him" (verses 9–10, ESV).

---

35. Joseph Smith, in "Discourse, between circa 26 June and circa 4 August 1839–A, as Reported by Willard Richards"; punctuation and spelling standardized.

THE ORDER OF PRIESTHOOD: BASED ON SPIRITUAL READINESS (7:11–28)

The Apostle makes an important point in verses 11–12. He asks, essentially, that if it was possible to become perfect through the Aaronic Priesthood—which continued with ancient Israel from the time of Moses until the coming of Jesus Christ—why would God rearrange things? Why would He send us a Savior, who was also the great Restorer, and thereby bring back the higher priesthood that had operated from the time of the Adamic dispensation until the Mosaic dispensation? Every gospel is administered by a priesthood. The *preparatory* gospel is administered by the lesser priesthood, while the *everlasting* gospel (the fullness of the gospel) is administered by the higher priesthood. To say this another way, the law of carnal commandments (the law of Moses) was administered by the Aaronic Order, while the power of an endless life (the law of Christ) is administered by the Order of Melchizedek.

Clearly, Paul notes, Jesus Christ did not come through the lineage of Levi, but rather through the tribe of Judah. When Jesus came to earth, He was, in a significant way, "after the similitude of Melchisedec," not Aaron (verse 15). God the Father Himself declared to His Only Begotten Son in the flesh, "Thou art a priest for ever after the order of Melchisedec" (verse 17; see also Psalm 110:4). "For the law [of Moses] made nothing perfect, but the bringing in of *a better hope* did; by the which we draw nigh unto God" (verse 19). Toward the end of his abridgment of the record of the Jaredites, Moroni spoke of this hope, writing, "And I also remember that thou [i.e., Jehovah, or Christ] hast said that thou hast prepared a house for man, yea, even among the mansions of thy Father, *in which man might have a more excellent hope*; wherefore man must hope, or he cannot receive an inheritance in the place which thou hast prepared" (Ether 12:32).

When a man has the Melchizedek Priesthood conferred upon him, he receives that priesthood with an oath and covenant. On the other hand, one who receives the Aaronic Priesthood does not receive it with an oath (verse 21).[36]

Thus Jesus, because He is everlasting, has an unchangeable priesthood, the holy priesthood after the order of the Son of God (Doctrine and Covenants 107:3). Through this priesthood, men and women may be saved "to the uttermost," meaning, perfectly and completely. How glorious it is to know that "he ever liveth to make intercession for them" (verse 25). Indeed, as the scriptures declare, we are invited to "come unto Christ" and, through His divine grace, "*be perfected in him*" (Moroni 10:32; see also Doctrine and Covenants 76:69).

Jesus the Christ was not like those [Aaronic] high priests "who offered up sacrifice daily, first for their own sins, and then for the sins of the people; for he needeth not offer sacrifice for his own sins, for he knew no sins; but for the sins of the people." And unlike the ancient Aaronic priests who offered numerous sacrifices through the years, Christ only did this "once, when he offered up himself" (Hebrews 7:26, JST).

FULFILLING JEREMIAH'S PROPHECY (8:6–13)

The law of Moses was not bad, evil, or lowly; it served its purpose extremely well, acting as a schoolmaster to bring ancient Israel to Christ (Galatians 3:24). But it was not the everlasting gospel. The covenant God made with Israel through Moses, who was their mediator with Jehovah, was just what was needed at the time, but the covenant associated with Christ's everlasting gospel is superior. In fact, it was of this gospel covenant that Jehovah spoke of prophetically through Jeremiah. Jesus would serve as the Mediator of that covenant, and the resulting blessings specified by the God of Israel were

- He will "put [His] law in their inward parts and write it in their hearts."
- He will be their God, and they will be His people.

---

36. See Joseph Smith, Journal, August 27, 1843.

- The people will no longer charge or challenge one another to know the Lord, for they will know Him, "from the least of them unto the greatest of them."[37]
- He will forgive their iniquity and remember their sins no more. (Jeremiah 31:31–34)

THE MEDIATOR OF THE NEW COVENANT (8:1–16)

For a discussion of Christ as our Mediator, see the commentary herein on 1 Timothy 2:5–6.

THE MINISTER OF THE TRUE TABERNACLE (9:1–8)

In chapter 9, the Apostle explains how the ancient tabernacle in the wilderness, built in the Mosaic dispensation (see Exodus 26:1–35), was a figure, type, or symbol that foreshadowed the kind of tabernacle Jesus would establish when He came to earth in the meridian of time. Paul lists the various parts of the holy tabernacle, including the table, the candlestick, and the shewbread (verse 2). He then reminds readers of what was found in the most sacred room within the ancient temple, the "Holiest of all," or Holy of Holies: the golden censer and the ark of the covenant (in which were stored Aaron's budding rod, the stone tablets containing the Ten Commandments, and a pot of manna). Above the ark of the covenant were two cherubim who figuratively guarded the ark (verses 3–5; Exodus 16:32–34; 25:16; 40:20; Numbers 17:10).

Paul explains that anciently the priests (those literal descendants of Aaron who officiated in the temple) performed their functions in the holy place. Professors Richard D. Draper and Michael D. Rhodes remind us that "according to the Mosaic law, a selected priest entered the holy place multiple times to carry out the services of offering incense

---

37. The Prophet Joseph Smith taught that the way the Saints will know the Lord is through receiving the blessings of the Second Comforter—through having a personal visitation of Jesus Christ Himself. "Discourse, between circa 26 June and circa 2 July 1839, as Reported by Wilford Woodruff."

at the time of both morning and evening prayers, filling the menorah lamps with oil, relighting them (Exodus 27:20–21), and, when necessary, changing the loaves of shewbread (Exodus 40:22–23)."[38] Once each year, on the Day of Atonement, "went the high priest alone . . . , [with] blood, which he offered for himself, and for the errors of the people [i.e., a sin offering]" (verse 7; see Leviticus 16:3–34). Specifically, the high priest would sprinkle the blood of animals seven times before the mercy seat.

Then Paul states, "The Holy Ghost this signifying, that the way into the holiest of all was not yet made manifest, while as the first tabernacle was yet standing" (verses 7–8). The tabernacle in the wilderness served its purpose well in the days of Moses, but, once again, this tabernacle—like the law of Moses, like the preparatory gospel—was inferior to that which Jesus Christ would bring when He restored the Melchizedek Priesthood and the everlasting gospel.

"AN HIGH PRIEST OF GOOD THINGS TO COME" (9:11–28)

In verses 11–12, Paul refers to Jesus as "an high priest of good things to come, by a greater and more perfect tabernacle, not made with hands, . . . neither by the blood of goats and calves, but by his own blood he entered in once into the holy place, having obtained eternal redemption for us." Later, in chapter 10, Paul states simply that "it is not possible that the blood of bulls and of goats should take away sins" (Hebrews 10:4). The "perfect tabernacle" seems to refer to heaven, the celestial kingdom, or to the mansions the faithful will inherit hereafter, and the Savior is the Builder and Preparer.

The Apostle continues: "For if the blood of bulls and of goats, and the ashes of an heifer sprinkling the unclean, sanctifieth to the purifying of the flesh: *How much more shall the blood of Christ*, who . . . offered himself without spot [i.e., blameless] to God, *purge your*

---

38. Draper and Rhodes, *Epistle to the Hebrews*, 463.

conscience from dead works to serve the living God? And for this cause he is the mediator of the new testament [i.e., covenant], that by means of [His] death, for the redemption of the transgressions . . . , they which are called might receive the promise of eternal inheritance" (verses 13–15). For people's consciences to be purged from dead works is for the Redeemer, by the power of His Holy Spirit, to open their spiritual eyes, reorient their thinking, and cause them to focus no longer on the outward performances and ordinances of the law of Moses, because, in fact, Jesus Christ has fulfilled the law.

To speak of Jesus as a "high priest of good things to come" is to emphasize that gospel hope will come only as the good news of Christ's Atonement lifts the spirits of all who turn to and trust in Him. "Every one of us has times when we need to know things will get better," declared Elder Jeffrey R. Holland.

> Moroni spoke of it in the Book of Mormon as "hope for a better world" (Ether 12:4). For emotional health and spiritual stamina, everyone needs to be able to look forward to some respite, to something pleasant and renewing and hopeful, whether that blessing be near at hand or still some distance ahead. It is enough just to know we can get there, that however measured or far away, there is the promise of "good things to come."
>
> My declaration is that this is precisely what the gospel of Jesus Christ offers us, especially in times of need. There is help. There is happiness. There really *is* light at the end of the tunnel. It is the Light of the World, the Bright and Morning Star, the "light that is endless, that can never be darkened" (Mosiah 16:9; see John 8:12; Revelation 22:16). It is the very Son of God Himself.[39]

---

39. Holland, "High Priest of Good Things to Come."

"And almost all things," Paul writes, "are by the law purged with blood; and without shedding of blood is no remission" (verse 22). In an epistle written to the Saints, the Prophet Joseph taught:

> By faith in [the Savior's] atonement or plan of redemption, Abel offered to God a sacrifice that was accepted, which was the firstlings of the flock [as commanded in Moses 5:4–5]. Cain offered of the fruit of the ground, and was not accepted, because he could not do it in faith: he could have no faith, or could not exercise faith contrary to the plan of heaven. It must be the shedding of the blood of the Only Begotten to atone for man; for this was the plan of redemption; and without the shedding of blood was no remission; and as the sacrifice was instituted for a type, by which man was to discern the great Sacrifice which God had prepared; to offer a sacrifice contrary to that, no faith could be exercised, because redemption was not purchased in that way, nor the power of atonement instituted after that order; consequently Cain could have no faith; and whatsoever is not of faith is sin.[40]

CHRIST ENTERS THE PRESENCE OF THE FATHER FOR US (9:24)

See the commentary herein on Hebrews 4:16.

JUDGMENT FOLLOWS DEATH (9:27)

"And as it is appointed unto men once to die, but after this the judgment" (verse 27). This verse has been used over the years by many Christians as evidence that there is no postmortal spirit world, no intermediate state into which spirits enter after they take their last breath on earth. The interpretation of this verse goes something like this: "Notice

---

40. Joseph Smith, in "Letter to the Church, circa March 1834."

that immediately after death comes the judgment." There is, however, nothing in the verse that states specifically that when we die, we go immediately into either heaven or hell. If we were to comply with this kind of logic, we could make the following statements, each of which would lead to confusion:

- After Creation comes the Millennium. (The Millennium *does* come after the Creation, doesn't it?)
- After we sin, we are forgiven. (That's true, but only if repentance takes place.)
- After Joseph Smith's First Vision, he was killed. (Yes, but a period of twenty-four years passed between these two events.)
- After Brigham Young's death, President Joseph F. Smith became the Prophet. (President Smith certainly did become the senior Apostle after Brigham Young died, some forty years later.)

There is, of course, a "partial judgment" that takes place at the time of death, but this is to determine whether the deceased goes into paradise or into that realm known variously as spirit prison, hell, or outer darkness (see 1 Peter 4:6; 2 Nephi 9:10–12; Alma 40:13–14).[41] The judgment of which our Christian friends speak is the Final Judgment, which takes place after the Second or Last Resurrection, to determine the degree of glory we will enjoy and thus what kingdom of glory we will inherit.

THE END OF ANIMAL SACRIFICES (10:6–14)

The repetition of religious rites can either enhance one's appreciation for what or whom they point to, or become empty acts, dead works, far more ritual than religion (see Doctrine and Covenants 22:2–3). Through the generations, too often the people of Israel, whom God had appointed to be a light unto the nations (Gentiles) and to be His

---

41. Joseph F. Smith, *Gospel Doctrine*, 448.

peculiar people, lost sight of what was behind animal sacrifices, especially the intricate offerings specified by the law of Moses.

Sadly, by the time of the prophet Malachi, some four hundred years before the coming of Jesus Christ, the sacrifices were being offered by priests who were unworthy to perform the sacred ordinances. In speaking of the Second Coming of the Messiah, Malachi asked: "But who may abide the day of his coming? and who shall stand when he appeareth? for he is like a refiner's fire, and like fullers' soap: And he shall sit as a refiner and purifier of silver: and *he shall purify the sons of Levi, and purge them as gold and silver, that they may offer unto the Lord an offering in righteousness*" (Malachi 3:2–3; compare Doctrine and Covenants 13).

In writing to the Hebrews, the Apostle Paul begins to quote or paraphrase from the Old Testament regarding animal sacrifice:

> Hath the Lord as great delight in burnt offerings and sacrifices, as in obeying the voice of the Lord? Behold, to obey is better than sacrifice, and to hearken than the fat of rams. (1 Samuel 15:22)

> Then said I, Lo, I come: in the volume of the book it is written of me, I delight to do thy will, O my God: yea, thy law is within my heart. (Psalm 40:7–8)

And to these passages we might well add the following:

> Thou desirest not sacrifice; else would I give it: thou delightest not in burnt offering. The sacrifices of God are a broken spirit: a broken and a contrite heart, O God, thou wilt not despise. (Psalm 51:16–17; compare 34:18; Doctrine and Covenants 59:8)

> Will the Lord be pleased with thousands of rams, or with ten thousands of rivers of oil? shall I give my firstborn for my transgression, the fruit of my body for the sin of my soul? He

hath shewed thee, O man, what is good; and what doth the Lord require of thee, but to do justly, and to love mercy, and to walk humbly with thy God? (Micah 6:7–8; compare Doctrine and Covenants 11:12)

We recall that following the death of Christ, massive and widespread destruction took place in the Americas (3 Nephi 8:5–25). Just before the Savior appeared to the more righteous in the Western Hemisphere, the Nephites heard His voice: "And ye shall offer up unto me no more the shedding of blood; yea, your sacrifices and your burnt offerings shall be done away, for I will accept none of your sacrifices and your burnt offerings." Then came this significant alteration to the law of sacrifice: "And *ye shall offer for a sacrifice unto me a broken heart and a contrite spirit.* And whoso cometh unto me with a broken heart and a contrite spirit, him will I baptize with fire and with the Holy Ghost" (3 Nephi 9:19–20). And again, in our dispensation, the Saints were instructed by the Lord, "Thou shalt thank the Lord thy God in all things. Thou shalt offer a sacrifice unto the Lord thy God in righteousness, even *that of a broken heart and a contrite spirit*" (Doctrine and Covenants 59:7–8).

In short, the Apostle teaches that the Lord "taketh away the first [i.e., animal sacrifice], that he may establish the second [i.e., broken heart, contrite spirit]" (verse 9). A modern Apostle explained that "real, personal sacrifice never was placing an animal on the altar. Instead, it is a willingness to put the animal in us upon the altar and letting it be consumed."[42]

Paul goes on to explain that in contrast to the ancient priests who offered sacrifices daily—sacrifices of animals which, of themselves, can never take away sins—"this man [i.e., Jesus], after he had offered one sacrifice for sins for ever, sat down on the right hand of God; . . . for by

---

42. Maxwell, "Deny Yourselves of All Ungodliness."

one offering he hath perfected for ever them that are sanctified" (verses 11–12, 14).

ENTERING GOD'S PRESENCE THROUGH CHRIST'S FLESH (10:19–24)

Paul here encourages the Saints, "Having therefore, brethren, boldness [i.e., license, authority] to enter into the holiest by the blood of Jesus, by a new and living way, which he hath consecrated for us, through *the veil, that is to say, his flesh*; and having an high priest over the house of God; let us draw near with a true heart in full assurance of faith, having our hearts sprinkled from an evil conscience, and our bodies washed with pure water" (verses 19–22). The Apostle is likening the Holy of Holies in the temple to what Latter-day Saints would describe as eternal life and exaltation in the celestial kingdom, life with our eternal families in the presence of God the Father and His Son, Jesus Christ.

The high priest was required to pass through the veil of the temple from the holy place into the Holy of Holies. Likewise, we are each required to pass from this mortal sphere into paradise and then the celestial world, doing so only by virtue of the broken and bruised body and shed blood of the Son of God. Whereas the high priest was allowed to pass through the veil of the temple into the Holy of Holies only one time each year, on the Day of Atonement, all faithful and obedient members of the Church of Jesus Christ can metaphorically pass through the flesh of the Redeemer again and again—that is, they can live daily in a state of repentance and obtain and retain a remission of sins from day to day by virtue of the atoning blood of Christ (see Mosiah 4:1–3, 11–12, 26; Alma 4:14). Further, if on the Sabbath day we attend our sacrament meeting with a humble and repentant heart and take the sacrament of the Lord's Supper in reverence, we may then pass through, as it were, the flesh and blood of the Holy One of Israel into the rest of God.

SINNING AGAINST GREAT LIGHT (10:26–31)

"For if we sin wilfully after that we have received the knowledge of the truth," the Apostle writes, "there remaineth no more sacrifice for sins, but a certain fearful looking for of judgment and fiery indignation, which shall devour the adversaries" (verses 26–27). This is a terribly strong statement, one that almost seems at odds with other scriptural passages. For instance, "As often as my people repent will I forgive them their trespasses against me" (Mosiah 26:30). And, "Behold, he who has repented of his sins, the same is forgiven, and I, the Lord, remember them no more" (Doctrine and Covenants 58:42).

In a revelation received on April 16, 1832, the Latter-day Saints were warned to "beware from henceforth, and refrain from sin, lest sore judgments fall upon your heads." And then followed a vital principle: "For of him unto whom much is given much is required; and *he who sins against the greater light shall receive the greater condemnation*" (Doctrine and Covenants 82:2–3). Paul's reference to the "knowledge of the truth" must mean more than an understanding of the gospel or even a strong testimony of that gospel.

The Prophet Joseph declared that "from apostates the faithful have received the severest persecutions. Judas was rebuked and immediately betrayed his Lord into the hands of His enemies, because Satan entered into him. *There is a supreme intelligence bestowed upon such as obey the gospel with full purpose of heart, which, if sinned against, the apostate is left naked and destitute of the Spirit of God*, and they are, in truth, nigh unto cursing, and their end is to be burned."[43]

Professors Draper and Rhodes have written regarding the "knowledge of the truth": "The noun [*knowledge*] denotes becoming fully acquainted with something known before that leads to an expanded and often an exact understanding of that thing. It suggests such a depth of

---

43. Joseph Smith, in "Letter to the Church, circa April 1834"; punctuation and spelling standardized.

participation between the 'knower' and the thing known that it has a powerful influence on the former. In the New Testament, that which can be known to this degree is limited to transcendent and moral matters. The word [*knowledge*] carries a strong connotation of a tender, deep, and abiding relationship with God."[44]

In verse 29 we read that one who sins against and defies a perfect knowledge of the truth is one who has "trodden under foot the Son of God, and hath counted the blood of the covenant, wherewith he was sanctified, an unholy thing, and hath done despite unto [i.e., rejected or violated] the Spirit of grace." Similar language is used in other scripture to describe the sons of perdition: "The blasphemy against the Holy Ghost, which shall not be forgiven in the world nor out of the world [i.e., on earth or in the postmortal spirit world], is in that ye *commit murder* wherein ye shed innocent blood, *and assent unto my death*, after ye have received my new and everlasting covenant, saith the Lord God; and he that abideth not this law can in nowise enter into my glory, but shall be damned, saith the Lord" (Doctrine and Covenants 132:27).

Indeed, "it is a fearful thing to fall into the hands of the living God" (verse 31). The God and Father of us all is filled with love and mercy and divine grace, but He is also a God of justice who must and will attend to those who have chosen to sin against major light and become an enemy of Christ and the gospel of salvation. These are the ones who will suffer the second death—the final spiritual death—and who will be cast out of the presence of the Father and the Son and remain in their unredeemed condition forever (Doctrine and Covenants 76:37–38).

TAKING JOYFULLY THE SPOILING OF ONE'S GOODS (10:34)

There is a cost associated with following Jesus Christ, a very real cost of discipleship. Life will not always be easy for faithful and devoted

---

44. Draper and Rhodes, *Epistle to the Hebrews*, 559.

believers. They must be willing to be caricatured, misunderstood, misrepresented, and repeatedly scorned, insulted, and ignored. In this verse, Paul refers here to those Hebrew Saints who "took joyfully the spoiling of [their] goods, knowing in [themselves] that [they] have in heaven a better and an enduring substance." In the words of another translation, "You had compassion for those who were in prison, and you cheerfully accepted the plundering of your possessions, knowing that you yourselves possessed something better and more lasting" (NRSV).

The early elders of this dispensation were taught:

> An actual knowledge to any person, that the course of life which he pursues is according to the will of God, is essentially necessary to enable him to have that confidence in God without which no person can obtain eternal life. It was this that enabled the ancient saints to endure all their afflictions and persecutions, and to take joyfully the spoiling of their goods, knowing (not believing merely) that they had a more enduring substance.
>
> Such was, and always will be, the situation of the saints of God, that unless they have an actual knowledge that the course they are pursuing is according to the will of God they will grow weary in their minds, and faint. . . . Nothing short of an actual knowledge of their being the favorites of heaven, and of their having embraced that order of things which God has established for the redemption of man, will enable them to exercise that confidence in him, necessary for them to overcome the world, and obtain that crown of glory which is laid up for them that fear God.[45]

"CAST NOT AWAY . . . YOUR CONFIDENCE" (10:35–36)

"Cast not away therefore your confidence," these verses read, "which hath great recompense of reward. For ye have need of patience,

---

45. *Lectures on Faith*, 6:2–4; pp. 67–68.

that, after ye have done the will of God, ye might receive the promise." Confidence in what? Confidence in whom? To have a Spirit-borne testimony of the divine Sonship of Christ is to have *confidence in Him*, confidence that (1) He is who the scriptures say He is—namely, the Only Begotten Son of God; (2) He identifies fully with our pains, sicknesses, infirmities, sorrows, temptations, disappointments, rejection, loneliness, and alienation, for He too has lived and walked and talked and ministered in this telestial, fallen world; (3) He loves every one of us tenderly and perfectly; (4) He has the power to forgive our sins, cleanse our souls, and make us into new creatures in Christ; and (5) He had the power, given to him by the Father, to rise triumphantly from the tomb, thereby making it possible for every mortal to likewise rise from the dead.

In a very real sense, we must have confidence *in ourselves*, in the assurance that all of our Heavenly Father's children are capable of gaining eternal life (see Articles of Faith 1:3). Further, we can have confidence that comes from knowing that our pursued course in life is according to the will of God. This is, of course, one of the prerequisites for the kind and quality of faith that leads to life and salvation.[46]

"I wish to encourage every one of us," Elder Jeffrey R. Holland beckoned to Brigham Young University students, "regarding the opposition that so often comes after enlightened decisions have been made, after moments of revelation and conviction have given us a peace and an assurance we thought we would never lose." Elder Holland then quoted Hebrews 10:35, in which Paul pleads with the Saints in the first century not to cast away their confidence. Elder Holland then added: "In Latter-day Saint talk that is to say, Sure it is tough—before you join the Church, while you are trying to join, and after you have joined. That is the way it has always been, Paul says, but don't draw back.

---

46. *Lectures on Faith*, 3:5; p. 38; and 6:5–6; pp. 68–69.

Don't panic and retreat. Don't lose your confidence. Don't forget how you once felt. Don't distrust the experience you had."[47]

"THE JUST SHALL LIVE BY FAITH" (10:38)

For a discussion of verse 38, see the commentary herein on Romans 1:17.

FAITH IS BASED ON ASSURANCE (11:1)

In this chapter, Paul briefly defines faith and then goes on to illustrate what true faith really looks like by referring to the great men and women through the centuries whose lives attested to their faith in the Lord and in His plan of salvation.

Let's first remind ourselves of what faith *is not*. Faith is neither weakness nor ignorance. Faith is not blind. Faith is not the absence of certitude. Faith is not simply the power of positive thinking, nor is it about willing something into existence. The Apostle writes, "Now faith is the substance [or "assurance," per the JST] of things hoped for, the evidence of things not seen" (verse 1). In other words, faith is the conviction that what we hope for is real and obtainable. And what do we hope for? We hope that Jesus Christ is our Lord and Redeemer; that no one of our Heavenly Father's spirit children comes to earth without the capacity to gain eternal life; that we will one day rise from the dead in glorious, immortal, resurrected bodies; and that through accepting the gospel of Jesus Christ and being true to our covenants, we will inherit life in the highest heaven hereafter. Faith in the Lord Jesus Christ consists in having a total *trust* in Him, a complete *confidence* in Him, and a ready *reliance* upon Him.

Perhaps a word about *trust* would be worthwhile. What does it mean to say that a husband truly trusts his wife? He trusts her in the sense that he knows she loves him, that she knows him well enough to understand his heart, his deepest desires and longings. He trusts her

---

47. Holland, *Trusting Jesus*, 170–71.

because she knows, only too well, his weaknesses and his inclination to be less than he should be, and yet she regularly displays patience and long-suffering. He trusts her because she is ever ready and willing to forgive him when he blunders. He trusts her because he knows he can share his heaviest burdens, darkest moments, and lingering doubts and that she will think no less of him. Finally, a husband trusts his wife because he knows that their companionship blesses and elevates his life and makes him so much more, so much better than he would be on his own. Further, he has trust in her because he knows she will always come through. And heaven only knows how much he relies on her wisdom, judgment, discernment, and unending devotion and loyalty.

The prophet Alma added an important ingredient to Paul's definition: "And now as I said concerning faith—faith is not to have a perfect knowledge of things; therefore if ye have faith ye hope for things which are not seen, *which are true*" (Alma 32:21). No person can exercise faith unto life and salvation in someone or something that is false. No matter the depth of their devotion, no matter the sincerity with which they approach their efforts, no matter how long or how intensely they worship, they cannot have true faith. Faith is always based on something or someone that actually exists.

When we come to know who Jesus is and recognize His great and marvelous powers and knowledge and the nature of His sacrificial offering—in other words, when we gain faith in Christ—then we gain a *hope* in Christ. We cannot "attain unto faith" except we shall have hope (Moroni 7:40). We need not speak of faith as something one either has in its fullness or does not have, because gaining faith is a process. And so it is with hope. Individuals, like the Zoramites, begin with the simple hope that there is a Savior (see Alma 32:27). On the other end of the continuum are those who know their Lord, have treasured up His word, and have been valiant in their witness. Their hope is for eternal life, for exaltation in the celestial kingdom (Moroni 7:40–42). Disciples of Christ have hope, not in the worldly sense of wishing or yearning, but rather in the sense of anticipation, expectation, and assurance that through the Divine Redeemer they can be cleansed and forgiven, empowered, and eventually saved in the highest heaven. They are motivated and directed by their confidence, or hope, in Christ.

GOD CREATED ALL THINGS BY FAITH (11:3)

Paul continues to speak on faith in verse 3: "Through faith we understand that the worlds were framed by the word of God, so that things which are seen were not made of things which do appear." Most who read this sentence assume it means that *by faith we come to know* that God created all things. That's certainly true. But the early elders of this dispensation were taught to look at this verse from a different perspective: that *by virtue of His faith, God created all things.* Having read verse 3, the elders were taught that "the principle of power which existed in the bosom of God, by which the worlds were framed, was faith; and that *it is by reason of this principle of power existing in the Deity, that all created things exist*; so that all things in heaven, on earth, or under the earth, exist *by reason of faith as it existed in Him.* . . . It is the principle by which Jehovah works, and through which he exercises power over all temporal as well as eternal things. Take this principle or attribute—for it is an attribute—from the Deity, and he would cease to exist."[48]

Faith and knowledge build upon one another. A certain degree of knowledge is necessary in order to exercise even "a particle of faith" (Alma 32:27). Then, after one begins to develop faith, new and added knowledge comes—new feelings and desires, new insights, and new perspectives. In one sense, as Alma suggested to the Zoramites, one's faith is replaced by knowledge whenever a testimony of a particular principle has been obtained (see Alma 32:34; Ether 3:19). In reality, however, faith has not disappeared but instead been added upon. Faith

---

48. *Lectures on Faith*, 1:15–16; p. 3.

is a principle of power and thus a divine attribute possessed by God in perfection; God is the embodiment of faith, just as He is the embodiment of love and justice and judgment and mercy.[49] And so mortals are not working toward that day when they will no longer live and act by faith, but rather toward that day, beyond the Resurrection, when they operate by perfect faith, the faith possessed by God the Father and Jesus Christ, His Son.[50]

The final great fruit of faith is eternal life. In the first estate we walked by sight *and* by faith. Those who were valiant in the premortal existence demonstrated "exceeding faith and good works" and were foreordained and foreappointed to significant assignments here on earth (Alma 13:1–6). In this life we walk by faith (see 2 Corinthians 5:7). That is, we proceed through life with the Spirit-given assurance that our actions are approved of God and will result in the salvation of our souls. To see with an "eye of faith" (Alma 5:15; 32:40) is thus to act according to the witness of the Spirit, to act as though one had seen and thus had perfect knowledge. The Saints of God view things with an eye of faith in this life, until one day, because of their faithful endurance, they see "with their eyes the things which they had [previously] beheld with an eye of faith" (Ether 12:19).

"The very name of the kind of life [God] lives," Elder Bruce R. McConkie explained, "is eternal life, and thus eternal life consists in living and being as he is. In other words, eternal life is to gain the power of God, which power is faith, and thus to be able to do what he does and to live as he lives. And the great and eternal plan of salvation that he has ordained and established consists of those laws, ordinances, and powers whereby faith is acquired and perfected until it is possessed in the same degree and to the same extent that it exists in Deity. Faith will thus dwell independently in every person who gains eternal life."[51]

---

49. *Lectures on Faith*, 1:15–17; pp. 3–4; and 7:2; p. 72.
50. See McConkie, *New Witness for the Articles of Faith*, 166–69, 209–10.
51. McConkie, *New Witness for the Articles of Faith*, 169.

The Prophet Joseph Smith and those who assisted him in preparing the *Lectures on Faith*, taught that "when men begin to live by faith they begin to draw near to God; and when faith is perfected they are like him; and because he is saved they are saved also; for they will be in the same situation he is in, because they have come to him; and when he appears they shall be like him, for they will see him as he is." In this sense, the plan of salvation is "a system of faith—it begins with faith, and continues by faith; and every blessing which is obtained in relation to it is the effect of faith, whether it pertains to this life or that which is to come. To this all the revelations of God bear witness."[52]

A CAVALCADE OF THE FAITHFUL (11:4–32)

Chapter 11 of the Epistle to the Hebrews is essentially a "who's who in faith," much like Ether 12 is in the Book of Mormon. In these verses, Paul lists many of the men and women through the centuries whose faith was solid and secure, whose faith enabled them to work mighty miracles and thereby bring to pass the otherwise impossible. Given space restrictions in this book, we will consider only a few of the examples given by Paul.

In verse 4 we read, "By faith **Abel** offered unto God a more excellent sacrifice than Cain, by which he obtained witness that he was righteous, God testifying of his gifts: and by it he being dead yet speaketh." In a lengthy letter written to the Saints in Kirtland, Ohio, the Prophet Joseph explained:

> It is said by Paul in his letter to the Hebrew brethren, that Abel obtained witness that he was righteous, God testifying of his gifts. To whom did God testify of the gifts of Abel, was it to Paul? We have very little on this important subject in the forepart of the Bible. But it is said that Abel himself obtained witness that he was righteous. Then certainly God spoke to

---

52. *Lectures on Faith*, 7:8, 17; pp. 74, 80.

him; indeed, it is said that God talked with him; and if He did, would He not, seeing that Abel was righteous deliver to him the whole plan of the Gospel? And is not the gospel the news of the redemption? How could Abel offer a sacrifice and look forward with faith on the Son of God for a remission of his sins, and not understand the Gospel? . . . And if Abel was taught of the coming of the Son of God, was he not taught also of His ordinances? We all admit that the Gospel has ordinances, and if so, had it not always ordinances, and were not its ordinances always the same?[53]

More than six years later, the Prophet again spoke of Abel, the son of Adam:

How doth he [i.e., Abel] yet speak? Why, he magnified the Priesthood which was conferred upon him, and died a righteous man, and therefore has become an angel of God by receiving his body from the dead, holding still the keys of his dispensation; and *was sent down from heaven unto Paul to minister consoling words, and to commit unto him a knowledge of the mysteries of godliness.*

And if this was not the case, I would ask, how did Paul know so much about Abel, and why should he talk about his speaking after he was dead? Hence that he spoke after he was dead must be by being sent down out of heaven to administer.[54]

Enoch is mentioned in verse 5, more specifically that he was translated. In chapters 6 and 7 of the book of Moses in the Pearl of Great Price, we learn of the early life of Enoch, his call as a prophet, his

---

53. Joseph Smith, in "Letter to the Church, circa March 1834."
54. Joseph Smith, in "Instruction on Priesthood, circa 5 October 1840"; punctuation and spelling standardized.

powerful ministry, and the translation of him and his city. In addition, Enoch is mentioned in sections 38, 45, 76, 84, and 107 of the Doctrine and Covenants. To aid our understanding of this verse, here are multiple English translations of verse 5:

> By faith Enoch was translated that he should not see death; and was not found, because God had translated him. (KJV)

> By faith Enoch was *taken up to another life without passing through death*; he was not to be found, because God had taken him. (REB)

> By faith Enoch was taken so that he did not experience death; and he was not found, because God had taken him. (NRSV)

> By faith *Enoch was taken from this life*. So that he did not experience death; he could not be found, because God had taken him away. (NIV)

Joseph Smith explained that God had "appointed unto [Enoch] *a ministry unto terrestrial bodies*, of whom there has been but little revealed. He is reserved also unto *the presidency of a dispensation*, and more shall be said of him and terrestrial bodies in another treatise. He is a ministering angel, to minister to those who shall be heirs of salvation, and appeared unto Jude as Abel did to Paul; therefore Jude spoke of him [Jude 1:14–15]. And Enoch, the seventh from Adam, revealed these sayings: 'Behold, the Lord cometh with ten thousands of His Saints.'"[55]

The Prophet Joseph also taught regarding translation:

> Now the doctrine of translation is a power which belongs to this [Melchizedek] Priesthood. . . . Many have supposed that

---

55. Joseph Smith, in "Instruction on Priesthood, circa 5 October 1840"; punctuation and spelling standardized.

the doctrine of translation was a doctrine whereby men were taken immediately into the presence of God, and into an eternal fulness, but this is a mistaken idea. *Their place of habitation is that of the terrestrial order*, and a place prepared for such characters He held in reserve to be ministering angels unto many planets, and who as yet have not entered into so great a fulness as those who are resurrected from the dead. . . . Translation obtains deliverance from the tortures and sufferings of the body [see 3 Nephi 28:7–9, 37–40], but their existence will prolong as to the labors and toils of the ministry, before they can enter into so great a rest and glory.[56]

Joseph further stated that "translated bodies cannot enter into rest until they have undergone a change equivalent unto death. Translated bodies are designed for future missions."[57]

Of **Abraham**, the Apostle Paul writes that "he looked for a city which hath foundations, whose builder and maker is God" (verse 10). That is, Abraham desired, just as Enoch and Melchizedek had, to participate in the building of the city of God, the holy city, Zion, a place where the pure in heart dwell (see Doctrine and Covenants 97:21; Moses 7:16–19).

Paul further explains that many of the ancients "died in faith, not having received the promises, but having seen them afar off [with an 'eye of faith'], and were persuaded of them, and embraced them, and confessed that they were strangers and pilgrims on the earth. For they that say such things declare plainly that they seek a country" (verses 13–14). In other words, many of the righteous ancients received the *promises* that the Almighty always makes to His obedient covenant people, but they

---

56. Joseph Smith, in "Instruction on Priesthood, circa 5 October 1840"; punctuation and spelling standardized.
57. Joseph Smith, in "Discourse, 3 October 1841, as Published in *Times and Seasons*."

did not live to see the *fulfillment* of those promises *in this life*. But those women and men who prove true and faithful to their covenants will inherit a better country—a heavenly one, the eternal Zion of our God.

Paul writes about a crucial moment in the life of Abraham, one for which he is known and beloved in both Judaism and Christianity—when he showed his willingness to obey God and offer his covenant son Isaac in sacrifice (verses 17–19; see Genesis 22). Why was Abraham willing? Because he was commanded to do so by Jehovah. It was to be through Isaac that the promises made to the fathers would be perpetuated (see Abraham 2:8–11). He was to be the means by which Abraham's posterity would be more numerous than the stars in the heavens, even more than the sands upon the seashore. Sacrificing Isaac thus seemed to be an impossible request from God; Abraham was commanded to obey in the face of what must have seemed like the absurd.

Professor Truman G. Madsen once spoke of an occasion when he was asked to serve as a guide to the Holy Land for President Hugh B. Brown. President Brown was a man who served as a member of the Quorum of the Twelve Apostles and also as a counselor to President David O. McKay. He was a person of deep intellect and profound wisdom. While standing in the valley of Hebron, Truman asked: "What are the blessings of Abraham, Isaac, and Jacob?" President Brown answered in one word: "posterity." Truman followed up: "Why, then, was Abraham commanded to go to Mount Moriah and offer his only hope of posterity?" "It was clear," Brother Madsen continued, that President Brown, "nearly ninety, had thought and prayed and wept over that question before. He finally said, '*Abraham needed to learn something about Abraham.*'"[58] Abraham needed to know, in his heart of hearts, that there was nothing that God would ask or require of him that he would not do.

The Apostle goes on to hold up **Isaac, Jacob, Joseph,** and **Moses** as

---

58. Madsen, *Highest in Us*, 49.

additional faithful examples. Of Moses, Paul writes that the Lawgiver "refused to be called the son of Pharaoh's daughter; choosing rather to suffer affliction with the people of God, than to enjoy the pleasures of sin for a season; esteeming the reproach of Christ greater riches than the treasures in Egypt" (verses 24–26). Another way of stating this is "preferring to share hardship with God's people rather than enjoy the transient pleasures of sin. He considered the stigma that rests on God's Anointed [i.e., Christ] greater wealth than the treasures of Egypt" (REB).

Paul then continues his "who's who in faith" by referring to **Rahab, Gideon, Barak, Samson, Jephthah, David,** and **Samuel**. And then Paul gives this sobering reminder: "Women received their dead raised to life again: and others were tortured, not accepting deliverance; that they might obtain a better resurrection" (verse 35; the JST renders the last part of this verse as "that they might obtain the first resurrection"). The Apostle adds this profound parenthetical insight: "*of whom the world was not worthy*" (verse 38). Indeed, when one considers that through the centuries, prophets and righteous, God-fearing women and men have consistently been ridiculed, rejected, tortured, and put to death because of their convictions, the Apostle's words ring painfully accurate and true. The world and the worldly simply aren't worthy of the pure hearted and single minded, those whom God sends to bless lives and to call others to look heavenward.

"THEY WITHOUT US SHOULD NOT BE MADE PERFECT" (11:39–40)

To conclude the chapter, Paul writes: "And these all, having obtained a good report [i.e., testimony or witness] through faith, received not the promise: God having provided some better thing for us, that *they without us should not be made perfect*" (verses 39–40). When Latter-day Saints read these words, particularly verse 40, our minds turn naturally to the importance of family history and temple work. And yet, when the Prophet Joseph and his scribe were engaged in the revision of the Bible, they came to verse 40 (sometime between February 16, 1832, and February 2, 1833) and rendered the verse as follows: "And these all, having obtained a good report through faith, received not the promise: God having provided some better things for them through their sufferings, *for without sufferings they could not be made perfect*" (JST).

One cannot read Hebrews carefully, particularly chapter 11, without realizing the vital importance of suffering in the sanctification of Saints' souls in all ages. It has been said that both Jesus and Melchizedek learned obedience *by the things which they suffered* and were thereby perfected (Hebrews 5:8–9). And so the alteration in the Joseph Smith Translation is just as true as it can be. Indeed, it fits the context of this chapter perfectly.

But as time passed—and as Joseph Smith and the Latter-day Saints learned and matured in their gospel understanding, line upon line, precept upon precept—new ideas, new concepts, and new perspectives burst upon their minds and hearts. On January 21, 1836, the Prophet received a vision of the celestial kingdom, in which he saw his older brother Alvin, who had died in 1823, in that highest heaven. Joseph must have wondered how that could be, given that Alvin had never been baptized by proper authority. In Joseph's words, "Thus came the voice of the Lord unto me, saying: All who have died without a knowledge of this gospel, who would have received it if they had been permitted to tarry, shall be heirs of the celestial kingdom of God; also all that shall die henceforth without a knowledge of it, who would have received it with all their hearts, shall be heirs of that kingdom; for I, the Lord, will judge all men according to their works, according to the desire of their hearts" (Doctrine and Covenants 137:7–9). Some four years later, on August 15, 1840, Joseph delivered his first public discourse on baptism for the dead at the funeral of Brother Seymour Brunson.

In a letter to the Saints in Nauvoo in September 1842, Joseph Smith wrote of the powers of the holy priesthood and particularly the sealing and binding powers. He referred to baptism for the dead and the vital importance of making salvation available to those who died without a knowledge of gospel truths, priesthood powers, covenants, and ordinances: "And now, my dearly beloved brethren and sisters, let me assure you that these are principles in relation to the dead and the living that cannot be lightly passed over, as pertaining to our salvation. For *their salvation is necessary and essential to our salvation, as Paul says concerning the fathers—that they without us cannot be made perfect—neither can we without our dead be made perfect*" (Doctrine and Covenants 128:15). In light of this statement, Joseph stated simply but powerfully in his King Follett sermon: "The greatest responsibility that God has laid upon us is to seek after our dead."[59]

Not everything of doctrinal importance was given to the boy prophet in the Sacred Grove in the spring of 1820. Nor was every doctrinal matter revealed and understood by Joseph and the Saints by 1833, during the time of his inspired Bible translation. This process of gradual revelation introduces us to a fascinating concept: a passage of scripture may be rendered in more ways than one. In short, a Joseph Smith Translation alteration need not invalidate the original passage in the King James Version.

"SO GREAT A CLOUD OF WITNESSES" (12:1)

In verse 1 of chapter 12, Paul refers to the many faithful people mentioned in the previous chapter, declaring that "we also are compassed about [i.e., surrounded by] so great a cloud of witnesses." Those men and women who have lived through the centuries and who were true and faithful to their covenants are only separated from us by a very thin veil. In other words, that "great cloud of witnesses" is busily

---

59. Joseph Smith, in "Discourse, 7 April 1844, as Reported by *Times and Seasons*."

engaged in the work of the Lord, just as we are on this side of the veil. They are striving to gather Israel where they are, just as we are striving to do so in mortality.

At the funeral for Brother James Adams, the Prophet Joseph Smith taught: "When men are prepared, they are better off to go hence," meaning, into the spirit world. "Brother Adams has gone to open up a more effectual door for the dead. The Spirits of the just are exalted to a greater and more glorious work—hence they are blessed in their departure to the world of Spirits. Enveloped in flaming fire, they are not far from us, and know and understand our thoughts, feelings, and motions, and are often pained therewith."[60]

President Joseph F. Smith, in an April 1916 conference address entitled "In the Presence of the Divine," made the following, deeply instructive remarks:

> Sometimes the Lord expands our vision from this point of view and this side of the veil, so that we feel and seem to realize that we can look beyond the thin veil which separates us from that other sphere. If we can see, by the enlightening influence of the Spirit of God and through the words that have been spoken by the holy prophets of God, beyond the veil that separates us from the spirit world, *surely those who have passed beyond, can see more clearly through the veil back here to us than it is possible for us to see to them from our sphere of action. I believe we move and have our being in the presence of heavenly messengers and of heavenly beings. We are not separate from them.* We begin to realize, more and more fully, as we become acquainted with the principles of the gospel, as they have been revealed anew in this dispensation, that *we are closely related to our kindred, to our ancestors, to our friends and associates and co-laborers who have preceded us into the spirit world.* We cannot forget them;

---

60. Joseph Smith, in "History, 1838–1856, volume E-1," 1751.

we do not cease to love them; we always hold them in our hearts, in memory....

They have advanced; we are advancing; we are growing as they have grown; we are reaching the goal that they have attained unto; and therefore, I claim that *we live in their presence, they see us, they are solicitous for our welfare, they love us now more than ever.* For now they see the dangers that beset us; they can comprehend, better than ever before, the weaknesses that are liable to mislead us into dark and forbidden paths. They see the temptations and the evils that beset us in life and the proneness of mortal beings to yield to temptation and to do wrong; hence their solicitude for us, and their love for us, and their desire for our well-being, must be greater than that which we feel for ourselves.[61]

President George Albert Smith likewise stressed that "those who are on the other side [of the veil] are . . . anxious about us. *They are praying for us and for our success. They are pleading, in their own way, for their descendants,* for their posterity who live upon the earth."[62]

"THE AUTHOR AND FINISHER OF OUR FAITH" (12:2–3)

Paul here writes of our Lord as the "author and finisher of our faith" (verse 2; compare Moroni 6:4). As we learned elsewhere, He is "the author of eternal salvation unto all them that obey him" (Hebrews 5:8), the Alpha and Omega, the beginning and the end, the first and the last of our faith (Moroni 6:4; Doctrine and Covenants 110:4). Jesus became the proponent and chief advocate of the Father's plan of salvation, the one sent to earth to put into effect the terms and conditions of that plan (see Moses 4:1–2).

Paul continues by declaring that "for the joy that was set before

---

61. Clark, *Messages of the First Presidency*, 5:6–7.
62. *Teachings of George Albert Smith*, 27.

him [i.e., the Savior] endured the cross, despising the shame, and is set down at the right hand of the throne of God" (verse 2). Jesus endured the unimaginable and unfathomable pain and anguish and alienation from the Father, both in Gethsemane and on Golgotha. He knew He was ministering in behalf of His spirit brothers and sisters, building for us a bridge over which we could pass from spiritual death to life eternal. "As in all things," President Russell M. Nelson taught, "Jesus Christ is our ultimate exemplar, 'who for the joy that was set before him endured the cross.' [Hebrews 12:2] Think of that! In order for Him to endure the most excruciating experience ever endured on earth, our Savior focused on joy. And what was the joy that was set before Him? Surely it included the joy of cleansing, healing, and strengthening us; the joy of paying for the sins of all who would repent; the joy of making it possible for you and me to return home—clean and worthy—to live with our Heavenly Parents and families."[63]

Jesus despised the shame of the world in that He cared precious little about how He was viewed or perceived by those with hardened, impenitent hearts. He despised the shame of the world in that He went to the cross willingly, in spite of the ignominy associated with death by crucifixion (see Deuteronomy 21:23). Jesus despised the shame of the world in that His eye was absolutely single to the glory of God the Father; He was oblivious to the world's telestial values and a sick society's pecking order.

In verse 3, the Apostle calls upon his readers to "consider him that endured such contradiction of sinners against himself." Other translations of this passage include the following:

> Consider him who endured such opposition from sinful men, so that you will not grow weary and lose heart. (NIV)

> Consider him who endured from sinners such hostility

---

63. Nelson, "Joy and Spiritual Survival."

against himself, so that you may not grow weary or fainthearted. (ESV)

He put up with enormous opposition from sinners. Weigh up in your minds just how severe it was; then you won't find yourselves getting weary and worn out. (KNT)

Those who attended the School of the Elders in Kirtland, Ohio, were taught that Jesus Christ "is called the Son because of the flesh, and descended in suffering below that which man can suffer; or, in other words, suffered greater sufferings, and was exposed to more powerful contradictions than any man can be. But, notwithstanding all this, he kept the law of God, and remained without sin."[64]

THE CHASTENING OF THE LORD (12:6–8, 11)

"For whom the Lord loveth," Paul writes, "he chasteneth, and scourgeth every son whom he receiveth" (verse 6). In most other translations, the word *chasteneth* is rendered *disciplines*, and the word *scourgeth* is translated as *rebukes* or *punishes*. Because God our Heavenly Father loves His children purely and infinitely and because He wants the very best for them, when they obey, He blesses and rewards them. When they disobey or stray from the covenant path, He corrects or punishes them. Indeed, this is what a true *disciple* is—one who seeks to be faithful and is, when needed, corrected or disciplined. In modern revelation, the Savior explained that "whom I love I also chasten that their sins may be forgiven, for with the chastisement I prepare a way for their deliverance in all things out of temptation" (Doctrine and Covenants 95:1). Likewise, the risen Lord taught John the Revelator that "as many as I love, I rebuke and chasten: be zealous therefore, and repent" (Revelation 3:19).

In verses 7 and 8, we learn that those who endure chastening—who

---

64. *Lectures on Faith*, 5:2; p. 59.

receive the Lord's gentle correction in a spirit of humility, acceptance, and even gratitude—become the sons and daughters of God. On the other hand, those who refuse the Lord's discipline, who bristle at their Father in Heaven's divine correction, become spiritually illegitimate children who have essentially declared that they have no desire to be a part of God's royal family. The King James translators were graphic in their translation of those who refuse to be the sons of God—spiritually speaking, they are *bastards* and not sons (verse 8). Other translations render this phrase as "illegitimate children and not sons."

Now to be sure, few of earth's inhabitants are eager to be corrected and set straight; it is often unsettling and occasionally painful to be chastened or disciplined. When seen from an eternal perspective, however, this kind of discipline yields "the peaceable fruit of righteousness unto them which are exercised [i.e., trained or disciplined] thereby" (verse 11).

GOD IS THE FATHER OF OUR SPIRITS (12:9–11)

Paul here reminds the Hebrew Saints that they had earthly, or mortal, fathers who corrected or disciplined them, "and [they] gave them reverence"—meaning, they showed their fathers respect. Why not, then, "be in subjection unto the Father of spirits, and live"—meaning, gain eternal life? (verse 9). This verse is one of a few scriptures that refer to the fact that Elohim, our Father in Heaven, is indeed the Father of our spirits and that we are the spirit sons and daughters of Deity. This is a singularly significant and spiritually satisfying teaching that is taught also in the Old Testament (see Numbers 16:22; 27:16).

President Lorenzo Snow, fifth President of the restored Church, explained that "we were born in the image of God our Father; he begat us like unto himself. There is the nature of deity in the composition of our spiritual organization; in our spiritual birth our Father transmitted to us the capabilities, powers and faculties which he himself possessed, as much so as the child on its mother's bosom possesses, although in an undeveloped state, the faculties, powers and susceptibilities of its parent."[65] On another occasion, President Snow remarked that "we have divinity within ourselves; our spiritual organism is immortal; it cannot be destroyed; it cannot be annihilated. We will live from all eternity to all eternity."[66]

The Apostle Paul continues: "For they verily for a few days chastened us after their own pleasure; but he for our profit, that we might be partakers of his holiness" (verse 10). To put this another way, our earthly fathers chastened or disciplined us when we were under their care, and they did so the best they could. No decent and rational father wants to do anything other than lead and guide his children in a manner that will best prepare them for life and for the challenges and struggles they will inevitably face. And no father who has an eternal perspective on life here and hereafter will do other than strive, with all the wisdom and love he possesses, to model the abundant life and encourage his posterity to enter and remain on the covenant path, which will result in a life of righteousness, even holiness.

FOLLOWING PEACE AND SEEKING HOLINESS (12:14–15)

"Follow peace with all men, and holiness, without which no man shall see the Lord" (verse 14). *Peace* and *holiness* are a fascinating spiritual combination. In a world like our own that is filled with contention, spiritual distractions, pessimism, and cynicism, nothing is more needed than the soft voice that turns away wrath (Proverbs 15:1); nothing is more welcome to honest truth seekers than the gentle voice of truth that declares in mildness but in power that there is a God and that He is in control. "Blessed are the peacemakers," the Savior said in His Sermon on the Mount, "for they shall be called the children of God" (Matthew 5:9).

To ancient Israel God issued this charge: "I am the Lord your God:

---

65. *Teachings of Presidents of the Church: Lorenzo Snow*, 84.
66. *Teachings of Presidents of the Church: Lorenzo Snow*, 84.

ye shall therefore sanctify yourselves, and ye shall be holy; for I am holy" (Leviticus 11:44). We understand that mortals cannot really sanctify themselves; such is accomplished only through the atoning blood of the Savior and the purifying power of the Holy Spirit. But there is another way of looking at the word *sanctify*. To sanctify is to separate oneself from wickedness, lewdness, harshness, and insensitivity. It is to separate oneself from the unholy and the profane, to draw the line between righteousness and wickedness, and to always stay on the Lord's side of the line.[67] In his first epistle, the Apostle Peter charged his readers, "As he which hath called you is holy, so be ye holy in all manner of conversation [i.e., conduct]" (1 Peter 1:15). Holiness is purity. Spiritual cleanliness. Godliness.

William Longstaff penned the words of a hymn that has become beloved to Christians throughout the world. Its simple message is deeply profound.

> *Take time to be holy, speak oft with thy Lord;*
> *Abide in Him always, and feed on His Word.*
> *Make friends of God's children, help those who are weak,*
> *Forgetting in nothing His blessing to seek.*
>
> *Take time to be holy, the world rushes on;*
> *Spend much time in secret, with Jesus alone.*
> *By looking to Jesus, like Him thou shalt be;*
> *Thy friends in thy conduct His likeness shall see.*
>
> *Take time to be holy, let Him be thy Guide;*
> *And run not before Him, whatever betide.*
> *In joy or in sorrow, still follow the Lord,*
> *And, looking to Jesus, still trust in His Word.*
>
> *Take time to be holy, be calm in thy soul,*
> *Each thought and each motive beneath His control.*

---

67. See George Albert Smith, *Sharing the Gospel with Others*, 42–43.

> *Thus led by His Spirit to fountains of love,*
> *Thou soon shalt be fitted for service above.*[68]

THE CHURCH OF THE FIRSTBORN (12:18–24)

Beginning in verse 18, Paul reminds the Hebrews that the holiness to which the followers of Christ are called is not attained in the same manner as it was when the ancient Israelites waited at the base of Mount Sinai, anticipating Jehovah to manifest Himself to the people. It is not about fire burning on the mountaintop, the sound of trumpets, or restrictions against beasts touching what had become the holy mountain (see Exodus 19:12–18). Rather, the Apostle writes, "Ye are come unto mount Sion [i.e., Zion], and unto the city of the living God, the heavenly Jerusalem, and to an innumerable company of angels, to the general assembly and church of the firstborn, [whose names are] written in heaven, and to God the Judge of all, and to the spirits of just men made perfect, and to Jesus the mediator of the new covenant" (verses 18–24). We learn in the vision of the degrees of glory that these are the blessings granted to those who inherit the celestial kingdom (Doctrine and Covenants 76:64–70).

Let's look more carefully at some of the transcendent blessings promised to those who "follow peace with all men, and [seek for] holiness, without which no man [or woman] shall see the Lord" (verse 14). First, they become celestial citizens of Zion, the heavenly Jerusalem, the final abode of the pure in heart (verse 22; compare Revelation 21:10, 22–27). Second, they are able to associate with "an innumerable company of angels, to the general assembly and church of the firstborn, which are written in heaven, and to God the judge of all, and to the spirits of just men made perfect, and to Jesus the mediator of the new covenant" (verses 22–24; compare Doctrine and Covenants 76:69).

---

68. *Cokesbury Worship Hymnal*, no. 57.

The scriptures speak of those who qualify for exaltation as being the Church of the Firstborn (see Doctrine and Covenants 76:54, 67, 102). The Church of the Firstborn is the inner circle of faithful Saints who have proven true and faithful to their covenants. As baptism is the gate to membership in the Church of Jesus Christ on earth, so celestial marriage opens the door to membership in the heavenly church.[69] The Church of the Firstborn is the Church beyond the veil, the organized body of Saints who qualify for full salvation. It is made up of those who qualify for the blessings of the Firstborn. Jesus is the literal firstborn of the Father and as such is entitled to the birthright. As an act of consummate mercy and grace, our blessed Savior makes it possible for us to inherit, receive, and possess the same blessings He receives, as though we were the firstborn (see Romans 8:17; Doctrine and Covenants 76:94–95; 84:38; 88:107; 132:20). President Brigham Young therefore stated that "the ordinances of the house of God are expressly for the Church of the Firstborn."[70]

"BETTER THINGS THAN THAT OF ABEL" (12:24)

Verse 24 speaks of those who are celestial coming into the presence of Christ, by means of the blood the Savior shed and sprinkled upon all those who come to Him humbly in faith and through repentance. The latter part of this verse declares that the blood of Christ "speaketh better things than that of Abel." This is a very strange expression, one that would have no meaning whatsoever were it not for the Joseph Smith Translation. One of the most important biblical passages on the Abrahamic covenant is Genesis 17. Verses 3–7 of the Joseph Smith Translation read: "And it came to pass, that Abram fell on his face, and called upon the name of the Lord. And God talked with him, saying, My people have gone astray from my precepts, and have not

---

69. See Joseph Fielding Smith, *Doctrines of Salvation*, 2:42; McConkie, *Promised Messiah*, 47; McConkie, *New Witness for the Articles of Faith*, 337.
70. Young, in *Journal of Discourses*, 8:154.

kept mine ordinances, which I gave unto their fathers; and they have not observed mine anointing, and the burial, or baptism wherewith I commanded them; but have turned from the commandment [to be baptized; see Moses 6:58–60], and *taken unto themselves the washing of children,* and the blood of sprinkling" (Genesis 17:3–6, JST). It appears that the people in the days of Abraham, some 1,800 years before the coming of Jesus Christ, fell into apostasy. They were guilty of what the prophet Mormon some 2,200 years later in the New World called a "gross error," "solemn mockery," and "awful wickedness"—namely, the baptism of little children (Moroni 8:6, 9, 16, 19–20). Such a practice is a perversion that denies the mercies of Christ and sets at naught the Lord's Atonement.

But then comes the following from the Joseph Smith Translation of Genesis 17:7: the people "have said that *the blood of the righteous Abel was shed for sins*; and have not known wherein they are accountable before me." Somehow, in some peculiar and bizarre manner, a group of apostates in Abraham's day had come to believe that it is the blood of Abel (shed by his brother Cain), the son of Adam and Eve, that cleanses from sin, that atones for the sins of the world.

This example is just one of many that illustrates the Joseph Smith Translation is one of the greatest evidences of the divine calling of Joseph Smith as the Prophet of the Restoration and the head of the dispensation of the fullness of times. The reference to Abel in Hebrews 12:24 is an enigma to many rank-and-file Bible readers and, to some extent, even to those who are serious students of the writings of the Apostle Paul.

SWEET AND PRACTICAL COUNSEL TO CHRISTIANS (13:1–25)

As is the case in a number of the Apostle's epistles, the end of this letter serves as a kind of catchall, in which Paul provides short bits of counsel. Among his parting words, Paul charges the Hebrew Saints to "be not forgetful to entertain strangers: for thereby some have entertained angels unawares" (verse 2). Some 124 years before the birth of the Savior, King Benjamin taught a related, deeply profound truth when he said: "I tell you these things that ye may learn wisdom; that ye may learn that *when ye are in the service of your fellow beings ye are only in the service of your God*" (Mosiah 2:17). In the meridian of time Jesus uttered a companion verity toward the end of His mortal ministry: "Verily I say unto you, *Inasmuch as ye have done it unto one of the least of these my brethren [and sisters], ye have done it unto me*" (Matthew 25:40).

One of the most beloved bits of counsel from C. S. Lewis has to do with how we treat one another. "It may be possible," Lewis has written,

> for each to think too much of his own potential glory hereafter; *it is hardly possible for him to think too often or too deeply about that of his neighbor.* The load, or weight, or burden of my neighbor's glory should be laid on my back, a load so heavy that only humility can carry it, and the backs of the proud will be broken. *It is a serious thing to live in a society of possible gods and goddesses,* to remember that the dullest and most uninteresting person you can talk to may one day be a creature which, if you saw it now, you would be strongly tempted to worship. . . . *There are no ordinary people. You have never talked to a mere mortal.* Nations, cultures, arts, civilizations—these are mortal, and their life is to ours as the life of a gnat. But it is immortals whom we joke with, work with, marry, snub, and exploit. . . . Next to the Blessed Sacrament itself, your neighbor is the holiest object presented to your senses.[71]

Paul then gives assorted bits of counsel in verses 3–17, including the following: Remember those who are in bonds. Marriage is

---

71. Lewis, "Weight of Glory," in *Weight of Glory and Other Addresses*, 39–40.

honorable, but God will judge the immoral. Avoid coveting and be content with what you have. Remember your Church leaders. Remember that Jesus is the same yesterday, today, and tomorrow. Avoid strange or false doctrine. Like the scapegoat in ancient times, Jesus suffered outside the gate of the city. Our world today is not our final home. Obey and follow the guidelines of those who lead you.

Conclusion

THE LENGTHENING SHADOW OF PAUL

I AM DEEPLY GRATEFUL TO have had the privilege over the last half century of coming to know the mind and heart of Paul, a man for whom I now have unbounded respect and admiration. It is given to but few to have the kind of impact on Christianity and, for that matter, on the religious world in general, as the Apostle Paul.

Let's reflect for a moment on how Paul's teachings impact our language today. Consider the following twenty expressions from Paul and how often these words continue to be employed by people in the twenty-first century:

- "The love of money is the root of all evil" (1 Timothy 6:10).
- "The powers that be" (Romans 13:1)
- "We brought nothing into this world, and it is certain [that] we can carry nothing out" (1 Timothy 6:7).
- It is better to give than to receive (actually the words of Jesus, quoted by Paul in Acts 20:35).
- "O death, where is thy sting? O grave, where is thy victory?" (1 Corinthians 15:55).
- "The times and the seasons" (1 Thessalonians 5:1)
- "A thief in the night" (1 Thessalonians 5:2)
- "Prove all things; hold fast that which is good" (1 Thessalonians 5:21).

- "Put on the whole armour of God" (Ephesians 6:11–17).
- "Work out your own salvation with fear and trembling" (Philippians 2:12).
- Faith, hope, and charity (1 Corinthians 13)
- "Let not the sun go down [on] your wrath" (Ephesians 4:26).
- The Lord is not far from any of us (Acts 17:27).
- "The letter killeth, but the spirit giveth life" (2 Corinthians 3:6).
- "Abstain from [the] appearance of evil" (1 Thessalonians 5:22).
- "A thorn in the flesh" (2 Corinthians 12:7)
- A labor of love (1 Thessalonians 1:3)
- There is one Lord, one faith, and one baptism (Ephesians 4:5).
- "I am . . . all things to all men" (1 Corinthians 9:22).
- "I have fought a good fight, I have finished my course, I have kept the faith" (2 Timothy 4:7).

Church leaders throughout the ages, as well as scholars, have paid beautiful tributes to the Apostle Paul. Clement, an early bishop of Rome, for example, wrote about Paul, observing, "After he had been seven times in chains, had been driven into exile, had been stoned, and had preached in the east and in the west, he won the genuine glory for his faith, having taught righteousness to the whole world and having reached the farthest limits of the west. Finally, when he had given his testimony before the rulers, he thus departed from the world and went to the holy place, having become an outstanding example of patient endurance."[1]

N. T. Wright and Michael F. Bird, two prominent New Testament scholars, said of the Apostle: "Paul's theological vision—which he says was rooted in his own literal vision of Jesus—was for the churches of Jews and gentiles to be united together in a common worship of God through Jesus the Messiah and in fellowship with the Holy Spirit." Wright and Bird added that, without Christian theology, "the church

---

1. 1 Clement 5:6–7; in Ehrman, *Apostolic Fathers*, 1:45.

would not be, could not be, what it was called to be. Without the constant prayerful and scriptural struggle to understand, in every generation, who God really is, what he's done in Jesus, and what it means for his people, the church easily slips away from its vocation to be united and holy and thereby to be a sign to the world of God's ultimate future. Paul left behind him a network of suffering, struggling, but growing churches. He left a small collection of explosive writings."[2]

Joseph Smith, the first Prophet and President of The Church of Jesus Christ of Latter-day Saints, wrote the following in an epistle to the members of the Church in Kirtland, Ohio:

> Though [Paul] once, according to his own word, persecuted the Church of God and wasted it, yet after embracing the faith, his labors were unceasing to spread the glorious news: and like a faithful soldier, when called to give his life in the cause which he had espoused, he laid it down, as he says, with an assurance of an eternal crown [2 Timothy 4:6–8]. Follow the labors of this Apostle from the time of his conversion to the time of his death, and you will have a fair sample of industry and patience in promulgating the Gospel of Christ. Derided, whipped, and stoned, the moment he escaped the hands of his persecutors he as zealously as ever proclaimed the doctrine of the Savior. . . .
>
> No one, we presume, will doubt the faithfulness of Paul to the end. None will say that he did not keep the faith, that he did not fight the good fight, that he did not preach and persuade to the last. And what was he to receive? A crown of righteousness. . . . Reflect for a moment . . . and enquire, whether you would consider yourselves worthy a seat at the marriage feast with Paul and others like him. . . . Have you a promise of receiving a crown of righteousness from the hand of the Lord,

---

2. Wright and Bird, *New Testament in Its World*, 393–94.

with the Church of the Firstborn? Here then, we understand, that Paul rested his hope in Christ, because he had kept the faith, and loved His [Christ's] appearing and from His hand he had a promise of receiving a crown of righteousness.[3]

President Spencer W. Kimball declared that "to see the forbearance and fortitude of Paul when he was giving his life to his ministry is to give courage to those who feel they have been injured and tried. . . . While starving, choking, freezing, poorly clothed, Paul was yet consistent in his service. He never wavered once after the testimony came to him following his supernatural experience." President Kimball tenderly added, "I love Paul, for he spoke the truth. He leveled with people. He was interested in them. I love Paul for his steadfastness, even unto death and martyrdom."[4]

The Apostle Paul's reach has been and will continue to be vast and impressive throughout the world. More personally, Paul has reached out to me—touched my heart, stimulated my mind, and fortified my faith in the Lord Jesus Christ. Paul's was an eloquent proclamation of the grand and galactic significance of our Lord's life, ministry, teachings, miracles, atoning sacrifice, and glorious Resurrection. Paul's writings have deepened my understanding of God's plan of salvation. I am fully convinced, by the power of the Holy Ghost, that Jesus of Nazareth was and is the Son of God, the Only Begotten in the flesh. I testify that the Jesus of history is indeed the Christ of faith—that the accounts of His life and ministry, as set forth in the four Gospels and in the writings of the Apostle Paul, are accurate and true and that they may be relied upon with confidence.

As a Latter-day Saint, I delight in the additional understanding and broadened perspective provided by latter-day prophets and seers, as well as the scriptures of the Restoration—the Book of Mormon,

---

3. Joseph Smith, in "Letter to the Church, circa March 1834."
4. *Teachings of Spencer W. Kimball*, 132, 482.

Doctrine and Covenants, and Pearl of Great Price. My soul resonates with the testimony borne in the 2020 bicentennial proclamation to the world from the First Presidency and Quorum of the Twelve Apostles: "We declare that The Church of Jesus Christ of Latter-day Saints, organized on April 6, 1830, is *Christ's New Testament Church restored*. This Church is anchored in the perfect life of its chief cornerstone, Jesus Christ, and in His infinite Atonement and literal Resurrection."[5]

I sincerely doubt that Paul had any idea that his fourteen epistles, his regulatory correspondence with those branches of the Church he helped to establish, would one day become a part—an indispensable part—of holy scripture. You and I are thereby the benefactors of a treasure trove of divine truth and wise counsel. What were once helpful letters to small pockets of former-day Saints are now a godsend to the Latter-day Saints and all those throughout the world who desire to come unto Christ, take upon them His precious name, and strive to live as He lived.

I can think of no more appropriate way to bring this volume to a close than to draw upon the words of Paul himself: "Now the God of peace, that brought again from the dead our Lord Jesus, that great shepherd of the sheep, through the blood of the everlasting covenant, make you perfect [i.e., whole, complete, spiritually mature] in every good work to do his will, working in you that which is well-pleasing in his sight, through Jesus Christ; to whom be glory for ever and ever. Amen" (Hebrews 13:20–21).

---

5. "Restoration of the Fulness of the Gospel of Jesus Christ."

SOURCES

Aburto, Reyna. "Thru Cloud and Sunshine, Lord, Abide with Me." *Ensign* or *Liahona*, November 2019.
Anderson, Richard Lloyd. *Understanding Paul*. Salt Lake City: Deseret Book, 1983.
Andrus, Hyrum L., and Helen Mae Andrus, comps. *They Knew the Prophet*. Salt Lake City: Bookcraft, 1974.
Ashton, Marvin J. "There Are Many Gifts." *Ensign*, November 1987.
Bainton, Roland H. *Here I Stand: A Life of Martin Luther*. New York: Meridian Books, 1995.
Ballard, Melvin J. *Melvin J. Ballard: Crusader for Righteousness*. Edited by Melvin R. Ballard. Salt Lake City: Bookcraft, 1966.
———. Sermon delivered at the Mutual Improvement Association annual conference, Sunday, June 1, 1919. In *The Improvement Era*, October 1919.
Ballard, M. Russell. "Building Bridges of Understanding." *Ensign*, June 1998.
———. "When Shall These Things Be?" Brigham Young University devotional address, Provo, UT, March 12, 1996.
Baugh, Alex. "The Practice of Baptism for the Dead Outside of Temples." *BYU Religious Studies Center Newsletter* 13, no. 1 (September 1998).
Bednar, David A. "We Believe in Being Chaste." *Ensign* or *Liahona*, May 2013.
Benson, Ezra Taft. *Teachings of Ezra Taft Benson*. Salt Lake City: Deseret Book, 1988.
———. *A Witness and a Warning: A Modern-Day Prophet Testifies of the Book of Mormon*. Salt Lake City: Deseret Book, 1988.
Blomberg, Craig L. *A New Testament Theology*. Waco, TX: Baylor University Press, 2018.
Brown, Raymond. *The Message of Hebrews*. Downers Grove, IL: IVP Academic, 1982.
Bruce, F. F. *The Books and the Parchments*. Westwood, NJ: Fleming H. Revell, 1963.
———. *Paul: Apostle of the Heart Set Free*. Grand Rapids, MI: Eerdmans, 1977.
———. *The Epistle to the Hebrews*. Grand Rapids, MI: Eerdmans, 1964.
Callister, Tad R. *The Inevitable Apostasy and the Promised Restoration*. Salt Lake City: Deseret Book, 2006.

Campbell, Douglas A. *Paul: An Apostle's Journey*. Grand Rapids, MI: Eerdmans, 2018.
Cannon, George Q. "Discourse by President George Q. Cannon." *Millennial Star* 56, no. 17 (April 23, 1894): 259–61.
———. *Gospel Truth: Discourses and Writings of George Q. Cannon*. Selected by Jerreld L. Newquist. 2 vols. in one. Salt Lake City: Deseret Book, 1987.
Children's Songbook. Salt Lake City: The Church of Jesus Christ of Latter-day Saints, 2017.
Christofferson, D. Todd. "Justification and Sanctification." *Ensign*, June 2001.
Clark, James R., ed. *Messages of the First Presidency*. 6 vols. Salt Lake City: Bookcraft, 1965–75.
The Cokesbury Worship Hymnal. Edited by C. A. Bowen. Nashville: Abingdon-Cokesbury Press, n.d.
Conference Report of The Church of Jesus Christ of Latter-day Saints, April 1921; April 1970.
Cook, Quentin L. "Valiant in the Testimony of Jesus." *Ensign* or *Liahona*, November 2016.
Cowdery, Oliver. In *Messenger and Advocate* 1, no. 1 (October 1834): 15–16.
Cowley, Matthias F., and Orson F. Whitney. *Cowley and Whitney on Doctrine*. Compiled by Forace Green. Salt Lake City: Bookcraft, 1963.
DeMarius, Richard E. "Corinthian Religion and Baptism for the Dead (1 Corinthians 15:29): Insights from Archaeology and Anthropology." *Journal of Biblical Literature* 114, no. 4 (1995): 678–79.
Draper, Richard D., and Michael D. Rhodes. *Epistle to the Hebrews*. Brigham Young University New Testament Commentary. Provo, UT: BYU Studies, 2021.
Dummelow, J. R., ed. *A Commentary on the Holy Bible*. New York: Macmillan, 1973.
Durant, Will. *The Story of Civilization*. Vol. 3, *Caesar and Christ*. New York: Simon & Schuster, 1944.
Ehrman, Bart D., ed. *The Apostolic Fathers*. The Loeb Classical Library. Cambridge, MA: Harvard University Press, 2003.
English Standard Version Study Bible. Wheaton, IL: Crossway Books, 2008.
Erickson, Millard J. *The Concise Dictionary of Christian Theology*. Rev. ed. Wheaton, IL: Crossway Books, 2001.
Eusebius. *The History of the Church*. Translated by G. A. Williamson. New York: Penguin Books, 1989.
Eyring, Henry B. *Because He First Loved Us*. Salt Lake City: Deseret Book, 2002.
"The Family: A Proclamation to the World." ChurchofJesusChrist.org.
Farrar, Frederick W. *The Life and Work of St. Paul*. 2 vols. New York: E. P. Dutton & Company, 1880.
Fee, Gordon D. *The First Epistle to the Corinthians*. Grand Rapids, MI: Eerdmans, 1987.
Fitzmyer, Joseph A. *Romans*. The Anchor Bible Series. New York: Doubleday, 1993.
Freedman, David Noel, ed. *Anchor Bible Dictionary*. 6 vols. New York: Doubleday, 1992.

Gigot, Francis E. *Outlines of New Testament History.* New York: Benziger Brothers, 1898.
Groberg, John H. "The Beauty and Importance of the Sacrament." *Ensign,* May 1989.
Guide to the Scriptures. scriptures.ChurchofJesusChrist.org.
Hafen, Bruce C. *The Broken Heart: Applying the Atonement to Life's Experiences.* Salt Lake City: Deseret Book, 1989.
Hagner, Donald A. *Encountering the Book of Hebrews.* Grand Rapids, MI: Baker Academic, 2002.
Hengel, Martin. *Crucifixion.* Philadelphia: Fortress Press, 1997.
Hilton, John, III. *Considering the Cross: How Calvary Connects Us with Christ.* Salt Lake City: Deseret Book, 2021.
Hinckley, Gordon B. *Teachings of Gordon B. Hinckley.* Salt Lake City: Deseret Book, 1997.
———. "We Bear Witness of Him." *Ensign,* May 1998.
Holland, Jeffrey R. *Christ and the New Covenant: The Messianic Message of the Book of Mormon.* Salt Lake City: Deseret Book, 1997.
———. "An High Priest of Good Things to Come." *Ensign,* November 1999.
———. "Lord, I Believe." *Ensign* or *Liahona,* May 2013.
———. "None Were with Him," *Ensign* or *Liahona,* May 2009.
———. "This Do in Remembrance of Me." *Ensign,* November 1995.
———. *Trusting Jesus.* Salt Lake City: Deseret Book, 2003.
Hunter, Howard W. "Being a Righteous Husband and Father." *Ensign,* November 1994.
———. "The Gospel, a Global Faith." *Ensign,* November 1991.
———. *"The Real Christmas."* Salt Lake City: Bookcraft, 1993.
Hymns of The Church of Jesus Christ of Latter-day Saints. Salt Lake City: The Church of Jesus Christ of Latter-day Saints, 1985.
Journal of Discourses. 26 vols. Liverpool: F. D. Richards & Sons, 1851–86.
Judd, Frank F., Jr. "The Epistles of the Apostle Paul." In *New Testament History, Culture, and Society,* edited by Lincoln H. Blumell, 419–20. Provo, UT: BYU Religion Studies Center; Salt Lake City: Deseret Book, 2019.
Keller, Timothy. *Hope in Times of Fear: The Resurrection and the Meaning of Easter.* New York: Viking, 2021.
Kimball, Spencer W. "Absolute Truth." *1977 BYU Fireside and Devotional Speeches of the Year.* Provo, UT: BYU Publications, 1978.
———. "Privileges and Responsibilities of Sisters." *Ensign,* November 1978.
———. *Teachings of Spencer W. Kimball.* Edited by Edward L. Kimball. Salt Lake City: Bookcraft, 1982.
The Kingdom New Testament: A Contemporary Translation. Translated by N. T. Wright. New York: HarperOne, 2011.
Larsen, Dean L. "Looking beyond the Mark." *Ensign,* November 1987.
Lectures on Faith. Salt Lake City: Deseret Book, 1985.
Lee, Harold B. "Put on the Whole Armor of God." *Improvement Era,* October 1962.
———. "Stand Ye in Holy Places." *Ensign,* July 1973.

———. *The Teachings of Harold B. Lee*. Compiled by Clyde J. Williams. Salt Lake City: Bookcraft, 1996.

Lee, Rex E. "Things that Change and Things that Don't." *1991–92 BYU Fireside and Devotional Speeches of the Year*. Provo, UT: BYU Publications, 1992.

Lewis, C. S. *Mere Christianity*. New York: Touchstone, 1996.

———. "The Weight of Glory." In *The Weight of Glory and Other Addresses*. New York: Touchstone, 1996.

Lund, Gerald N. *Jesus Christ: Key to the Plan of Salvation*. Salt Lake City: Deseret Book, 1991.

———. "Salvation: By Grace or by Works?" *Ensign*, April 1981.

MacArthur, John F. *Hard to Believe: The High Cost and Infinite Value of Following Christ*. Nashville: Thomas Nelson, 2003.

MacArthur Study Bible. English Standard Version. Wheaton, IL: Crossway Books, 2010.

Madsen, Truman G. *Four Essays on Love*. Salt Lake City: Deseret Book, 2007.

———. *The Highest in Us*. Salt Lake City: Bookcraft, 1978.

Matthews, Robert J. *Behold the Messiah: New Testament Insights from Latter-day Revelation*. Salt Lake City: Bookcraft, 1994.

———. *"A Plainer Translation": Joseph Smith's Translation of the Bible, A History and Commentary*. Provo, UT: Brigham Young University Press, 1975.

———. *Unto All Nations: A Guide to the Book of Acts and the Writings of Paul*. Salt Lake City: Deseret Book, 1975.

Maxwell, Neal A. *All These Things Shall Give Thee Experience*. Salt Lake City: Deseret Book, 1979.

———. "Deny Yourselves of All Ungodliness." *Ensign*, May 1995.

———. *Even as I Am*. Salt Lake City: Deseret Book, 1982.

———. *"For the Power Is in Them": Mormon Musings*. Salt Lake City: Deseret Book, 1973.

———. "The Great Plan of the Eternal God." *Ensign*, May 1984.

———. "Lest Ye Be Wearied and Faint in Your Minds." *Ensign*, May 1991.

———. "Meeting the Challenges of Today." *1978 Devotional Speeches of the Year*. Provo, UT: BYU Publications, 1979.

———. *Moving in His Majesty and Power*. Salt Lake City: Deseret Book, 2004.

———. *Things as They Really Are*. Salt Lake City: Deseret Book, 1978.

———. *We Will Prove Them Herewith*. Salt Lake City: Deseret Book, 1982.

———. "What Should We Pray For?" In *Prayer*. Salt Lake City: Deseret Book, 1978.

———. "Willing to Submit." *Ensign*, May 1985.

McConkie, Bruce R. Address delivered at the funeral of S. Dilworth Young, July 13, 1981, typescript.

———. *Doctrinal New Testament Commentary*. 3 vols. Salt Lake City: Bookcraft, 1965–73.

———. "The Doctrinal Restoration." In *The Joseph Smith Translation: The Restoration of Plain and Precious Things*. Edited by Monte S. Nyman and Robert L. Millet. Provo, UT: BYU Religious Studies Center, 1985.

———. "The Doctrine of the Priesthood." *Ensign*, May 1982.

———. *Doctrines of the Restoration: Sermons and Writings of Bruce R. McConkie*. Edited by Mark L. McConkie. Salt Lake City: Bookcraft, 1989.

———. "Jesus Christ and Him Crucified." *1976 BYU Speeches of the Year*. Provo, UT: BYU Publications, 1977.

———. *The Millennial Messiah: The Second Coming of Christ*. Salt Lake City: Deseret Book, 1982.

———. *The Mortal Messiah: From Bethlehem to Calvary*. 4 vols. Salt Lake City: Deseret Book, 1979–81.

———. "The Mystery of Godliness." *1984–85 Brigham Young University Devotional and Fireside Speeches*. Provo, UT: BYU Publications, 1985.

———. *A New Witness for the Articles of Faith*. Salt Lake City: Deseret Book, 1985.

———. *The Promised Messiah: The First Coming of Christ*. Salt Lake City: Deseret Book, 1978.

———. "Think on These Things." *Ensign*, January 1974.

———. "What Think Ye of Salvation by Grace?" *1984 BYU Speeches of the Year*. Provo, UT: BYU Publications, 1984.

McGrath, Alister. *In the Beginning: The Story of the King James Bible and How It Changed a Nation, a Language, and a Culture*. New York: Anchor Books, 2001.

McKay, David O. *Ancient Apostles*. Salt Lake City: Deseret Book, 1965.

———. *Gospel Ideals: Selections from the Discourses of David O. McKay*. Salt Lake City: The Improvement Era, 1953.

———. "Unity in the Home—the Church—the Nation." *Improvement Era*, February 1954.

McKim, Donald K. *Westminster Dictionary of Theological Terms*. Louisville, KY: Westminster John Knox Press, 1996.

Miller, Adam S. *An Early Resurrection: Life in Christ Before You Die*. Salt Lake City: Deseret Book; Provo, UT: Neal A. Maxwell Institute for Religious Scholarship, 2018.

———. *Grace Is Not God's Backup Plan: An Urgent Paraphrase of Paul's Letter to the Romans*. N.p., 2015.

Millet, Robert L. *I Saw a Pillar of Light: Sacred, Saving Truths from Joseph Smith's First Vision*. Salt Lake City: Deseret Book, 2020.

———. *Whole in Christ*. Salt Lake City: Deseret Book, 2021.

Millet, Robert L., Camille Fronk Olson, Andrew C. Skinner, and Brent L. Top. *LDS Beliefs: A Doctrinal Reference*. Salt Lake City: Deseret Book, 2011.

Monson, Thomas S. *The Teachings of Thomas S. Monson*. Compiled by Lynne E. Cannegieter. Salt Lake City: Deseret Book, 2011.

Morris, Leon. *Epistle to the Romans*. Grand Rapids, MI: Eerdmans, 1988.

Murphy-O'Connor, Jerome. *Paul: A Critical Life*. Oxford: Clarendon Press, 1996.

———. *Paul: His Story*. Oxford: Oxford University Press, 2004.

"Nauvoo Baptisms for the Dead." Book A. Church Family History Archives, Salt Lake City.

Nelson, Russell M. "Decisions for Eternity." *Ensign* or *Liahona*, November 2013.

———. "Doors of Death." *Ensign*, May 1992.
———. "Joy and Spiritual Survival." *Ensign* or *Liahona*, November 2016.
———. "The Love and Laws of God." Brigham Young University devotional address, Provo, UT, September 17, 2019.
———. *Perfection Pending*. Salt Lake City: Deseret Book, 1998.
———. "Prophets, Leadership, and Divine Law." Worldwide devotional for young adults, January 8, 2017.
———. *Teachings of Russell M. Nelson*. Salt Lake City: Deseret Book, 2018.
———. "We Can Do Better and Be Better." *Ensign*, May 2019.
New International Version. Grand Rapids, MI: Zondervan, 1978.
New International Version Study Bible. Grand Rapids, MI: Zondervan, 2011.
New Revised Standard Version. Oxford: Oxford University Press, 1989.
Nibley, Hugh W. *Approaching Zion*. Vol. 9 of the Collected Works of Hugh Nibley. Salt Lake City: Deseret Book; Provo, UT: Foundation for Ancient Research and Mormon Studies, 1989.
———. *The Prophetic Book of Mormon*. Vol. 8 of the Collected Works of Hugh Nibley. Salt Lake City: Deseret Book; Provo, UT: Foundation for Ancient Research and Mormon Studies, 1987.
———. *Since Cumorah*. 2nd ed. Vol. 7 of the Collected Works of Hugh Nibley. Salt Lake City: Deseret Book; Provo, UT: Foundation for Ancient Research and Mormon Studies, 1981.
———. *The World and the Prophets*. Vol. 3 of the Collected Works of Hugh Nibley. Salt Lake City: Deseret Book; Provo, UT: Foundation for Ancient Research and Mormon Studies, 1987.
Oaks, Dallin H. "The Great Plan of Happiness." *Ensign*, November 1993.
———. "Have You Been Saved?" *Ensign*, May 1998.
———. "He Heals the Heavy Laden." *Ensign*, November 2006.
———. "'Judge Not' and Judging." *Ensign*, August 1999.
———. *The Lord's Way*. Salt Lake City: Deseret Book, 1991.
———. "Truth and the Plan." *Ensign*, November 2018.
Packer, Boyd K. "The Brilliant Morning of Forgiveness." *Ensign*, November 1995.
———. "The Fountain of Life." Brigham Young University devotional address, Provo, UT, 1992.
———. "Inspiring Music—Worthy Thoughts." *Ensign*, January 1974.
———. *Let Not Your Heart Be Troubled*. Salt Lake City: Bookcraft, 1991.
———. "The Mediator." *Ensign*, May 1977.
———. *Mine Errand from the Lord: Selections from the Sermons and Writings of Boyd K. Packer*. Compiled by Clyde J. Williams. Salt Lake City: Bookcraft, 2008.
———. "The Only True Church." *Ensign*, November 1985.
———. "What Every Elder Should Know—and Every Sister as Well: A Primer on Principles of Priesthood Government." *Ensign*, February 1993.
Pagels, Elaine. *Adam, Eve, and the Serpent*. New York: Random House, 1988.
Peterson, Eugene H. *The Message: The Bible in Contemporary Language*. Colorado Springs, CO: NavPress, 2002.

Pratt, Orson. *The True Faith. A Series of Pamphlets.* Liverpool, 1852.
Pratt, Parley P. *Key to the Science of Theology.* Salt Lake City: Deseret Book, 1978.
The Random House College Dictionary. Rev. ed. New York: Random House, 1988.
"The Restoration of the Fulness of the Gospel of Jesus Christ: A Bicentennial Proclamation to the World." ChurchofJesusChrist.org.
The Revised English Bible. Oxford: Oxford University Press, 1989.
Rhodes, Michael J. "Paul and Prejudice: How the Apostle's Words to the Corinthians Speak to Inequity in Churches Today." *Christianity Today* 65, no. 2 (March 2021).
Roberts, Alexander, and James Donaldson, eds. *The Ante-Nicene Fathers.* 10 vols. Peabody, MA: Hendrickson, 1994.
Robinson, Benjamin Willard. *The Life of Paul.* 2nd ed. Chicago: University of Chicago Press, 1928.
Robinson, Stephen E. *Believing Christ: The Parable of the Bicycle and Other Good News.* Salt Lake City: Deseret Book, 1991.
Sanders, E. P. *Paul: A Very Short Introduction.* New York: Oxford University Press, 2001.
Smith, George Albert. *Sharing the Gospel with Others.* Compiled by Preston Nibley. Salt Lake City: Deseret Book, 1948.
———. *The Teachings of George Albert Smith.* Edited by Robert and Susan McIntosh. Salt Lake City: Bookcraft, 1996.
Smith, Joseph. "Baptism." *Times and Seasons* 3 (September 1, 1842): 904.
———. "Baptism for the Dead." *Times and Seasons* 3 (April 15, 1842): 760.
———. "Copy of a Letter from J. Smith Jr. to Mr. Galland." *Times and Seasons* 1 (February 1840): 54.
———. "Discourse, between circa 26 June and circa 2 July 1839, as Reported by Wilford Woodruff." The Joseph Smith Papers. https://www.josephsmith papers.org/paper-summary/discourse-between-circa-26-june-and-circa-2-july -1839-as-reported-by-wilford-woodruff/1.
———. "Discourse, between circa 26 June and circa 4 August 1839–A, as Reported by Willard Richards." The Joseph Smith Papers. https://www.josephsmith papers.org/paper-summary/discourse-between-circa-26-june-and-circa-4 -august-1839-a-as-reported-by-willard-richards/1.
———. "Discourse, 5 January 1841, as Reported by William Clayton." The Joseph Smith Papers. https://www.josephsmithpapers.org/paper-summary /discourse-5-january-1841-as-reported-by-william-clayton/1.
———. "Discourse, 16 May 1841, as Published in *Times and Seasons*." The Joseph Smith Papers. https://www.josephsmithpapers.org/paper-summary /discourse-16may-1841-as-published-in-times-and-seasons/1.
———. "Discourse, 16 May 1841, as Reported by Unidentified Scribe." The Joseph Smith Papers. https://www.josephsmithpapers.org/paper-summary /discourse-16may-1841-as-reported-by-unidentified-scribe/1.
———. "Discourse, 3 October 1841, as Published in *Times and Seasons*." The Joseph Smith Papers. https://www.josephsmithpapers.org/paper-summary /discourse-3-october-1841-as-published-in-times-and-seasons/1.

———."Discourse, 10 April 1842, as Reported by Wilford Woodruff." The Joseph Smith Papers. https://www.josephsmithpapers.org/paper-summary/discourse-10-april-1842-as-reported-by-wilford-woodruff/1.

———. "Discourse, 28 April 1842." The Joseph Smith Papers. https://www.josephsmithpapers.org/paper-summary/discourse-28-april-1842/1.

———. "Discourse, 7 April 1844, as Reported by *Times and Seasons*." The Joseph Smith Papers. https://www.josephsmithpapers.org/paper-summary/discourse-7-april-1844-as-reported-by-times-and-seasons/1. See also "Accounts of the 'King Follett Sermon,'" The Joseph Smith Papers. https://www.josephsmithpapers.org/site/accounts-of-the-king-follett-sermon?p=1&highlight=accounts%20of%20king%20follett%20sermon.

———. "Discourse, 12 May 1844, as Reported by George Laub." The Joseph Smith Papers. https://www.josephsmithpapers.org/paper-summary/discourse-12-may-1844-as-reported-by-george-laub/1.

———. "*Elders' Journal*, July 1838." The Joseph Smith Papers. https://www.josephsmithpapers.org/paper-summary/elders-journal-july-1838/1.

———. "Extract from the Private Journal of Joseph Smith Jr." *Times and Seasons* 1, no. 1 (November 1839): 8.

———."Gift of the Holy Ghost." *Times and Seasons* 3 (June 15, 1842): 824–25.

———. "History, 1838–1856, volume A-1 [23 December 1805–30 August 1834]." The Joseph Smith Papers. https://www.josephsmithpapers.org/paper-summary/history-1838-1856-volume-a-1-23-december-1805-30-august-1834/1.

———. "History, 1838–1856, volume C-1 [2 November 1838–31 July 1842]." The Joseph Smith Papers. https://www.josephsmithpapers.org/paper-summary/history-1838-1856-volume-c-1-2-november-1838-31-july-1842/1.

———. "History, 1838–1856, volume C-1 Addenda." The Joseph Smith Papers. https://www.josephsmithpapers.org/paper-summary/history-1838-1856-volume-c-1-addenda/1.

———. "History, 1838–1856, volume D-1 [1 August 1842–1 July 1843]." The Joseph Smith Papers. https://www.josephsmithpapers.org/paper-summary/history-1838-1856-volume-d-1-1-august-1842-1-july-1843/1.

———. "History, 1838–1856, volume E-1 [1 July 1843–30 April 1844]." The Joseph Smith Papers. https://www.josephsmithpapers.org/paper-summary/history-1838-1856-volume-e-1-1-july-1843-30-april-1844/1.

———. "History, 1838–1856, volume F-1 [1 May 1844–8 August 1844]." The Joseph Smith Papers. https://www.josephsmithpapers.org/paper-summary/history-1838-1856-volume-f-1-1-may-1844-8-august-1844/1.

———. "Instruction on Priesthood, circa 5 October 1840." The Joseph Smith Papers. https://www.josephsmithpapers.org/paper-summary/instruction-on-priesthood-circa-5-october-1840/20.

———. "Journal, December 1841–December 1842." The Joseph Smith Papers. https://www.josephsmithpapers.org/paper-summary/journal-december-1841-december-1842/1.

———. "Journal, December 1842–June 1844; Book 1, 21 December 1842–10

March 1843." The Joseph Smith Papers. https://www.josephsmithpapers.org/paper-summary/journal-december-1842-june-1844-book-1-21-december-1842-10-march-1843/1.

———. "Journal, December 1842–June 1844; Book 2, 10 March 1843–14 July 1843." The Joseph Smith Papers. https://www.josephsmithpapers.org/paper-summary/journal-december-1842-june-1844-book-2-10-march-1843-14-july-1843/1.

———. "Journal, December 1842–June 1844; Book 3, 15 July 1843–29 February 1844." The Joseph Smith Papers. https://www.josephsmithpapers.org/paper-summary/journal-december-1842-june-1844-book-3-15-july-1843-29-february-1844/1.

———. "Letter to Church Leaders in Jackson County, Missouri, 25 June 1833." The Joseph Smith Papers. https://www.josephsmithpapers.org/paper-summary/letter-to-church-leaders-in-jackson-county-missouri-25-june-1833/1.

———. "Letter to Edward Partridge and the Church, circa 22 March 1839." The Joseph Smith Papers. https://www.josephsmithpapers.org/paper-summary/letter-to-edward-partridge-and-the-church-circa-22-march-1839/1.

———. "Letter to the Church, circa March 1834." The Joseph Smith Papers. https://www.josephsmithpapers.org/paper-summary/letter-to-the-church-circa-march-1834/1.

———. "Letter to the Church, circa April 1834." The Joseph Smith Papers. https://www.josephsmithpapers.org/paper-summary/letter-to-the-church-circa-april-1834/1.

———. "Letter to the Church and Edward Partridge, 20 March 1839." The Joseph Smith Papers. https://www.josephsmithpapers.org/paper-summary/letter-to-the-church-and-edward-partridge-20-march-1839/1.

———. "Minutes and Discourse, 28 April 1842." The Joseph Smith Papers. https://www.josephsmithpapers.org/paper-summary/minutes-and-discourse-28-april-1842/1.

———. *The Papers of Joseph Smith*. 2 vols. Edited by Dean C. Jessee. Salt Lake City: Deseret Book, 1989.

———. *Teachings of Presidents of the Church: Joseph Smith*. Salt Lake City: The Church of Jesus Christ of Latter-day Saints, 2007.

———. *The Words of Joseph Smith: The Contemporary Accounts of the Nauvoo Discourses of the Prophet Joseph*. Edited by Andrew F. Ehat and Lyndon W. Cook. Provo, UT: BYU Religious Studies Center, 1980.

Smith, Joseph F. *Gospel Doctrine*. Salt Lake City: Deseret Book, 1971.

Smith, Joseph Fielding. *Doctrines of Salvation*. 3 vols. Compiled by Bruce R. McConkie. Salt Lake City: Bookcraft, 1954–56.

———. *The Progress of Man*. Salt Lake City: Deseret Book, 1964.

———. *Take Heed to Yourselves*. Salt Lake City: Deseret Book, 1966.

———. *The Way to Perfection*. Salt Lake City: Deseret Book, 1972.

Smith, Lucy Mack. *History of Joseph Smith by His Mother*. Salt Lake City: Bookcraft, n.d.

Snow, Lorenzo. "Man's Destiny." *Improvement Era* 22, no. 8 (June 1919): 660; originally written January 11, 1892.
———. *Teachings of Presidents of the Church: Lorenzo Snow*. Salt Lake City: The Church of Jesus Christ of Latter-day Saints, 2012.
Sperry, Sidney B. *Paul's Life and Letters*. Salt Lake City: Bookcraft, 1955.
Stackhouse, John G. *Humble Apologetics*. New York: Oxford University Press, 2002.
Stott, John. *Life in Christ*. Wheaton, IL: Tyndale House Publishers, 1991.
Svartvik, Jesper. "A Dangerous Book: Reading Hebrews without Supercessionism." *The Christian Century* 138, no. 19 (September 21, 2021).
Talmage, James E. *Jesus the Christ*. Salt Lake City: Deseret Book, 1916.
Taylor, John. "The Living God." *Times and Seasons* 6 (February 15, 1845): 809.
Top, Brent L. *The Life Before*. Salt Lake City: Bookcraft, 1988.
Uchtdorf, Dieter F. "Fellow Travelers, Brothers and Sisters, Children of God." Address delivered at the inaugural symposium of the John A. Widtsoe Foundation, Los Angeles, April 24, 2015.
———. "The Gift of Grace." *Ensign*, May 2015.
Wilken, Robert Louis. *The First Thousand Years: A Global History of Christianity*. New Haven, CN: Yale University Press, 2012.
Williams, Peter. *America's Religions: From Their Origins to the Twenty-first Century*. Urbana: University of Illinois Press, 2002.
Witherington, Ben, III. *The Paul Quest: The Renewed Search for the Jew of Tarsus*. Downers Grove, IL: InterVarsity Press, 1998.
Woodruff, Wilford. *Discourses of Wilford Woodruff*. Edited by G. Homer Durham. Salt Lake City: Bookcraft, 1969.
Wright, N. T. *Paul: A Biography*. New York: HarperOne, 2018.
———. *Paul for Everyone: Romans*. 2 vols. Louisville, KY: Westminster John Knox Press, 2004.
———. *Surprised by Hope: Rethinking Heaven, the Resurrection, and the Mission of the Church*. New York: HarperOne, 2008.
———. *Surprised by Scripture: Engaging Temporary Issues*. New York: HarperOne, 2014.
———. *What Saint Paul Really Said: Was Paul of Tarsus the Real Founder of Christianity?* Grand Rapids, MI: Eerdmans, 1997.
Wright, N. T., and Michael F. Bird. *The New Testament in Its World: An Introduction to the History, Literature, and Theology of the First Christians*. Grand Rapids, MI: Zondervan, 2019.
Young, Brigham. Vision, February 17, 1847. In Brigham Young Office Files, 1832–1878. Church History Library, Salt Lake City.
Zondervan New American Standard Study Bible. Edited by Kenneth Barker. Grand Rapids, MI: Zondervan, 1999.

INDEX

Aaron, 379
Aaronic Priesthood, 197–98, 392, 393
Abba, 204
Abel, 397, 410–11, 426–27
Abraham: as justified by faith, 30–32; children of, 194–97, 208; gospel preached to, 196–97, 374–75; as mediator, 314; Melchizedek and, 390, 391; promises made to, 413–14
Abrahamic covenant, 66, 197–98, 386–89, 426–27
Absolute truth, 177–78
Aburto, Reyna, 175
Accountability, 26, 136, 209
Adam, 292–94
Adamic language, 127–29
Adams, James, 418
Addictive patterns, 38
Adoption: as children of God, 40–42; into divine family, 203–4; "articles of," 227
Afterlife, 139–40. *See also* spirit world
Agency, 22–23, 135, 304
Alma the Younger, 268
Ammon, 268
Anderson, Richard Lloyd, 12–13, 221
Angels: tongue of, 129–30; worship of, 279–80; Jesus as higher than, 364–65
Animal sacrifice, 398–400
Antichrists, 111
Apostasy, 223, 302–5, 320–23, 332, 343–44, 427
Apostle(s): Paul's calling as, 179–81; as foundation of Church, 230–31; material assistance for, 306; Jesus Christ as, 371–72
Appearance of evil, abstaining from, 299
Aquinas, Thomas, 12

Argument, 275–76
Aristarchus, 285
Armor of God, wielding, 245–49
"Articles of adoption," 227
Asceticism, 98
Ashton, Marvin J., 118–19
Assurance, faith as based on, 406–8
Atonement: reconciliation to God through, 33–34; receiving, 34–35; Fall overcome through, 35; and continuing in sin, 35–36; salvation through, 47; cross as token of, 72–76; and worth of souls, 95–96; and sacrament, 113–14; importance of, 132–34; for sin, 162–63, 180–81; change through, 193–94; as "emptying" of Christ, 252–57; death abolished through, 337; as centerpiece of plan of salvation, 353–54; scope of, 362; withdrawal of Spirit during, 363; Alma's prophecy of, 370–71; entering God's presence through, 401; focus on joy in, 420. *See also* reconciliation
Augustine, 11–12

Baker, Simon, 138–39
Ballard, Melvin J., 57, 115
Ballard, M. Russell, 295–96, 353
Baptism, 36–37, 209, 227–28, 277–78, 354–55
Baptism for the dead, 137–39, 416–17
Barak, 415
Barnabas, 187, 188–89, 190–91, 346
Bednar, David A., 96
Benson, Ezra Taft, 26, 32
Biblical corruption, 304
Bird, Michael F., 431–32
Bishop(s): counsel to author as, 85; standards

for, 250–51; qualifications for, 317–18, 349–50; duties of, 349–50
Blessings: and nature of God and Jesus, 48; of Jews and Gentiles, 65–67; unconditional, 135; of obedience, 151–52
Blomberg, Craig L., 5
Blood, 141
Body: as temple of God, 93–94; points of view on, 97–98, 134; nature of resurrected, 139–41, 157; changed, 262–63. *See also* Resurrection
Book of Life, 264
Born again, 42, 158–63, 204, 220
Brown, Hugh B., 414
Brown, Raymond, 12
Bruce, F. F., 2, 346–47
Brunson, Seymour, 138, 416
Busybodies, 307

Cain, 397
Calling, 379–80
Calling and election made sure, 345–46
Campbell, Douglas, 4, 131–32
Cannon, George Q., 120–21
Carnally minded, 39–40
Celestial glory, 29, 163–64
Celestial kingdom, 172–73, 225, 401
Celibacy, 321–23
Change, through Atonement, 193–94
Change of heart, 24
Charity, 59–60, 121–26, 324
Chastening, 421–22
Chastity, 22–23, 99, 290–91, 321–23
Cheerful giving, 166–67
Childbearing, 316
Children: accountability of, 26, 136, 209; teaching gospel to, 333–35
Children of God: adoption as, 40–42; and worth of souls, 95; put on Christ, 202–3; Gentiles as, 229–30; preservation of, 281; salvation of, 312–13; spiritual station of, 365–66
Children of light, walking as, 240, 296–97
Children of promise, 208
Christians: Jewish, 6, 11, 181, 182, 187, 190–92, 300, 360; behavior of, 87, 125, 212, 239, 265, 323–24; and dispute resolution, 92; live by power of God, 175–76; opposition to Paul, 184–85; Gentile, 190–92; conversion of, 287; persecution of, 337–38; to discuss Christ's teachings, 365; counsel to, 427–29
Christlike life, 282–83
Christofferson, D. Todd, 28–29

Church of Jesus Christ: as temple of God, 84–86; love in, 234; need for organized, 236–38; spiritual knowledge of members of, 283–84; alteration of ordinances of, 303–4; cautions to men and women in, 315–17
Church of Jesus Christ of Latter-day Saints, The: understanding for, 234–35; responsibilities of members of, 284
Church of the Firstborn, 425–26
Circumcision, 25–26, 72, 188, 189, 208–10, 259
Circumspect, 240
Clayton, William, 282
Clement of Alexandria, 11, 12, 431
Cloak, 346–47
Colossae, 269
Colossians, epistle to, 269; gospel to go to all nations, 269–70; translated into kingdom of God, 270–71; Jesus as Firstborn of every creature, 271–72; fullness dwells in Christ, 272–73, 277–78; life grounded and settled in Christ, 274–75; philosophies of men, 275–76; completion in Jesus Christ, 278–79; avoid worship of angels, 279–80; putting on new man, 280–82; Christlike life, 282–83; conversing with those of other faiths, 283–85; Paul sends love to friends, 285
Comfort, 215–16
Commandment(s): obedience to, 54–55, 78, 239–40, 266; to love others, 210–11, 324
Conceitedness, 59
Concision, 259
Confidence, casting not away, 404–6
Contention, 70–71. *See also* divisiveness
Contrite spirit, 399–400
Cook, Quentin L., 304
Corinthians, first epistle to, 69; plea for unity, 69–72; Atonement, 72–76, 132–34; spiritual knowledge, 76–78; gaining mind of Christ, 78–79; gospel learning, 79–82; Jesus Christ as foundation / rock, 83–84, 104–5; spiritual growth, 83–84; Church as temple of God, 84–86; judgment, 86–87; acknowledging limitations, 87–90; confrontation of wickedness, 90–91; excessive and unnecessary litigation, 91–93; body as temple of God, 93–94; marriage and missions, 96–100; God's nature, 100–102; material assistance for Paul, 102–3; Paul's versatility, 103–4; temptation, 105–6; head coverings, 106–9; interdependence of men and women, 109–10; usefulness of heresies, 110–11; sacrament, 111–13; Last

Supper, 113–14; worthily taking sacrament, 114–16; revelation on Christ's divinity, 116–18; spiritual gifts, 118–21, 126–30; charity, 121–26; gift of prophecy, 126–27; gift of tongues, 127–30; women speaking in church, 131–32; resurrection, 134–36; God as supreme, 136–37; baptisms for the dead, 137–39; nature of resurrected bodies, 139–41; victory through Christ, 141–42; works and hope for future, 142–43

Corinthians, second epistle to, 144; turning to God, 144–46; Holy Ghost as spiritual barometer, 146–47; triumph in Christ, 147–48; fruits of gospel, 148; Christian life, 148–50; blindness of Jews, 150–51; Holy Ghost as liberator, 151; blessings of obedience, 151–52; Satan seeks to blind us, 152–53; Jesus Christ as missionary message, 153–54; pressing on through trials, 154–56; looking to Resurrection, 156–58; walking by faith, 158; spiritual rebirth, 158–63; day / time of salvation, 163–64; associating with unbelievers, 164–65; godly sorrow leads to repentance, 165–66; condescension of Jesus Christ, 166; cheerful giving, 166–67; spiritual warfare, 167–68; righteousness as measured by God's standards, 168–69; simplicity, 169–70; Paul's persecution and suffering, 170–71; Paul's spiritual experiences, 171–73; strength through God's grace, 173–75; living by power of God, 175–76; self-examination, 176–77; absolute truth, 177–78

Covel, James, 354

Covenant, versus oath, 388

Covenant path, 110

Covetousness, 330. *See also* envy

Creation, 272, 362, 408–10

Cross, 72, 74–75, 218–20

Crucifixion, 73–76

Cynicism, 266–67

Damascus, 5, 184–85

David, King, 58, 415

Day of Atonement, 369, 371, 395

Deacons, 250–51, 317–18

Dead: baptisms for, 137–39, 416–17; fate of righteous, 292–94

Death: sorrow in, 293; abolished by Jesus Christ, 337; in faith, 345–46; judgment following, 397–98

Degrees of glory, 71, 139–41, 172–73, 214, 352, 416

Deification, 100–101, 428

"Destroyed in the flesh," 91

Diploma, 8

Discouragement, 214

Dispensation(s), 223; final dispensation, 223–25; dispensation of the fulness of times, 224–25

Divine impassibility, 376

Divinization, 100–101

Divisiveness, 67–68. *See also* contention

Doctrine: false, 309–10; teaching sound, 351

Dogs, 259

Doubts, 263

Draper, Richard D., 389, 394–95, 402–3

Drunkenness, 241

Dummelow, J. R., 108

Durant, Will, 304

Duty, doing, 148–49

"Earnest of the Spirit" / "earnest of our inheritance," 146–47, 225, 337

Economic disparity, of Corinthian members, 111–13

Election, of Israel, 48–49. *See also* foreordination

Enduring, 345–46

Enoch, 389–90, 411–12

Envy, 123–24, 330

Epaphras, 285

Ephesians, epistle to, 221; foreordination, 221–23; final dispensation, 223–25; "earnest of our inheritance," 225; Godhead hierarchy, 226; salvation by grace, 226–29; Gentiles as children of God, 229–30; Apostles and prophets as foundation of Church, 230–31; mystery concerning Gentiles, 231–32; Jesus dwells in us by faith, 232–34; unity in Church, 234–35; Jesus's postmortal descent, 235–36; need for church organization, 236–38; putting off old man, 238–39; walking as children of light, 240; redeeming the time, 240–41; psalms, hymns, and spiritual songs, 241–43; submission in marriage, 243–44; harmony and love in home, 244–45; wielding armor of God, 245–49

Ephesus, 221

Epistles, 9–15; Thessalonians, first epistle to; chronological order of, 10–11. *See also* Colossians, epistle to; Corinthians, first epistle to; Corinthians, second epistle to; Ephesians, epistle to; Galatians, epistle to; Hebrews, epistle to; Philemon, epistle to; Philippians, epistle to; Romans, epistle to;

Thessalonians, first epistle to; Thessalonians, second epistle to; Timothy, first epistle to; Timothy, second epistle to; Titus, epistle to
Esau, 50–51
Eternal life: sealing up to, 61–62; path to, 110; hope and assurance of, 146–47, 225, 281; premortal promise of, 348–49; through Atonement, 401; as fruit of faith, 409. *See also* immortality
Evangelist, 344
Eve, 316–17
Evil: abstaining from appearance of, 299; root of, 326–28
Exaltation, 101–2, 109, 401, 426
Example, serving as, 323–25
Eyesight, of Paul, 206–7
Eyring, Henry B., 237

Faith: living by, 20–21; justification by, 21, 27–29; Abraham as justified by, 30–32; in Jesus Christ, 31, 406, 407; Gentiles made righteous by, 51–52; by hearing, 52–55; as manifest in faithfulness, 53–54; and witness of Spirit, 77–78; trials and, 154–56; walking by, 158; salvation by grace through, 226–29; Gentiles as children of God through, 229–30; Jesus dwells in us by, 232–34; as spiritual weapon, 247; hope and, 248; doubts and, 263; acting as example of, 324; defined, 406; as based on assurance, 406–8; creation through, 408–10; Jesus as author and finisher of our, 419–21
Faithfulness: faith as manifest in, 53–54; in premortal state, 56–57
"Faith package," 227
Fallen, lifting, 212–13
Fallenness, 27, 35, 39, 40, 93, 214–15
Fall from grace, 146–47
Fall of Adam, 35, 316–17
False doctrine, 309–10
False teachers, 338–39
Family: roles in, 243–44; love in, 244–45; harmony in, 283; transmitting gospel through, 333–35
Farrar, Frederick W., 8
"Father and the Son, The: A Doctrinal Exposition," 272
Fear, 335–37
Fee, Gordon D., 84–85
Final dispensation, 223–25
Final Judgment, 397–98
Financial disparity, of Corinthian members, 111–13

Firstborn, Church of the, 425–26
First Vision, 362–63
Fitzmyer, Joseph A., 67
"Flesh, destroyed in the," 91
Flesh, works of, 211–12
Foolish speculations, 340
Foreign languages, 129
Foreordination, 46–47, 55–57, 221–23
Forgiveness, 115, 134–35, 145, 261–62. *See also* repentance; sin
Fornication, 290–91
Foundation, Jesus Christ as, 83–84, 104–5
Freedom, 151
Fruit of the Spirit, 211–12
Frustration, 214
Future, hope for, 142–43

Gains, become losses, 259–61
Galatia, 179
Galatians, epistle to, 179; Paul's calling, 179–81; warnings against another gospel, 181–83; source of gospel, 183–84; Paul travels to Arabia, 184–86; Paul visits Jerusalem, 186–87; Jerusalem conference, 187–90; Paul confronts Peter, 190–92; Jesus as fulfillment of Mosaic law, 192–94; children of Abraham, 194–97; Jesus as fulfillment of Abrahamic covenant, 197–98; Mosaic law as schoolmaster to bring us to Christ, 198–202; children of God put on Christ, 202–3; adoption into divine family, 203–4; knowing and being known by God, 204–6; Paul's "infirmity of the flesh," 206–7; Jesus as formed in us, 207–8; children of promise, 208; circumcision, 208–10; commandment to love others, 210–11; works of the flesh and fruit of the Spirit, 211–12; lifting others, 212–13; law of the harvest, 213–14; weariness in well-doing, 214–17; doing good to all, 217–18; glorying in cross, 218–20
Gamaliel, 2–3
Generations, transmitting truth through, 333–35
Gentile Christians, 190–92
Gentiles: laws of God obeyed by, 24–25; made righteous by faith, 51–52; blessings of, 65–67; and children of Abraham, 194–97; as children of God, 229–30; God's mystery concerning, 231–32
Gentleness, 264–65
Gideon, 415
Gifts of the Spirit, 118–21, 126–30
Giving, cheerful, 166–67

Glory: degrees of, 71, 139–41, 172–73, 214, 352, 416; of Jesus Christ, 366–67
Gnostics and Gnosticism, 97, 98, 134, 279–80, 310, 331–32
God: in Godhead, 19; and plan of salvation, 19; righteousness of, 20; wrath of, against ungodliness, 21–23; as no respecter of persons, 23–24; presence of, 30, 141, 327, 401; turning life over to, 32; reconciliation to, 33–34; children of, 40–42, 95, 202–3; sons and daughters of, 40–42; works things for our good, 44–46; and foreordination of Christ, 46–47; love of, 47–48, 50–51; no unrighteousness with, 50–51; existence of, 53; love for, 54–55, 76; and foreordination of Israel, 55–57; wisdom and knowledge of, 57–58; wisdom of, 57–58; submission to, 58–59; knowing things of, 76–78; spiritual growth through, 83–84; Church as temple of, 84–86; acknowledging unworthiness before, 87–90; body as temple of, 93–94; body of, 94; becoming like, 100–102, 428; grace of, 135, 353–54; Jesus's submission to, 136–37, 225–26; as supreme, 136–37; turning to, 144–46; knowledge of mysteries of, 152–53; righteousness as measured by standards of, 168–69; strength through grace of, 173–75; living by power of, 175–76; drawing closer to, 204; knowing, and being known by, 204–6; worshipping, 232–33; imitating, 240; armor of, 245–49; working within us, 250–51; work of, 252; Jesus's relationship with, 254–56; will of, 270; Jesus as Firstborn of, 271–72; walking worthy of, 287–89; vengeance upon those who know not, 300–302; understanding mysteries of, 318–19; as King of Kings, 328–29; scripture as given by inspiration of, 341–43; Jesus as in likeness of, 362–64; "rest of," 372–74; empathy of, 376; Jesus's authority from, 379–81; denial of power of, 380; oaths and covenants with, 388–89; created all things through faith, 408–10; as Father of our spirits, 422–23. *See also* children of God; kingdom of God; word of God
God-fearers, 6–7
Godhead, 18–19, 100, 136, 225–26, 277–78. *See also* God; Holy Ghost; Jesus Christ
Godliness: mystery of, 318–20; denial of power of, 380
Godly sorrow, 165–66
Good: from trials, 44–46; doing, 217–18; from unfortunate or tragic, 251–52; focusing on, 266–67; holding fast to, 299
Gospel: shame of, 19–20, 336; given to Jews and Gentiles, 65–67; learning, 79–82; purpose of, 123; evidence of truthfulness of, 148; fruits of, 148; complicating, 169; source of, 183–84; early knowledge of, 196; preached to Abraham, 196–97; leveling effect of, 203; hope in, 215–16, 396; as spiritual weapon, 247; preparation for, 268; to go to all nations, 269–70; as global faith, 284; comes by power, 286–87; transmitting, through generations, 333–35; preached from beginning, 374–75; building on first principles of, 384
Gospel prerequisites, 79–82
Government, submission to, 60–61
Grace: salvation through, 20–21, 54–55, 226–29, 257–58; of God, 135, 353–54; and unconditional blessings, 135; falling from, 146–47; strength through, 173–75; availability of, 351–52; confidence in Christ's, 377–78
"Grace and peace to you," 19
Gratitude, 297–98
Great Apostasy, 303–5, 332
Greek philosophy, 304
Grief, 293
Groberg, John H., 115–16

Habit, 38
Hafen, Bruce C., 123
Hagar, 208
Harmony, in home, 244–45, 283
Harvest, law of, 213–14
Head coverings, 106–9
Healing, 174
Hearing, faith by, 52–55
Heart: change of, 24; circumcision of, 25–26, 259; hardened, 58; believing, 153; desires of, 311; broken, and contrite spirit, 399–400
Hebrews, epistle to, 360–61; authorship, 11–15; will of God manifested through Jesus Christ, 361–62; Jesus as in likeness of Father, 362–63; Atonement, 363; Jesus's spiritual station, 364–65; discussing Christ's teachings, 365; man's spiritual station, 365–66; glory and honor for Jesus Christ, 366–67; Jesus identifies with and succors us, 367–71; Jesus as Apostle and High Priest, 371–72; Jesus as even greater than Moses, 372; rest of the Lord, 372–74; gospel preached from beginning, 374–75; word of God, 375–76;

450 INDEX

empathy of Jesus Christ, 376–77; confidence in Christ's mercy and grace, 377–78; authority of Jesus Christ, 379–81; obedience of Melchizedek, 381–84; building on first principles, 384; unpardonable sin, 385–86; Abrahamic covenant, 386–89; Melchizedek Priesthood, 389–91; order of priesthood, 392–93; fulfillment of Jeremiah's prophecy, 393–94; minister of true tabernacle, 394–95; Jesus as high priest of good things to come, 395–97; judgment following death, 397–98; end of animal sacrifices, 398–400; entering God's presence, 401; sinning against great light, 402–3; trials in discipleship, 403–4; keeping confidence, 404–6; faith as based on assurance, 406–8; creation through faith, 408–10; list of faithful, 410–15; suffering and sanctification, 415–17; spirit world, 417–19; Jesus as author and finisher of our faith, 419–21; chastening of the Lord, 421–22; God as Father of our spirits, 422–23; following peace and seeking holiness, 423–25; Church of the Firstborn, 425–26; salvation through Christ, 426–27; counsel to Christians, 427–29
Hedonism, 98
Hengel, Martin, 74
Heresies, 110–11
High priest, 369, 371–72, 395
High priest of good things to come, 395–97
Hillel, 3, 184
Hinckley, Gordon B., 284–85, 310
Holiness: call to, 290–91; seeking, 423–25
Holland, Jeffrey R., 48, 113–14, 125–26, 215, 253–54, 263, 396, 405–6
Holy Ghost: and repentance, 39–40; prayer and, 42–44; witness of, 77–78; and mind of Christ, 78–79; revelation through, 116–18; and gift of tongues, 129–30; as spiritual barometer, 146–47; and Christian life, 148–50; as liberator, 151; spiritual knowledge through, 152–53, 275–76; Jesus dwells in us through, 233–34; confirmation of truth through, 287; quenching, 298; baptism of fire and, 354–55; withdrawal of, 363; denial of, 385
Holy of Holies, 394, 401
Home: roles in, 243–44; love in, 244–45; harmony in, 283; transmitting truth in, 333–35
Hope, 76–77, 215–16, 248, 396, 407–8
Hunter, Howard W., 207–8, 244, 284
Hyde, Orson, 363

Hymenaeus, 339
Hymns, 215–16, 241–43
Hypocrisy, 320–21

Idle, withdrawing from, 305–7
Idolatry, 22
Immorality, 94, 96–97, 98, 290–91, 385
Immortality, 328–30. *See also* eternal life
Impassibility, divine, 376
Imperfection, 121
Impute, 31
Incarnation, 166
"In Christ," 39–40
Infant baptism, 209
"Infirmity of the flesh," 206–7
Innocence, of Jesus Christ, 273
Integrity, 212
Isaac, 208, 414, 415–16
Ishmael, 208
Israel: election of, 48–49, 55–57; true members of, 49–50; sacred moments in history of, as shadow of Christ, 104–5; priesthood held by, 197–98; hardheartedness of, 372–73; gospel preached to, 375. *See also* Jews

Jacob (son of Isaac), 415–16
Jacob (son of Lehi), 20
Jambres, 341
James, 186–87
Jannes, 341
Jephthah, 415
Jeremiah, 393–94
Jerome, 11–12
Jerusalem, Paul visits, 186–87
Jerusalem conference, 187–90, 348, 360
Jesus (Justus), 285
Jesus Christ: and plan of salvation, 19; righteousness of, 20–21; salvation through, 20–21, 31–32, 47, 52–53, 54–55, 353–54, 426–27; and need for salvation, 26–27; faith in, 31, 406, 407; reconciliation to God through, 33–34; "in Christ," 39–40; acceptance of, 41; foreordination of, 46–47; confessing and calling upon, 53–54; brings gospel to Israel, 66; crucifixion of, 73–75; hope in, 76–77, 396, 407–8; waiting on and hoping in, 76–77; gaining mind of, 78–79; as foundation, 83–84; judging righteously like, 86–87; coming to know, 89; desiring closeness with, 89–90; as rock, 104–5; and Last Supper, 113–14; revelation on divinity of, 116–17; becoming like, 123, 194; as embodiment of charity, 123–24; as Mediator, 132–33, 313–15, 372, 394;

submits to Father, 136–37, 225–26;
Second Coming of, 141–42, 211, 265,
293, 294–96, 301–2, 352, 399; victory
through, 141–42; triumph in, 147–48; as
fulfillment of Mosaic law, 150–51, 192–94,
204, 230, 280, 393–94; as missionary
message, 153–54; suffering of, 155–56,
416, 420; and spiritual rebirth, 158–63;
being in, 160, 275; condescension of,
166; as standard of salvation, 176; bears
burden of sins, 180–81; submission to,
193; as fulfillment of Abrahamic covenant,
197–98; Mosaic law as schoolmaster to
bring us to, 198–202; putting on, 202–3;
drawing closer to, 204; as formed in us,
207–8; law of circumcision done away in,
209; Jewish rejection of, 231–32; dwells in
us by faith, 232–34; postmortal descent of,
235–36, 364; "emptied" himself, 252–57;
God's relationship with, 254–56; doing
all things through, 267–68; as Firstborn
of every creature, 271–72; fullness dwells
in, 272–73, 277–78; innocence of, 273;
life grounded and settled in, 274–75;
baptism in name of, 277–78; forsaking,
278; completion in, 278–79; Christlike
life, 282–83; standing fast in, 289–90;
ministry of, 312; and mystery of godliness,
318–20; death abolished by, 337; purity of,
350–51; titles of, 360–61, 367; will of God
manifested through, 361–62; in likeness of
Father, 362–64; spiritual station of, 364–65;
discussing teachings of, 365; glory and
honor for, 366–67; early years of, 367–68;
identifies with and succors us, 367–71;
development of, 368–69; as Apostle and
High Priest, 371–72; as even greater
than Moses, 372; empathy of, 376–77;
confidence in, 377–78, 404–5; authority
of, 379–81; Melchizedek as type of, 382;
lineage of, 392; as high priest of good things
to come, 395–97; entering God's presence
through, 401; as author and finisher of our
faith, 419–21; focuses on joy, 420. *See also*
Atonement; Godhead; Light of Christ
Jewish Christians, 6, 11, 181, 182, 187,
190–92, 300, 360
Jews: encountered by Paul, 6; Paul preaches to,
9; advantages of, 26; blessings of, 65–67;
blindness of, 150–51; reject Jesus Christ,
231–32. *See also* Israel
Johnson, Benjamin F., 282
Joseph of Egypt, 415–16

Joy, 216, 289, 420
Judaizers, 11, 182, 210, 300
Judd, Frank F., 9–10
Judgment, 24–25, 86–87, 168–69, 205, 277,
311, 313, 397–98
Justification, 21, 27–33

Keller, Timothy, 94, 162
Kenosis, 253
Kimball, Spencer W., 177, 244, 433
Kindness, 264–65
Kingdom of God: seeking, 266; translated into,
270–71
King James Version (KJV), 15–16
King of Kings, 328–29
Kirtland Temple, 129
Knowledge: of God, 57–58; through
revelation, 116–18; faith and, 408. *See also*
spiritual knowledge

Language: Adamic, 127–29; and gift of
tongues, 127–30
Larsen, Dean L., 150–51
Last dispensation, 223
Last Supper, 113–14
Law of Moses: Jesus as fulfillment of, 150–51,
192–94, 204, 230, 280, 393–94; leaving
behind ordinances of, 181–82; as
schoolmaster to bring us to Christ, 198–
202; Paul's observance of, 259; purpose of,
310–11
Lectures on Faith, 78
Lee, Harold B., 212–13, 246, 327, 333–34
Lee, Rex E., 178
Lewis, C. S., 33, 239, 258, 428
Liberty, 151
Lifting others, 212–13
Light, sinning against great, 402–3
Light of Christ, 24, 87, 95
Limitations, acknowledging, 87–90
Litigation, avoiding unnecessary, 91–93
Longstaff, William, 424–25
Losses, gains become, 259–61
Love: of God, 23–24, 47–48, 50–51; for God,
54–55, 76; commandment concerning,
210–11, 324; for others, 218; in Church of
Jesus Christ, 234; in home, 244–45
"Love Divine, All Loves Excelling," 151–52
Luke, 285, 346
Lund, Gerald N., 88
Luther, Martin, 21

MacArthur, John, 73
Madsen, Truman G., 45–46, 414

Man / men: interdependence of women and, 109–10; spiritual station of, 365–66
Mark, 188–89, 285, 346
Marriage, 90, 96–100, 107, 243–44, 321–23
Matthews, Robert J., 38, 99–100, 186–87, 203, 309, 382
Maxwell, Neal A., 43–44, 154–55, 169, 274, 295, 336–37, 362
McConkie, Bruce R.: on Paul's challenge in preaching gospel, 51–52; on salvation, 63; on marriage prohibitions under Mosaic law, 90; on marriage of Paul, 99; on God, 100; on writings on charity, 124–25; on Saints as epistles of truth, 148; on Paul's confrontation of Peter, 191–92; on keeping commandments, 239–40; on Second Coming, 265; on righteous thoughts, 267; on perfection, 273; on rejoicing, 297–98; on doctrine, 310; on mystery of godliness, 320; on conferral of Holy Ghost, 355; on man's spiritual station, 366; on Jesus as High Priest, 372; on Jesus's priesthood authority, 381; on oaths and covenants, 388–89; on eternal life, 409
McGrath, Alister, 15–16
McKay, David O., 4–5, 245, 303
Meat: offered as sacrifice, 64–65; milk before, 79–82, 384; abstaining from, 322–23
Mediator, Jesus Christ as, 132–33, 313–15, 372, 394
Melchizedek, 381–84, 389–91, 416
Melchizedek Priesthood, 109–10, 198, 372, 381, 388, 389–91, 392–93
Mercy, 166–67, 377–78
Michael, 292–94
Millennium, 141, 211
Miller, Adam, 160, 354
Missionary work, 161, 287–89
Missions, 99–100
Modesty, 123–24, 315
Money, 326–28, 330–31
Mortality: purpose of, 27, 110; salvation in, 61; value of, 143; trials as part of, 214–15; work of God in, 252; perfection in, 273
Moses, 198–200, 314, 341, 415–16
Motives, pure, 167
Mourning, 293
Murphy-O'Connor, Jerome, 185

Natural man, 238–39
Nature, changed, 193–94
Nelson, Russell M.: on law of chastity, 22–23; on repentance, 63–64, 247; on body as temple of God, 96; on joy, 216; on mourning dead, 293; on learning about Jesus Christ, 361; on Atonement, 362, 420
Nephi, 152–53
New and everlasting covenant, 270
New man, putting on, 238–39, 280–82
Nibley, Hugh, 50, 276, 328
Nyman, Jane, 139

Oaks, Dallin H., 62, 77–78, 87, 92–93, 174, 316–17
Oaths, 387–88
Obedience: blessings of, 23–24, 151–52; to commandments, 54–55, 78, 239–40, 266; of Melchizedek, 381–84
Old man, putting off, 238–39
Olive Leaf revelation, 214
Onesimus, 285, 356, 357–59
Ordinances, 41, 303–4, 372, 387, 426
Origen, 12
"Origin of Man, The," 271–72
Orthodox, 110
Ostrikinos, 153–54
Other faiths, conversing with those of, 283–85
Others: treatment of, 65, 428; judgment of, 86–87; love for, 210–11, 218, 324; lifting, 212–13; doing good to, 217–18; looking after, 263–65, 284

Packer, Boyd K.: on learning gospel, 79; on Jesus as Mediator, 132–33, 314–15; on forgiveness, 145; on truthfulness of Church, 234–35; on controlling thoughts, 242–43; on judgment, 313; on fear, 336; on oath and covenant of priesthood, 388
Paganism, 304
Pagels, Elaine, 316
Parable, of rich fool, 330–31
Parchments, 346–47
Partisanship, in Corinth, 69–70
Passover, 113
Patriarchal blessings, 349
Patriarchs, 344
Paul: background of, 1–2, 183–84; education of, 2–3; as Pharisee, 2–3, 184; conversion of, 3–6, 19–20, 185–86; types of people encountered by, 6–7; as Roman citizen, 7–8; appearance of, 8–9; missionary efforts of, 9; following conversion, 38; marriage of, 99; material assistance for, 102–3, 306; versatility of, 103–4; challenges facing, 154; persecution and suffering of, 170–71; spiritual experiences of, 171–73; "thorn in the flesh" of, 173–74; calling of, 179–81;

travels to Arabia, 184–86; visits Jerusalem, 186–87; attends Jerusalem conference, 187–90; confronts Peter, 190–92; "infirmity of the flesh" of, 206–7; glories in cross, 218–20; imprisonment of, 251–52; as prepared to face the end, 344–46; continuing influence of, 430–34; tributes to, 431–32. *See also* epistles
Peace: brought by justification, 32–33; that passes understanding, 265–66; following, 423–25
Peculiar people, 352
Penrose, Charles W., 109
Perfection, 30, 237, 261, 273, 290, 350–51, 415–17
Perilous times, 340–41
Persecution: of Paul, 170–71; of Saints, 337–38
Peter, 186–87, 190–92
Peterson, Eugene, 231, 288–89
Pharisee, Paul as, 2–3, 184
Philemon, epistle to, 356–59
Philetus, 339
Philippi, 250
Philippians, epistle to, 250; God working within us, 250–51; good from unfortunate or tragic, 251–52; Atonement, 252–57; salvation through works versus grace, 257–58; gains become losses, 259–61; looking back following forgiveness, 261–62; bodies to be changed, 262–63; looking after others, 263–65; peace that passes understanding, 265–66; focusing on good, 266–67; doing all things through Christ, 267–68
Philosophies of men, 275–76
Plan of salvation, 18–19, 96, 221–22, 312, 353–54, 410
Poor, division of rich and, in Corinth, 111–13
Pornos, 94
Potentate, 328–29
Poverty, of Jesus Christ, 166
Pratt, Orson, 41, 227, 362
Pratt, Parley P., 137, 158–59, 363
Prayer: and Holy Spirit, 42–44; without ceasing, 298
Premortal state, 56–57, 221–22, 348–49
Pride, 39
Priesthood, 109–10, 174, 197–98, 372, 379–81, 388, 389–92
Priests: celibacy of, 321–22; at tabernacle, 394–95. *See also* high priest
Promise, children of, 208
Prophecy, gift of, 126–27
Prophesyings, despising, 298–99

Prophets, 230–31, 295
Propitiation, 29–30
Proselytes, 6
Prosperity, 327
Protestant Reformation, 21
Proto-Gnostic ideas, 97–98, 134
Psalms, 241–43
Pure / purity, 324–25, 350–51

"Quiet, study to be," 291–92

Rahab, 415
Ransom, 315
Reason, 275–76
Rebirth, 42, 158–63, 204, 220
Reconciliation, 33–34, 160–62, 274, 314. *See also* Atonement
Redeeming the time, 240–41
Redemption, 271
Reformation, 21
Rejoicing, 297–98
Religions, conversing with those of other, 283–85
Repentance: and reconciliation, 33–34, 161–62; and coming unto Christ, 39–40; possibility of, 47–48; righteousness and, 49–50; as process, 63–64; and worthily taking sacrament, 114–15; as possible through Resurrection, 134–35; and godly sorrow, 165–66; and lifting those who have fallen, 212–13; and salvation by grace, 227–28; looking back following, 261–62. *See also* forgiveness; sin
Restitution, 145
"Rest of the Lord," 372–74
Resurrection: baptism as in similitude of, 36–37; and body as temple of God, 93–94; women as witnesses of, 131; importance of, 133–34; repentance possible through, 134–35; as universal, 135–36; nature of resurrected bodies, 139–41; following Second Coming, 142; and value of mortality, 143; looking to, 156–58; degrees of glory in, 214; Jesus receives fullness of glory following, 273; judgment following, 277; and fate of righteous dead, 292–94; and immortality, 330; Christian versus Jewish conception of, 339; of ancient faithful, 415
Revelation, 116–18
Rhodes, Michael D., 389, 394–95, 402–3
Rich fool, parable of, 330–31
Righteousness: of God and Jesus Christ, 20–21; repentance and, 49–50; of Gentiles by faith, 51–52; as measured by God's

standards, 168–69; as spiritual weapon, 247; fate of righteous dead, 292–94
Righteous thoughts, 266–67
Robinson, Benjamin Willard, 186
Robinson, Stephen, 29–30
Rock, Jesus Christ as, 83–84, 104–5
Roman citizenship, 7–8
Romans, epistle to, 18; Godhead and plan of salvation, 18–19; greeting, 19; Paul's confidence in conversion, 19–20; God's wrath against ungodliness, 21–23; love of God and blessings of obedience, 23–24; judgment, 24–25; circumcision, 25–26; advantages of being Jew, 26; need for salvation, 26–27; justification by faith, 27–29; propitiation, 29–30; justification of Abraham, 30–32; peace brought by justification, 32–33; reception of Atonement, 34–35; continuing in sin, 35–36; baptism, 36–37; "servant of sin," 37–38; Paul pre- and post-conversion, 38; spiritual-mindedness, 39–40; adoption as children of God, 40–42; prayer and Holy Ghost, 42–44; trials worked for our good, 44–46; foreordination, 46–47, 55–57; love of God, 47–48, 50–51; election of Israel, 48–49; repentance, 49–50; righteousness by faith, 51–52; faith by hearing, 52–55; wisdom and knowledge of God, 57–58; sacrificing of will, 58–59; call to Christian charity, 59–60; submission to government, 60–61; salvation as process, 61–64; sacrificial meat, 64–65; treatment of others, 65; blessings of Jews and Gentiles, 65–67; divisiveness, 67–68
Rooted and grounded, 274–75

Sacrament, 111–16, 401
Sacrifice(s): of will, 58–59; eating meat offered as, 64–65; and opening of windows of heaven, 327; of Abel and Cain, 397; end of animal, 398–400; of Isaac, 414
Salt, speech seasoned with, 283
Salvation: through Jesus Christ, 20–21, 31–32, 47, 52–53, 54–55, 353–54, 426–27; through works, 20–21, 51–52, 257–58, 353; need for, 26–27; as gift, 54–55; as process, 61–64; for dead, 137–39, 416–17; and reconciliation, 161; day / time of, 163–64; Jesus Christ as standard of, 176; through grace, 226–29, 257–58; as spiritual weapon, 247–48; for sinners, 312; of children of God, 312–13; availability of grace bringing, 351–52

Samson, 415
Samuel, 415
Sanctification, 28–29, 290, 415–17, 424
Sanders, E. P., 131
Sarah, 208
Satan, 105–6, 152–53, 303
Saul. See Paul
School of the Elders, 78, 100, 421
Scripture study, 341–43
Sealing up to eternal life, 61–62
Second Coming, 141–42, 211, 265, 293, 294–96, 301–2, 352, 399
"Seducing spirits," 320
Self-examination, 176–77
"Servant of sin," 37–38
Service, 148–49, 284, 428
Sexual immorality, 94, 96–97, 98, 290–91, 385
Shakers, 323
Shame, 19–20, 336
Shammai, 3, 184
Shammaites, 184
Shortcomings, acknowledging, 87–90
Simplicity, 169–70
Sin: God's wrath against, 21–23; and reconciliation to God, 33–34; continuing in, 35–36, 62; "servant of," 37–38; in Church, 85–86; atonement for, 162–63, 180–81; and lifting those who have fallen, 212–13; remission of, 228; redemption from, 271; and sanctification, 290; salvation for sinners, 312; unpardonable, 385–86; against great light, 402–3. See also forgiveness; repentance
Skinner, Andrew C., 200–201
Slaves / slavery, 245, 326, 356. See also Onesimus
Smith, Alvin, 139, 416
Smith, George Albert, 419
Smith, Hyrum, 139
Smith, Joseph: on Paul's appearance, 8–9; on Paul as author of Hebrews, 14; trials of, 45; on predestination, 47; on possibility of repentance, 47–48; on election of Israel, 49; on faith, 53; on trifling with souls of men, 68; on teaching gospel, 80; on corporeal nature of God, 94; on plurality of gods, 100–101; material assistance for, 102–3; on Satan, 105; on spiritual gifts, 119–20; on charity, 122; on gift of tongues, 128–29, 130; on Atonement, 132; on Resurrection, 136, 157, 294; on baptism for the dead, 138–39; on degrees of glory, 140–41, 172–73; on presence of God, 141; on self-examination, 176–77; on Paul's confrontation of Peter,

191; on children of Abraham, 195; on early knowledge of gospel, 196–97; on loving others, 218; on premortal existence, 222; called to preside over last dispensation, 223; on new dispensations, 224; on dispensation of fulness of times, 224–25; on Godhead, 226; on adoption to Lord's family, 227; on perfection of Jesus Christ, 273; on sealing up to eternal life, 282; on Bible, 304; on ordinances, 304; on immortality, 329–30; on evangelists, 344; on baptism, 354–55; First Vision of, 362–63; on Jesus as High Priest, 371–72; on gospel preached to Israelites, 375; on authority and ordination, 379; on denying Holy Ghost, 385–86; on Melchizedek, 390; on priesthood, 391; on sacrifices of Abel and Cain, 397; on sinning against great light, 402; on Abel, 410–11; on translation, 412–13; on salvation of dead, 416–17; on spirit world, 418; on Paul's faithfulness, 432–33

Smith, Joseph F., 76, 157–58, 168, 291, 418–19

Smith, Joseph Fielding, 91, 127–28, 180, 199, 261–62, 317

Smith, Joseph Sr., 139

Snow, Lorenzo, 256–57, 422

Songs, spiritual, 241–43

Soul, worth of, 95–96

Speculations, foolish, 340

Speech, seasoned with salt, 283

Sperry, Sidney B., 12, 186, 303

Spirit(s): "seducing," 320; immortality of, 329–30; contrite, 399–400; God as Father of, 422–23

Spiritual gifts, 118–21, 126–30

Spiritual knowledge: source of, 76–78, 183–84; timing in receiving, 79–82; through revelation, 116–18; through Holy Ghost, 152–53, 275–76; of Church members, 283–84

Spiritually minded, 39–40

Spiritual progress, 79–82, 83–84, 201, 213–14, 384

Spiritual rebirth, 42, 158–63, 204, 220

Spiritual warfare, 167–68, 245–49

Spirit world, 236, 252, 364, 417–19. *See also* afterlife

Stackhouse, John Jr., 265

Step-parent, marriage to, 90

Stott, John, 194

Strength: through God's grace, 173–75; through trials, 174–75, 216

"Study to be approved," 338–39

Submission: as sacrifice, 58–59; to government, 60–61; of Jesus to Father, 136–37, 225–26; to Jesus Christ, 193; in marriage, 243–44; of women, 315–16; of slaves to masters, 326

Success, 327

Suffering, 155–56, 170–71, 415–17, 420

Swearing oaths, 387–88

Tabernacle, 394–95

Talmage, James E., 35

Tarsus, 1–2

Taylor, John, 226

Teachers, false, 338–39

Teaching, simplicity in, 169–70

Telestial kingdom, 352

Telestial peoples, 71, 140

Temple of God: Church as, 84–86; body as, 93–94

Temptation, 105–6

Testimony, 333–34, 337–38, 374

Thanksgiving, 298

Theosis, 100–101

Thessalonians, first epistle to, 286; gospel comes by power, 286–87; walking worthy of God, 287–89; standing fast in Lord, 289–90; call to holiness, 290–91; "study to be quiet," 291–92; fate of righteous dead, 292–94; Second Coming, 294–96; walking as children of light, 296–97; closing counsel, 297–99

Thessalonians, second epistle to: vengeance upon those who know not God, 300–302; apostasy, 302–5; withdrawing from idle, 305–7; weariness in well-doing, 307–8

Thessalonica, 286

Third heaven, 172–73

"Thorn in the flesh," 173–74

Thoughts: controlling, 242–43; righteous, 266–67

Time: righteous use of, 240–41; wasting, in debating trivialities, 338

Timothy, 189, 309, 325–26

Timothy, first epistle to, 309; false doctrine, 309–10; law of Moses, 310–11; plan of salvation and Jesus' ministry, 312; salvation of God's children, 312–13; Jesus Christ as Mediator, 313–15; cautions to Church members, 315–17; qualifications for bishops and deacons, 317–18; mystery of godliness, 318–20; warnings of apostasy, 320–23; serving as example, 323–25; Timothy's responsibilities, 325–26; submission of slaves, 326; "root of all evil,"

326–28; light of immortality, 328–30; works, 330–32
Timothy, second epistle to, 333; transmitting truth through generations, 333–35; fear, 335–37; perfection, 337–38; "study to be approved," 338–39; perilous times, 340–41; scriptures as Godsend, 341–43; apostasy, 343–44; Paul's preparation to face the end, 344–46; Paul's final instructions, 346–47
Titus, 188, 189, 348
Titus, epistle to, 348; premortal promise of eternal life, 348–49; qualifications and duties of bishops, 349–50; "unto the pure all things are pure," 350–51; charge to teach sound doctrine, 351; availability of grace, 351–52; "washing of regeneration," 353–55
Tongues, gift of, 127–30
Top, Brent L., 57
Translation, 172, 411–13
Treatment of others, 65, 428
Trials: good from, 44–46; turning to God during, 144–46; pressing on in, 154–56; strength through, 174–75, 216; as part of mortality, 214–15; in discipleship, 403–4
Trust, 406–7
Truth, 177–78, 246, 333–35, 403
Tychicus, 285

Uchtdorf, Dieter F., 54–55, 217
Unbelievers, associating with, 164–65
Ungodliness, God's wrath against, 21–23
United Society of Believers in Christ's Second Appearing, 323
Unity, 69–72, 234–35, 238
Unpardonable sin, 385–86
Unrighteous dominion, 243–44
Unrighteousness, 50–51
Unworthiness, acknowledging, 87–90

Vengeance, upon those who defy God, 300–302

Ward, counsel for author's, 85
Warfare, spiritual, 167–68, 245–49
War in heaven, 167
"Washing of regeneration," 353–55
Watts, Isaac, 219–20
Weak, bearing infirmities of, 65
"Weak brethren," 7
Weaknesses, 173–75
Wealth, 326–28, 330–31
Weariness in well-doing, 214–17, 307–8
Weber, Max, 327
Well-doing, weariness in, 214–17, 307–8
Wesley, Charles, 151–52, 264
Whitney, Orson F., 316
Wickedness, confrontation of, 90–91
Will, sacrificing, 58–59
Williams, Peter, 327
Will of God: knowing and carrying out, 270; manifested through Jesus Christ, 361–62
Women: head coverings for, 106–9; interdependence of men and, 109–10; as principal witnesses of Resurrection, 131; speaking in church, 131–32; submission of, 243–44, 315–16; cautions to, 315–16
Word of God: as spiritual weapon, 248–49; as sharper than two-edged sword, 375–76
Work ethic, 327
Works: salvation through, 20–21, 51–52, 257–58, 353; and hope for future, 142–43; rich in good, 330–32
Works of the flesh, 211–12
World, being in but not of, 305–6
Wright, N. T.: on Tarsus, 1–2; on Gamaliel, 3; on Paul's epistles, 13; on agency, 23; on head coverings, 108; on works and future, 143; on Shammaites, 184; on changed bodies, 262–63; on Colossians 2:8, 275; on first-century conceptions of resurrection, 339; on Paul's influence, 431–32

Young, Brigham, 128–29, 287, 426